CHURCHILL

WINSTON S.
CHURCHILL

THE SECOND WORLD WAR

BOOK I

THE GATHERING STORM
FROM WAR TO WAR
1919—1939

*Illustrations researched and selected
by Roger Jean Ségalat*

Distributed by
HERON BOOKS

First published 1948
Ninth Edition 1967
Copyright Cassell and Company Limited
Edito-Service S.A., Geneva, Publishers

MORAL OF THE WORK

IN WAR: RESOLUTION
IN DEFEAT: DEFIANCE
IN VICTORY: MAGNANIMITY
IN PEACE: GOODWILL

PREFACE

I MUST regard these volumes as a continuation of the story of the First World War which I set out in *The World Crisis*, *The Eastern Front*, and *The Aftermath*. Together, if the present work is completed, they will cover an account of another Thirty Years War.

I have followed, as in previous volumes, the method of Defoe's *Memoirs of a Cavalier*, as far as I am able, in which the author hangs the chronicle and discussion of great military and political events upon the thread of the personal experiences of an individual. I am perhaps the only man who has passed through both the two supreme cataclysms of recorded history in high executive office. Whereas however in the First World War I filled responsible but subordinate posts, I was in this second struggle with Germany for more than five years the head of His Majesty's Government. I write therefore from a different standpoint and with more authority than was possible in my earlier books.

Nearly all my official work was transacted by dictation to secretaries. During the time I was Prime Minister I issued Memoranda, Directives, Personal Telegrams, and Minutes which amount to nearly a million words. These documents, composed from day to day under the stress of events and with the knowledge available at the moment, will no doubt show many shortcomings. Taken together, they nevertheless give a current account of these tremendous events as they were viewed at the time by one who bore the chief responsibility for the war and policy of the British Empire and Commonwealth. I doubt whether any similar record exists or has ever existed of the day-to-day conduct of war and administration. I do not describe it as history, for that belongs to another generation. But I claim with confidence that it is a contribution to history which will be of service to the future.

These thirty years of action and advocacy comprise and express my life-effort, and I am content to be judged upon them. I have adhered to my rule of never criticising any measure of war or policy after the event unless I had before expressed publicly or formally my opinion or warning about it. Indeed in the after-light I have softened many of the severities of contemporary controversy. It has given me pain to record these disagreements with so many men whom I liked or respected; but it would be wrong not to lay the lessons of the past before the future. Let no one look down on those honourable, well-meaning men whose actions are chronicled in these pages without searching his own heart, reviewing his own discharge of public duty, and applying the lessons of the past to his future conduct.

It must not be supposed that I expect everybody to agree with what I say, still less that I only write what will be popular. I give my testimony according to the lights I follow. Every possible care has been taken to verify the facts; but much is constantly coming to light from the disclosure of captured documents or other revelations which may present a new aspect to the conclusions which I have drawn. This is why it is important to rely upon authentic contemporary records and the expressions of opinion set down when all was obscure.

One day President Roosevelt told me that he was asking publicly for suggestions about what the war should be called. I said at once "the Unnecessary War." There never was a war more easy to stop than that which has just wrecked what was left of the world from the previous struggle. The human tragedy reaches its climax in the fact that after all the exertions and sacrifices of hundreds of millions of people and the victories of the Righteous Cause we have still not found Peace or Security, and that we lie in the grip of even worse perils than those we have surmounted. It is my earnest hope that pondering upon the past may give guidance in days to come, enable a new generation to repair some of the errors of former years, and thus govern, in accordance with the needs and glory of man, the awful unfolding scene of the future.

WINSTON SPENCER CHURCHILL

Chartwell,
Westerham,
Kent

March 1948

NOTE TO THE NEW EDITION

THE opportunity of a reprint enables various errors in detail to be corrected. I am grateful to those who have drawn attention to these and offered suggestions for improvement. I must express my appreciation also of the generous reception given to the work, and extend my cordial thanks to the many persons who have written to me concerning it.

For this new issue the publishers have found it possible to reset the entire book in a larger type, a change which it is hoped will be found agreeable to all readers.

WINSTON S. CHURCHILL

Chartwell,
June 14, 1949

ACKNOWLEDGMENTS

I HAVE been greatly assisted in the establishment of the story in its military aspect by Lieutenant-General Sir Henry Pownall; in naval matters by Commodore G. R. G. Allen; and on European and general questions by Colonel F. W. Deakin, of Wadham College, Oxford, who also helped me in my work *Marlborough: His Life and Times*. I have had much assistance from Sir Edward Marsh in matters of diction. I must in addition make my acknowledgments to the very large numbers of others who have kindly read these pages and commented upon them.

Lord Ismay has also given me his invaluable aid, and with my other friends will continue to do so in the future.

I record my obligations to His Majesty's Government for permission to reproduce the text of certain official documents of which the Crown Copyright is legally vested in the Controller of His Majesty's Stationery Office.

TABLE OF CONTENTS

Chapter   *Page*

    I   The Follies of the Victors, 1919–1929 . . 3

   II   Peace at its Zenith, 1922–1931 . . . 18

  III Lurking Dangers 35

  IV Adolf Hitler 47

   V The Locust Years, 1931–1935 60

  VI The Darkening Scene, 1934 81

 VII Air Parity Lost, 1934–1935 99

VIII Challenge and Response, 1935 . . . 117

  IX Problems of Air and Sea, 1935–1939 . . 132

   X Sanctions against Italy, 1935 . . . 148

  XI Hitler Strikes, 1936 169

 XII The Loaded Pause. Spain, 1936–1937 . . 186

XIII Germany Armed, 1936–1938 202

XIV Mr. Eden at the Foreign Office. His Resigna-
       tion 215

 XV The Rape of Austria, February 1938 . . 232

XVI Czechoslovakia 250

XVII The Tragedy of Munich 268

XVIII Munich Winter 289

XIX Prague, Albania, and the Polish Guarantee . 305

 XX The Soviet Enigma 322

XXI On the Verge 341

Appendices:

A. A Conversation with Count Grandi . . . 361

B. My Note on the Fleet Air Arm . . . 362

C. Memorandum on Supply Organisation . . 365

D. My Statement on the Occasion of the Deputation of Conservative Members of Both Houses to the Prime Minister, July 28, 1936 . . . 367

E. Comparative Output of First-line Aircraft . . 373

INDEX 375

MAPS

Europe, 1921—After the Peace Treaties . . . 7

The Hitlerite Aggressions 265

BOOK I

THE GATHERING STORM
FROM WAR TO WAR

1919—1939

THEME OF THE BOOK

HOW THE ENGLISH-SPEAKING PEOPLES
THROUGH THEIR UNWISDOM
CARELESSNESS AND GOOD NATURE
ALLOWED THE WICKED
TO REARM

CHAPTER I

THE FOLLIES OF THE VICTORS

1919-1929

The War to End War – A Blood-drained France – The Rhine Frontier – The Economic Clauses of the Versailles Treaty – Ignorance about Reparations – Destruction of the Austro-Hungarian Empire by the Treaties of St. Germain and of Trianon – The Weimar Republic – The Anglo-American Guarantee to France Repudiated by the United States – The Fall of Clemenceau – Poincaré Invades the Ruhr – The Collapse of the Mark – American Isolation – End of the Anglo-Japanese Alliance – Anglo-American Naval Disarmament – Fascism the Child of Communism – How Easy to Prevent a Second Armageddon – The One Solid Security for Peace – The Victors Forget – The Vanquished Remember – Moral Havoc of the Second World War – Failure to Keep Germany Disarmed the Cause.

AFTER the end of the World War of 1914 there was a deep conviction and almost universal hope that peace would reign in the world. This heart's desire of all the peoples could easily have been gained by steadfastness in righteous convictions, and by reasonable common sense and prudence. The phrase "the war to end war" was on every lip, and measures had been taken to turn it into reality. President Wilson, wielding, as was thought, the authority of the United States, had made the conception of a League of Nations dominant in all minds. The British Delegation at Versailles moulded and shaped his idea into an Instrument which will for ever constitute a milestone in the hard march of man. The victorious Allies were at that time all-powerful, so far as their outside enemies were concerned. They had to face grave internal difficulties and many riddles to which they did not know the answer, but the Teutonic Powers in the great mass of Central Europe which had made the upheaval were prostrate before them, and Russia, already shattered by the German flail, was convulsed by civil war and falling into the grip of the Bolshevik or Communist Party.

*　　*　　*

In the summer of 1919 the Allied Armies stood along the Rhine, and their bridgeheads bulged deeply into defeated, disarmed, and hungry Germany. The chiefs of the victor Powers debated and disputed the future in Paris. Before them lay the map of Europe to be redrawn almost as they might resolve. After fifty-two months of agony and hazards the Teutonic coalition lay at their mercy, and not one of its four members could offer the slightest resistance to their will. Germany, the head and front of the offence, regarded by all as the prime cause of the catastrophe which had fallen upon the world, was at the mercy or discretion of conquerors, themselves reeling from the torment they had endured. Moreover, this had been a war not of Governments, but of peoples. The whole life-energy of the greatest nations had been poured out in wrath and slaughter. The war leaders assembled in Paris had been borne thither upon the strongest and most furious tides that have ever flowed in human history. Gone were the days of the treaties of Utrecht and Vienna, when aristocratic statesmen and diplomats, victor and vanquished alike, met in polite and courtly disputation, and, free from the clatter and babel of democracy, could reshape systems upon the fundamentals of which they were all agreed. The peoples, transported by their sufferings and by the mass teachings with which they had been inspired, stood around in scores of millions to demand that retribution should be exacted to the full. Woe betide the leaders now perched on their dizzy pinnacles of triumph if they cast away at the conference table what the soldiers had won on a hundred blood-soaked battlefields.

France, by right alike of her efforts and her losses, held the leading place. Nearly a million and a half Frenchmen had perished defending the soil of France on which they stood against the invader. Five times in a hundred years, in 1814, 1815, 1870, 1914, and 1918, had the towers of Nôtre Dame seen the flash of Prussian guns and heard the thunder of their cannonade. Now for four horrible years thirteen provinces of France had lain in the rigorous

4

grip of Prussian military rule. Wide regions had been systematically devastated by the enemy or pulverised in the encounter of
the armies. There was hardly a cottage or a family from Verdun
to Toulon that did not mourn its dead or shelter its cripples. To
those Frenchmen—and there were many in high authority—who
had fought and suffered in 1870 it seemed almost a miracle that
France should have emerged victorious from the incomparably
more terrible struggle which had just ended. All their lives they
had dwelt in fear of the German Empire. They remembered the
preventive war which Bismarck had sought to wage in 1875; they
remembered the brutal threat which had driven Delcassé from
office in 1905; they had quaked at the Moroccan menace in 1906,
at the Bosnian dispute of 1908, and at the Agadir crisis of 1911.
The Kaiser's "mailed fist" and "shining armour" speeches might
be received with ridicule in England and America: they sounded a
knell of horrible reality in the hearts of the French. For fifty years
almost they had lived under the terror of the German arms. Now,
at the price of their life-blood, the long oppression had been rolled
away. Surely here at last was peace and safety. With one passionate spasm the French people cried "Never again!"

But the future was heavy with foreboding. The population of
France was less than two-thirds that of Germany. The French
population was stationary, while the German grew. In a decade
or less the annual flood of German youth reaching the military
age must be double that of France. Germany had fought nearly
the whole world, almost single-handed, and she had almost conquered. Those who knew the most knew best the several occasions when the result of the Great War had trembled in the
balance, and the accidents and chances which had turned the fateful scale. What prospect was there in the future that the Great
Allies would once again appear in their millions upon the battlefields of France or in the East? Russia was in ruin and convulsion,
transformed beyond all semblance of the past. Italy might be
upon the opposite side. Great Britain and the United States were
separated by the seas or oceans from Europe. The British Empire
itself seemed knit together by ties which none but its citizens could
understand. What combination of events could ever bring back
again to France and Flanders the formidable Canadians of the
Vimy Ridge; the glorious Australians of Villers-Bretonneux; the
dauntless New Zealanders of the crater-fields of Passchendaele;

the steadfast Indian Corps which in the cruel winter of 1914 had held the line by Armentières? When again would peaceful, care-less, anti-militarist Britain tramp the plains of Artois and Picardy with armies of two or three million men? When again would the ocean bear two millions of the splendid manhood of America to Champagne and the Argonne? Worn down, doubly decimated, but undisputed masters of the hour, the French nation peered into the future in thankful wonder and haunting dread. Where then was that SECURITY without which all that had been gained seemed valueless, and life itself, even amid the rejoicings of victory, was almost unendurable? The mortal need was Security at all costs and by all methods, however stern or even harsh.

★   ★   ★

On Armistice Day the German armies had marched homeward in good order. "They fought well." said Marshal Foch, Generalis-simo of the Allies, with the laurels bright upon his brow, speaking in soldierly mood: "let them keep their weapons." But he de-manded that the French frontier should henceforth be the Rhine. Germany might be disarmed; her military system shivered in fragments; her fortresses dismantled: Germany might be im-poverished; she might be loaded with measureless indemnities; she might become a prey to internal feuds: but all this would pass in ten years or in twenty. The indestructible might "of all the German tribes" would rise once more and the unquenched fires of warrior Prussia glow and burn again. But the Rhine, the broad, deep, swift-flowing Rhine, once held and fortified by the French Army, would be a barrier and a shield behind which France could dwell and breathe for generations. Very different were the sentiments and views of the English-speaking world, without whose aid France must have succumbed. The territorial provi-sions of the Treaty of Versailles left Germany practically intact. She still remained the largest homogeneous racial block in Europe. When Marshal Foch heard of the signing of the Peace Treaty of Versailles he observed with singular accuracy: "This is not Peace. It is an Armistice for twenty years."

★   ★   ★

The economic clauses of the Treaty were malignant and silly to an extent that made them obviously futile. Germany was con-demned to pay reparations on a fabulous scale. These dictates

6

EUROPE 1921—AFTER THE PEACE TREATIES

gave expression to the anger of the victors, and to the failure of their peoples to understand that no defeated nation or community can ever pay tribute on a scale which would meet the cost of modern war.

The multitudes remained plunged in ignorance of the simplest economic facts, and their leaders, seeking their votes, did not dare to undeceive them. The newspapers, after their fashion, reflected and emphasised the prevailing opinions. Few voices were raised to explain that payment of reparations can only be made by services or by the physical transportation of goods in wagons across land frontiers or in ships across salt water; or that when these goods arrive in the demanding countries they dislocate the local industry except in very primitive or rigorously-controlled societies. In practice, as even the Russians have now learned, the only way of pillaging a defeated nation is to cart away any movables which are wanted, and to drive off a portion of its manhood as permanent or temporary slaves. But the profit gained from such processes bears no relation to the cost of the war. No one in great authority had the wit, ascendancy, or detachment from public folly to declare these fundamental, brutal facts to the electorates; nor would anyone have been believed if he had. The triumphant Allies continued to assert that they would squeeze Germany "till the pips squeaked". All this had a potent bearing on the prosperity of the world and the mood of the German race.

In fact, however, these clauses were never enforced. On the contrary, whereas about £1,000 millions of German assets were appropriated by the victorious Powers, more than £1,500 millions were lent a few years later to Germany principally by the United States and Great Britain, thus enabling the ruin of the war to be rapidly repaired in Germany. As this apparently magnanimous process was still accompanied by the machine-made howlings of the unhappy and embittered populations in the victorious countries, and the assurances of their statesmen that Germany should be made to pay "to the uttermost farthing", no gratitude or goodwill was to be expected or reaped.

Germany only paid, or was only able to pay, the indemnities later extorted because the United States was profusely lending money to Europe, and especially to her. In fact, during the three years 1926 to 1929 the United States was receiving back in the form of debt-instalment indemnities from all quarters about one-fifth of the money which she was lending to Germany with no chance of repayment. However, everybody seemed pleased and appeared to think this might go on for ever.

History will characterise all these transactions as insane. They helped to breed both the martial curse and the "economic blizzard", of which more later. Germany now borrowed in all directions, swallowing greedily every credit which was lavishly offered her. Misguided sentiment about aiding the vanquished nation, coupled with a profitable rate of interest on these loans, led British investors to participate, though on a much smaller scale than those of the United States. Thus Germany gained about fifteen hundred million pounds sterling in loans as against the one thousand millions of indemnities which she paid in one form or another by surrender of capital assets and *valuta* in foreign countries, or by juggling with the enormous American loans. All this is a sad story of complicated idiocy in the making of which much toil and virtue was consumed.

*　*　*

The second cardinal tragedy was the complete break-up of the Austro-Hungarian Empire by the Treaties of St. Germain and Trianon. For centuries this surviving embodiment of the Holy Roman Empire had afforded a common life, with advantages in trade and security, to a large number of peoples, none of whom in our own time had the strength or vitality to stand by themselves in the face of pressure from a revivified Germany or Russia. All these races wished to break away from the Federal or Imperial structure, and to encourage their desires was deemed a liberal policy. The Balkanisation of South-eastern Europe proceeded apace, with the consequent relative aggrandisement of Prussia and the German Reich, which, though tired and war-scarred, was intact and locally overwhelming. There is not one of the peoples or provinces that constituted the Empire of the Habsburgs to whom gaining their independence has not brought the tortures which ancient poets and theologians had reserved for the damned. The noble capital of Vienna, the home of so much long-defended culture and tradition, the centre of so many roads, rivers, and railways, was left stark and starving, like a great emporium in an impoverished district whose inhabitants have mostly departed.

The victors imposed upon the Germans all the long-sought

ideals of the liberal nations of the West. They were relieved from
the burden of compulsory military service and from the need of
keeping up heavy armaments. The enormous American loans
were presently pressed upon them, though they had no credit. A
democratic constitution, in accordance with all the latest improvements, was established at Weimar. Emperors having been driven
out, nonentities were elected. Beneath this flimsy fabric raged the
passions of the mighty, defeated, but substantially uninjured
German nation. The prejudice of the Americans against
monarchy, which Mr. Lloyd George made no attempt to counter-
act, had made it clear to the beaten Empire that it would have
better treatment from the Allies as a republic than as a monarchy.
Wise policy would have crowned and fortified the Weimar
Republic with a constitutional sovereign in the person of an infant
grandson of the Kaiser, under a Council of Regency. Instead, a
gaping void was opened in the national life of the German people.
All the strong elements, military and feudal, which might have
rallied to a constitutional monarchy and for its sake respected
and sustained the new democratic and Parliamentary processes
were for the time being unhinged. The Weimar Republic, with
all its liberal trappings and blessings, was regarded as an imposition of the enemy. It could not hold the loyalties or the imagination of the German people. For a spell they sought to cling as in
desperation to the aged Marshal Hindenburg. Thereafter mighty
forces were adrift, the void was open, and into that void after a
pause there strode a maniac of ferocious genius, the repository
and expression of the most virulent hatreds that have ever cor-
roded the human breast—Corporal Hitler.

★   ★   ★

France had been bled white by the war. The generation that
had dreamed since 1870 of a war of revenge had triumphed, but
at a deadly cost in national life-strength. It was a haggard France
that greeted the dawn of victory. Deep fear of Germany pervaded the French nation on the morrow of their dazzling success.
It was this fear that had prompted Marshal Foch to demand the
Rhine frontier for the safety of France against her far larger
neighbour. But the British and American statesmen held that the
absorption of German-populated districts in French territory was
contrary to the Fourteen Points and to the principles of

nationalism and self-determination upon which the Peace Treaty was to be based. They therefore withstood Foch and France. They gained Clemenceau by promising, first, a joint Anglo-American guarantee for the defence of France; secondly, a demilitarised zone; and, thirdly, the total, lasting disarmament of Germany. Clemenceau accepted this in spite of Foch's protests and his own instincts. The Treaty of Guarantee was signed accordingly by Wilson and Lloyd George and Clemenceau. The United States Senate refused to ratify the treaty. They repudiated President Wilson's signature. And we, who had deferred so much to his opinions and wishes in all this business of peace-making, were told without much ceremony that we ought to be better informed about the American Constitution.

In the fear, anger, and disarray of the French people the rugged, dominating figure of Clemenceau, with his world-famed authority, and his special British and American contacts, was incontinently discarded. "Ingratitude towards their great men," says Plutarch, "is the mark of strong peoples." It was imprudent for France to indulge this trait when she was so grievously weakened. There was little compensating strength to be found in the revival of the group intrigues and ceaseless changes of Governments and Ministers which were the characteristic of the Third Republic, however profitable or diverting they were to those engaged in them.

Poincaré, the strongest figure who succeeded Clemenceau, attempted to make an independent Rhineland under the patronage and control of France. This had no chance of success. He did not hesitate to try to enforce reparations on Germany by the invasion of the Ruhr. This certainly imposed compliance with the Treaties on Germany; but it was severely condemned by British and American opinion. As a result of the general financial and political disorganisation of Germany, together with reparation payments during the years 1919 to 1923, the mark rapidly collapsed. The rage aroused in Germany by the French occupation of the Ruhr led to a vast, reckless printing of paper notes with the deliberate object of destroying the whole basis of the currency. In the final stages of the inflation the mark stood at forty-three million millions to the pound sterling. The social and economic consequences of this inflation were deadly and far-reaching. The savings of the middle classes were wiped out, and a natural following was thus provided for the banners of National Socialism. The whole structure of German industry was distorted by the growth of mushroom trusts. The entire working capital of the country disappeared. The internal national debt and the debt of industry in the form of fixed capital charges and mortgages were of course simultaneously liquidated or repudiated. But this was no compensation for the loss of working capital. All led directly to the large-scale borrowings of a bankrupt nation abroad which were the feature of ensuing years. German sufferings and bitterness marched forward together—as they do to-day.

The British temper towards Germany, which at first had been so fierce, very soon went as far astray in the opposite direction. A rift opened between Lloyd George and Poincaré, whose bristling personality hampered his firm and far-sighted policies. The two nations fell apart in thought and action, and British sympathy or even admiration for Germany found powerful expression.

★　★　★

The League of Nations had no sooner been created than it received an almost mortal blow. The United States abandoned President Wilson's offspring. The President himself, ready to do battle for his ideals, suffered a paralytic stroke just as he was setting forth on his campaign, and lingered henceforward a futile wreck for a great part of two long and vital years, at the end of which his party and his policy were swept away by the Republican Presidential victory of 1920. Across the Atlantic on the morrow of the Republican success isolationist conceptions prevailed. Europe must be left to stew in its own juice, and must pay its lawful debts. At the same time tariffs were raised to prevent the entry of the goods by which alone these debts could be discharged. At the Washington Conference of 1921 far-reaching proposals for naval disarmament were made by the United States, and the British and American Governments proceeded to sink their battleships and break up their military establishments with gusto. It was argued in odd logic that it would be immoral to disarm the vanquished unless the victors also stripped themselves of their weapons. The finger of Anglo-American reprobation was presently to be pointed at France, deprived alike of the Rhine frontier and of her Treaty guarantee, for maintaining, even on a greatly reduced scale, a French Army based upon universal service.

The United States made it clear to Britain that the continuance of her alliance with Japan, to which the Japanese had punctiliously conformed, would constitute a barrier in Anglo-American relations. Accordingly this alliance was brought to an end. The annulment caused a profound impression in Japan, and was viewed as the spurning of an Asiatic Power by the Western world. Many links were sundered which might afterwards have proved of decisive value to peace. At the same time, Japan could console herself with the fact that the downfall of Germany and Russia had, for a time, raised her to the third place among the world's naval Powers, and certainly to the highest rank. Although the Washington Naval Agreement prescribed a lower ratio of strength in capital ships for Japan than for Britain and the United States (five: five: three), the quota assigned to her was well up to her building and financial capacity for a good many years, and she watched with an attentive eye the two leading naval Powers cutting each other down far below what their resources would have permitted and what their responsibilities enjoined. Thus, both in Europe and in Asia, conditions were swiftly created by the victorious Allies which, in the name of peace, cleared the way for the renewal of war.

While all these untoward events were taking place, amid a ceaseless chatter of well-meant platitudes on both sides of the Atlantic, a new and more terrible cause of quarrel than the Imperialism of Czars and Kaisers became apparent in Europe. The Civil War in Russia ended in the absolute victory of the Bolshevik Revolution. The Soviet armies which advanced to subjugate Poland were indeed repulsed in the Battle of Warsaw, but Germany and Italy nearly succumbed to Communist propaganda and designs, and Hungary actually fell for a while under the control of the Communist dictator Bela Kun. Although Marshal Foch wisely observed that "Bolshevism had never crossed the frontiers of victory", the foundations of European civilisation trembled in the early post-war years. Fascism was the shadow or ugly child of Communism. While Corporal Hitler was making himself useful to the German officer-class in Munich by arousing soldiers and workers to fierce hatred of Jews and Communists, on whom he laid the blame for Germany's defeat, another adventurer, Benito Mussolini, provided Italy with a new theme of government which, while it claimed to save the Italian people from Communism, raised himself to dictatorial power. As Fascism sprang from Communism, so Nazism developed from Fascism. Thus were set on foot those kindred movements which were destined soon to plunge the world into even more hideous strife, which none can say has ended with their destruction.

★   ★   ★

Nevertheless one solid security for peace remained. Germany was disarmed. All her artillery and weapons were destroyed. Her fleet had already sunk itself in Scapa Flow. Her vast army was disbanded. By the Treaty of Versailles only a professional long-service army, not exceeding one hundred thousand men, and unable on this basis to accumulate reserves, was permitted to Germany for purposes of internal order. The annual quotas of recruits no longer received their training; the cadres were dissolved. Every effort was made to reduce to a tithe the Officer Corps. No military air force of any kind was allowed. Submarines were forbidden, and the German Navy was limited to a handful of vessels under 10,000 tons. Soviet Russia was barred off from Western Europe by a cordon of violently anti-Bolshevik States, who had broken away from the former Empire of the Czars in its new and more terrible form. Poland and Czechoslovakia raised independent heads, and seemed to stand erect in Central Europe. Hungary had recovered from her dose of Bela Kun. The French Army, resting upon its laurels, was incomparably the strongest military force in Europe, and it was for some years believed that the French Air Force was also of a high order.

Up till the year 1934 the power of the conquerors remained unchallenged in Europe, and indeed throughout the world There was no moment in these sixteen years when the three former Allies, or even Britain and France with their associates in Europe, could not in the name of the League of Nations and under its moral and international shield have controlled by a mere effort of the will the armed strength of Germany. Instead, until 1931 the victors, and particularly the United States, concentrated their efforts upon extorting by vexatious foreign controls their annual reparations from Germany. The fact that these payments were made only from far larger American loans reduced the whole process to the absurd Nothing was reaped except ill-will. On the other hand, the strict enforcement at any time till 1934 of the Disarmament Clauses of the Peace Treaty would have guarded indefinitely, without violence or bloodshed, the peace and safety of mankind. But this was neglected while the infringements remained petty, and shunned as they assumed serious proportions. Thus the final safeguard of a long peace was cast away. The crimes of the vanquished find their background and their explanation, though not, of course, their pardon, in the follies of the victors. Without these follies crime would have found neither temptation nor opportunity.

★   ★   ★

In these pages I attempt to recount some of the incidents and impressions which form in my mind the story of the coming upon mankind of the worst tragedy in its tumultuous history. This presented itself not only in the destruction of life and property inseparable from war. There had been fearful slaughters of soldiers in the First World War, and much of the accumulated treasure of the nations was consumed. Still, apart from the excesses of the Russian Revolution, the main fabric of European civilisation remained erect at the close of the struggle. When the storm and dust of the cannonade passed suddenly away, the nations, despite their enmities, could still recognise each other as historic racial personalities. The laws of war had on the whole been respected. There was a common professional meeting-ground between military men who had fought one another. Vanquished and victors alike still preserved the semblance of civilised States. A solemn peace was made which, apart from unenforceable financial aspects, conformed to the principles which in the nineteenth century had increasingly regulated the relations of enlightened peoples. The reign of law was proclaimed, and a World Instrument was formed to guard us all, and especially Europe, against a renewed convulsion.

In the Second World War every bond between man and man was to perish. Crimes were committed by the Germans under the Hitlerite domination to which they allowed themselves to be subjected which find no equal in scale and wickedness with any that have darkened the human record. The wholesale massacre by systematised processes of six or seven millions of men, women, and children in the German execution camps exceeds in horror

15

the rough-and-ready butcheries of Genghis Khan, and in scale reduces them to pigmy proportions. Deliberate extermination of whole populations was contemplated and pursued by both Germany and Russia in the Eastern war. The hideous process of bombarding open cities from the air, once started by the Germans, was repaid twenty-fold by the ever-mounting power of the Allies, and found its culmination in the use of the atomic bombs which obliterated Hiroshima and Nagasaki.

We have at length emerged from a scene of material ruin and moral havoc the like of which had never darkened the imagination of former centuries. After all that we suffered and achieved we find ourselves still confronted with problems and perils not less but far more formidable than those through which we have so narrowly made our way.

It is my purpose, as one who lived and acted in these days, to show how easily the tragedy of the Second World War could have been prevented; how the malice of the wicked was reinforced by the weakness of the virtuous; how the structure and habits of democratic States, unless they are welded into larger organisms, lack those elements of persistence and conviction which can alone give security to humble masses; how, even in matters of self-preservation, no policy is pursued for even ten or fifteen years at a time. We shall see how the counsels of prudence and restraint may become the prime agents of mortal danger; how the middle course adopted from desires for safety and a quiet life may be found to lead direct to the bull's-eye of disaster. We shall see how absolute is the need of a broad path of international action pursued by many States in common across the years, irrespective of the ebb and flow of national politics.

It was a simple policy to keep Germany disarmed and the victors adequately armed for thirty years, and in the meanwhile, even if a reconciliation could not be made with Germany, to build ever more strongly a true League of Nations capable of making sure that treaties were kept, or changed only by discussion and agreement. When three or four powerful Governments acting together have demanded the most fearful sacrifices from their peoples, when these have been given freely for the common cause, and when the longed-for result has been attained, it would seem reasonable that concerted action should be preserved so that at least the essentials would not be cast away. But this modest requirement the might, civilisation, learning, knowledge, science, of the victors were unable to supply. They lived from hand to mouth and from day to day, and from one election to another, until, when scarcely twenty years were out, the dread signal of the Second World War was given, and we must write of the sons of those who had fought and died so faithfully and well:

> Shoulder to aching shoulder, side by side,
> They trudged away from life's broad wealds of light.*

* Siegfried Sasson.

CHAPTER II

PEACE AT ITS ZENITH

1922-1931

Mr. Baldwin's Arrival – Fall of Lloyd George – The Revival of Protection – The First Socialist Government in Britain – Mr. Baldwin's Victory – I Become Chancellor of the Exchequer – War Debts and Reparations – Steady Progress at Home for All Classes – Hindenburg Elected President of Germany – The Conference at Locarno – Austen Chamberlain's Achievement – Peace at its Zenith – A Tranquil Europe – Revival of German Prosperity – The General Election of 1929 – My Differences with Mr. Baldwin – India – The Economic Blizzard – A Fine Hope Dies – Unemployment – Fall of Mr. MacDonald's Second Administration – My Political Exile from Office Begins – The British Financial Convulsion – The General Election of 1931.

*D*URING the year 1922 a new leader arose in Britain. Mr. Stanley Baldwin had been unknown or unnoticed in the world drama and played a modest part in domestic affairs. He had been Financial Secretary to the Treasury during the war, and was at this time President of the Board of Trade. He became the ruling force in British politics from October 1922, when he ousted Mr. Lloyd George, until May 1937, when, loaded with honours and enshrined in public esteem, he laid down his heavy task and retired in dignity and silence to his Worcestershire home. My relations with this statesman are a definite part of the tale I have to tell. Our differences at times were serious, but in all these years and later I never had an unpleasant personal interview or contact with him, and at no time did I feel we could not talk together in good faith and understanding as man to man.

★   ★   ★

The party stresses which the Irish Settlement had created inside Mr. Lloyd George's Coalition were growing with the approach

18

of an inevitable General Election. The issue arose whether we should go to the country as a Coalition Government or break up beforehand. It seemed more in accordance with the public interest and the decencies of British politics that parties and Ministers who had come through so much together and bore a mass of joint responsibilities should present themselves unitedly to the nation. In order to make this easy for the Conservatives, who were by far the larger and stronger party, the Prime Minister and I had written earlier in the year offering to resign our offices and give our support from a private station to a new Government to be formed by Mr. Austen Chamberlain. The Conservative leaders, having considered this letter, replied firmly that they would not accept that sacrifice from us and that we must all stand or fall together. This chivalrous attitude was not endorsed by their followers in the party, which now felt itself strong enough to resume undivided power in the State.

By an overwhelming vote the Conservative Party determined to break with Lloyd George and end the National Coalition Government. The Prime Minister resigned that same afternoon. In the morning we had been friends and colleagues of all these people. By nightfall they were our party foes, intent on driving us from public life. With the solitary and unexpected exception of Lord Curzon, all the prominent Conservatives who had fought the war with us, and the majority of all the Ministers, adhered to Lloyd George. These included Arthur Balfour, Austen Chamberlain, Robert Horne, and Lord Birkenhead, the four ablest figures in the Conservative Party. At the crucial moment I was prostrated by a severe operation for appendicitis, and in the morning when I recovered consciousness I learned that the Lloyd George Government had resigned, and that I had lost not only my appendix but my office as Secretary of State for the Dominions and Colonies, in which I conceived myself to have had some Parliamentary and administrative success. Mr. Bonar Law, who had left us a year before for serious reasons of health, reluctantly became Prime Minister. He formed a Government of what one might call "the Second Eleven". Mr. Baldwin, the outstanding figure, was Chancellor of the Exchequer. The Prime Minister asked the King for a Dissolution. The people wanted a change. Mr. Bonar Law, with Mr. Baldwin at his side, and Lord Beaverbrook as his principal stimulant and mentor, gained a majority of seventy-three, with all the expectations of a five-year tenure of power. Early in the year 1923 Mr. Bonar Law resigned the Premiership and retired to die of his fell affliction. Mr. Baldwin succeeded him as Prime Minister, and Lord Curzon reconciled himself to the office of Foreign Secretary in the new Administration.

Thus began that period of fourteen years which may well be called "the Baldwin-MacDonald Régime". At first in alternation but eventually in political brotherhood, these two statesmen governed the country. Nominally the representatives of opposing parties, of contrary doctrines, of antagonistic interests, they proved in fact to be more nearly akin in outlook, temperament, and method than any other two men who had been Prime Ministers since that office was known to the Constitution. Curiously enough, the sympathies of each extended far into the territory of the other. Ramsay MacDonald nursed many of the sentiments of the old Tory. Stanley Baldwin, apart from a manufacturer's ingrained approval of Protection, was by disposition a truer representative of mild Socialism than many to be found in the Labour ranks.

*　　*　　*

Mr. Baldwin was by no means dazzled by his suddenly-acquired political eminence. "Give me your prayers," he said, when congratulations were offered. He was however soon disquieted by the fear that Mr. Lloyd George would rally, upon the cry of Protection, the numerous dissentient Conservative leaders who had gone out of office with the War Cabinet, and thus split the Government majority and even challenge the party leadership. He therefore resolved, in the autumn of 1923, to forestall his rivals by raising the Protectionist issue himself. He made a speech at Plymouth on October 25 which could only have the effect of bringing the newly-elected Parliament to an untimely end. He protested his innocence of any such design; but to accept this would be to underrate his profound knowledge of British party politics. Parliament was accordingly on his advice dissolved in October, and a second General Election was held within barely a twelvemonth.

The Liberal Party, rallying round the standard of Free Trade, to which I also adhered, gained a balancing position at the polls, and, though in a minority, might well have taken office had Mr. Asquith wished to do so. In view of his disinclination, Mr. Ramsay MacDonald, at the head of little more than two-fifths of the House, became the first Socialist Prime Minister of Great Britain, and lived in office for a year by the sufferance and on the quarrels of the two older parties. The nation was extremely restive under minority Socialist rule, and the political weather became so favourable that the two Oppositions—Liberal and Conservative—picked an occasion to defeat the Socialist Government on a major issue. There was another General Election—the third in less than two years. The Conservatives were returned by a majority of 222 over all other parties combined.* At the beginning of this election Mr. Baldwin's position was very weak, and he made no particular contribution to the result. He had however previously maintained himself as party leader, and as the results were declared it became certain that he would become again Prime Minister.

At this time I stood fairly high in Tory popularity. At the Westminster by-election six months later I proved my hold upon Conservative forces. Although I stood as an Independent Constitutionalist, great numbers of Tories worked and voted for me. In charge of each of my thirty-four committee rooms was a Conservative M.P. defying his leader Mr. Baldwin and the party machine. This was unprecedented. I was defeated only by forty-three votes out of over twenty thousand cast. At the General Election I was returned for Epping by a ten thousand majority, but as a "Constitutionalist". I would not at that time adopt the name "Conservative". I had had some friendly contacts with Mr. Baldwin in the interval; but I did not think he would survive to be Prime Minister. Now on the morrow of his victory I had no idea how he felt towards me. I was surprised, and the Conservative Party dumbfounded, when he invited me to become Chancellor of the Exchequer, the office which my father had once held. A year later, with the approval of my constituents, not having been pressed personally in any way, I formally rejoined the Conservative Party and the Carlton Club, which I had left twenty years before.

★   ★   ★

* Conservatives 413, Liberal 40, Labour 151.

My first question at the Treasury of an international character was our American debt. At the end of the war the European Allies owed the United States about ten thousand million dollars, of which four thousand million were owed by Britain. On the other hand, we were owed by the other Allies, principally by Russia, seven thousand million dollars. In 1920 Britain had proposed an all-round cancellation of war debts. This involved, on paper at least, a sacrifice by us of about seven hundred and fifty million pounds sterling. As the value of money has halved since then, the figures could in fact be doubled. No settlement was reached. On August 1, 1922, in Mr. Lloyd George's day, the Balfour Note had declared that Great Britain would collect no more from her debtors, Ally or former enemy, than the United States collected from her. This was a worthy statement. In December of 1922 a British delegation under Mr. Baldwin, Chancellor of the Exchequer in Mr. Bonar Law's Government, visited Washington; and as the result Britain agreed to pay the whole of her war debt to the United States at a rate of interest that had been reduced from 5 to $3\frac{1}{2}$ per cent., irrespective of receipts from her debtors.

This agreement caused deep concern in many instructed quarters, and to no one more than the Prime Minister himself. It imposed upon Great Britain, much impoverished by the war, in which, as she was to do once again, she had fought from the first day to the last, the payment of thirty-five millions sterling a year for sixty-two years. The basis of this agreement was considered, not only in this Island, but by many disinterested financial authorities in America, to be a severe and improvident condition for both borrower and lender. "They hired the money, didn't they?" said President Coolidge. This laconic statement was true, but not exhaustive. Payments between countries which take the form of the transfer of goods and services, or still more of their fruitful exchange, are not only just but beneficial. Payments which are only the arbitrary, artificial transmission across the exchange of such very large sums as arise in war finance cannot fail to derange the whole process of world economy. This is equally true whether the payments are exacted from an ally who shared the victory and bore much of the brunt or from a defeated enemy nation. The enforcement of the Baldwin-Coolidge debt settlement is a recognisable factor in the economic collapse which was presently to overwhelm the world, to prevent its recovery and inflame its hatreds.

The service of the American debt was particularly difficult to render to a country which had newly raised its tariffs to even higher limits, and was soon to bury in its vaults nearly all the gold yet dug up. Similar but lighter settlements were imposed upon the other European Allies. The first result was that every-one put the screw on Germany. I was in full accord with the policy of the Balfour Note of 1922, and had argued for it at the time; and when I became Chancellor of the Exchequer I reiterated it, and acted accordingly. I thought that if Great Britain were thus made not only the debtor but the debt-collector of the United States the unwisdom of the debt collection would become apparent at Washington. However, no such reaction followed. Indeed, the argument was resented. The United States continued to insist upon its annual repayments from Great Britain, albeit at a reduced rate of interest.

It therefore fell to me to make settlements with all our Allies which, added to the German payments, which we had already scaled down, would enable us to produce the thirty-five millions annually for the American Treasury. Severest pressure was put upon Germany, and a vexatious *régime* of international control of German internal affairs was imposed. The United States received from England three payments in full, and these were extorted from Germany by indemnities on the modified Dawes scale.

★　　★　　★

For almost five years I lived next door to Mr. Baldwin at No. 11 Downing Street, and nearly every morning on my way through his house to the Treasury I looked in upon him for a few minutes' chat in the Cabinet Room As I was one of his leading colleagues, I take my share of responsibility for all that happened. These five years were marked by very considerable recovery at home. This was a capable, sedate Government during a period in which marked improvement and recovery were gradually effected year by year. There was nothing sensational or contro-versial to boast about on the platforms, but, measured by every test, economic and financial, the mass of the people were definitely better off, and the state of the nation and of the world was easier and more fertile by the end of our term than at its beginning. Here is a modest but a solid claim.

It was in Europe that the distinction of the Administration was achieved.

★　　★　　★

Hindenburg now rose to power in Germany. At the end of February 1925 Friedrich Ebert, leader of the pre-war German Social-Democrat Party, and first President of the German Republic after the defeat, died. A new President had to be chosen. All Germans had long been brought up under paternal despotism, tempered by far-reaching customs of free speech and Parliamentary opposition. Defeat had brought them on its scaly wings democratic forms and liberties in an extreme degree. But the nation was rent and bewildered by all it had gone through, and many parties and groups contended for precedence and office. Out of the turmoil emerged a strong desire to turn to old Field-Marshal von Hindenburg, who was dwelling in dignified retirement. Hindenburg was faithful to the exiled Emperor, and favoured a restoration of the Imperial monarchy "on the English model". This of course was much the most sensible though least fashionable thing to do. When he was besought to stand as a candidate for the Presidency under the Weimar Constitution he was profoundly disturbed. "Leave me in peace," he said again and again.

However, the pressure was continuous, and only Grand-Admiral von Tirpitz at last was found capable of persuading him to abandon both his scruples and his inclinations at the call of duty, which he had always obeyed. Hindenburg's opponents were Marx of the Catholic Centre and Thaelmann the Communist. On Sunday, April 26, all Germany voted. The result was unexpectedly close: Hindenburg, 14,655,766; Marx, 13,751,615; Thaelmann, 1,931,151. Hindenburg, who towered above his opponents by being illustrious, reluctant, and disinterested, was elected by less than a million majority, and with no absolute majority on the total poll. He rebuked his son Oskar for waking him at seven to tell him the news: "Why did you want to wake me up an hour earlier? It would still have been true at eight." And with this he went to sleep again till his usual calling-time.

In France the election of Hindenburg was at first viewed as a renewal of the German challenge. In England there was an easier reaction. Always wishing as I did to see Germany recover her honour and self-respect and to let war-bitterness die, I was not at all distressed by the news. "He is a very sensible old man," said Lloyd George to me when we next met; and so indeed he proved as long as his faculties remained. Even some of his most bitter opponents were forced to admit "Better a Zero than a Nero".* However, he was seventy-seven, and his term of office was to be seven years. Few expected him to be returned again. He did his best to be impartial between the various parties, and certainly his tenure of the Presidency gave a sober strength and comfort to Germany without menace to her neighbours.

★   ★   ★

Meanwhile in February 1925 the German Government had addressed itself to M. Herriot, then French Premier. Their memorandum stated that Germany was willing to declare her acceptance of a pact by virtue of which the Powers interested in the Rhine, above all England, France, Italy, and Germany, would enter into a solemn obligation for a lengthy period towards the Government of the United States, as trustees, not to wage war against a contracting State. Furthermore, a pact expressly guaranteeing the existing territorial status on the Rhine would be acceptable to Germany. This was a remarkable event. The French Government undertook to consult their Allies. Mr. Austen Chamberlain made the news public in the House of Commons on March 5. Parliamentary crises in France and Germany delayed the process of negotiations, but after consultation between London and Paris a formal Note was handed to Herr Stresemann, the German Foreign Minister, by the French Ambassador in Berlin on June 16, 1925. The Note declared that no agreement could be reached unless as a prior condition Germany entered the League of Nations. There could be no suggestion in any proposed agreement of a modification of the conditions of the Peace Treaty. Belgium must be included among the contracting Powers, and finally the natural complement of a Rhineland Pact would be a Franco-German Arbitration Treaty.

The British attitude was debated in the House of Commons on

* Theodore Lessing (murdered by the Nazis, September 1933).

June 24. Mr. Chamberlain explained that British commitments under the Pact would be limited to the West. France would probably define her special relationships with Poland and Czechoslovakia; but Great Britain would not assume any obligations other than those specified in the Covenant of the League. The British Dominions were not enthusiastic about a Western Pact. General Smuts was anxious to avoid regional arrangements. The Canadians were lukewarm, and only New Zealand was unconditionally prepared to accept the view of the British Government. Nevertheless we persevered. To me the aim of ending the thousand-year strife between France and Germany seemed a supreme object. If we could only weave Gaul and Teuton so closely together economically, socially, and morally as to prevent the occasion of new quarrels, and make old antagonisms die in the realisation of mutual prosperity and interdependence, Europe would rise again. It seemed to me that the supreme interest of the British people in Europe lay in the assuagement of the Franco-German feud, and that they had no other interests comparable or contrary to that. This is still my view to-day.

Mr. Austen Chamberlain, as Foreign Secretary, had an outlook which was respected by all parties, and the whole Cabinet was united in his support. In July the Germans replied to the French Note, accepting the linking up of a Western Pact with the entry of Germany into the League of Nations, but stating the prior need for agreement upon general disarmament. M. Briand came to England, and prolonged discussions were held upon the Western Pact and its surroundings. In August the French, with the full agreement of Great Britain, replied officially to Germany. Germany must enter the League without reservations as the first and indispensable step. The German Government accepted this stipulation. This meant that the conditions of the Treaties were to continue in force unless or until modified by mutual arrangement, and that no specific pledge for a reduction of Allied armaments had been obtained. Further demands by the Germans, put forward under intense nationalistic pressure and excitement, for the eradication from the Peace Treaty of the War Guilt clause, for keeping open the issue of Alsace-Lorraine, and for the immediate evacuation of Cologne by Allied troops, were not pressed by the German Government, and would not have been conceded by the Allies.

On this basis the Conference at Locarno was formally opened on October 4. By the waters of this calm lake the delegates of Britain, France, Germany, Belgium, and Italy assembled. The Conference achieved: first, the Treaty of Mutual Guarantee between the five Powers; secondly, Arbitration Treaties between Germany and France, Germany and Belgium, Germany and Poland, Germany and Czechoslovakia; thirdly, special agreements between France and Poland, and France and Czechoslovakia, by which France undertook to afford them assistance if a breakdown of the Western Pact were followed by an unprovoked resort to arms. Thus did the Western European democracies agree to keep the peace among themselves in all circumstances, and to stand united against any one of their number who broke the contract and marched in aggression upon a brother land. As between France and Germany, Great Britain became solemnly pledged to come to the aid of whichever of these two States was the object of unprovoked aggression. This far-reaching military commitment was accepted by Parliament and endorsed warmly by the nation. The histories may be searched in vain for a parallel to such an undertaking.

The question whether there was any obligation on the part of France or Britain to disarm, or to disarm to any particular level, was not affected. I had been brought into these matters as Chancellor of the Exchequer at an early stage. My own view about this two-way guarantee was that while France remained armed and Germany disarmed Germany could not attack her; and that on the other hand France would never attack Germany if that automatically involved Britain becoming Germany's ally. Thus although the proposal seemed dangerous in theory—pledging us in fact to take part on one side or the other in any Franco-German war that might arise—there was little likelihood of such a disaster ever coming to pass; and this was the best means of preventing it. I was therefore always equally opposed to the disarmament of France and to the rearmament of Germany, because of the much greater danger this immediately brought on Great Britain. On the other hand, Britain and the League of Nations, which Germany joined as part of the agreement, offered a real protection to the German people. Thus there was a balance created in which Britain, whose major interest was the cessation of the quarrel between Germany and France, was to a large extent umpire and arbiter. One hoped that this equilibrium might have lasted twenty years, during which the Allied armaments would gradually and naturally have dwindled under the influence of a long peace, growing confidence, and financial burdens. It was evident that danger would arise if ever Germany became more or less equal with France, still more if she became stronger than France. But all this seemed excluded by solemn treaty obligations.

*   *   *

The pact of Locarno was concerned only with peace in the West, and it was hoped that what was called an "Eastern Locarno" might be its successor. We should have been very glad if the danger of some future war between Germany and Russia could have been controlled in the same spirit and by similar measures as the possibility of war between Germany and France. Even the Germany of Stresemann was however disinclined to close the door on German claims in the East, or to accept the territorial treaty position about Poland, Danzig, the Corridor, and Upper Silesia. Soviet Russia brooded in her isolation behind the *Cordon Sanitaire* of anti-Bolshevik States. Although our efforts were continued, no progress was made in the East. I did not at any time close my mind to an attempt to give Germany greater satisfaction on her eastern frontier. But no opportunity arose during these brief years of hope.

*   *   *

There were great rejoicings about the treaty which emerged at the end of 1925 from the Conference at Locarno. Mr. Baldwin was the first to sign it at the Foreign Office. The Foreign Secretary, having no official residence, asked me to lend my dining-room at No. 11 Downing Street for his intimate friendly luncheon with Herr Stresemann. We all met together in great amity, and thought what a wonderful future would await Europe if its greatest nation became truly united and felt themselves secure. After this memorable instrument had received the cordial assent of Parliament, Mr. Austen Chamberlain was given the Garter and the Nobel Peace Prize. His achievement was the high-water mark of Europe's restoration, and it inaugurated three years of peace and recovery. Although old antagonisms were but sleeping, and the drumbeat of new levies was already heard, we were justified in hoping that the ground thus solidly gained would open the road to a further forward march.

At the end of the second Baldwin Administration the state of Europe was tranquil, as it had not been for twenty years, and was not to be for at least another twenty. A friendly feeling existed towards Germany following upon our Treaty of Locarno, and the evacuation of the Rhineland by the French Army and Allied contingents at a much earlier date than had been prescribed at Versailles. The new Germany took her place in the truncated League of Nations. Under the genial influence of American and British loans Germany was reviving rapidly. Her new ocean liners gained the Blue Riband of the Atlantic. Her trade advanced by leaps and bounds, and internal prosperity ripened. France and her system of alliances also seemed secure in Europe. The disarmament clauses of the Treaty of Versailles were not openly violated. The German Navy was non-existent. The German Air Force was prohibited and still unborn. There were many influences in Germany strongly opposed, if only on grounds of prudence, to the idea of war, and the German High Command could not believe that the Allies would allow them to rearm. On the other hand, there lay before us what I later called the "Economic Blizzard". Knowledge of this was confined to rare financial circles, and these were cowed into silence by what they foresaw.

*　　*　　*

The General Election of May 1929 showed that the "swing of the pendulum" and the normal desire for change were powerful factors with the British electorate. The Socialists had a small majority over the Conservatives in the new House of Commons. The Liberals, with about sixty seats, held the balance, and it was plain that under Mr. Lloyd George's leadership they would, at the outset at least, be hostile to the Conservatives. Mr. Baldwin and I were in full agreement that we should not seek to hold office in a minority or on precarious Liberal support. Accordingly, although there were some differences of opinion in the Cabinet and the party about the course to be taken, Mr. Baldwin tendered his resignation to the King. We all went down to Windsor in a special train to give up our seals and offices; and on June 7 Mr. Ramsay MacDonald became for the second time Prime Minister at the head of a minority Government depending upon Liberal votes.

★   ★   ★

The Socialist Prime Minister wished his new Labour Government to distinguish itself by large concessions to Egypt, by a far-reaching constitutional change in India, and by a renewed effort for world, or at any rate British, disarmament. These were aims in which he could count upon Liberal aid, and for which he therefore commanded a Parliamentary majority. Here began my differences with Mr. Baldwin, and thereafter the relationship in which we had worked since he chose me for Chancellor of the Exchequer five years before became sensibly altered. We still of course remained in easy personal contact, but we knew we did not mean the same thing. My idea was that the Conservative Opposition should strongly confront the Labour Government on all great Imperial and national issues, should identify itself with the majesty of Britain as under Lord Beaconsfield and Lord Salisbury, and should not hesitate to face controversy, even though that might not immediately evoke a response from the nation. So far as I could see, Mr. Baldwin felt that the times were too far gone for any robust assertion of British Imperial greatness, and that the hope of the Conservative Party lay in accommodation with Liberal and Labour forces and in adroit, well-timed manœuvres to detach powerful moods of public opinion and large blocks of voters from them. He certainly was very successful. He was the greatest party manager the Conservatives had ever had. He fought, as their leader, five General Elections, of which he won three. History alone can judge these general issues.

It was on India that our definite breach occurred. The Prime Minister, strongly supported and even spurred by the Conservative Viceroy, Lord Irwin, afterwards Lord Halifax, pressed forward with his plan of Indian self-government. A portentous conference was held in London, of which Mr. Gandhi, lately released from commodious internment, was the central figure. There is no need to follow in these pages the details of the controversy which occupied the sessions of 1929 and 1930. On the release of Mr. Gandhi in order that he might become the envoy of Nationalist India to the London conference I reached the breaking-point in my relations with Mr. Baldwin. He seemed

30

quite content with these developments, was in general accord with the Prime Minister and the Viceroy, and led the Conservative Opposition decidedly along this path. I felt sure we should lose India in the final result and that measureless disasters would come upon the Indian peoples. I therefore after a while resigned from the Shadow Cabinet upon this issue. On January 27, 1931, I wrote to Mr. Baldwin:

Now that our divergence of view upon Indian policy has become public, I feel that I ought not any longer to attend the meetings of your Business Committee, to which you have hitherto so kindly invited me. I need scarcely add that I will give you whatever aid is in my power in opposing the Socialist Government in the House of Commons, and I shall do my utmost to secure their defeat at the General Election.

★   ★   ★

The year 1929 reached almost the end of its third quarter under the promise and appearance of increasing prosperity, particularly in the United States. Extraordinary optimism sustained an orgy of speculation. Books were written to prove that economic crisis was a phase which expanding business organisation and science had at last mastered. "We are apparently finished and done with economic cycles as we have known them," said the President of the New York Stock Exchange in September. But in October a sudden and violent tempest swept over Wall Street. The intervention of the most powerful agencies failed to stem the tide of panic sales. A group of leading banks constituted a milliard-dollar pool to maintain and stabilise the market. All was vain.

The whole wealth so swiftly gathered in the paper values of previous years vanished. The prosperity of millions of American homes had grown upon a gigantic structure of inflated credit, now suddenly proved phantom. Apart from the nation-wide speculation in shares which even the most famous banks had encouraged by easy loans, a vast system of purchase by instalment of houses, furniture, cars, and numberless kinds of household conveniences and indulgences had grown up. All now fell together. The mighty production plants were thrown into confusion and paralysis. But yesterday there had been the urgent question of parking the motor-cars in which thousands of artisans and craftsmen were beginning to travel to their daily work. To-day the grievous pangs of falling wages and rising unemployment afflicted the whole community, engaged till this moment in the most active creation of all kinds of desirable articles for the enjoyment of millions. The American banking system was far less concentrated and solidly based than the British. Twenty thousand local banks suspended payment. The means of exchange of goods and services between man and man was smitten to the ground, and the crash on Wall Street reverberated in modest and rich households alike.

It should not however be supposed that the fair vision of far greater wealth and comfort ever more widely shared which had entranced the people of the United States had nothing behind it but delusion and market frenzy. Never before had such immense quantities of goods of all kinds been produced, shared, and exchanged in any society. There is in fact no limit to the benefits which human beings may bestow upon one another by the highest exertion of their diligence and skill. This splendid manifestation had been shattered and cast down by vain imaginative processes and greed of gain which far outstripped the great achievement itself. In the wake of the collapse of the stock market came during the years between 1929 and 1932 an unrelenting fall in prices and consequent cuts in production causing widespread unemployment.

The consequences of this dislocation of economic life became world-wide. A general contraction of trade in the face of unemployment and declining production followed. Tariff restrictions were imposed to protect the home markets. The general crisis brought with it acute monetary difficulties, and paralysed internal credit. This spread ruin and unemployment far and wide throughout the globe. Mr. MacDonald's Government, with all their promises behind them, saw unemployment during 1930 and 1931 bound up in their faces from one million to nearly three millions. It was said that in the United States ten million persons were without work. The entire banking system of the great Republic was thrown into confusion and temporary collapse. Consequential disasters fell upon Germany and other European countries. However, nobody starved in the English-speaking world.

★   ★   ★

It is always difficult for an Administration or party which is founded upon attacking capital to preserve the confidence and credit so important to the highly artificial economy of an island like Britain. Mr. MacDonald's Labour-Socialist Government were utterly unable to cope with the problems which confronted them. They could not command the party discipline or produce the vigour necessary even to balance the Budget. In such conditions a Government already in a minority and deprived of all financial confidence could not survive.

The failure of the Labour Party to face this tempest, the sudden collapse of British financial credit, and the break-up of the Liberal Party, with its unwholesome balancing power, led to a National Coalition. It seemed that only a Government of all parties was capable of coping with the crisis. Mr. MacDonald and his Chancellor of the Exchequer, on a strong patriotic emotion, attempted to carry the mass of the Labour Party into this combination. Mr. Baldwin, always content that others should have the function so long as he retained the power, was willing to serve under Mr. MacDonald. It was an attitude which, though deserving respect, did not correspond to the facts. Mr. Lloyd George was still recovering from an operation—serious at his age, and Sir Herbert Samuel led the bulk of the Liberals into the all-party combination.

I was not invited to take part in the Coalition Government. I was politically severed from Mr. Baldwin about India. I was an opponent of the policy of Mr. MacDonald's Labour Government. Like many others, I had felt the need of a national concentration. But I was neither surprised nor unhappy when I was left out of it. Indeed, I remained painting at Cannes while the political crisis lasted. What I should have done if I had been asked to join I cannot tell. It is superfluous to discuss doubtful temptations that have never existed. Certainly during the summer I had talked to MacDonald about a National Administration, and he had shown some interest. But I was awkwardly placed in the political scene. I had had fifteen years of Cabinet office, and was now busy with my life of Marlborough. Political dramas are very exciting at the time to those engaged in the clatter and whirlpool of politics, but I can truthfully affirm that I never felt resentment, still less pain, at being so decisively discarded in a moment of national stress. There was however an inconvenience. For all these years since 1905 I had sat on one or the other of the Front

Benches, and always had the advantage of speaking from the box, on which you can put your notes and pretend with more or less success to be making it up as you go along. Now I had to find with some difficulty a seat below the gangway on the Government side, where I had to hold my notes in my hand whenever I spoke, and take my chance in debate with other well-known ex-Cabinet Ministers. However, from time to time I got called.

* * *

The formation of the new Government did not end the financial crisis, and I returned from abroad to find everything unsettled in the advent of an inevitable General Election. The verdict of the electorate was worthy of the British nation. A National Government had been formed under Mr. Ramsay MacDonald, the founder of the Labour-Socialist Party. They proposed to the people a programme of severe austerity and sacrifice. It was an earlier version of "blood, toil, tears, and sweat", without the stimulus or the requirements of war and mortal peril. The sternest economy must be practised. Everyone would have his wages, salary, or income reduced. The mass of the people were asked to vote for a *régime* of self-denial. They responded as they always do when caught in the heroic temper. Although, contrary to their declarations, the Government abandoned the Gold Standard, and although Mr. Baldwin was obliged to suspend, as it proved for ever, those very payments on the American debt which he had forced on the Bonar Law Cabinet of 1923, confidence and credit were restored. There was an overwhelming majority for the new Administration. Mr. MacDonald as Prime Minister was only followed by seven or eight members of his own party; but barely fifty of his Labour opponents and former followers were returned to Parliament. His health and powers were failing fast, and he reigned in increasing decrepitude at the summit of the British system for nearly four fateful years. And very soon in these four years came Hitler.

CHAPTER III

LURKING DANGERS

My Reflections in 1928 – Annihilating Terrors of Future War – Some Technical Predictions – Allied Hatred of War and Militarism – "Ease Would Recant" – The German Army – The Hundred Thousand Volunteer Limit – General von Seeckt, His Work and Theme – "A Second Scharnhorst" – The Withdrawal of the Allied Mission of Control, January 1927 – German Aviation – Encroachment and Camouflage – The German Navy – Rathenau's Munitions Scheme – Convertible Factories – The "No Major War for Ten Years" Rule.

IN MY BOOK *The Aftermath* I have set down some reflections on the four years which elapsed between the Armistice and the change of Government in Britain at the end of 1922. Writing in 1928, I was deeply under the impression of a future catastrophe.

It was not until the dawn of the twentieth century of the Christian era that war began to enter into its kingdom as the potential destroyer of the human race. The organisation of mankind into great States and Empires, and the rise of nations to full collective consciousness, enabled enterprises of slaughter to be planned and executed upon a scale and with a perseverance never before imagined. All the noblest virtues of individuals were gathered to strengthen the destructive capacity of the mass. Good finances, the resources of world-wide credit and trade, the accumulation of large capital reserves, made it possible to divert for considerable periods the energies of whole peoples to the task of devastation. Democratic institutions gave expression to the will-power of millions. Education not only brought the course of the conflict within the comprehension of everyone, but rendered each person serviceable in a high degree for the purpose in hand. The Press afforded a means of unification and of mutual stimulation. Religion, having discreetly avoided conflict on the fundamental issues. offered its encouragements and consolations, through all its forms, impartially to all the combatants. Lastly, Science unfolded her treasures and her secrets to the desperate demands of men, and placed in their hands agencies and apparatus almost decisive in their character.

In consequence many novel features presented themselves. Instead of merely fortified towns being starved whole nations were methodically subjected, or sought to be subjected, to the process of reduction by famine. The entire population in one capacity or another took part in the war; all were equally the object of attack. The air opened paths along which death and terror could be carried far behind the lines of the actual armies, to women, children, the aged, the sick, who in earlier struggles would perforce have been left untouched. Marvellous organisations of railroads, steamships, and motor vehicles placed and maintained tens of millions of men continuously in action. Healing and surgery in their exquisite developments returned them again and again to the shambles. Nothing was wasted that could contribute to the process of waste. The last dying kick was brought into military utility.

But all that happened in the four years of the Great War was only a prelude to what was preparing for the fifth year. The campaign of the year 1919 would have witnessed an immense accession to the powers of destruction. Had the Germans retained the morale to make good their retreat to the Rhine, they would have been assaulted in the summer of 1919 with forces and by methods incomparably more prodigious than any yet employed. Thousands of aeroplanes would have shattered their cities. Scores of thousands of cannon would have blasted their front. Arrangements were being made to carry simultaneously a quarter of a million men, together with all their requirements, continuously forward across country in mechanical vehicles moving ten or fifteen miles each day. Poison gases of incredible malignity, against which only a secret mask (which the Germans could not obtain in time) was proof, would have stifled all resistance and paralysed all life on the hostile front subjected to attack. No doubt the Germans too had their plans. But the hour of wrath had passed. The signal of relief was given, and the horrors of 1919 remained buried in the archives of the great antagonists.

The war stopped as suddenly and as universally as it had begun. The world lifted its head, surveyed the scene of ruin, and victors and vanquished alike drew breath. In a hundred laboratories, in a thousand arsenals, factories, and bureaux, men pulled themselves up with a jerk, and turned from the task in which they had been absorbed. Their projects were put aside unfinished, unexecuted; but their knowledge was preserved; their data, calculations, and discoveries were hastily bundled together and docketed "for future reference" by the War Offices in every country. The campaign of 1919 was never fought; but its ideas go marching along. In every army they are being explored, elaborated, refined under the surface of peace, and should war come again to the world it is not with the weapons and agencies prepared for 1919 that it will be fought, but with developments and extensions of these which will be incomparably more formidable and fatal.

It is in these circumstances that we entered upon that period of exhaustion which has been described as Peace. It gives us, at any rate, an opportunity to consider the general situation. Certain sombre facts emerge, solid, inexorable, like the shapes of mountains from drifting mist. It is established that henceforward whole populations will take part in war, all doing their utmost, all subjected to the fury of the enemy. It is established that nations who believe their life is at stake will not be restrained from using any means to secure their existence. It is probable—nay, certain—that among the means which will next time be at their disposal will be agencies and processes of destruction wholesale, unlimited, and perhaps, once launched, uncontrollable.

Mankind has never been in this position before. Without having improved appreciably in virtue or enjoying wiser guidance, it has got into its hands for the first time the tools by which it can unfailingly accomplish its own extermination. That is the point in human destinies to which all the glories and toils of men have at last led them. They would do well to pause and ponder upon their new responsibilities. Death stands at attention, obedient, expectant, ready to serve, ready to shear away the peoples *en masse*; ready, if called on, to pulverise, without hope of repair, what is left of civilisation. He awaits only the word of command. He awaits it from a frail, bewildered being, long his victim, now—for one occasion only—his Master.

*   *   *

All this was published on January 1, 1929. Now, on another New Year's Day eighteen years later, I could not write it differently. All the words and actions for which I am accountable between the wars had as their object only the prevention of a second World War; and, of course, of making sure that if the worst happened we won, or at least survived. There can hardly ever have been a war more easy to prevent than this second Armageddon. I have always been ready to use force in order to defy tyranny or ward off ruin. But had our British, American, and Allied affairs been conducted with the ordinary consistency and common sense usual in decent households there was no need

37

for Force to march unaccompanied by Law; and Strength, more-over, could have been used in righteous causes with little risk of bloodshed. In their loss of purpose, in their abandonment even of the themes they most sincerely espoused, Britain, France, and most of all, because of their immense power and impartiality, the United States, allowed conditions to be gradually built up which led to the very climax they dreaded most. They have only to repeat the same well-meaning, short-sighted behaviour towards the new problems which in singular resemblance confront us to-day to bring about a third convulsion from which none may live to tell the tale.

★ ★ ★

I had written even earlier, in 1925, some thoughts and queries of a technical character which it would be wrong to omit in these days:

May there not be methods of using explosive energy incomparably more intense than anything heretofore discovered? Might not a bomb no bigger than an orange be found to possess a secret power to destroy a whole block of buildings—nay, to concentrate the force of a thousand tons of cordite and blast a township at a stroke? Could not explosives even of the existing type be guided automatically in flying machines by wireless or other rays, without a human pilot, in ceaseless procession upon a hostile city, arsenal, camp, or dockyard?

As for poison gas and chemical warfare in all its forms, only the first chapter has been written of a terrible book. Certainly every one of these new avenues to destruction is being studied on both sides of the Rhine with all the science and patience of which man is capable. And why should it be supposed that these resources will be limited to inorganic chemistry? A study of disease—of pestilences methodically prepared and deliberately launched upon man and beast—is certainly being pursued in the laboratories of more than one great country. Blight to destroy crops, anthrax to slay horses and cattle, plague to poison not armies only but whole districts—such are the lines along which military science is remorselessly advancing.

All this is nearly a quarter of a century old.

★ ★ ★

It is natural that a proud people vanquished in war should strive to rearm themselves as soon as possible. They will not respect more than they can help treaties exacted from them under duress.

38

> ... Ease would recant
> Vows made in pain, as violent and void.

The responsibility therefore of imposing a continual state of military disarmament upon a beaten foe rests upon the victors. For this purpose they must pursue a twofold policy. First, while remaining sufficiently armed themselves, they must enforce with tireless vigilance and authority the clauses of the treaty which forbid the revival of their late antagonist's military power. Secondly, they should do all that is possible to reconcile the defeated nation to its lot by acts of benevolence designed to procure the greatest amount of prosperity in the beaten country, and labour by every means to create a basis of true friendship and of common interests, so that the incentive to appeal again to arms will be continually diminished. In these years I coined the maxim, "The redress of the grievances of the vanquished should precede the disarmament of the victors." As will be seen, the reverse process was, to a large extent, followed by Britain, the United States, and France. And thereby hangs this tale.

★   ★   ★

It is a prodigious task to make an army embodying the whole manhood of a mighty nation. The victorious Allies had at Mr. Lloyd George's suggestion limited the German Army to a hundred thousand men, and conscription was forbidden. This force therefore became the nucleus and the crucible out of which an army of millions of men was if possible to be re-formed. The hundred thousand men were a hundred thousand leaders. Once the decision to expand was taken, the privates could become sergeants, the sergeants officers. None the less, Mr. Lloyd George's plan for preventing the re-creation of the German Army was not ill-conceived. No foreign inspection could in times of peace control the quality of the hundred thousand men allowed to Germany. But the issue did not turn on this. Three or four millions of trained soldiers were needed merely to hold the German frontiers. To make a nation-wide army which could compare with, still more surpass, the French Army required not only the preparation of the leaders and the revival of the old regiments and formations, but the national compulsory service of each annual quota of men reaching the military age. Volunteer corps, youth movements, extensions of the police and constabu-

39

lary forces, old-comrades associations, all kinds of non-official and indeed illegal organisations, might play their part in the interim period. But without universal national service the bones of the skeleton could never be clothed with flesh and sinew.

There was therefore no possibility of Germany creating an army which could face the French Army until conscription had been applied for several years. Here was a line which could not be transgressed without an obvious, flagrant breach of the Treaty of Versailles. Every kind of concealed, ingenious, elaborate preparation could be made beforehand, but the moment must come when the Rubicon would have to be crossed and the conquerors defied. Mr. Lloyd George's principle was thus sound. Had it been enforced with authority and prudence there could have been no new forging of the German war-machine. The class called up for each year, however well schooled beforehand, would also have to remain for at least two years in the regimental or other units, and it was only after this period of training that the reserves without which no modern army is possible could be gradually formed and accumulated. France, though her manhood had been depleted in a horrible degree by the previous war, had nevertheless maintained a regular uninterrupted routine of training annual quotas and of passing the trained soldiers into a reserve which comprised the whole fighting man-power of the nation. For fifteen years Germany was not allowed to build up a similar reserve. In all these years the German Army might nourish and cherish its military spirit and tradition, but it could not possibly even dream of entering the lists against the long-established unbroken developments of the armed, trained, organised manpower which flowed and gathered naturally from the French military system.

*   *   *

The creator of the nucleus and structure of the future German Army was General von Seeckt. As early as 1921 Seeckt was busy planning, in secret and on paper, a full-size German army, and arguing deferentially about his various activities with the Inter-Allied Military Commission of Control. His biographer, General von Rabenau, wrote in the triumphant days of 1940: "It would have been difficult to do the work of 1935-39 if from 1920-34 the centre of leadership had corresponded to the needs of the small army." For instance, the Treaty demanded a decrease in the Officer Corps from thirty-four thousand to four thousand. Every device was used to overcome this fatal barrier, and in spite of the efforts of the Allied Control Commission the process of planning for a revived German Army went forward. "The enemy," says Seeckt's biographer, "did his best to destroy the General Staff, and was supported by the political parties within Germany. The Inter-Allied Control had rightly, from its standpoint, tried for years to make the training in higher staffs so primitive that there could be no General Staff. They tried in the boldest ways to discover how General Staff officers were being trained, but we succeeded in giving nothing away, neither the system nor what was taught. Seeckt never gave in, for had the General Staff been destroyed it would have been difficult to re-create it. . . . Although the form had to be broken, the content was saved. . . ." In fact, under the pretence of being Departments of Reconstruction, Research, and Culture, several thousand staff officers in plain clothes and their assistants were held together in Berlin, thinking deeply about the past and the future.

Rabenau makes an illuminating comment: "Without Seeckt there would to-day [in 1940] be no General Staff in the German sense, for which generations are required and which cannot be achieved in a day, however gifted or industrious officers may be. Continuity of conception is imperative to safeguard leadership in the nervous trials of reality. Knowledge or capacity in individuals is not enough. In war the organically-developed capacity of a majority is necessary, and for this decades are needed. . . . In a small hundred-thousand army, if the generals were not also to be small, it was imperative to create a great theoretical framework. To this end large-scale practical exercises or war games were introduced . . . not so much to train the General Staff, but rather to create a class of higher commanders." These would be capable of thinking in full-scale military terms.

Seeckt insisted that false doctrines, springing from personal experiences of the Great War, should be avoided. All the lessons of that war were thoroughly and systematically studied. New principles of training and instructional courses of all kinds were introduced. All the existing manuals were rewritten, not for the hundred-thousand army, but for the armed might of the German Reich. In order to baffle the inquisitive Allies, whole sections of these manuals were printed in special type and made public.

Those for internal consumption were secret. The main principle
inculcated was the need for the closest co-operation of *all* vital
arms. Not only were the main services—infantry, motorised
cavalry, and artillery—to be tactically interwoven, but machine-
gun, trench mortar, and tommy-gun units, anti-tank weapons,
army air squadrons, and much else were all to be blended. It is
to this theme that the German war leaders attributed their tactical
successes in the campaigns of 1939 and 1940. By 1924 Seeckt could
feel that the strength of the German army was slowly increasing
beyond the hundred-thousand limit. "The fruits of this," said his
biographer, "were born only ten years later." In 1925 the old
Field-Marshal von Mackensen congratulated Seeckt on his building up of the Reichswehr, and compared him, not unjustly, to
the Scharnhorst who had secretly prepared the Prussian counter-
stroke against Napoleon during the years of the French occupation of Germany after Jena. "The old fire burns still, and the
Allied Control had not destroyed any of the lasting elements of
German strength."

In the summer of 1926 Seeckt conducted his largest military
exercise for commanders with staffs and signals. He had no
troops, but practically all the generals, commanding officers, and
General Staff officers of the army were introduced to the art of
war and its innumerable technical problems on the scale of a
German army which, when the time came, could raise the German
nation to its former rank.

For several years short-service training of soldiers beyond the
official establishments was practised on a small scale. These men
were known as "black", *i.e.*, illegal. From 1925 onwards the
whole sphere of "black" was centralised in the Reichswehr
Ministry and sustained by national funds. The General Staff plan
of 1925 for an extension and improvement of the army outside
Treaty limits was to double and then to treble the existing legal
seven infantry divisions. But Seeckt's ultimate aim was a minimum of sixty-three. From 1926 the main obstacle to this planning
was the opposition of the Prussian Socialist Government. This
was swept away in 1932. It was not till April 1933 that the
establishment of the hundred-thousand army was officially exceeded, though its strength had for some time been rising steadily
above that figure.

* * *

Amid the goodwill and hopes following Locarno a questionable, though by no means irremediable, decision was taken by the British and French Governments. The Inter-Allied Control Commission was to be withdrawn, and in substitution there should be an agreed scheme of investigation by the League of Nations ready to be put into operation when any of the parties desired. It was thought that some such arrangement might form a complement to the Locarno Treaty. This hope was not fulfilled. Marshal Foch reported that effective disarmament of Germany had taken place; but it had to be recognised that the disarmament of a nation of sixty-five millions could not be permanent, and that certain precautions were necessary. In January 1927 the Control Commission was nevertheless withdrawn from Germany. It was already known that the Germans were straining the interpretation of the Treaty in many covert and minor ways, and no doubt they were making paper plans to become a military nation once again. There were Boy Scouts, Cadet Corps, and many volunteer unarmed organisations both of youth and of veterans. But nothing could be done on a large scale in the Army or Navy which would not become obvious. The introduction of compulsory national service, the establishment of a Military Air Force, or the laying down of warships beyond the Treaty limits would be an open breach of German obligations which could at any time have been raised in the League of Nations, of which Germany was now a member.

The Air was far less definable. The Treaty prohibited a German Military Air Force, and it was officially dissolved in May 1920. In his farewell order Seeckt said he hoped that it would again rise, and meanwhile its spirit would still live. He gave it every encouragement to do so. His first step had been to create within the Reichswehr Ministry a special group of experienced ex-Air Force officers, whose existence was hidden from the Allied Commission and protected against his own Government. This was gradually expanded until within the Ministry there were "air cells" in the various offices or inspectorates, and air personnel were gradually introduced throughout the cadres of the Army. The Civil Aviation Department was headed by an experienced war-time officer, a nominee of Seeckt's, who made sure that the control and development of civil aviation took place in harmony with military needs. This department, together with the German

Civil Air Transport, and various camouflaged military or naval air establishments, was to a great extent staffed by ex-flying officers without knowledge of commercial aviation.

Even before 1924 the beginnings of a system of airfields and civil aircraft factories and the training of pilots and instruction in passive air defence had come into existence throughout Germany. There was already much reasonable show of commercial flying, and very large numbers of Germans, both men and women, were encouraged to become "air-minded" by the institution of a network of gliding clubs. Severe limitations were observed, on paper, about the number of service personnel permitted to fly. But these rules, with so many others, were circumvented by Seeckt, who, with the connivance of the German Transport Ministry, succeeded in building up a sure foundation for an efficient industry and a future air arm. It was thought by the Allies, in the mood of 1926, derogatory to German national pride to go too far in curbing these German encroachments, and the victors rested on the line of principle which forbade a German Military Air Force. This proved a very vague and shadowy frontier.

In the naval sphere similar evasions were practised. By the Versailles Treaty Germany was allowed only to retain a small naval force with a maximum strength of fifteen thousand men. Subterfuges were used to increase this total. Naval organisations were covertly incorporated into civil Ministries. The coastal defences in Heligoland, although destroyed in accordance with the Treaty, were soon reconstructed. U-boats were illicitly built, and their officers and men trained in other countries. Everything possible was done to keep the Kaiser's Navy alive, and to prepare for the day when it could openly resume a place upon the sea.

Important progress was also made in another decisive direction. Herr Rathenau had, during his tenure of the Ministry of Reconstruction in 1919, set on foot on the broadest lines the reconstruction of German war industry. "They have destroyed your weapons," he had told the generals, in effect. "But these weapons would in any case have become obsolete before the next war. That war will be fought with brand-new ones, and the army which is least hampered with obsolete material will have a great advantage."

Nevertheless the struggle to preserve weapons from destruction was waged persistently by the German staffs throughout the years of control. Every form of deception and every obstacle baffled the Allied Commission. The work of evasion became thoroughly organised. The German police, which at first had interfered, presently became accessories of the Reichswehr in the amassing of arms. Under a civilian camouflage an organisation was set up to safeguard reserves of weapons and equipment. From 1926 this organisation had representatives all over Germany, and there was a network of depots of all kinds. Even more was ingenuity used to create machinery for future production of war material. Lathes which had been set up for war purposes and were capable of being reconverted to that use were retained for civil production in far greater numbers than were required for ordinary commercial work. State arsenals built for war were not closed down in accordance with the Treaty.

A general scheme had thus been put into action by which all the new factories, and many of the old, founded with American and British loans for reconstruction were designed from the outset for speedy conversion to war, and volumes could be written on the thoroughness and detail with which this was planned. Herr Rathenau had been brutally murdered in 1922 by anti-Semite and nascent Nazi secret societies, who fastened their hatred upon this Jew—Germany's faithful servant. When he came to power in 1929 Herr Bruening carried on the work with zeal and discretion. Thus, while the victors reposed on masses of obsolescent equipment an immense German potential of new munitions production was, year by year, coming into being.

*   *   *

It had been decided by the War Cabinet in 1919 that as part of the economy campaign the Service departments should frame their estimates on the assumption that "the British Empire will not be engaged in any great war during the next ten years, and that no Expeditionary Force will be required". In 1924, when I became Chancellor of the Exchequer, I asked the Committee of Imperial Defence to review this rule; but no recommendations were made for altering it. In 1927 the War Office suggested that the 1919 decision should be extended for the Army only to cover ten years "from the present date". This was approved by the Cabinet and Committee of Imperial Defence. The matter was next discussed on July 5, 1928, when I proposed with acceptance "that the basis of estimates for the Service departments should rest upon the statement that there would be no major war for a period of ten years, and that this basis should advance from day to day, but that the assumption should be reviewed every year by the Committee of Imperial Defence". It was left open for any Service department or Dominion Government to raise the issue at their discretion if they thought fit.

It has been contended that the acceptance of this principle lulled the fighting departments into a false sense of security, that research was neglected, and only short-term views prevailed, especially where expense was involved. Up till the time when I left office in 1929 I felt so hopeful that the peace of the world would be maintained that I saw no reason to take any new decision; nor in the event was I proved wrong. War did not break out till the autumn of 1939. Ten years is a long time in this fugitive world. The ten-year rule with its day-to-day advance remained in force until 1932, when, on March 23, Mr. MacDonald's Government rightly decided that its abandonment could be assumed.

All this time the Allies possessed the strength, and the right, to prevent any visible or tangible German rearmament, and Germany must have obeyed a strong united demand from Britain, France, and Italy to bring her actions into conformity with what the Peace Treaties had prescribed. In reviewing again the history of the eight years from 1930 to 1938 we can see how much time we had. Up till 1934 at least German rearmament could have been prevented without the loss of a single life. It was not time that was lacking.

CHAPTER IV

ADOLF HITLER

*The Blinded Corporal – The Obscure Fuehrer – The Munich Putsch,
1923 – "Mein Kampf" – Hitler's Problems – Hitler and the Reichswehr – The Schleicher Intrigue – The Impact of the Economic Blizzard
– Chancellor Bruening – A Constitutional Monarchy – Equality of
Armaments – Schleicher Intervenes – The Fall of Bruening.*

IN OCTOBER 1918 a German corporal had been temporarily blinded by mustard gas in a British attack near
Comines. While he lay in hospital in Pomerania defeat and
revolution swept over Germany. The son of an obscure Austrian
customs official, he had nursed youthful dreams of becoming a
great artist. Having failed to gain entry to the Academy of Art in
Vienna, he had lived in poverty in that capital and later in
Munich. Sometimes as a house-painter, often as a casual labourer,
he suffered physical privations and bred a harsh though concealed
resentment that the world had denied him success. These mis-
fortunes did not lead him into Communist ranks. By an honourable inversion he cherished all the more an abnormal sense of
racial loyalty and a fervent and mystic admiration for Germany
and the German people. He sprang eagerly to arms at the outbreak of the war, and served for four years with a Bavarian regiment on the Western Front. Such were the early fortunes of
Adolf Hitler.

As he lay sightless and helpless in hospital during the winter of
1918 his own personal failure seemed merged in the disaster of the
whole German people. The shock of defeat, the collapse of law
and order, the triumph of the French, caused this convalescent
regimental orderly an agony which consumed his being, and
generated those portentous and measureless forces of the spirit
which may spell the rescue or the doom of mankind. The down-

47

fall of Germany seemed to him inexplicable by ordinary processes. Somewhere there had been a gigantic and monstrous betrayal. Lonely and pent within himself, the little soldier pondered and speculated upon the possible causes of the catastrophe, guided only by his narrow personal experiences. He had mingled in Vienna with extreme German Nationalist groups, and here he had heard stories of sinister, undermining activities of another race, foes and exploiters of the Nordic world—the Jews. His patriotic anger fused with his envy of the rich and successful into one overpowering hate.

When at length, as an unnoted patient, he was released from hospital, still wearing the uniform in which he had an almost school-boyish pride, what scenes met his newly unscaled eyes! Fearful are the convulsions of defeat. Around him in the atmosphere of despair and frenzy glared the lineaments of Red Revolution. Armoured cars dashed through the streets of Munich scattering leaflets or bullets upon the fugitive wayfarers. His own comrades, with defiant red arm-bands on their uniform, were shouting slogans of fury against all that he cared for on earth. As in a dream everything suddenly became clear. Germany had been stabbed in the back and clawed down by the Jews, by the profiteers and intriguers behind the Front, by the accursed Bolsheviks in their international conspiracy of Jewish intellectuals. Shining before him he saw his duty, to save Germany from these plagues, to avenge her wrongs, and lead the master race to its long-decreed destiny.

The officers of his regiment, deeply alarmed by the seditious and revolutionary temper of their men, were very glad to find one, at any rate, who seemed to have the root of the matter in him. Corporal Hitler desired to remain mobilised, and found employment as a "political education officer" or agent. In this guise he gathered information about mutinous and subversive designs. Presently he was told by the Security officer for whom he worked to attend meetings of the local political parties of all complexions. One evening in September 1919 the Corporal went to a rally of the German Workers' Party in a Munich brewery, and here he heard for the first time people talking in the style of his secret convictions against the Jews, the speculators, the "November Criminals" who had brought Germany into the abyss. On September 16 he joined this party, and shortly afterwards, in

48

harmony with his military work, undertook its propaganda. In February 1920 the first mass meeting of the German Workers' Party was held in Munich, and here Adolf Hitler himself dominated the proceedings and in twenty-five points outlined the party programme. He had now become a politician. His campaign of national salvation had been opened. In April he was demobilised, and the expansion of the party absorbed his whole life. By the middle of the following year he had ousted the original leaders, and by his passion and genius forced upon the hypnotised company the acceptance of his personal control. Already he was "the Fuehrer". An unsuccessful newspaper, the *Voelkischer Beobachter*, was bought as the party organ.

The Communists were not long in recognising their foe. They tried to break up Hitler's meetings, and in the closing days of 1921 he organised his first units of storm-troopers. Up to this point all had moved in local circles in Bavaria. But in the tribulation of German life during these first post-war years many began here and there throughout the Reich to listen to the new gospel. The fierce anger of all Germany at the French occupation of the Ruhr in 1923 brought what was now called the National Socialist Party a broad wave of adherents. The collapse of the mark destroyed the basis of the German middle class, of whom many in their despair became recruits of the new party and found relief from their misery in hatred, vengeance, and patriotic fervour.

At the beginning Hitler had made it clear that the path to power lay through aggression and violence against a Weimar Republic born from the shame of defeat. By November 1923 "the Fuehrer" had a determined group around him, among whom Goering, Hess, Rosenberg, and Roehm were prominent. These men of action decided that the moment had come to attempt the seizure of authority in the State of Bavaria. General von Ludendorff lent the military prestige of his name to the venture, and marched forward in the *Putsch*. It used to be said before the war: "In Germany there will be no revolution, because in Germany all revolutions are strictly forbidden." This precept was revived on this occasion by the local authorities in Munich. The police troops fired, carefully avoiding the General, who marched straight forward into their ranks and was received with respect. About twenty of the demonstrators were killed. Hitler threw himself upon the ground, and presently escaped with other leaders from the scene. In April 1924 he was sentenced to four years' imprisonment.

Although the German authorities had maintained order, and the German court had inflicted punishment, the feeling was widespread throughout the land that they were striking at their own flesh and blood, and were playing the foreigners' game at the expense of Germany's most faithful sons. Hitler's sentence was reduced from four years to thirteen months. These months in the Landsberg fortress were however sufficient to enable him to complete in outline *Mein Kampf*, a treatise on his political philosophy inscribed to the dead of the recent *Putsch*. When eventually he came to power there was no book which deserved more careful study from the rulers, political and military, of the Allied Powers. All was there—the programme of German resurrection, the technique of party propaganda; the plan for combating Marxism; the concept of a National-Socialist State; the rightful position of Germany at the summit of the world. Here was the new Koran of faith and war: turgid, verbose, shapeless, but pregnant with its message.

The main thesis of *Mein Kampf* is simple. Man is a fighting animal; therefore the nation, being a community of fighters, is a fighting unit. Any living organism which ceases to fight for its existence is doomed to extinction. A country or race which ceases to fight is equally doomed. The fighting capacity of a race depends on its purity. Hence the need for ridding it of foreign defilements. The Jewish race, owing to its universality, is of necessity pacifist and internationalist. Pacifism is the deadliest sin, for it means the surrender of the race in the fight for existence. The first duty of every country is therefore to nationalise the masses. Intelligence in the case of the individual is not of first importance; will and determination are the prime qualities. The individual who is born to command is more valuable than countless thousands of subordinate natures. Only brute force can ensure the survival of the race; hence the necessity for military forms. The race must fight; a race that rests must rust and perish. Had the German race been united in good time it would have been already master of the globe. The new Reich must gather within its fold all the scattered German elements in Europe. A race which has suffered defeat can be rescued by restoring its self-confidence.

Above all things the army must be taught to believe in its own invincibility. To restore the German nation the people must be convinced that the recovery of freedom by force of arms is possible. The aristocratic principle is fundamentally sound. Intellectualism is undesirable. The ultimate aim of education is to produce a German who can be converted with the minimum of training into a soldier. The greatest upheavals in history would have been unthinkable had it not been for the driving force of fanatical and hysterical passions. Nothing could have been effected by the bourgeois virtues of peace and order. The world is now moving towards such an upheaval, and the new German State must see to it that the race is ready for the last and greatest decisions on this earth.

Foreign policy may be unscrupulous. It is not the task of diplomacy to allow a nation to founder heroically, but rather to see that it can prosper and survive. England and Italy are the only two possible allies for Germany. No country will enter into an alliance with a cowardly pacifist State run by democrats and Marxists. So long as Germany does not fend for herself, nobody will fend for her. Her lost provinces cannot be regained by solemn appeals to Heaven or by pious hopes in the League of Nations, but only by force of arms. Germany must not repeat the mistake of fighting all her enemies at once. She must single out the most dangerous and attack him with all her forces. The world will only cease to be anti-German when Germany recovers equality of rights and resumes her place in the sun. There must be no sentimentality about Germany's foreign policy. To attack France for purely sentimental reasons would be foolish. What Germany needs is increase of territory in Europe. Germany's pre-war colonial policy was a mistake and should be abandoned. Germany must look for expansion to Russia, and especially to the Baltic States. No alliance with Russia can be tolerated. To wage war together with Russia against the West would be criminal, for the aim of the Soviets is the triumph of international Judaism.

Such were the "granite pillars" of his policy.

*　　*　　*

The ceaseless struggles and gradual emergence of Adolf Hitler as a national figure were little noticed by the victors, oppressed and harassed as they were by their own troubles and party strife.

A long interval passed before National Socialism, or the "Nazi Party", as it came to be called, gained so strong a hold of the masses of the German people, of the armed forces, of the machinery of the State, and among industrialists not unreasonably terrified of Communism, as to become a power in German life of which world-wide notice had to be taken. When Hitler was released from prison at the end of 1924 he said that it would take him five years to reorganise his movement.

★ ★ ★

One of the democratic provisions of the Weimar Constitution prescribed elections to the Reichstag every four years. It was hoped by this provision to make sure that the masses of the German people should enjoy a complete and continuous control over their Parliament. In practice of course it only meant that they lived in a continual atmosphere of febrile political excitement and ceaseless electioneering. The progress of Hitler and his doctrines is thus registered with precision. In 1928 he had but twelve seats in the Reichstag. In 1930 this became 107; in 1932, 230. By that time the whole structure of Germany had been permeated by the agencies and discipline of the National Socialist Party, and intimidation of all kinds and insults and brutalities towards the Jews were rampant.

It is not necessary in this account to follow year by year this complex and formidable development, with all its passions and villainies and all its ups and downs. The pale sunlight of Locarno shone for a while upon the scene. The spending of the profuse American loans induced a sense of returning prosperity. Marshal Hindenburg presided over the German State, and Stresemann was his Foreign Minister. The stable decent majority of the German people, responding to their ingrained love of massive and majestic authority, clung to him till his dying gasp. But other powerful factors were also active in the distracted nation to which the Weimar Republic could offer no sense of security, and no satisfaction of national glory or revenge.

Behind the veneer of republican governments and democratic institutions, imposed by the victors and tainted with defeat, the real political power in Germany and the enduring structure of the nation in the post-war years had been the General Staff of the Reichswehr. They it was who made and unmade Presidents and

Cabinets. They had found in Marshal Hindenburg a symbol of
their power and an agent of their will. But Hindenburg in 1930
was eighty-three years of age. From this time his character and
mental grasp steadily declined. He became increasingly preju-
diced, arbitrary, and senile. An enormous image had been made
of him in the war, and patriots could show their admiration by
paying for a nail to drive into it. This illustrates effectively what
he had now become—"the Wooden Titan". It had for some
time been clear to the generals that a satisfactory successor to the
aged Marshal would have to be found. The search for the new
man was however overtaken by the vehement growth and force
of the National-Socialist movement. After the failure of the 1923
Putsch in Munich Hitler had professed a programme of strict
legality within the framework of the Weimar Republic. Yet at
the same time he had encouraged and planned the expansion of
the military and para-military formations of the Nazi Party.
From very small beginnings the S.A., the Storm Troops or
Brownshirts, with their small disciplinary core, the S.S., grew
in numbers and vigour to the point where the Reichswehr viewed
their activities and potential strength with grave alarm.

At the head of the Storm Troop formations stood a German
soldier of fortune, Ernst Roehm, the comrade and hitherto the
close friend of Hitler through all the years of struggle. Roehm,
Chief of the Staff of the S.A., was a man of proved ability and
courage, but dominated by personal ambition and sexually per-
verted. His vices were no barrier to Hitler's collaboration with
him along the hard and dangerous path to power. The Storm
Troops had, as Bruening complains, absorbed most of the old
German Nationalist formations, such as the Free Companies
which had fought in the Baltic and Poland against the Bolsheviks
in the 1920's, and also the Nationalist Veterans' Organisation of
the Steel Helmets (Stahlhelm).

Pondering most carefully upon the tides that were flowing in
the nation, the Reichswehr convinced themselves with much
reluctance that, as a military caste and organisation in opposition
to the Nazi movement, they could no longer maintain control of
Germany. Both factions had in common the resolve to raise
Germany from the abyss and avenge her defeat; but while the
Reichswehr represented the ordered structure of the Kaiser's
Empire, and gave shelter to the feudal, aristocratic, land-owning

and well-to-do classes in German society, the S.A. had become to a large extent a revolutionary movement fanned by the discontents of temperamental or embittered subversives and the desperation of ruined men. They differed from the Bolsheviks whom they denounced no more than the North Pole does from the South.

For the Reichswehr to quarrel with the Nazi Party was to tear the defeated nation asunder. The Army chiefs in 1931 and 1932 felt they must, for their own sake and for that of the country, join forces with those to whom in domestic matters they were opposed with all the rigidity and severeness of the German mind. Hitler, for his part, although prepared to use any battering-ram to break into the citadels of power, had always before his eyes the leadership of the great and glittering Germany which had commanded the admiration and loyalty of his youthful years. The conditions for a compact between him and the Reichswehr were therefore present and natural on both sides. The Army chiefs had gradually realised that the strength of the Nazi Party was such that Hitler was the only possible successor to Hindenburg as head of the German nation. Hitler on his side knew that to carry out his programme of German resurrection an alliance with the governing *élite* of the Reichswehr was indispensable. A bargain was struck, and the German Army leaders began to persuade Hindenburg to look upon Hitler as eventual Chancellor of the Reich. Thus by agreeing to curtail the activities of the Brownshirts, to subordinate them to the General Staff, and ultimately, if unavoidable, to liquidate them, Hitler gained the allegiance of the controlling forces in Germany, official executive dominance, and the apparent reversion of the Headship of the German State. The Corporal had travelled far.

*　　*　　*

There was however an inner and separate complication. If the key to any master-combination of German internal forces was the General Staff of the Army, several hands were grasping for that key. General Kurt von Schleicher at this time exercised a subtle and on occasions a decisive influence. He was the political mentor of the reserved and potentially dominating military circle. He was viewed with a measure of distrust by all sections and factions, and regarded as an adroit and useful political agent possessed of much knowledge outside the General Staff manuals and not usually accessible to soldiers. Schleicher had long been convinced of the significance of the Nazi movement and of the need to stem and control it. On the other hand, he saw that in this terrific mob-thrust, with its ever-growing private army of S.A., there was a weapon which, if properly handled by his comrades of the General Staff, might reassert the greatness of Germany, and perhaps even establish his own. In this intention during the course of 1931 Schleicher began to plot secretly with Roehm, Chief of the Staff of the Nazi Storm Troopers. There was thus a major double process at work, the General Staff making their arrangements with Hitler, and Schleicher in their midst pursuing his personal conspiracy with Hitler's principal lieutenant and would-be rival, Roehm. Schleicher's contacts with the revolutionary element of the Nazi Party, and particularly with Roehm, lasted until both he and Roehm were shot by Hitler's orders three years later. This certainly simplified the political situation, and also that of the survivors.

* * *

Meanwhile the Economic Blizzard smote Germany in her turn. The United States banks, faced with increasing commitments at home, refused to increase their improvident loans to Germany. This reaction led to the widespread closing of factories and the sudden ruin of many enterprises on which the peaceful revival of Germany was based. Unemployment in Germany rose to 2,300,000 in the winter of 1930. At the same time Reparations entered a new phase. For the previous three years the American Agent-General, Mr. S. Parker Gilbert, had acted as Allied representative in the collection of the heavy payments demanded by the Allies, including the payments to Britain which I transmitted automatically to the United States Treasury. It was certain this system could not last. Already in the summer of 1929 Mr. Young, the American Commissioner, had framed, proposed, and negotiated in Paris an important scheme of mitigation, which not only put a final limit to the period of Reparation payments but freed both the Reichsbank and the German railways from Allied control, and abolished the Reparations Commission in favour of the Bank for International Settlements. Hitler and his National-Socialist movement joined forces with the business and commercial interests, which were represented, and to some extent led, by the truculent and transient figure of the commercial magnate Hugenberg. A vain but savage campaign was launched against this far-reaching and benevolent easement proffered by the Allies. The German Government succeeded by a dead-lift effort in procuring the assent of the Reichstag to the "Young Plan" by no more than 224 votes to 206. Stresemann, the Foreign Minister, who was now a dying man, gained his last success in the agreement for the complete evacuation of the Rhineland by the Allied armies, long before the Treaty required.

But the German masses were largely indifferent to the remarkable concessions of the victors. Earlier, or in happier circumstances, these would have been acclaimed as long steps upon the path of reconciliation and a return to true peace. But now the ever-present overshadowing fear of the German masses was unemployment. The middle classes had already been ruined and driven into violent courses by the flight from the mark. Stresemann's internal political position was undermined by the international economic stresses, and the vehement assaults of Hitler's Nazis and Hugenberg's capitalist magnates led to his overthrow. On March 28, 1930, Bruening, the leader of the Catholic Centre Party, became Chancellor.

* * *

Bruening was a Catholic from Westphalia and a patriot, seeking to re-create the former Germany in modern democratic guise. He pursued continuously the scheme of factory preparation for war which had been devised by Herr Rathenau before his murder. He had also to struggle towards financial stability amid mounting chaos. His programme of economy and reduction of Civil Service numbers and salaries was not popular. The tides of hatred flowed ever more turbulently. Supported by President Hindenburg, Bruening dissolved a hostile Reichstag, and the election of 1930 left him with a majority. He now made the last recognisable effort to rally what remained of the old Germany against the resurgent, violent, and debased nationalist agitation. For this purpose he had first to secure the re-election of Hindenburg as President. Chancellor Bruening looked to a new but obvious solution. He saw the peace, safety, and glory of Germany only in the restoration of an Emperor. Could he then induce the aged Marshal Hindenburg, if and when re-elected, to act for his last term of office as Regent for a restored monarchy to come into effect upon his death? This policy, if achieved, would have filled the void at the summit of the German nation towards which Hitler was now evidently making his way. In all the circumstances this was the right course. But how could Bruening lead Germany to it? The Conservative element, which was drifting to Hitler, might have been recalled by the return of Kaiser Wilhelm; but neither the Social Democrats nor the trade union forces would tolerate the return of the old Kaiser or the Crown Prince. Bruening's plan was not to recreate a Second Reich. He desired a constitutional monarchy on English lines. He hoped that one of the sons of the Crown Prince might be a suitable candidate.

In November 1931 he confided his plans to Hindenburg, on whom all depended. The aged Marshal's reaction was at once vehement and peculiar. He was astonished and hostile. He said that he regarded himself solely as trustee of the Kaiser. Any other solution was an insult to his military honour. The monarchical conception, to which he was devoted, could not be reconciled with picking and choosing among royal princes. Legitimacy must not be violated. Meanwhile, as Germany would not accept the return of the Kaiser, there was nothing left but he himself, Hindenburg. On this he rested. No compromise for him! "J'y suis, j'y reste." Bruening argued vehemently and perhaps over-long with the old veteran. The Chancellor had a strong case. Unless Hindenburg would accept this monarchical solution, albeit unorthodox, there must be a revolutionary Nazi dictatorship. No agreement was reached. But whether or not Bruening could convert Hindenburg, it was imperative to get him re-elected as President, in order at least to stave off an immediate political collapse of the German State. In its first stage Bruening's plan was successful. At the Presidential elections held in March 1932 Hindenburg was returned, after a second ballot, by a majority over his rivals, Hitler and the Communist Thaelmann. Both the economic position in Germany and her relations with Europe had now to be faced. The Disarmament Conference was sitting at Geneva, and Hitler throve upon a roaring campaign against the humiliation of Germany under Versailles.

In careful meditation Bruening drafted a far-reaching plan of

Treaty revision; and in April 1932 he went to Geneva and found
an unexpectedly favourable reception. In conversations between
him and MacDonald, Stimson, and Norman Davis it seemed that
agreement could be reached. The extraordinary basis of this was
the principle, subject to various reserved interpretations, of
"equality of armaments" between Germany and France. It is
indeed surprising, as future chapters will explain, that anyone in
his senses should have imagined that peace could be built on such
foundations. If this vital point were conceded by the victors, it
might well pull Bruening out of his plight; and then the next
step—and this one wise—would be the cancelling of Reparations for the sake of European revival. Such a settlement would
of course have raised Bruening's personal position to one of
triumph.

Norman Davis, the American Ambassador-at-Large, telephoned to the French Premier, Tardieu, to come immediately
from Paris to Geneva. But, unfortunately for Bruening, Tardieu
had other news. Schleicher had been busy in Berlin, and had just
warned the French Ambassador not to negotiate with Bruening
because his fall was imminent. It may well be also that Tardieu
was concerned with the military position of France on the formula
of "equality of armaments". At any rate, Tardieu did not come to
Geneva, and on May 1 Bruening returned to Berlin. To arrive
there empty-handed at such a moment was fatal to him. Drastic
and even desperate measures were required to cope with the
threatened economic collapse inside Germany. For these measures
Bruening's unpopular Government had not the necessary
strength. He struggled on through May, and meanwhile Tardieu,
in the kaleidoscope of French Parliamentary politics, was replaced
by M. Herriot.

The new French Premier declared himself ready to discuss the
formula reached in the Geneva conversations. The American
Ambassador in Berlin was instructed to urge the German Chancellor to go to Geneva without a moment's delay. This message
was received by Bruening early on May 30. But meanwhile
Schleicher's influence had prevailed. Hindenburg had already
been persuaded to dismiss the Chancellor. In the course of that
very morning, after the American invitation, with all its hope and
imprudence, had reached Bruening, he learned that his fate was
settled, and by midday he resigned to avoid actual dismissal. So

ended the last Government in post-war Germany which might have led the German people into the enjoyment of a stable and civilised constitution and opened peaceful channels of intercourse with their neighbours. The offers which the Allies had made to Bruening would, but for Schleicher's intrigue and Tardieu's delay, certainly have saved him. These offers had presently to be discussed with a different System and a different man.

CHAPTER V

THE LOCUST YEARS*

1931-1935

The MacDonald-Baldwin Coalition – The Indian Collapse – All Germany Astir – Hindenburg and Hitler – Schleicher Fails as a Stop-gap – Hitler Becomes Chancellor – The Burning of the Reichstag, February 27, 1933 – Hitler Wins a Majority at the Elections – The New Master – Qualitative Disarmament – 1932 in Germany – British Air Estimates of 1933 – Equality of Status in Armaments – "The MacDonald Plan" – "Thank God for the French Army" – Hitler Quits the League of Nations – A New York Adventure – Peace at Chartwell – Some Wise Friends – The Marlborough Battlefield – Putzi – The Attitude of the Conservative Party – Dangers in the Far East – Japan Attacks China – Accountability.

THE British Government which resulted from the General Election of 1931 was in appearance one of the strongest and in fact one of the weakest in British records. Mr. Ramsay MacDonald, the Prime Minister, had severed himself, with the utmost bitterness on both sides, from the Socialist Party which it had been his life's work to create. Henceforward he brooded supinely at the head of an Administration which, though nominally National, was in fact overwhelmingly Conservative. Mr. Baldwin preferred the substance to the form of power, and reigned placidly in the background. The Foreign Office was filled by Sir John Simon, one of the leaders of the Liberal contingent. The main work of the Administration at home was done by Mr. Neville Chamberlain, who soon succeeded Mr.

* Four years later Sir Thomas Inskip, Minister for Co-ordination of Defence, who was well versed in the Bible, used the expressive phrase about this dismal period, of which he was the heir: "The years that the locust hath eaten" (Joel, ii, 25).

Snowden as Chancellor of the Exchequer. The Labour Party, blamed for its failure in the financial crisis and sorely stricken at the polls, was led by the extreme pacifist, Mr. George Lansbury. During the period of four and a quarter years of this Administration, from August 1931 to November 1935, the entire situation on the Continent of Europe was reversed.

On the first return of the new Parliament the Government demanded a Vote of Confidence upon their Indian policy. To this I moved an Amendment as follows:

Provided that nothing in the said policy shall commit this House to the establishment in India of a Dominion Constitution as defined by the Statute of Westminster. . . . And that no question of self-government in India at this juncture shall impair the ultimate responsibility of Parliament for the peace, order, and good government of the Indian Empire.

On this occasion I spoke for as much as an hour and a half, and was heard with attention. But on this issue, as later upon Defence, nothing that one could say made the slightest difference. We have now along this subsidiary Eastern road also reached our horrible consummation in the slaughter of hundreds of thousands of poor people who only sought to earn their living under conditions of peace and justice. I ventured to tell the ignorant Members of all parties:

As the British authority passes for a time into collapse, the old hatreds between the Moslems and the Hindus revive and acquire new life and malignancy. We cannot easily conceive what these hatreds are. There are in India mobs of neighbours, people who have dwelt together in the closest propinquity all their lives, who when held and dominated by these passions will tear each other to pieces, men, women, and children, with their fingers. Not for a hundred years have the relations between Moslems and Hindus been so poisoned as they have been since England was deemed to be losing her grip, and was believed to be ready to quit the scene if told to go.

We mustered little more than forty in the Lobby against all the three parties in the House of Commons. This must be noted as a sad milestone on the downward path.

*   *   *

Meanwhile all Germany was astir and great events marched forward.

Much had happened in the year which followed the fall of the Bruening Cabinet in May 1932. Papen and the political general, Schleicher, had hitherto attempted to govern Germany by cleverness and intrigue. The time for these had now passed. Papen, who succeeded Bruening as Chancellor, hoped to rule with the support of the entourage of President Hindenburg and of the extreme Nationalist group in the Reichstag. On July 20 a decisive step was taken. The Socialist Government in Prussia was forcibly ousted from office. But Papen's rival was eager for power. In Schleicher's calculations the instrument lay in the dark, hidden forces storming into German politics behind the rising power and name of Adolf Hitler. He hoped to make the Hitler Movement a docile servant of the Reichswehr, and in so doing to gain the control of both himself. The contacts between Schleicher and Roehm, the leader of the Nazi Storm Troopers, which had begun in 1931, were extended in the following year to more precise relations between Schleicher and Hitler himself. The road to power for both men seemed to be obstructed only by Papen and by the confidence displayed by Hindenburg in him.

In August 1932 Hitler came to Berlin on a private summons from the President. The moment for a forward step seemed at hand. Thirteen million German voters stood behind the Fuehrer. A vital share of office must be his for the asking. He was now in somewhat the position of Mussolini on the eve of the march on Rome. But Papen did not care about recent Italian history. He had the support of Hindenburg and had no intention of resigning. The old Marshal saw Hitler. He was not impressed. "*That* man for Chancellor? I'll make him a postmaster and he can lick stamps with my head on them." In palace circles Hitler had not the influence of his competitors.

In the country the vast electorate was restless and adrift. In November 1932, for the fifth time in a year, elections were held throughout Germany. The Nazis lost ground and their 230 seats were reduced to 196, the Communists gaining the balance. The bargaining power of the Fuehrer was thus weakened. Perhaps General Schleicher would be able to do without him after all. The General gained favour in the circle of Hindenburg's advisers. On November 17 Papen resigned and Schleicher became Chancellor in his stead. But the new Chancellor was found to have

Peace maintained by Force of Arms

1 Clemenceau signs the Treaty of Versailles 28th June, 1919.
2 The occupation of the Rhineland, 1920.

3 A session of the League of Nations, under the chairmanship of Mr. Viviani, February 1923.
4 Gandhi in London, surrounded by crowds.

5 The anti-tank defences of the Maginot Line.
6 An armoured gun emplacement in action on the Maginot Line.

7 The underground caverns of the Maginot Line.

been more apt at pulling wires behind the scenes than at the open summit of power. He had quarrelled with too many people. Hitler, together with Papen and the Nationalists, now ranged themselves against him; and the Communists, fighting the Nazis in the streets and the Government by their strikes, helped to make his rule impossible. Papen brought his personal influence to bear on President Hindenburg. Would not after all the best solution be to placate Hitler by thrusting upon him the responsibilities and burdens of office? Hindenburg at last reluctantly consented. On January 30, 1933, Adolf Hitler took office as Chancellor of Germany.

The hand of the Master was soon felt upon all who would or might oppose the New Order. On February 2 all meetings or demonstrations of the German Communist Party were forbidden, and throughout Germany a round-up of secret arms belonging to the Communists began. The climax came on the evening of February 27, 1933. The building of the Reichstag broke into flames. Brownshirts, Blackshirts, and their auxiliary formations were called out. Four thousand arrests, including the Central Committee of the Communist Party, were made overnight. These measures were entrusted to Goering, now Minister of the Interior of Prussia. They formed the preliminary to the forthcoming elections and secured the defeat of the Communists, the most formidable opponents of the new *régime*. The organising of the electoral campaign was the task of Goebbels, and he lacked neither skill nor zeal.

But there were still many forces in Germany reluctant, obstinate, or actively hostile to Hitlerism. The Communists, and many who in their perplexity and distress voted with them, obtained 81 seats, the Socialists 118, the Centre party 73, and the Nationalist allies of Hitler under Papen and Hugenberg 52. Thirty-three seats were allotted to minor Right Centre groups. The Nazis obtained a vote of 17,300,000, with 288 seats. These results gave Hitler and his Nationalist allies control of the Reichstag. Thus, and thus only, did Hitler obtain by hook and crook a majority vote from the German people. Under the ordinary processes of civilised Parliamentary government, so large a minority would have had great influence and due consideration in the State. But in the new Nazi Germany minorities were now to learn that they had no rights.

On March 21, 1933, Hitler opened, in the Garrison Church at Potsdam, hard by the tomb of Frederick the Great, the first Reichstag of the Third Reich. In the body of the church sat the representatives of the Reichswehr, the symbol of the continuity of German might, and the senior officers of the S.A. and S.S., the new figures of resurgent Germany. On March 24 the majority of the Reichstag, overbearing or overawing all opponents, confirmed by 441 votes to 94 complete emergency powers to Chancellor Hitler for four years. As the result was announced Hitler turned to the benches of the Socialists and cried, "And now I have no further need of you."

Amid the excitement of the election the exultant columns of the National Socialist Party filed past their leader in the pagan homage of a torchlight procession through the streets of Berlin. It had been a long struggle, difficult for foreigners, especially those who had not known the pangs of defeat, to comprehend. Adolf Hitler had at last arrived. But he was not alone. He had called from the depths of defeat the dark and savage furies latent in the most numerous, most serviceable, ruthless, contradictory, and ill-starred race in Europe. He had conjured up the fearful idol of an all-devouring Moloch of which he was the priest and incarnation. It is not within my scope to describe the inconceivable brutality and villainy by which this apparatus of hatred and tyranny had been fashioned and was now to be perfected. It is necessary, for the purpose of this account, only to present to the reader the new and fearful fact which had broken upon the still unwitting world: GERMANY UNDER HITLER, AND GERMANY ARMING.

While these deadly changes were taking place in Germany the MacDonald-Baldwin Government felt bound to enforce for some time the severe reductions and restrictions which the financial crisis had imposed upon our already modest armaments, and steadfastly closed their eyes and ears to the disquieting symptoms in Europe. In vehement efforts to procure a disarmament of the victors equal to that which had been enforced upon the vanquished by the Treaty of Versailles, Mr. MacDonald and his Conservative and Liberal colleagues pressed a series of proposals forward in the League of Nations and through every other channel that was open. The French, although their political affairs still remained in constant flux and in motion without particular significance, clung tenaciously to the French Army as the centre and prop of the life of France and of all her alliances. This attitude earned them rebukes both in Britain and in the United States. The opinions of the Press and public were in no way founded upon reality; but the adverse tide was strong.

When in May 1932 the virtues of disarmament were extolled in the House of Commons by all parties, the Foreign Secretary opened a new line in the classification of weapons which should be allowed or discouraged. He called this "qualitative disarmament". It was easier to expose the fallacy than to convince the Members. I said:

The Foreign Secretary told us that it was difficult to divide weapons into offensive and defensive categories. It certainly is, because almost every conceivable weapon may be used in defence or offence; either by an aggressor or by the innocent victim of his assault. To make it more difficult for the invader, heavy guns, tanks, and poison gas are to be relegated to the evil category of offensive weapons. The invasion of France by Germany in 1914 reached its climax without the employment of any of these weapons. The heavy gun is to be described as "an offensive weapon". It is all right in a fortress; there it is virtuous and pacific in its character; but bring it out into the field—and, of course, if it were needed, it would be brought out into the field—and it immediately becomes naughty, peccant, militaristic, and has to be placed under the ban of civilisation. Take the tank. The Germans, having invaded France, entrenched themselves; and in a couple of years they shot down 1,500,000 French and British soldiers who were trying to free the soil of France. The tank was invented to overcome the fire of the machine-guns with which the Germans were maintaining themselves in France, and it saved a lot of life in clearing the soil of the invader. Now, apparently, the machine-gun, which was the German weapon for holding on to thirteen provinces of France, is to be the virtuous, defensive machine-gun, and the tank, which was the means by which these Allied lives were saved, is to be placed under the censure and obloquy of all just and righteous men. . . .

A truer classification might be drawn in banning weapons which tend to be indiscriminate in their action and whose use entails death and wounds, not merely on the combatants in the fighting zones, but on the civil population, men, women, and children, far removed from those areas. There indeed, it seems to me, would be a direction in which the united nations assembled at Geneva might advance with hope. . . .

At the end I gave my first formal warning of approaching war:

I should very much regret to see any approximation in military strength between Germany and France. Those who speak of that as though it were right, or even a question of fair dealing, altogether underrate the gravity of the European situation. I would say to those who would like to see Germany and France on an equal footing in armaments: "Do you wish for war?" For my part, I earnestly hope that no such approximation will take place during my lifetime or that of my children. To say that is not in the least to imply any want of regard or admiration for the great qualities of the German people, but I am sure that the thesis that they should be placed in an equal military position with France is one which, if it ever emerged in fact, would bring us within practical distance of almost measureless calamity.

The British Air Estimates of March 1933 revealed a total lack of comprehension alike by the Government and the Oppositions, Labour and Liberal, of what was going on. I had to say (March 14, 1933):

I regretted to hear the Under-Secretary say that we were only the fifth air Power, and that the ten-year programme was suspended for another year. I was sorry to hear him boast that the Air Ministry had not laid down a single new unit this year. All these ideas are being increasingly stultified by the march of events, and we should be well advised to concentrate upon our air defences with greater vigour.

* * *

Under the so-called National Government British public opinion showed an increasing inclination to cast aside all care about Germany. In vain the French had pointed out correctly in a memorandum of July 21, 1931, that the general assurance given at Versailles that a universal limitation of armaments should follow the one-sided disarmament of Germany did not constitute a Treaty obligation. It certainly was not an obligation enforceable apart from time and circumstance. Yet when in 1932 the German delegation to the Disarmament Conference categorically demanded the removal of all restrictions upon their right to re-arm they found much support in the British Press. The *Times* spoke of "the timely redress of inequality", and the *New Statesman* of "the unqualified recognition of the principle of the equality of States". This meant that the seventy million Germans ought to be allowed to rearm and prepare for war without the victors in the late fearful struggle being entitled to make any objection. Equality of status between victors and vanquished; equality between a France of thirty-nine millions and a Germany of nearly double that number!

The German Government were emboldened by the British demeanour. They ascribed it to the fundamental weakness and inherent decadence imposed even upon a Nordic race by the democratic and Parliamentary form of society. With all Hitler's national drive behind them, they took a haughty line. In July their delegation gathered up its papers and quitted the Disarmament Conference. To coax them back then became the prime political objective of the victorious Allies. In November the French, under severe and constant British pressure, proposed what was somewhat unfairly called "the Herriot Plan". The essence of this was the reconstitution of all European defence forces as short-service armies with limited numbers, admitting equality of status but not necessarily accepting equality of strength. In fact and in principle, the admission of equality of status made it impossible ultimately not to accept equality of strength. This enabled the Allied Governments to offer to Germany "Equality of rights in a system which would provide security for all nations". Under certain safeguards of an illusory character the French were reduced to accepting this meaningless formula. On this the Germans consented to return to the Disarmament Conference. This was hailed as a notable victory for peace.

Fanned by the breeze of popularity, His Majesty's Government now produced on March 16, 1933, what was called after its author and inspirer "the MacDonald Plan". It accepted as its starting-point the adoption of the French conception of short-service armies—in this case of eight months' service—and proceeded to prescribe exact figures for the troops of each country. The French Army should be reduced from its peace-time establishment of 500,000 men to 200,000 and the Germans should increase to parity at that figure. By this time the German military forces, though not yet provided with the mass of trained reserves which only a succession of annual conscripted quotas could supply, may well have amounted to the equivalent of over a million ardent volunteers, partially equipped, and with many forms of the latest weapons coming along through the convertible and partially-converted factories to arm them.

At the end of the First World War, France, like Great Britain, had an enormous mass of heavy artillery, whereas the cannon of the German Army had in fact been blown to bits according to Treaty. Mr. MacDonald sought to remedy this evident inequality by proposing to limit the calibre of mobile artillery guns to 105 mm., or 4.2 inches. Existing guns up to 6 inches could be retained, but all replacements were to be limited to 4.2 inches. British interests, as distinct from those of France, were to be protected by the maintenance of the Treaty restrictions against German naval armaments until 1935, when it was proposed that a new Naval Conference should meet. Military aircraft were prohibited to Germany for the duration of the agreement; but the three Allied Powers were to reduce their own Air Forces to 500 planes apiece.

I viewed this attack upon the French armed forces and the attempt to establish equality between Germany and France with strong aversion; and on March 23, 1933, I had the opportunity of saying to Parliament:

I doubt the wisdom of pressing this plan upon France at the present time. I do not think the French will agree. They must be greatly concerned at what is taking place in Germany, as well as at the attitude of some others of their neighbours. I dare say that during this anxious month there are a good many people who have said to themselves, as I have been saying for several years: "Thank God for the French Army." When we read about Germany, when we watch with surprise and distress the tumultuous insurgence of ferocity and war spirit, the pitiless ill-treatment of minorities, the denial of the normal protections of civilised society, the persecution of large numbers of individuals solely on the ground of race—when we see all that occurring in one of the most gifted, learned, and scientific and formidable nations in the world, one cannot help feeling glad that the fierce passions that are raging in Germany have not yet found any other outlet but upon themselves. It seems to me that at a moment like this to ask France to halve her Army while Germany doubles hers, to ask France to halve her Air Force while the German Air Force remains whatever it is, is a proposal likely to be considered by the French Government, at present at any rate, as somewhat unseasonable. The figures that are given in the plan of the strength of armies and aeroplanes secure to France only as many aeroplanes as would be possessed by Italy, leaving any air-power possessed by Germany entirely out of consideration.

And again in April:

The Germans demand equality in weapons and equality in the organisation of armies and fleets, and we have been told, "You cannot keep so great a nation in an inferior position. What others have, they must have." I have never agreed. It is a most dangerous demand to make. Nothing in life is eternal, but as surely as Germany acquires full military equality with her neighbours while her own grievances are still unredressed and while she is in the temper which we have unhappily seen, so surely shall we see ourselves within a measurable distance of the renewal of general European war.

. . . One of the things which we were told after the Great War would be a security for us was that Germany would be a democracy with Parliamentary institutions. All that has been swept away. You have most grim dictatorship. You have militarism and appeals to every form of fighting spirit, from the reintroduction of duelling in the colleges to the Minister of Education advising the plentiful use of the cane in the elementary schools. You have these martial or pugnacious manifestations, and also this persecution of the Jews of which so many members have spoken. . . .

I will leave Germany and turn to France. France is not only the sole great surviving democracy in Europe; she is also the strongest military Power, I am glad to say, and she is the head of a system of States and nations. France is the guarantor and protector of the whole crescent of small States which runs right round from Belgium to Yugoslavia and Roumania. They all look to France. When any step is taken, by England or any other Power, to weaken the diplomatic or military security of France, all these small nations tremble with fear and anger. They fear that the central protective force will be weakened, and that then they will be at the mercy of the great Teutonic Power.

When one considers that the facts were hardly in dispute, the actions of a responsible Government of respectable men and the public opinion which so flocculently supported them are scarcely comprehensible. It was like being smothered by a feather-bed. I remember particularly the look of pain and aversion which I saw on the faces of Members in all parts of the House when I said, "Thank God for the French Army." Words were vain.

However, the French had the hardihood to insist that there should be a delay of four years before the destruction of their heavy war material. The British Government accepted this modification provided that the French agreement about the destruction of their artillery was specified in a document for immediate signature. France bowed to this, and on October 12, 1933, Sir John Simon, after complaining that Germany had shifted her ground in the course of the preceding weeks, brought these draft proposals before the Disarmament Conference. The result was unexpected. Hitler, now Chancellor and Master of all Germany, having already given orders on assuming power to drive ahead boldly on a nation-wide scale, both in the training-camps and the factories, felt himself in a strong position. He did not even trouble to accept the quixotic offers pressed upon him. With a gesture of disdain he directed the German Government to withdraw both from the Conference and from the League of Nations. Such was the fate of the MacDonald Plan.

★　★　★

It is difficult to find a parallel to the unwisdom of the British and weakness of the French Governments, who none the less reflected the opinion of their Parliaments in this disastrous period. Nor can the United States escape the censure of history. Absorbed in their own affairs and all the abounding interests, activities, and accidents of a free community, they simply gaped at the vast changes which were taking place in Europe, and imagined they were no concern of theirs. The considerable corps of highly competent, widely-trained professional American officers formed their own opinions, but these produced no noticeable effect upon the improvident aloofness of American foreign policy. If the influence of the United States had been exerted, it might have galvanised the French and British politicians into action. The League of Nations, battered though it had been, was still an august instrument which would have invested any challenge to the new Hitler war-menace with the sanctions of International Law. Under the strain the Americans merely shrugged their shoulders, so that in a few years they had to pour out the blood and treasures of the New World to save themselves from mortal danger.

Seven years later when at Tours I witnessed the French agony all this was in my mind, and that is why, even when proposals for a separate peace were mentioned, I spoke only words of comfort and reassurance, which I rejoice to feel have been made good.

★　★　★

I had arranged at the beginning of 1931 to undertake a considerable lecture tour in the United States, and travelled to New

York. Here I suffered a serious accident, which nearly cost me my life. On December 13, when on my way to visit Mr. Bernard Baruch, I got out of my car on the wrong side, and walked across Fifth Avenue without bearing in mind the opposite rule of the road which prevails in America, or the red lights, then unused in Britain. There was a shattering collision. For two months I was a wreck. I gradually regained at Nassau in the Bahamas enough strength to crawl around. In this condition I undertook a tour of forty lectures throughout the United States, living all day on my back in a railway compartment, and addressing in the evening large audiences. On the whole I consider this was the hardest time I have had in my life. I lay pretty low all through this year, but in time my strength returned.

Meanwhile at home our life flowed placidly downstream. At Westminster Mr. Baldwin adopted and espoused the main principles of Mr. MacDonald's India Bill, the conduct of which in the Commons was entrusted to the new Secretary of State for India, Sir Samuel Hoare. The report of the Simon Commission was ignored, and no opportunity of debating it was given to Parliament. With about seventy other Conservatives I formed a group called "the India Defence League", which during the next four years resisted the Government's policy on India in so far as it went beyond the recommendations of the Commission. We fought the matter out at party conferences with a considerable measure of support, sometimes running very close, but always in a minority. The Labour Opposition voted in Parliament with the Government on the Indian issue, and it became, like Disarmament, a link between the two Front Benches. Their followers presented an overwhelming majority against our group, and derided us as "Die-hards". The rise of Hitler to power, the domination of the Nazi Party over all Germany, and the rapid, active growth of German armed power, led to further differences between me and the Government and the various political parties in the State.

The years from 1931 to 1935, apart from my anxiety on public affairs, were personally very pleasant to me. I earned my livelihood by dictating articles which had a wide circulation not only in Great Britain and the United States, but also, before Hitler's shadow fell upon them, in the most famous newspapers of sixteen

71

European countries. I lived in fact from mouth to hand. I produced in succession the various volumes of the life of Marlborough. I meditated constantly upon the European situation and the rearming of Germany. I lived mainly at Chartwell, where I had much to amuse me. I built with my own hands a large part of two cottages and extensive kitchen-garden walls, and made all kinds of rockeries and waterworks and a large swimming-pool which was filtered to limpidity and could be heated to supplement our fickle sunshine. Thus I never had a dull or idle moment from morning till midnight, and with my happy family around me dwelt at peace within my habitation.

During these years I saw a great deal of Frederick Lindemann, Professor of Experimental Philosophy at Oxford University. Lindemann was already an old friend of mine. I had met him first at the close of the previous war, in which he had distinguished himself by conducting in the air a number of experiments, hitherto reserved for daring pilots, to overcome the then almost mortal dangers of a "spin". We came much closer together from 1932 onwards, and he frequently motored over from Oxford to stay with me at Chartwell. Here we had many talks into the small hours of the morning about the dangers which seemed to be gathering upon us. Lindemann, "the Prof.", as he was called among his friends, became my chief adviser on the scientific aspects of modern war and particularly air defence, and also on questions involving statistics of all kinds. This pleasant and fertile association continued throughout the war.

Another of my close friends was Desmond Morton.* When in 1917 Field-Marshal Haig filled his personal staff with young officers fresh from the firing line, Desmond was recommended to him as the pick of the Artillery. He had commanded the most advanced field battery in Arras during the severe spring fighting of that year. To his Military Cross he added the unique distinction of having been shot through the heart, and living happily ever afterwards with the bullet in him. When I became Minister of Munitions in July 1917 I frequently visited the front as the Commander-in-Chief's guest, and he always sent his trusted aide-de-camp, Desmond Morton, with me. Together we visited many parts of the line. During these sometimes dangerous excursions, and at the Commander-in-Chief's house, I formed a

* Now Major Sir Desmond Morton, K.C.B., M.C.

great regard and friendship for this brilliant and gallant officer, and in 1919, when I became Secretary of State for War and Air, I appointed him to a key position in the Intelligence, which he held for many years. He was a neighbour of mine, dwelling only a mile away from Chartwell. He obtained from the Prime Minister, Mr. MacDonald, permission to talk freely to me and keep me well informed. He became, and continued during the war to be, one of my most intimate advisers till our final victory was won.

I had also formed a friendship with Ralph Wigram, then the rising star of the Foreign Office and in the centre of all its affairs. He had reached a level in that department which entitled him to express responsible opinions upon policy, and to use a wide discretion in his contacts, official and unofficial. He was a charming and fearless man, and his convictions, based upon profound knowledge and study, dominated his being. He saw as clearly as I did, but with more certain information, the awful peril which was closing in upon us. This drew us together. Often we met at his little house in North Street, and he and Mrs. Wigram came to stay with us at Chartwell. Like other officials of high rank, he spoke to me with complete confidence. All this helped me to form and fortify my opinion about the Hitler Movement. For my part, with the many connections which I now had in France, in Germany, and other countries, I had been able to send him a certain amount of information which we examined together.

From 1933 onwards Wigram became keenly distressed at the policy of the Government and the course of events. While his official chiefs formed every day a higher opinion of his capacity, and while his influence in the Foreign Office grew, his thoughts turned repeatedly to resignation. He had so much force and grace in his conversation that all who had grave business with him, and many others, gave ever-increasing importance to his views.

*   *   *

It was of great value to me, and it may be thought also to the country, that I should have the means of conducting searching and precise discussions for so many years in this very small circle. On my side however I gathered and contributed a great deal of information from foreign sources. I had confidential contacts with several of the French Ministers and with the successive chiefs of the French Government. Mr. Ian Colvin, the son of the famous leader-writer of the *Morning Post*, was the *News Chronicle* correspondent in Berlin. He plunged very deeply into German politics, and established contacts of a most secret character with some of the important German generals, and also with independent men of character and quality in Germany who saw in the Hitler Movement the approaching ruin of their native land. Several visitors of consequence came to me from Germany and poured their hearts out in their bitter distress. Most of these were executed by Hitler during the war. From other directions I was able to check and furnish information on the whole field of our air defence. In this way I became as well instructed as many Ministers of the Crown. All the facts I gathered from every source, including especially foreign connections, I reported to the Government from time to time. My personal relations with Ministers and also with many of their high officials were close and easy, and although I was often their critic we maintained a spirit of comradeship. Later on, as will be seen, I was made officially party to much of their most secret technical knowledge. From my own long experience in high office I was also possessed of the most precious secrets of the State. All this enabled me to form and maintain opinions which did not depend on what was published in the newspapers, though these brought many items to the discriminating eye.

*   *   *

At Westminster I pursued my two themes of India and the German menace, and went to Parliament from time to time to deliver warning speeches, which commanded attention, but did not, unhappily, wake to action the crowded, puzzled Houses which heard them. On the German danger, as on India, I found myself working in Parliament with a group of friends. It was composed differently from the India Defence League. Sir Austen Chamberlain, Sir Robert Horne, Sir Edward Grigg, Lord Winterton, Mr. Bracken, Sir Henry Croft, and several others formed our circle. We met regularly and to a large extent pooled our information. The Ministers eyed this significant but not unfriendly body of their own supporters and former colleagues or seniors with respect. We could at any time command the attention of Parliament and stage a full-dress debate.

*   *   *

74

The reader will pardon a personal digression in a lighter vein.

In the summer of 1932 for the purposes of my life of Marl-borough I visited his old battlefields in the Low Countries and Germany. Our family expedition, which included "the Prof.", journeyed agreeably along the line of Marlborough's celebrated march in 1705 from the Netherlands to the Danube, passing the Rhine at Coblenz. As we wended our way through these beauti-ful regions from one ancient, famous city to another, I naturally asked questions about the Hitler Movement, and found it the prime topic in every German mind. I sensed a Hitler atmosphere. After passing a day on the field of Blenheim, I drove into Munich, and spent the best part of a week there.

At the Regina Hotel a gentleman introduced himself to some of my party. He was Herr Hanfstaengl, and spoke a great deal about "the Fuehrer", with whom he appeared to be intimate. As he seemed to be a lively and talkative fellow, speaking excellent English, I asked him to dine. He gave a most interesting account of Hitler's activities and outlook. He spoke as one under the spell. He had probably been told to get in touch with me. He was evidently most anxious to please. After dinner he went to the piano and played and sang many tunes and songs in such remark-able style that we all enjoyed ourselves immensely. He seemed to know all the English tunes that I liked. He was a great enter-tainer, and at that time, as is known, a favourite of the Fuehrer. He said I ought to meet him, and that nothing would be easier to arrange. Herr Hitler came every day to the hotel about five o'clock, and would be very glad indeed to see me.

I had no national prejudices against Hitler at this time. I knew little of his doctrine or record and nothing of his character. I admire men who stand up for their country in defeat, even though I am on the other side. He had a perfect right to be a patriotic German if he chose. I always wanted England, Germany, and France to be friends. However, in the course of conversation with Hanfstaengl I happened to say, "Why is your chief so violent about the Jews? I can quite understand being angry with Jews who have done wrong or are against the country, and I understand resisting them if they try to monopolise power in any walk of life; but what is the sense of being against a man simply because of his birth? How can any man help how he is born?" He must have repeated this to Hitler, because about noon the next day he came round with rather a serious air and said that the appointment he had made with me to meet Hitler could not take place as the Fuehrer would not be coming to the hotel that afternoon. This was the last I saw of "Putzi"—for such was his pet name—although we stayed several more days at the hotel. Thus Hitler lost his only chance of meeting me. Later on, when he was all-powerful, I was to receive several invitations from him. But by that time a lot had happened, and I excused myself.

* * *

All this while the United States remained intensely preoccupied with its own vehement internal affairs and economic problems. Europe and far-off Japan watched with steady gaze the rise of German warlike power. Disquietude was increasingly expressed in Scandinavian countries and the States of the Little Entente and in some Balkan countries. Deep anxiety ruled in France, where a large amount of knowledge of Hitler's activities and of German preparations had come to hand. There was, I was told, a catalogue of breaches of the treaties of immense and formidable gravity, but when I asked my French friends why this matter was not raised in the League of Nations, and Germany invited, or even ultimately summoned, to explain her action and state precisely what she was doing, I was answered that the British Government would deprecate such an alarming step. Thus, while Mr. MacDonald, with Mr. Baldwin's full authority, preached disarmament to the French and practised it upon the British, the German might grew by leaps and bounds, and the time for overt action approached.

In justice to the Conservative Party it must be mentioned that at each of the Conferences of the National Union of Conservative Associations from 1932 onwards resolutions proposed by such worthies as Lord Lloyd and Sir Henry Croft in favour of an immediate strengthening of our armaments to meet the growing danger from abroad were carried almost unanimously. But the Parliamentary control by the Government Whips in the House of Commons was at this time so effective, and the three parties in the Government, as well as the Labour Opposition, so sunk in lethargy and blindness, that the warnings of their followers in the country were as ineffective as were the signs of the times and the evidence of the Secret Service. This was one of those awful periods which recur in our history, when the noble British nation seems to fall from its high estate, loses all trace of sense or purpose, and appears to cower from the menace of foreign peril, frothing pious platitudes while foemen forge their arms.

In this dark time the basest sentiments received acceptance or passed unchallenged by the responsible leaders of the political parties. In 1933 the students of the Oxford Union, under the inspiration of a Mr. Joad, passed their ever-shameful resolution, "That this House will in no circumstances fight for its King and Country." It was easy to laugh off such an episode in England, but in Germany, in Russia, in Italy, in Japan, the idea of a decadent, degenerate Britain took deep root and swayed many calculations. Little did the foolish boys who passed the resolution dream that they were destined quite soon to conquer or fall gloriously in the ensuing war, and prove themselves the finest generation ever bred in Britain. Less excuse can be found for their elders, who had no chance of self-redemption in action.*

★   ★   ★

In November 1933 we had another debate in the House of Commons. I returned to my main theme:

We read of large importations of scrap iron and nickel and war metals, quite out of the ordinary. We read all the news which accumulates of the military spirit which is rife throughout the country; we see that a philosophy of blood-lust is being inculcated into their youth to which no parallel can be found since the days of barbarism. We see all these forces on the move, and we must remember that this is the same mighty Germany which fought all the world and almost beat the world; it is the same mighty Germany which took two and a half lives for every German life that was taken.† No wonder, when you have these preparations, these doctrines, and these assertions openly made, that there is alarm throughout the whole circle of nations which surround Germany. . . .

★   ★   ★

* I cannot resist telling this story. I was asked to address the University Conservative Association in the Oxford Union. I declined to do so, but said I would give them an hour to ask me questions. One of the questions was, "Do you think Germany was guilty of making the last war?" I said, "Yes, of course." A young German Rhodes scholar rose from his place and said, "After this insult to my country I will not remain here." He then stalked out amid roars of applause. I thought him a spirited boy. Two years later it was found out in Germany that he had a Jewish ancestor. This ended his career in Germany.

† This excludes the Russian losses.

While this fearful transformation in the relative war-power of victors and vanquished was taking place in Europe, a complete lack of concert between the non-aggressive and peace-loving States had also developed in the Far East. This story forms a counterpart to the disastrous turn of events in Europe, and arose from the same paralysis of thought and action among the leaders of the former and future Allies.

The Economic Blizzard of 1929 to 1931 had affected Japan not less than the rest of the world. Since 1914 her population had grown from fifty to seventy millions. Her metallurgical factories had increased from fifty to one hundred and forty-eight. The cost of living had risen steadily. The production of rice was stationary, and its importation expensive. The need for raw material and for external markets was clamant. In the violent depression Britain and forty other countries felt increasingly compelled, as the years passed, to apply restrictions or tariffs against Japanese goods produced under labour conditions unrelated to European or American standards. China was more than ever Japan's principal export market for cotton and other manufactures, and almost her sole source of coal and iron. A new assertion of control over China became therefore the main theme of Japanese policy.

In September 1931, on a pretext of local disorders, the Japanese occupied Mukden and the zone of the Manchurian Railway. In January 1932 they demanded the dissolution of all Chinese associations of an anti-Japanese character. The Chinese Government refused, and on the 28th the Japanese landed to the north of the International Concession at Shanghai. The Chinese resisted with spirit, and, although without aeroplanes or anti-tank guns or any of the modern weapons, maintained their resistance for more than a month. At the end of February, after suffering very heavy losses, they were obliged to retire from their forts in the bay of Wu-Sung, and took up positions about twelve miles inland. Early in 1932 the Japanese created the puppet State of Manchukuo. A year later the Chinese province of Jehol was annexed to it, and Japanese troops, penetrating deeply into defenceless regions, had reached the Great Wall of China. This aggressive action corresponded to the growth of Japanese power in the Far East and her new naval position on the oceans.

From the first shot the outrage committed upon China aroused the strongest hostility in the United States. But the policy of Isolation cut both ways. Had the United States been a member of the League of Nations, she could undoubtedly have led that assembly into collective action against Japan, of which the United States would herself have been the principal mandatory. The British Government on their part showed no desire to act with the United States alone; nor did they wish to be drawn into antagonism with Japan further than their obligations under the League of Nations Charter required. There was a rueful feeling in some British circles at the loss of the Japanese Alliance and the consequential weakening of the British position with all its long-established interests in the Far East. His Majesty's Government could hardly be blamed if in their grave financial and growing European embarrassments they did not seek a prominent *rôle* at the side of the United States in the Far East without any hope of corresponding American support in Europe.

China however was a member of the League, and although she had not paid her subscription to that body she appealed to it for what was no more than justice. On September 30, 1931, the League called on Japan to remove her troops from Manchuria. In December a Commission was appointed to conduct an inquiry on the spot. The League of Nations entrusted the chairmanship of the Commission to the Earl of Lytton, the worthy descendant of a gifted line. He had had many years' experience in the East as Governor of Bengal and as acting Viceroy of India. The report, which was unanimous, was a remarkable document, and forms the basis of any serious study of the conflict between China and Japan. The whole background of the Manchurian affair was carefully presented. The conclusions drawn were plain: Manchukuo was the artificial creation of the Japanese General Staff, and the wishes of the population had played no part in the formation of this puppet State. Lord Lytton and his colleagues in their report not only analysed the situation, but put forward concrete proposals for an international solution. These were for the declaration of an autonomous Manchuria. It would still remain part of China, under the ægis of the League, and there would be a comprehensive treaty between China and Japan regulating their interests in Manchuria. The fact that the League could not follow up these proposals in no way detracts from the value of the Lytton report. The American Secretary of State, Stimson, wrote of the document: "It became at once and remains to-day the outstanding impartial authority upon the subject which it covers." In February 1933 the League of Nations declared that the State of Manchukuo could not be recognised. Although no sanctions were imposed upon Japan, nor any other action taken, Japan, on March 27, 1933, withdrew from the League of Nations. Germany and Japan had been on opposite sides in the war; they now looked towards each other in a different mood. The moral authority of the League was shown to be devoid of any physical support at a time when its activity and strength were most needed.

★　　★　　★

We must regard as deeply blameworthy before history the conduct not only of the British National and mainly Conservative Government, but of the Labour-Socialist and Liberal Parties, both in and out of office, during this fatal period. Delight in smooth-sounding platitudes, refusal to face unpleasant facts, desire for popularity and electoral success irrespective of the vital interests of the State, genuine love of peace and pathetic belief that love can be its sole foundation, obvious lack of intellectual vigour in both leaders of the British Coalition Government, marked ignorance of Europe and aversion from its problems in Mr. Baldwin, the strong and violent pacifism which at this time dominated the Labour-Socialist Party, the utter devotion of the Liberals to sentiment apart from reality, the failure and worse than failure of Mr. Lloyd George, the erstwhile great war-time leader, to address himself to the continuity of his work, the whole supported by overwhelming majorities in both Houses of Parliament: all these constituted a picture of British fatuity and fecklessness which, though devoid of guile, was not devoid of guilt, and, though free from wickedness or evil design, played a definite part in the unleashing upon the world of horrors and miseries which, even so far as they have unfolded, are already beyond comparison in human experience.

CHAPTER VI

THE DARKENING SCENE

1934

Spring Warnings – The German Blood Purge of June 30 – The End of Disarmament – The Murder of Dr. Dollfuss, July 25 – The Death of Hindenburg – Hitler Head of the German State, August 2 – The Italian Dilemma – The Murder of King Alexander and M. Barthou at Marseilles, October 9 – M. Laval, French Foreign Minister, November – Italian-Abyssinian Clash at Wal-Wal, December – Franco-Italian Agreement, January 6, 1935 – The Saar Plebiscite, January 13, 1935.

HITLER'S accession to the Chancellorship in 1933 had not been regarded with enthusiasm in Rome. Nazism was viewed as a crude and brutalised version of the Fascist theme. The ambitions of a Greater Germany towards Austria and in South-eastern Europe were well known. Mussolini foresaw that in neither of these regions would Italian interests coincide with those of the new Germany. Nor had he long to wait for confirmation.

*   *   *

The acquisition of Austria by Germany was one of Hitler's most cherished ambitions. The first page of *Mein Kampf* contains the sentence, "German Austria must return to the great German Motherland." From the moment, therefore, of the acquisition of power in January 1933, the Nazi German Government cast its eyes upon Vienna. Hitler could not afford as yet to clash with Mussolini, whose interests in Austria had been loudly proclaimed. Even infiltration and underground activities had to be applied with caution by a Germany as yet militarily weak. Pressure on Austria however began in the first few months. Unceasing demands were made on the Austrian Government to force members of the satellite Austrian Nazi Party both into the Cabinet and into key posts in the Administration. Austrian Nazis were trained in an Austrian legion organised in Bavaria. Bomb outrages on the railways and at tourist centres, German aeroplanes showering leaflets over Salzburg and Innsbruck, disturbed the daily life of the republic. The Austrian Chancellor Dollfuss was equally opposed both by Socialist pressure within and external German designs against Austrian independence. Nor was this the only menace to the Austrian State. Following the evil example of their German neighbours, the Austrian Socialists had built up a private army with which to override the decision of the ballot-box. Both dangers loomed upon Dollfuss during 1933. The only quarter to which he could turn for protection and whence he had already received assurances of support was Fascist Italy. In August 1933 he met Mussolini at Riccione. A close personal and political understanding was reached between them. Dollfuss, who believed that Italy would hold the ring, felt strong enough to move against one set of his opponents—the Austrian Socialists.

In January 1934 Suvich, Mussolini's principal adviser on foreign affairs, visited Vienna as a gesture of warning to Germany. On January 21 he made the following public statement:

The importance of Austria, due to her position in the heart of Central Europe and in the Danube basin, far exceeds, as is well known, her territorial and numerical size. If she is to fulfil in the interests of all the mission accorded her by centuries-old tradition and geographical situation, the normal conditions of independence and peaceful life must first of all be secured. That is the standpoint which Italy has long maintained in regard to both political and economic conditions on the basis of unchangeable principles.

Three weeks later the Dollfuss Government took action against the Socialist organisations of Vienna. The Heimwehr, under Major Fey, belonging to Dollfuss's own party, received orders to disarm the equivalent and equally illegal body controlled by the Austrian Socialists. The latter resisted forcibly, and on February 12 street fighting broke out in the capital. Within a few hours the Socialist forces were broken. This event not only brought Dollfuss closer to Italy, but strengthened him in the next stage of his task against the Nazi penetration and conspiracy. On the other hand, many of the defeated Socialists or Communists swung over to the Nazi camp in their bitterness. In Austria as in Germany the Catholic-Socialist feud helped the Nazis.

★　　★　　★

Until the middle of 1934 the control of events was still largely in the hands of His Majesty's Government without the risk of war. They could at any time, in concert with France and through the agency of the League of Nations, have brought an overwhelming power to bear upon the Hitler Movement, about which Germany was profoundly divided. This would have involved no bloodshed. But this phase was passing. An armed Germany under Nazi control was approaching the threshold. And yet, incredible though it may seem, far into this cardinal year Mr. MacDonald, armed with Mr. Baldwin's political power, continued to work for the disarmament of France. I cannot but quote the unavailing protest which I made in Parliament on February 7:

What happens, for instance, if, after we have equalised and reduced the army of France to the level of that of Germany, and got an equality for Germany, and with all the reactions which will have followed in the sentiment of Europe upon such a change, Germany then proceeds to say, "How can you keep a great nation of seventy millions in a position in which it is not entitled to have a navy equal to the greatest of the fleets upon the seas?" You will say, "No; we do not agree. Armies—they belong to other people. Navies—that question affects Britain's interests and we are bound to say, 'No'." But what position shall we be in to say that "No"?

Wars come very suddenly. I have lived through a period when one looked forward, as we do now, with great anxiety and uncertainty to what would happen in the future. Suddenly something did happen— tremendous, swift, overpowering, irresistible. Let me remind the House of the sort of thing that happened in 1914. There was absolutely no quarrel between Germany and France. One July afternoon the German Ambassador drove down to the Quai d'Orsay and said to the French Prime Minister, "We have been forced to mobilise against Russia, and war will be declared. What is to be the position of France?" The French Premier made the answer which his Cabinet had agreed upon, that France would act in accordance with what she considered to be her own interests. The Ambassador said, "You have an alliance with Russia, have you not?" "Quite so," said the French Premier. And that was the process by which, in a few minutes, the area of the struggle, already serious in the East, was enormously widened and multiplied by the throwing in of the two great nations of the West on either side. But sometimes even a declaration of neutrality does not suffice. On this very occasion, as we now know, the German Ambassador was authorised by his Government, in case the French did not do their duty by their Russian ally, in case they showed any disposition to back out of the conflict which had been resolved on by Germany, to demand that the fortresses of Toul and Verdun should be handed over to German troops as a guarantee that the French, having declared neutrality, would not change their mind at a subsequent moment. . . .

We may ourselves, in the lifetime of those who are here, if we are not in a proper state of security, be confronted on some occasion with a visit from an Ambassador, and may have to give an answer, and if that answer is not satisfactory, within the next few hours the crash of bombs exploding in London and cataracts of masonry and fire and smoke will warn us of any inadequacy which has been permitted in our aerial defences. We are vulnerable as we have never been before. I often heard criticisms of the Liberal Government before the war. . . . A far graver case rests upon those who now hold power if by any chance, against our wishes and against our hopes, trouble should come.

Not one of the lessons of the past has been learned, not one of them has been applied, and the situation is incomparably more dangerous. Then we had the Navy and no air menace. Then the Navy was the "sure shield" of Britain. . . . We cannot say that now. This cursed, hellish invention and development of war from the air has revolutionised our position. We are not the same kind of country we used to be when we were an island, only twenty years ago.

I then asked for three definite decisions to be taken without delay. For the Army, the reorganisation of our civil factories, so that they could be turned over rapidly to war purposes, should be begun in Britain, as all over Europe. For the Navy we should regain freedom of design. We should get rid of this London Treaty which had crippled us in building the kind of ships we wanted, and had stopped the United States from building a great battleship which she probably needed, and to which we should not have had the slightest reason to object. We should be helped in doing this by the fact that another of the parties to that treaty* was resolved to regain her freedom too. Thirdly, the air. We ought to have an Air Force as strong as the Air Force of France or Germany, whichever was the stronger. The Government

* Japan.

commanded overwhelming majorities in both branches of the Legislature, and nothing would be denied to them. They had only to make their proposals with confidence and conviction for the safety of the country, and their countrymen would sustain them.

★ ★ ★

There was at this moment a flicker of European unity against the German menace. On February 17, 1934, the British, French, and Italian Governments made a common declaration upon the maintenance of Austrian independence. On March 14 I spoke again in Parliament:

The awful danger of our present foreign policy is that we go on perpetually asking the French to weaken themselves. And what do we say is the inducement? We say, "Weaken yourselves," and we always hold out the hope that if they do it and get into trouble we will then in some way or other go to their aid, although we have nothing with which to go to their aid. I cannot imagine a more dangerous policy. There is something to be said for isolation; there is something to be said for alliances. But there is nothing to be said for weakening the Power on the Continent with whom you would be in alliance, and then involving yourself more [deeply] in Continental tangles in order to make it up to them. In that way you have neither the one thing nor the other; you have the worst of both worlds.

The Romans had a maxim, "Shorten your weapons and lengthen your frontiers." But our maxim seems to be, "Diminish your weapons and increase your obligations." Aye, and diminish the weapons of your friends.

★ ★ ★

Italy now made a final attempt to carry out the aforesaid maxim. On March 17 Italy, Hungary, and Austria signed the so-called Rome Protocols, providing for mutual consultation in the event of a threat to any of the three parties. But Hitler was growing steadily stronger, and in May and June subversive activities increased throughout Austria. Dollfuss immediately sent reports on these terrorist acts to Suvich, with a note deploring their depressive effect upon Austrian trade and tourists.

It was with this dossier in his hand that Mussolini went to Venice on June 14 to meet Hitler for the first time. The German Chancellor stepped from his aeroplane in a brown mackintosh and Homburg hat into an array of sparkling Fascist uniforms, with a resplendent and portly Duce at their head. As Mussolini caught sight of his guest, he murmured to his aide, "*Non mi piace.*" ("I don't like the look of him.") At this strange meeting only a general exchange of ideas took place, with mutual lectures upon the virtues of dictatorship on the German and Italian models. Mussolini was clearly perplexed both by the personality and language of his guest. He summed up his final impression in these words, "A garrulous monk." He did however extract some assurances of relaxation of German pressure upon Dollfuss. Ciano told the journalists after the meeting, "You see. Nothing more will happen."

But the pause in German activities which followed was due not to Mussolini's appeal, but to Hitler's own internal preoccupations.

★ ★ ★

The acquisition of power had opened a deep divergence between the Fuehrer and many of those who had borne him forward. Under Roehm's leadership the S.A. increasingly represented the more revolutionary elements of the party. There were senior members of the party, such as Gregor Strasser, ardent for social revolution, who feared that Hitler in arriving at the first place would simply be taken over by the existing hierarchy, the Reichswehr, the bankers, and the industrialists. He would not have been the first revolutionary leader to kick down the ladder by which he had risen to exalted heights. To the rank and file of the S.A. ("Brownshirts") the triumph of January 1933 was meant to carry with it the freedom to pillage not only the Jews and profiteers, but also the well-to-do, established classes of society. Rumours of a great betrayal by their leader soon began to spread in certain circles of the party. Chief-of-Staff Roehm acted on this impulse with energy. In January 1933 the S.A. had been four hundred thousand strong. By the spring of 1934 he had recruited and organised nearly three million men. Hitler in his new situation was uneasy at the growth of this mammoth machine, which, while professing fervent loyalty to his name, and being for the most part deeply attached to him, was beginning to slip from his own personal control. Hitherto he had possessed a private army. Now he had the national Army. He did not intend to exchange the one for the other. He wanted both, and to use each, as events required, to control the other. He had now therefore to deal with Roehm. "I am resolved," he declared to the leaders of the S.A. in these days, "to repress severely any attempt to overturn the existing order. I will oppose with the sternest energy a second revolutionary wave, for it would bring with it inevitable chaos. Whoever raises his head against the established authority of the State will be severely treated, whatever his position."

In spite of his misgivings Hitler was not easily convinced of the disloyalty of his comrade of the Munich *Putsch*, who for the last seven years had been the Chief of Staff of his Brownshirt army. When, in December 1933, the unity of the party with the State had been proclaimed Roehm became a member of the German Cabinet. One of the consequences of the union of the party with the State was to be the merging of the Brownshirts with the Reichswehr. The rapid progress of national rearmament forced the issue of the status and control of all the German armed forces into the forefront of politics. In February 1934 Mr. Eden arrived in Berlin, and in the course of conversation Hitler agreed provisionally to give certain assurances about the non-military character of the S.A. Roehm was already in constant friction with General von Blomberg, the Chief of the General Staff. He now feared the sacrifice of the party army he had taken so many years to build, and, in spite of warnings of the gravity of his conduct, he published on April 18 an unmistakable challenge:

The Revolution we have made is not a national revolution, but a National *Socialist* Revolution. We would even underline this last word, "Socialist". The only rampart which exists against reaction is represented by our Assault Groups, for they are the absolute incarnation of the revolutionary idea. The militant in the Brown Shirt from the first day pledged himself to the path of revolution, and he will not deviate by a hairbreadth until our ultimate goal has been achieved.

He omitted on this occasion the "Heil Hitler!" which had been the invariable conclusion of Brownshirt harangues.

During the course of April and May Blomberg continually complained to Hitler about the insolence and activities of the S.A. The Fuehrer had to choose between the generals who hated him and the Brownshirt thugs to whom he owed so much. He chose the generals. At the beginning of June Hitler, in a five-hour conversation, made a last effort to conciliate and come to terms with Roehm. But with this abnormal fanatic, devoured by ambition, no compromise was possible. The mystic hierarchic Greater Germany of which Hitler dreamed and the Proletarian Republic of the People's Army desired by Roehm were separated by an impassable gulf.

Within the framework of the Brownshirts there had been formed a small and highly-trained *élite*, wearing black uniforms and known as the S.S., or later as Blackshirts. These units were intended for the personal protection of the Fuehrer and for special and confidential tasks. They were commanded by an unsuccessful ex-poultry-farmer, Heinrich Himmler. Foreseeing the impending clash between Hitler and the Army on the one hand and Roehm and the Brownshirts on the other, Himmler took care to carry the S.S. into Hitler's camp. On the other hand, Roehm had supporters of great influence within the party, who, like Gregor Strasser, saw their ferocious plans for Social Revolution being cast aside. The Reichswehr also had its rebels. Ex-Chancellor von Schleicher had never forgiven his disgrace in January 1933 and the failure of the Army chiefs to choose him as successor to Hindenburg. In a clash between Roehm and Hitler Schleicher saw an opportunity. He was imprudent enough to drop hints to the French Ambassador in Berlin that the fall of Hitler was not far off. This repeated the action he had taken in the case of Bruening. But the times had become more dangerous.

It will long be disputed in Germany whether Hitler was forced to strike by the imminence of the Roehm plot, or whether he and the generals, fearing what might be coming, resolved on a clean-cut liquidation while they had the power. Hitler's interest and that of the victorious faction was plainly to establish the case for a plot. It is improbable that Roehm and the Brownshirts had actually got as far as this. They were a menacing movement rather than a plot, but at any moment this line might have been crossed. It is certain they were drawing up their forces. It is also certain they were forestalled.

Events now moved rapidly. On June 25 the Reichswehr was confined to barracks, and ammunition was issued to the Blackshirts. On the opposite side the Brownshirts were ordered to stand in readiness, and Roehm with Hitler's consent called a meeting for June 30 of all their senior leaders to meet at Wiessee, in the Bavarian lakes. Hitler received warning of grave danger on the 29th. He flew to Godesberg, where he was joined by Goebbels, who brought alarming news of impending mutiny in Berlin. According to Goebbels, Roehm's adjutant, Karl Ernst, had been given orders to attempt a rising. This seems unlikely. Ernst was actually at Bremen, about to embark from that port on his honeymoon.

On this information, true or false, Hitler took instant decisions. He ordered Goering to take control in Berlin. He boarded his aeroplane for Munich, resolved to arrest his main opponents personally. In this life or death climax, as it had now become, he showed himself a terrible personality. Plunged in dark thought, he sat in the co-pilot's seat throughout the journey. The plane landed at an airfield near Munich at 4 o'clock in the morning of June 30. Hitler had with him, besides Goebbels, about a dozen of his personal bodyguard. He drove to the Brown House in Munich, summoned the leaders of the local S.A. to his presence, and placed them under arrest. At 6 o'clock, with Goebbels and his small escort only, he motored to Wiessee.

Roehm was ill in the summer of 1934 and had gone to Wiessee to take a cure. The establishment he had selected was a small chalet belonging to the doctor in charge of his case. No worse headquarters could have been chosen from which to organise an immediate revolt. The chalet stands at the end of a narrow cul-de-sac lane. All arrivals and departures could be easily noted. There was no room large enough to hold the alleged impending meeting of Brownshirt leaders. There was only one telephone. This ill accords with the theory of an imminent uprising. If Roehm and his followers were about to revolt, they were certainly careless.

At seven o'clock the Fuehrer's procession of cars arrived in front of Roehm's chalet. Alone and unarmed, Hitler mounted the stairs and entered Roehm's bedroom. What passed between the two men will never be known. Roehm was taken completely by surprise, and he and his personal staff were arrested without incident. The small party, with its prisoners, now left by road for Munich. It happened that they soon met a column of lorries of armed Brownshirts on their way to acclaim Roehm at the conference convened at Wiessee for noon. Hitler stepped out of his car, called for the commanding officer, and, with confident authority, ordered him to take his men home. He was instantly obeyed. If he had been an hour later, or they had been an hour earlier, great events would have taken a different course.

On arrival at Munich Roehm and his entourage were imprisoned in the same gaol where he and Hitler had been confined together ten years before. That afternoon the executions began. A revolver was placed in Roehm's cell, but as he disdained the invitation the cell door was opened within a few minutes and he was riddled with bullets. All the afternoon the executions proceeded in Munich at brief intervals. The firing parties of eight had to be relieved from time to time on account of the mental stress of the soldiers. But for several hours the recurrent volleys were heard every ten minutes or so.

Meanwhile in Berlin Goering, having heard from Hitler, followed a similar procedure. But here, in the capital, the killing spread beyond the hierarchy of the S.A. Schleicher and his wife, who threw herself in front of him, were shot in their house. Gregor Strasser was arrested and put to death. Papen's private secretary and immediate circle were also shot; but for some unknown reason he himself was spared. In the Lichterfelde barracks in Berlin Karl Ernst, clawed back from Bremen, met his fate; and here, as in Munich, the volleys of the executioners were heard all day. Throughout Germany, during these twenty-four hours, many men unconnected with the Roehm plot disappeared as the victims of private vengeance, sometimes for very old scores. Otto von Kahr, for instance, who as head of the Bavarian Government had broken the 1923 *Putsch*, was found dead in the woods near Munich. The total number of persons "liquidated" is variously estimated as between five and seven thousand.

Late in the afternoon of this bloody day Hitler returned by air to Berlin. It was time to put an end to the slaughter, which was spreading every moment. That evening a certain number of the S.S., who through excess of zeal had gone a little far in shooting prisoners, were themselves led out to execution. About one o'clock in the morning of July 1 the sounds of firing ceased. Later in the day the Fuehrer appeared on the balcony of the Chancellery to receive the acclamations of the Berlin crowds, many of whom thought that he had himself been a victim. Some say he looked haggard, others triumphant. He may well have been both. His promptitude and ruthlessness had saved his purpose and no doubt his life. In that "Night of the Long Knives", as it was called, the unity of National-Socialist Germany had been preserved to carry its curse throughout the world.

A fortnight later the Fuehrer addressed the Reichstag, who sat in loyalty or awe before him. In the course of two hours he delivered a reasoned defence of his action. The speech reveals his knowledge of the German mind and his own undoubted powers of argument. Its climax was:

The necessity for acting with lightning speed meant that in this decisive hour I had very few men with me. . . . Although only a few days before I had been prepared to exercise clemency, at this hour there was no place for any such consideration. Mutinies are suppressed in accordance with laws of iron which are eternally the same. If anyone reproaches me and asks why I did not resort to the regular Courts of Justice for conviction of the offenders, then all that I can say to him is this: In this hour I was responsible for the fate of the German people, and thereby I became the supreme Justiciar of the German people. . . . I did not wish to deliver up the Young Reich to the fate of the Old Reich. I gave the order to shoot those who were the ringleaders in this treason. . . .

Then followed this mixed but expressive metaphor:

And I further gave the order to burn out down to the raw flesh the ulcers of this poisoning of the wells in our domestic life, and of the poisoning of the outside world.

This massacre, however explicable by the hideous forces at work, showed that the new Master of Germany would stop at nothing, and that conditions in Germany bore no resemblance to those of a civilised State. A Dictatorship based upon terror and reeking with blood had confronted the world. Anti-Semitism was ferocious and brazen, and the concentration-camp system was already in full operation for all obnoxious or politically dissident classes. I was deeply affected by the episode, and the whole process of German rearmament, of which there was now overwhelming evidence, seemed to me invested with a ruthless, lurid tinge. It glittered and it glared.

★   ★   ★

We may now return for a moment to the House of Commons. In the course of June 1934 the Standing Committee of the Disarmament Conference at Geneva was adjourned indefinitely. On July 13 I said:

I am very glad that the Disarmament Conference is passing out of life into history. It is the greatest mistake to mix up disarmament with peace. When you have peace you will have disarmament. But there has been during these recent years a steady deterioration in the relations between different countries, a steady growth of ill-will, and a steady, indeed a rapid increase in armaments that has gone on through all these years in spite of the endless flow of oratory, of perorations, of well-meaning sentiments, of banquets, which have marked this epoch.

Europe will be secure when nations no longer feel themselves in great danger, as many of them do now. Then the pressure and the burden of armaments will fall away automatically, as they ought to have done in a long peace; and it might be quite easy to seal a movement of that character by some general agreement. I hope, indeed, that we have now also reached the end of the period of the Government pressing France—this peaceful France with no militarism—to weaken her armed forces. I rejoice that the French have not taken the advice which has been offered to them so freely from various quarters, and which the Leader of the Opposition [Mr. Lansbury] no doubt would strongly endorse.

This is not the only Germany which we shall live to see, but we have to consider that at present two or three men, in what may well be a desperate position, have the whole of that mighty country in their grip, have that wonderful scientific, intelligent, docile, valiant people in their grip, a population of seventy millions; that there is no dynastic interest such as the monarchy brings as a restraint upon policy, because it looks long ahead and has much to lose; and that there is no public opinion except what is manufactured by those new and terrible engines—broadcasting and a controlled Press. Politics in Germany are not as they are over here. There you do not leave office to go into Opposition. You do not leave the Front Bench to sit below the Gangway. You may well leave your high office at a quarter of an hour's notice to drive to the police station, and you may be conducted thereafter very rapidly to an even graver ordeal.

It seems to me that men in that position might very easily be tempted to do what even a military dictatorship would not do, because a military dictatorship, with all its many faults, at any rate is one that is based on a very accurate study of the real facts; and there is more danger in this kind of dictatorship than there would be in a military dictatorship, because you have men who, to relieve themselves from the great peril which confronts them at home, might easily plunge into a foreign adventure of the most dangerous and catastrophic character to the whole world.

★　　★　　★

The first temptation to such an adventure was soon to be revealed.

During the early part of July 1934 there was much coming and going over the mountain paths leading from Bavaria into Austrian territory. At the end of July a German courier fell into the hands of the Austrian frontier police. He carried documents, including cipher keys, which showed that a complete plan of revolt was reaching fruition. The organiser of the *coup d'état* was to be Anton von Rintelen, at that time Austrian Minister to Italy. Dollfuss and his Ministers were slow to respond to the warnings of an impending crisis, and to the signs of imminent revolt which became apparent in the early hours of July 25. The Nazi adherents in Vienna mobilised during the morning. Just before one o'clock in the afternoon a party of armed rebels entered the Chancellery, and Dollfuss, hit by two revolver bullets, was left to bleed slowly to death. Another detachment of Nazis seized the broadcasting station and announced the resignation of the Dollfuss Government and the assumption of office by Rintelen.

But the other members of the Dollfuss Cabinet reacted with firmness and energy. President Dr. Miklas issued a formal command to restore order at all costs. Dr. Schuschnigg assumed the administration. The majority of the Austrian Army and police rallied to his Government, and besieged the Chancellery building, where, surrounded by a small party of rebels, Dollfuss was dying. The revolt had also broken out in the provinces, and parties from the Austrian legion in Bavaria crossed the frontier. Mussolini had by now heard the news. He telegraphed at once to Prince Starhemberg, the head of the Austrian Heimwehr, promising Italian support for Austrian independence. Flying specially to Venice, the Duce received the widow of Dr. Dollfuss with every circumstance of sympathy. At the same time three Italian divisions were dispatched to the Brenner Pass. On this Hitler, who knew the limits of his strength, recoiled. The German Minister in Vienna, Rieth, and other German officials implicated in the rising, were recalled or dismissed. The attempt had failed. A longer process was needed. Papen, newly spared from the blood-bath, was appointed as German Minister to Vienna, with instructions to work by more subtle means.

Papen had been appointed German Minister to Vienna for the explicit purpose of organising the overthrow of the Austrian

Republic. He had a double task: the encouragement of the underground Austrian Nazi Party, which received henceforth a monthly subsidy of 200,000 marks; and the undermining or winning over of leading personalities in Austrian politics. In the early days of his appointment he expressed himself with frankness verging upon indiscretion to his American colleagues in Vienna. "In the boldest and most cynical manner," says the American Minister, "Papen proceeded to tell me that all South-eastern Europe to the borders of Turkey was Germany's natural hinterland, and that he had been charged with the mission of effecting German economic and political control over the whole of this region. He blandly and directly said that getting control of Austria was to be the first step. He intended to use his reputation as a good Catholic to gain influence with Austrians like Cardinal Innitzer. The German Government was determined to gain control of South-eastern Europe. There was nothing to stop them. The policy of the United States, like that of France and England, was not 'realistic'."

Amid these tragedies and alarms the aged Marshal Hindenburg, who had for some months been almost completely senile, and so more than ever a tool of the Reichswehr, expired. Hitler became the head of the German State while retaining the office of Chancellor. He was now the Sovereign of Germany. His bargain with the Reichswehr had been sealed and kept by the bloodpurge. The Brownshirts had been reduced to obedience and reaffirmed their loyalty to the Fuehrer. All foes and potential rivals had been extirpated from their ranks. Henceforward they lost their influence and became a kind of special constabulary for ceremonial occasions. The Blackshirts, on the other hand, increased in numbers, and, strengthened by privileges and discipline, became under Himmler a Prætorian Guard for the person of the Fuehrer, a counterpoise to the Army leaders and military caste, and also political troops to arm with considerable military force the activities of the expanding Secret Police or Gestapo. It was only necessary to invest these powers with the formal sanction of a managed plebiscite to make Hitler's dictatorship absolute and perfect.

★　　★　　★

Events in Austria drew France and Italy together, and the shock of the Dollfuss assassination led to General Staff contacts. The

Different Aspects of Peace

8 Before the scuttling of the captured German Fleet at Scapa Flow, 21st June, 1919.
9 Mussolini's entry into Rome (centre foreground), 29th October, 1922.

10 The assassination of the President of the French Republic, Paul Doumer, by
Gorguloff, 12th May, 1932.
11 The assassination of King Alexander of Yugoslavia, 10th October, 1934.
The photo shows the body of the assassin at the feet of police agents.

12 The ceremonial laying of the first stone of the Maginot Line at Bar-le-Duc.
   In the centre, Maginot (with walking-stick); right, President Poincaré.
13 The financial crash of 1929 at the New York Stock Exchange.

14 Stanley Baldwin.

menace to Austrian independence promoted a revision of Franco-Italian relations, and this had to comprise not only the balance of power in the Mediterranean and North Africa, but the relative positions of France and Italy in South-eastern Europe. But Mussolini was anxious not only to safeguard Italy's position in Europe against the potential German threat, but also to secure her imperial future in Africa. Against Germany, close relations with France and Great Britain would be useful; but in the Mediterranean and Africa disagreements with both these Powers might be inevitable. The Duce wondered whether the common need for security felt by Italy, France, and Great Britain might not induce the two former allies of Italy to accept the Italian Imperialist programme in Africa. At any rate this seemed a hopeful course for Italian policy.

* * *

In France, after the Stavisky scandal and the riots of February, M. Daladier had been succeeded as Premier by a Government of the Right Centre under M. Doumergue, with M. Barthou as Foreign Minister. Ever since the signature of the Locarno treaties France had been anxious to reach formal agreement on security measures in the East. British reluctance to undertake commitments beyond the Rhine, the German refusal to make binding agreements with Poland and Czechoslovakia, the fears of the Little Entente as to Russian intentions, Russian suspicion of the capitalist West, all united to thwart such a programme. In September 1934, however, Louis Barthou determined to go forward. His original plan was to propose an Eastern Pact, grouping together Germany, Russia, Poland, Czechoslovakia, and the Baltic States on the basis of a guarantee by France of the European frontiers of Russia, and by Russia of the eastern borders of Germany. Both Germany and Poland were opposed to an Eastern Pact; but Barthou succeeded in obtaining the entry of Russia into the League of Nations on September 18, 1934. This was an important step. Litvinov, who represented the Soviet Government, was versed in every aspect of foreign affairs. He adapted himself to the atmosphere of the League of Nations and spoke its moral language with so much success that he soon became an outstanding figure.

In her search for allies against the new Germany that had been allowed to grow up, it was natural that France should turn her eyes to Russia and try to re-create the balance of power which had existed before the war. But in October a tragedy occurred. In pursuance of French policy in the Balkans King Alexander of Yugoslavia had been invited to pay an official visit to Paris. He landed at Marseilles, was met by M. Barthou, and drove with him and General Georges through the welcoming crowds who thronged the streets, gay with flags and flowers. Once again from the dark recesses of the Serbian and Croat underworld a hideous murder-plot sprang upon the European stage, and, as at Sarajevo in 1914, a band of assassins, ready to give their lives, were at hand. The French police arrangements were loose and casual. A figure darted from the cheering crowds, mounted the running-board of the car, and discharged his automatic pistol into the King and its other occupants, all of whom were stricken. The murderer was immediately cut down and killed by the mounted Republican guardsman behind whom he had slipped. A scene of wild confusion occurred. King Alexander expired almost immediately. General Georges and M. Barthou stepped out of the carriage streaming with blood. The General was too weak to move, but soon received medical aid. The Minister wandered off into the crowd. It was twenty minutes before he was attended to. He was made to walk upstairs to the Prefect's office before he could be given medical care; the doctor then applied the tourniquet *below* the wound. He had already lost much blood; he was seventy-two, and he died in a few hours. This was a heavy blow to French foreign policy, which under him was beginning to take a coherent form. He was succeeded as Foreign Secretary by Pierre Laval.

Laval's later shameful record and fate must not obscure the fact of his personal force and capacity. He had a clear and intense view. He believed that France must at all costs avoid war, and he hoped to secure this by arrangements with the Dictators of Italy and Germany, against whose systems he entertained no prejudice. He distrusted Soviet Russia. Despite his occasional protestations of friendship, he disliked England and thought her a worthless ally. At that time indeed British repute did not stand very high in France. Laval's first object was to reach a definite understanding with Italy, and he deemed the moment ripe. The French Government was obsessed by the German danger, and was prepared to make solid concessions to gain Italy. In January 1935 M. Laval went to Rome and signed a series of agreements with the object of removing the main obstacles between the two countries. Both Governments were united upon the illegality of German rearmament. They agreed to consult each other in the event of future threats to the independence of Austria. In the colonial sphere France undertook to make administrative concessions about the status of Italians in Tunisia, and handed over to Italy certain tracts of territory on the borders both of Libya and of Somaliland, together with a 20 per cent. share in the Jibuti—Addis-Ababa railway. These conversations were designed to lay the foundations for more formal discussions between France, Italy, and Great Britain about a common front against the growing German menace. Across them all there cut in the ensuing months the fact of Italian aggression in Abyssinia.

*   *   *

In December 1934 a clash took place between Italian and Abyssinian soldiers at the wells of Wal Wal, on the borders of Abyssinia and Italian Somaliland. This was to be the pretext for the ultimate presentation before the world of Italian claims upon the Ethiopian kingdom. Thus the problem of containing Germany in Europe was henceforth confused and distorted by the fate of Abyssinia.

*   *   *

There is one more incident at this juncture which should be mentioned. Under the terms of the Treaty of Versailles, the Saar Valley, a small strip of German territory, possessing rich coal-mines and important iron-works, was to decide at the end of fifteen years by a plebiscite whether the population wished to return to Germany or not. The date fixed for this event was in January 1935. There could be no doubt of the outcome. The majority would certainly vote for reincorporation into the German Fatherland; and, to make assurance doubly sure, the valley, though nominally governed by a League of Nations Commission, was in fact under the control of the local Nazi Party centre. Barthou realised that ultimately the Saar was bound to return to Germany, but was inclined to insist upon some guarantees to those who might vote against immediate incorporation with Germany. His assassination changed the tone of French policy. On December 3, 1934, Laval made a direct bargain with the Germans over the coal-mines, and three days later announced publicly before the League Council that France would not oppose the return of the Saar to Germany. The actual plebiscite was held on January 13, 1935, under international supervision, in which a British brigade took part; and this little enclave—except Danzig, the only territorial embodiment of League sovereignty—voted by 90.3 per cent. for return to Germany. This moral triumph for National Socialism, although the result of a normal and inevitable procedure, added to Hitler's prestige, and seemed to crown his authority with an honest sample of the will of the German people. He was not at all conciliated, still less impressed, by the proof of the League's impartiality or fair play. No doubt it confirmed his view that the Allies were decadent fools. For his own part he proceeded to concentrate on his main objective, the expansion of the German forces.

CHAPTER VII

AIR PARITY LOST

1934-1935

The German Short Cut – The East Fulham Election, October 25, 1933 – Debate of February 7, 1934 – Mr. Baldwin's Pledge of Air Parity – The Labour Vote of Censure against Air Increases – Liberal Hostility – My Precise Warning, November 28, 1934 – Mr. Baldwin's Contradiction – Hitler Claims that Germany Has Air Parity, March 1935 – Mr. MacDonald's Alarm – Mr. Baldwin's Confession, May 22 – The Labour and Liberal Attitudes – The Air Ministry View – Lord Londonderry Presently Succeeded by Sir Philip Cunliffe-Lister.

*T*HE German General Staff did not believe that the German Army could be formed and matured on a scale greater than that of France, and suitably provided with arsenals and equipment, before 1943. The German Navy, except for U-boats, could not be rebuilt in its old state under twelve or fifteen years, and in the process would compete heavily with all other plans. But owing to the unlucky discovery by an immature civilisation of the internal combustion engine and the art of flying, a new weapon of national rivalry had leapt upon the scene capable of altering much more rapidly the relative war-power of States. Granted a share in the ever-accumulating knowledge of mankind and in the march of Science, only four or five years might be required by a nation of the first magnitude, devoting itself to the task, to create a powerful, and perhaps a supreme, Air Force. This period would of course be shortened by any preliminary work and thought.

As in the case of the German Army, the re-creation of the German air power was long and carefully prepared in secret. As early as 1923 Seeckt had decided that the future German Air

Force must be a part of the German war-machine. For the time being he was content to build inside the "airforceless army" a well-articulated Air Force skeleton which could not be discerned, or at any rate was not discerned in its early years, from without. Air-power is the most difficult of all forms of military force to measure, or even to express in precise terms. The extent to which the factories and training-grounds of civil aviation have acquired a military value and significance at any given moment cannot easily be judged and still less exactly defined. The opportunities for concealment, camouflage, and treaty-evasion are numerous and varied. The air, and the air alone, offered Hitler the chance of a short cut, first to equality and next to predominance, in a vital military arm over France and Britain. But what would France and Britain do?

By the autumn of 1933 it was plain that neither by precept nor still less by example would the British effort for disarmament succeed. The pacifism of the Labour and Liberal Parties was not affected even by the grave event of the German withdrawal from the League of Nations. Both continued in the name of Peace to urge British disarmament, and anyone who differed was called "warmonger" and "scaremonger". It appeared that their feeling was endorsed by the people, who of course did not understand what was unfolding. At a by-election which occurred in East Fulham on October 25 a wave of pacifist emotion increased the Socialist vote by nearly 9,000, and the Conservative vote fell by over 10,000. The successful candidate, Mr. Wilmot, said after the poll that "British people demand . . . that the British Government shall give a lead to the whole world by initiating immediately a policy of general disarmament." And Mr. Lansbury, then Leader of the Labour Party, said that all nations must "disarm to the level of Germany as a preliminary to total disarmament". This election left a deep impression upon Mr. Baldwin, and he referred to it in a remarkable speech three years later. In November came the Reichstag election, at which no candidates except those endorsed by Hitler were tolerated, and the Nazis obtained 95 per cent. of the votes polled.

It would be wrong in judging the policy of the British Government not to remember the passionate desire for peace which animated the uninformed, misinformed majority of the British people, and seemed to threaten with political extinction any party or politician who dared to take any other line. This, of course, is no excuse for political leaders who fall short of their duty. It is much better for parties or politicians to be turned out of office than to imperil the life of the nation. Moreover, there is no record in our history of any Government asking Parliament and the people for the necessary measures for defence and being refused. Nevertheless, those who scared the timid MacDonald-Baldwin Government from their path should at least keep silent.

The Air Estimates of March 1934 totalled only twenty millions, and contained provision for four new squadrons, or an increase in our first-line air strength from 850 to 890. The financial cost involved in the first year was £130,000.

On this I said:

We are, it is admitted, the fifth air Power only—if that. We are but half the strength of France, our nearest neighbour. Germany is arming fast and no one is going to stop her. That seems quite clear. No one proposes a preventive war to stop Germany breaking the Treaty of Versailles. She is going to arm; she is doing it; she has been doing it. I have no knowledge of the details, but is is well known that those very gifted people, with their science and with their factories—with what they call their "Air-Sport"—are capable of developing with great rapidity the most powerful Air Force for all purposes, offensive and defensive, within a very short period of time.

I dread the day when the means of threatening the heart of the British Empire should pass into the hands of the present rulers of Germany. We should be in a position which would be odious to every man who values freedom of action and independence, and also in a position of the utmost peril for our crowded, peaceful population engaged in their daily toil. I dread that day, but it is not perhaps far distant. It is perhaps only a year, or perhaps eighteen months distant. It has not come yet—at least, so I believe or I hope and pray; but it is not far distant. There is time for us to take the necessary measures, but it is the measures we want. We want the measures to achieve parity. No nation playing the part we play and aspire to play in the world has a right to be in a position where it can be blackmailed. . . .

None of the grievances between the victors and the vanquished have been redressed. The spirit of aggressive Nationalism was never more rife in Europe and in the world. Far away are the days of Locarno, when we nourished bright hopes of the reunion of the European family. . . .

I called upon Mr. Baldwin, as the man who possessed the power, for action. His was the power, and his the responsibility. In the course of his reply Mr. Baldwin said:

If all our efforts for an agreement fail, and if it is not possible to obtain this equality in such matters as I have indicated, then any Government of this country—a National Government more than any, and *this* Government—will see to it that in air strength and air power this country shall no longer be in a position inferior to any country within striking distance of its shores.

Here was a most solemn and definite pledge, given at a time when it could almost certainly have been made good by vigorous action on a large scale.

* * *

Although Germany had not yet openly violated the clauses of the Treaty which forbade her a military Air Force, civil aviation and an immense development of gliding had now reached a point where they could very rapidly reinforce and extend the secret and illegal military Air Force already formed. The blatant denunciations of Communism and Bolshevism by Hitler had not prevented the clandestine sending by Germany of arms to Russia. On the other hand, from 1927 onwards a number of German pilots had been trained by the Soviets for military purposes. There were fluctuations, but in 1932 the British Ambassador in Berlin reported that the Reichswehr had close technical liaison with the Red Army. Just as the Fascist dictator of Italy had, almost from his accession to power, been the first to make a trade agreement with Soviet Russia, so now the relations between Nazi Germany and the vast Soviet State appeared to be unprejudiced by public ideological controversy.

* * *

Nevertheless, when on July 20, 1934, the Government brought forward some belated and inadequate proposals for strengthening the Royal Air Force by 41 squadrons, or about 820 machines, *only to be completed in five years*, the Labour Party, supported by the Liberals, moved a Vote of Censure upon them in the House of Commons.

The motion regretted that

His Majesty's Government should enter upon a policy of rearmament neither necessitated by any new commitment nor calculated to add to the security of the nation, but certain to jeopardise the prospects of international disarmament and to encourage a revival of dangerous and wasteful competition in preparation for war.

In support of this complete refusal by the Opposition to take any measures to strengthen our air-power Mr. Attlee, speaking in their name, said: "We deny the need for increased air armaments. . . . We deny the proposition that an increased British Air Force will make for the peace of the world, and we reject altogether the claim to parity." The Liberal Party supported this Censure Motion, although they would have preferred their own, which ran as follows:

That this House views with grave concern the tendency among the nations of the world to resume the competitive race of armaments which has always proved a precursor of war; it will not approve any expansion of our own armaments unless it is clear that the Disarmament Conference has failed and unless a definite case is established; and these conditions not being present as regards the proposed additional expenditure of £20,000,000 upon air armaments, the House declines its assent.

In his speech the Liberal Leader, Sir Herbert Samuel, said: "What is the case in regard to Germany? Nothing we have so far seen or heard would suggest that our present Air Force is not adequate to meet any peril at the present time from this quarter."

When we remember that this was language used after careful deliberation by the responsible heads of parties, the danger of our country becomes apparent. This was the formative time when by extreme exertions we could have preserved the air strength on which our independence of action was founded. If Great Britain and France had each maintained quantitative parity with Germany they would together have been double as strong, and Hitler's career of violence might have been nipped in the bud without the loss of a single life. Thereafter it was too late. We cannot doubt the sincerity of the Leaders of the Socialist and Liberal Parties. They were completely wrong and mistaken, and they bear their share of the burden before history. It is indeed astonishing that the Socialist Party should have endeavoured in after years to claim superior foresight and should have reproached their opponents with failing to provide for national safety.

* * *

I now enjoyed for once the advantage of being able to urge rearmament in the guise of a defender of the Government. I therefore received an unusually friendly hearing from the Conservative Party.

One would have thought that the character of His Majesty's Government and the record of its principal Ministers would have induced the Opposition to view the request for an increase in the national defence with some confidence and some consideration. I do not suppose there has ever been such a pacifist-minded Government. There is the Prime Minister, who in the war proved in the most extreme manner and with very great courage his convictions and the sacrifices he would make for what he believed was the cause of pacifism. The Lord President of the Council is chiefly associated in the public mind with the repetition of the prayer "Give peace in our time". One would have supposed that when Ministers like these come forward and say that they feel it their duty to ask for some small increase in the means they have of guaranteeing the public safety, it would weigh with the Opposition and would be considered as a proof of the reality of the danger from which they seek to protect us.

Then look at the apologies which the Government have made. No one could have put forward a proposal in more extremely inoffensive terms. Meekness has characterised every word which they have spoken since this subject was first mooted. We are told that we can see for ourselves how small is the proposal. We are assured that it can be stopped at any minute if Geneva succeeds. And we are also assured that the steps we are taking, although they may to some lower minds have associated with them some idea of national self-defence, are really only associated with the great principle of collective security.

But all these apologies and soothing procedures are most curtly repulsed by the Opposition. Their only answer to these efforts to conciliate them is a Vote of Censure, which is to be decided to-night. It seems to me that we have got very nearly to the end of the period when it is worth while endeavouring to conciliate some classes of opinion upon this subject. We are in the presence of an attempt to establish a kind of tyranny of opinion, and if its reign could be perpetuated the effect might be profoundly injurious to the stability and security of this country. We are a rich and easy prey. No country is so vulnerable, and no country would better repay pillage than our own. . . . *With our enormous metropolis here, the greatest target in the world, a kind of tremendous, fat, valuable cow tied up to attract the beast of prey*, we are in a position in which we have never been before, and in which no other country is at the present time.

Let us remember this: our weakness does not only involve ourselves; our weakness involves also the stability of Europe.

I then proceeded to argue that Germany was already approaching air parity with Britain:

I first assert that Germany has already, in violation of the Treaty, created *a military Air Force which is now nearly two-thirds as strong as our present home defence Air Force.* That is the first statement which I put before the Government for their consideration. The second is that Germany is rapidly increasing this Air Force, not only by large sums of money which figure in her estimates, but also by public subscriptions—very often almost forced subscriptions—which are in progress and have been in progress for some time all over Germany. *By the end of* 1935 *the German Air Force will be nearly equal in numbers and efficiency to our home defence Air Force at that date even if the Government's present proposals are carried out.*

The third statement is that if Germany continues this expansion and if we continue to carry out our scheme, then some time in 1936 Germany will be definitely and substantially stronger in the air than Great Britain. Fourthly, and this is the point which is causing anxiety, once they have got that lead we may never be able to overtake them. If these assertions cannot be contradicted, then there is cause for the anxiety which exists in all parts of the House, not only because of the physical strength of the German Air Force, but I am bound to say also because of the character of the present German dictatorship. *If the Government have to admit at any time in the next few years that the German air forces are stronger than our own, then they will be held, and I think rightly held, to have failed in their prime duty to the country.*

I ended as follows:

The Opposition are very free-spoken, as most of us are in this country, on the conduct of the German Nazi Government. No one has been more severe in criticism than the Labour Party or that section of the Liberal Party which I see opposite. And their great newspapers, now united in the common cause, have been the most forward in the severity of their strictures. But these criticisms are fiercely resented by the powerful men who have Germany in their hands. So that we are to disarm our friends, we are to have no allies, we are to affront powerful nations, and we are to neglect our own defences entirely. That is a miserable and perilous situation. Indeed, the position to which they seek to reduce us by the course which they have pursued and by the vote which they ask us to take is one of terrible jeopardy, and in voting against them to-night we shall hope that a better path for national safety will be found than that along which they would conduct us.

The Labour Party's Vote of Censure was of course defeated by a large majority, and I have no doubt that the nation, had it been appealed to with proper preparation on these issues, would equally have sustained the measures necessary for national safety.

*　*　*

It is not possible to tell this story without recording the milestones which we passed on our long journey from security to the jaws of Death. Looking back, I am astonished at the length of time that was granted to us. It would have been possible in 1933, or even in 1934, for Britain to have created an air-power which would have imposed the necessary restraints upon Hitler's ambition, or would perhaps have enabled the military leaders of Germany to control his violent acts. More than five whole years had yet to run before we were to be confronted with the supreme ordeal. Had we acted even now with reasonable prudence and healthy energy, it might never have come to pass. Based upon superior air-power, Britain and France could safely have invoked the aid of the League of Nations, and all the States of Europe would have gathered behind them. For the first time the League would have had an Instrument of Authority.

When the winter session opened on November 28, 1934, I moved in the name of some of my friends* an Amendment to the Address, declaring that "the strength of our national defences and especially of our air defences is no longer adequate to secure the peace, safety, and freedom of Your Majesty's faithful subjects". The House was packed and very ready to listen. After using all the arguments which emphasised the heavy danger to us and to the world, I came to precise facts:

I assert, first, that Germany already, at this moment, has a military Air Force—that is to say, military squadrons, with the necessary ground services, and the necessary reserves of trained personnel and material—which only awaits an order to assemble in full open combination; and that this illegal Air Force is rapidly approaching equality with our own. Secondly, by this time next year, if Germany executes her existing programme without acceleration, and if we execute our existing

---

* The amendment stood in the names of Mr. Churchill, Sir Robert Horne, Mr. Amery, Captain F. E. Guest, Lord Winterton, and Mr. Boothby.

programme on the basis which now lies before us without slowing down, and carry out the increases announced to Parliament in July last, the German military Air Force will this time next year be in fact at least as strong as our own, and it may be even stronger. Thirdly, on the same basis—that is to say, both sides continuing with their existing programmes as at present arranged—by the end of 1936, that is, one year further on, and two years from now, the German military Air Force will be nearly 50 per cent. stronger, and in 1937 nearly double. All this is on the assumption, as I say, that there is no acceleration on the part of Germany, and no slowing down on our part.

Mr. Baldwin, who followed me at once, faced this issue squarely, and, on the case made out by his Air Ministry advisers, met me with direct contradiction:

It is not the case that Germany is rapidly approaching equality with us. I pointed out that the German figures are total figures, not first-line strength figures, and I have given our own first-line figures and said they are only first-line figures, with a considerably larger reserve at our disposal behind them, even if we confine the comparison to the German air strength and the strength of the Royal Air Force immediately available in Europe. Germany is actively engaged in the production of service aircraft, but her real strength is not 50 per cent. of our strength in Europe to-day. As for the position this time next year, if she continues to execute her air programme without acceleration, and if we continue to carry out at the present approved rate the expansion announced to Parliament in July, *so far from the German military Air Force being at least as strong as, and probably stronger than, our own, we estimate that we shall still have a margin in Europe alone of nearly 50 per cent.* I cannot look farther forward than the next two years. Mr. Churchill speaks of what may happen in 1937. Such investigations as I have been able to make lead me to believe that his figures are considerably exaggerated.

*   *   *

This sweeping assurance from the virtual Prime Minister soothed most of the alarmed, and silenced many of the critics. Everyone was glad to learn that my precise statements had been denied upon unimpeachable authority. I was not at all convinced. I believed that Mr. Baldwin was not being told the truth by his advisers, and anyhow that he did not know the facts.

*   *   *

Thus the winter months slipped away, and it was not till the spring that I again had the opportunity of raising the issue. I gave full and precise notice.

Mr. Churchill to Mr. Baldwin   17.III.35

On the Air Estimates on Tuesday I propose to renew our discussion of last November and to analyse as far as I can your figures of British and German air strength for home defence at the various dates in question, viz.: then, now, at the end of the year 1935 calendar and financial, etc. I believe that the Germans are already as strong as we are and possibly stronger, and that if we carry out our new programme as prescribed Germany will be 50 per cent. stronger than we by the end of 1935 or the beginning of 1936. This, as you will see, runs counter to your statement of November, that we should have a 50 per cent. superiority at that date. I shall of course refer to your under-taking of March 1934 that "this country shall no longer be in a position inferior to any country within striking distance of its shores", and I shall argue that according to such knowledge as I have been able to acquire this is not being made good, as will rapidly be proved by events.

I thought it would be convenient to you if I let you know before-hand as I did on the last occasion what my general line will be, and if whoever speaks for the Government is able to prove the contrary no one will be better pleased than I.

On March 19 the Air Estimates were presented to the House. I reiterated my statement of November, and again directly challenged the assurances which Mr. Baldwin had then given. A very confident reply was made by the Under-Secretary for Air. However, at the end of March the Foreign Secretary and Mr. Eden paid a visit to Herr Hitler in Germany, and in the course of an important conversation, the text of which is on record, they were told personally by him that the German Air Force had already reached parity with Great Britain. This fact was made public by the Government on April 3. At the beginning of May the Prime Minister wrote an article in his own organ, *The News-letter*, in which he emphasised the dangers of German rearmament in terms akin to those which I had so often expressed since 1932. He used the revealing word "ambush", which must have sprung from the anxiety of his heart. We had indeed fallen into an ambush. Mr. MacDonald himself opened the debate. After referring to the declared German intention to build a Navy beyond the Treaty and submarines in breach of it, he came to the air position:

In the debate last November certain estimates were put forward on the basis of our then estimates as to the strength of the German Air Force, and the assurance was given by the Lord President, on behalf of the Government, that in no circumstances would we accept any position of inferiority with regard to whatever Air Force might be raised in Germany in the future. If it were not so, that would put us in an impossible position, of which the Government and the Air Ministry are fully aware. In the course of the visit which the Foreign Secretary and the Lord Privy Seal paid to Berlin at the end of March, the German Chancellor stated, as the House was informed on April 3, that Germany had reached parity with Great Britain in the air. Whatever may be the exact interpretation of this phrase in terms of air strength, it undoubtedly indicated that the German force has been expanded to a point considerably in excess of the estimates which we were able to place before the House last year. That is a grave fact, with regard to which both the Government and the Air Ministry have taken immediate notice.

When in due course I was called I said:

Even now we are not taking the measures which would be in true proportion to our needs. The Government have proposed these increases. They must face the storm. They will have to encounter every form of unfair attack. Their motives will be misrepresented. They will be calumniated and called warmongers. Every kind of attack will be made upon them by many powerful, numerous, and extremely vocal forces in this country. They are going to get it anyway. Why, then, not fight for something that will give us safety? Why, then, not insist that the provision for the Air Force should be adequate, and then, however severe may be the censure and however strident the abuse which they have to face, at any rate there will be this satisfactory result—that His Majesty's Government will be able to feel that in this, of all matters the prime responsibility of a Government, they have done their duty.

Although the House listened to me with close attention, I felt a sensation of despair. To be so entirely convinced and vindicated in a matter of life and death to one's country, and not to be able to make Parliament and the nation heed the warning, or bow to the proof by taking action, was an experience most painful. I went on:

I confess that words fail me. In the year 1708 Mr. Secretary St. John, by a calculated Ministerial indiscretion, revealed to the House the fact that the Battle of Almanza had been lost in the previous summer because only 8,000 English troops were actually in Spain out of the 29,000 that had been voted by the House of Commons for this service. When a month later this revelation was confirmed by the Government, it is recorded that the House sat in silence for half an hour, no Member caring to speak or wishing to make a comment upon so staggering an announcement. And yet how incomparably small that event was to what we have now to face. That was merely a frustration of policy. Nothing that could happen to Spain in that war could possibly have contained in it any form of danger which was potentially mortal. . . .

There is a wide measure of agreement in the House to-night upon our foreign policy. We are bound to act in concert with France and Italy and other Powers, great and small, who are anxious to preserve peace. I would not refuse the co-operation of any Government which plainly conformed to that test, so long as it was willing to work under the authority and sanction of the League of Nations. Such a policy does not close the door upon a revision of the treaties, but it procures a sense of stability, and an adequate gathering together of all reasonable Powers for self-defence, before any inquiry of that character [*i.e.*, Treaty revision] can be entered upon. In this august association for collective security we must build up defence forces of all kinds and combine our action with that of friendly Powers, so that we may be allowed to live in quiet ourselves and retrieve the woeful miscalculations of which we are at present the dupes, and of which, unless we take warning in time, we may some day be the victims.

There lay in my memory at this time some lines from an unknown writer about a railway accident. I had learnt them from a volume of *Punch* cartoons which I used to pore over when I was eight or nine years old at school at Brighton.

> Who is in charge of the clattering train?
> The axles creak and the couplings strain,
> And the pace is hot, and the points are near,
> And Sleep has deadened the driver's ear;
> And the signals flash through the night in vain,
> For Death is in charge of the clattering train.

However, I did not repeat them.

*   *   *

It was not until May 22 that Mr. Baldwin made his celebrated confession. I am forced to cite it:

First of all, with regard to the figure I gave in November of German aeroplanes, nothing has come to my knowledge since that makes me think that figure was wrong. I believed at that time it was right. *Where I was wrong was in my estimate of the future. There I was completely wrong. We were completely misled on that subject.* . . .

I would repeat here that there is no occasion, in my view, in what we are doing, for panic. But I will say this deliberately, with all the knowledge I have of the situation, that I would not remain for one moment in any Government which took less determined steps than we are taking to-day. I think it is only due to say that there has been a great deal of criticism, both in the Press and verbally, about the Air Ministry, as though they were responsible for possibly an inadequate programme, for not having gone ahead faster, and for many other things. I only want to repeat that whatever responsibility there may be—and we are perfectly ready to meet criticism—*that responsibility is not that of any single Minister; it is the responsibility of the Government as a whole, and we are all responsible, and we are all to blame.*

I hoped that this shocking confession would be a decisive event, and that at the least a Parliamentary Committee of all parties would be set up to report upon the facts and upon our safety. The House of Commons had a different reaction. The Labour and Liberal Oppositions, having nine months earlier moved or supported a Vote of Censure even upon the modest steps the Government had taken, were ineffectual and undecided. They were looking forward to an election against "Tory armaments". Neither the Labour nor the Liberal spokesmen had prepared themselves for Mr. Baldwin's disclosures and admission, and they did not attempt to adapt their speeches to this outstanding episode. Mr. Attlee said:

As a party we do not stand for unilateral disarmament. . . . We stand for Collective Security through the League of Nations. We reject the use of force as an instrument of policy. We stand for the reduction of armaments and pooled security. . . . We have stated that this country must be prepared to make its contribution to collective security. Our policy is not one of seeking security through rearmament, but through disarmament. Our aim is the reduction of armaments, and then the complete abolition of all national armaments and the creation of an International Police Force under the League.

What was to happen if this spacious policy could not be immediately achieved or till it was achieved he did not say. He complained that the White Paper on defence justified increases in the Navy by reference to the United States, and increases in our Air Force by references to the Air Forces of Russia, Japan, and the United States. "All that was old-fashioned talk and right outside the collective system." He recognised that the fact of German rearmament had become dominating, but "The measure of the counterweight to any particular armed forces is not the forces of this country or of France, but the combined force of all loyal Powers in the League of Nations. An aggressor must be made to realise that if he challenges the world he will be met by the co-ordinated forces of the world, not by a number of disjointed national forces." The only way was to concentrate all airpower in the hands of the League, which must be united and become a reality. Meanwhile he and his party voted against the measure proposed.

For the Liberals, Sir Archibald Sinclair asked the Government to summon "a fresh economic conference, and to bring Germany not only within the political comity of nations but also into active co-operation with ourselves in all the works of civilisation and in raising the standards of life of both peoples. . . . Let the Government table detailed and definite proposals for the abolition of military air forces and the control of civil aviation. If the proposals are resisted let the responsibility be clearly and properly fixed."

Nevertheless [said he], while disarmament ought vigorously to be pursued as the chief objective of the Government, a situation in which a great country not a member of the League of Nations possesses the most powerful Army and perhaps the most powerful Air Force in Western Europe, with probably a greater coefficient of expansion than any other Air Force . . . cannot be allowed to endure. . . . The Liberal Party will feel bound to support measures of national defence when clear proof is afforded of their necessity. . . . I cannot therefore agree that to increase our national armaments is necessarily inconsistent with our obligations under the collective peace system.

He then proceeded to deal at length with "the question of private profits being made out of the means of death", and quoted a recent speech by Lord Halifax, President of the Board of Education, who had said that the British people were "disposed to regard the preparation of instruments of war as too high and too grave a thing to be entrusted to any hands less responsible than those of the State itself". Sir Archibald Sinclair thought that there ought to be national factories for dealing with the rapid expansion in air armaments, for which expansion, he said, a case had been made out.

The existence of private armament firms had long been a bugbear to Labour and Liberal minds, and it lent itself readily to the making of popular speeches. It was of course absurd to suppose that at this time our air expansion, recognised as necessary, could be achieved through national factories only. A large part of the private industry of the country was urgently required for immediate adaptation and to reinforce our existing sources of manufacture. Nothing in the speeches of the Opposition leaders was in the slightest degree related to the emergency in which they admitted we stood, or to the far graver facts which we now know lay behind it.

The Government majority for their part appeared captivated by Mr. Baldwin's candour. His admission of having been utterly wrong, with all his sources of knowledge, upon a vital matter for which he was responsible was held to be redeemed by the frankness with which he declared his error and shouldered the blame. There was even a strange wave of enthusiasm for a Minister who did not hesitate to say that he was wrong. Indeed, many Conservative Members seemed angry with me for having brought their trusted leader to a plight from which only his native manliness and honesty had extricated him; but not, alas, his country.

*　　*　　*

My kinsman, Lord Londonderry, a friend from childhood days, the direct descendant of the famous Castlereagh of Napoleonic times, was a man of unquestionable loyalty and patriotism. He had presided over the Air Ministry since the formation of the Coalition. In this period the grave changes which have been described had overshadowed our affairs, and the Air Ministry had become one of the most important offices in the State. During the years of retrenchment and disarmament he and his Ministry had tried to keep and get as much as they could from a severe and arbitrary Chancellor of the Exchequer. They were overjoyed when in the summer of 1934 an air programme of forty-one additional squadrons was conceded to them by the Cabinet. But in British politics the hot fits very quickly succeed the cold. When the Foreign Secretary returned from Berlin, profoundly startled by Hitler's assertion that his Air Force was equal to that of Britain, the whole Cabinet became deeply concerned. Mr. Baldwin had to face, in the light of what was now generally accepted as a new situation, his assertions of November, when he had contradicted me. The Cabinet had no idea they had been overtaken in the air, and turned, as is usually the case, inquisitorial looks upon the department involved and its Minister.

The Air Ministry did not realise that a new inheritance awaited them. The Treasury's fetters were broken. They had but to ask for more. Instead of this they reacted strongly against Hitler's claim to air parity. Londonderry, who was their spokesman, even rested upon the statement that *"when Simon and Eden went to Berlin there was only one German operation squadron in being. From their training establishments they hoped to form fifteen to twenty squadron formations by the end of the month."** All this is a matter of nomenclature. It is of course very difficult to classify Air Forces, because of the absence of any common "yardstick" and all the variations in defining "first-line air strength" and "operational units". The Air Ministry now led its chief into an elaborate vindication of their own past conduct, and in consequence were entirely out of harmony with the new mood of a genuinely alarmed Government and public. The experts and officials at the Air Ministry had given Mr. Baldwin the figures and forecasts with which he had answered me in November. They wished him to go into action in defence of these statements; but this was no longer practical politics. There seems no doubt that these experts and officials of the Air Ministry at this time were themselves misled and misled their chief. A great air Power, at least the equal of our own, long pent up, had at last sprung into daylight in Germany.

It was an odd and painful experience for Londonderry, as his book describes, after having gone through several years of asking for more, to be suddenly turned out for not asking enough. But apart from all this his political standing was not sufficient to enable him to head a department now at the very centre and

---

* The Marquess of Londonderry, *Wings of Destiny*, 1943, p. 128.

almost at the summit of our affairs. Besides, everyone could see
that in such times the Air Minister must be in the House of
Commons. Accordingly Mr. Ramsay MacDonald's vacation of
the Premiership later in the year became also the occasion for the
appointment of Sir Philip Cunliffe-Lister, then Secretary of State
for the Colonies, as Air Minister, as part of a new policy for
vigorous air expansion. Lord Londonderry with much reluctance
became Lord Privy Seal and Leader of the House of Lords; but
after the General Election Mr. Baldwin dispensed with his services
in both these capacities. The great achievement of his period in
office was the designing and promotion of the ever-famous
Hurricane and Spitfire fighters. The first prototypes of these
flew in November 1935 and March 1936 respectively. Londonderry does not mention this in his defence, but he might well
have done so, since he took the blame for so much that he had
not done. The new Secretary of State, wafted by favourable
breezes and fresh tides, ordered immediate large-scale production
of these types, and they were ready in some numbers none too
soon. Cunliffe-Lister was a much more potent political figure
than his predecessor, and had a better chance and a more inspirit-
ing task. He brought an altogether more powerful force to bear
upon our air policy and administration, and set himself actively
to work to make up for the time lost by the Cabinet from 1932
to 1934. He however made the serious mistake of quitting the
House of Commons for the House of Lords in November 1935,
thus stultifying one of the arguments for his transfer to the
Secretaryship of State for Air. This was to cost him his office
a few years later.

*　*　*

A disaster of the first magnitude had fallen upon us. Hitler had
already obtained parity with Great Britain. Henceforward he
had merely to drive his factories and training-schools at full speed
not only to keep his lead in the air, but steadily to improve it.
Henceforward all the unknown, immeasurable threats which
overhung London from air attack would be a definite and com-
pelling factor in all our decisions. Moreover, we could never
catch up; or at any rate the Government never did catch up.
Credit is due to them and to the Air Ministry for the high
efficiency of the Royal Air Force. But the pledge that air parity
would be maintained was irretrievably broken. It is true that

the immediate further expansion of the German Air Force did not proceed at the same rate as in the period when they gained parity. No doubt a supreme effort had been made by them to achieve at a bound this commanding position and to assist and exploit it in their diplomacy. It gave Hitler the foundation for the successive acts of aggression which he had planned and which were now soon to take place. Very considerable efforts were made by the British Government in the next four years, and there is no doubt that we excelled in air quality; but quantity was henceforth beyond us. The outbreak of the war found us with barely half the German numbers.

CHAPTER VIII

CHALLENGE AND RESPONSE

1935

Hitler Decrees Conscription, March 16, 1935 – Two Years' Military Service in France, March 16 – Sir John Simon and Mr. Eden in Berlin, March 24 – The Stresa Conference – The Franco-Soviet Pact, May 2 – Mr. Baldwin Becomes Prime Minister, June 7 – Sir Samuel Hoare, Foreign Secretary – Mr. Eden Appointed Minister for League of Nations Affairs – The Anglo-German Naval Agreement – Its Dangers – Far-reaching Effects in Europe – The Foreign Secretary's Defence – The Growth of the German Army – French and German Man-power.

*T*HE years of underground burrowings, of secret or disguised preparations, were now over, and Hitler at length felt himself strong enough to make his first open challenge. On March 9, 1935, the official constitution of the German Air Force was announced, and on the 16th it was declared that the German Army would henceforth be based on national compulsory service. The laws to implement these decisions were soon promulgated, and action had already begun in anticipation. The French Government, who were well informed of what was coming, had actually declared the consequential extension of their own military service to two years a few hours earlier on the same momentous day. The German action was an open formal affront to the treaties of peace upon which the League of Nations was founded. As long as the breaches had taken the form of evasions or calling things by other names, it was easy for the responsible victorious Powers, obsessed by pacifism and preoccupied with domestic politics, to avoid the responsibility of declaring that the Peace Treaty was being broken or repudiated. Now the issue came with blunt and brutal force. Almost on the same day the Ethiopian Government appealed to the League of Nations against the threatening demands of Italy. When, on March 24, against this background, Sir John Simon with the Lord Privy Seal, Mr. Eden, visited Berlin at Hitler's invitation, the French Government thought the occasion ill-chosen. They had now themselves at once to face, not the reduction of their Army, so eagerly pressed upon them by Mr. MacDonald the year before, but the extension of compulsory military service from one year to two. In the prevailing state of public opinion this was a heavy task. Not only the Communists but the Socialists had voted against the measure. When M. Léon Blum said, "The workers of France will rise to resist Hitlerite aggression," Thorez replied, amid the applause of his Soviet-bound faction, "We will not tolerate the working classes being drawn into a so-called war in defence of Democracy against Fascism."

The United States had washed their hands of all concern with Europe, apart from wishing well to everybody, and were sure they would never have to be bothered with it again. But France, Great Britain, and also—decidedly—Italy, in spite of their discordances, felt bound to challenge this definite act of treaty-violation by Hitler. A Conference of the former principal Allies was summoned under the League of Nations at Stresa, and all these matters were brought to debate.

* * *

Anthony Eden had for nearly ten years devoted himself almost entirely to the study of foreign affairs. Taken from Eton at eighteen to the World War, he had served for four years with distinction in the 60th Rifles through many of the bloodiest battles, and risen to the position of Brigade-Major, with the Military Cross. Shortly after entering the House of Commons in 1925, he became Parliamentary Private Secretary to Austen Chamberlain at the Foreign Office during Mr. Baldwin's second Administration. In the MacDonald-Baldwin Coalition of 1931 he was appointed Under-Secretary of State and served under the new Foreign Secretary, Sir John Simon. The duties of an Under-Secretary are often changed, but his responsibilities are always limited. He has to serve his chief in carrying out the policy settled in the Cabinet, of which he is not a member and to which he has no access. Only in an extreme case where conscience and honour are involved is he justified in carrying any difference about foreign policy to the point of public controversy or resignation.

Eden had however during all these years obtained a wide view of the foreign scene, and he was intimately acquainted with the life and thought of the great department upon which so much depends. Sir John Simon's conduct of foreign affairs was not in 1935 viewed with favour either by the Opposition or in influential circles of the Conservative Party. Eden, with all his knowledge and exceptional gifts, began therefore to acquire prominence. For this reason, after becoming Lord Privy Seal at the end of 1934, he had retained by the desire of the Cabinet an informal but close association with the Foreign Office, and thus had been invited to accompany his former chief, Sir John Simon, on the inopportune, but not unfruitful, visit to Berlin. The Foreign Secretary returned to London after the interview with Hitler, bringing with him the important news, already mentioned, that, according to Hitler, Germany *had now gained air parity with Britain*. Eden was sent on to Moscow, where he established contacts with Stalin which were to be revived with advantage after some years. On the homeward journey his aeroplane ran into a severe and prolonged storm, and when after a dangerous flight they landed he was almost in a state of collapse. The doctors declared that he was not fit to go with Simon to the Stresa Conference, and indeed for several months he was an invalid. In these circumstances the Prime Minister decided himself to accompany the Foreign Secretary, although at this time his own health, eyesight, and mental powers were evidently failing. Great Britain was therefore weakly represented at this all-important meeting, which MM. Flandin and Laval attended on behalf of France, and Signors Mussolini and Suvich on behalf of Italy.

There was general agreement that open violation of solemn treaties, for the making of which millions of men had died, could not be borne. But the British representatives made it clear at the outset that they would not consider the possibility of sanctions in the event of treaty-violation. This naturally confined the Conference to the region of words. A resolution was passed unanimously to the effect that "unilateral"—by which they meant one-sided—breaches of treaties could not be accepted, and the Executive Council of the League of Nations was invited to pronounce upon the situation disclosed. On the second afternoon of the Conference Mussolini strongly supported this action, and was outspoken against aggression by one Power upon another. The final declaration was as follows:

The three Powers, the object of whose policy is the collective maintenance of peace within the framework of the League of Nations, find themselves in complete agreement in opposing, by all practicable means, any unilateral repudiation of treaties which may endanger the peace of Europe, and will act in close and cordial collaboration for this purpose.

The Italian Dictator in his speech had stressed the words "*peace of Europe*", and paused after "Europe" in a noticeable manner. This emphasis on Europe at once struck the attention of the British Foreign Office representatives. They pricked up their ears, and well understood that while Mussolini would work with France and Britain to prevent Germany from rearming he reserved for himself any excursion in Africa against Abyssinia on which he might later resolve. Should this point be raised or not? Discussions were held that night among the Foreign Office officials. Everyone was so anxious for Mussolini's support in dealing with Germany that it was felt undesirable at that moment to warn him off Abyssinia, which would obviously have very much annoyed him. Therefore the question was not raised; it passed by default, and Mussolini felt, and in a sense had reason to feel, that the Allies had acquiesced in his statement and would give him a free hand against Abyssinia. The French remained mute on the point, and the Conference separated.

In due course, on April 15–17, the Council of the League of Nations examined the alleged breach of the Treaty of Versailles committed by Germany in decreeing universal compulsory military service. The following Powers were represented on the Council: the Argentine Republic, Australia, Great Britain, Chile, Czechoslovakia, Denmark, France, Italy, Mexico, Poland, Portugal, Spain, Turkey, and the U.S.S.R. All these Powers voted for the principle that treaties should not be broken by "unilateral" action, and referred the issue to the Plenary Assembly of the League. At the same time the Foreign Ministers of the three Scandinavian countries, Sweden, Norway, and Denmark, being deeply concerned about the naval balance in the Baltic, also met together in general support. In all nineteen countries formally protested. But how vain was all their voting without the readiness of any single Power or any group of Powers to contemplate the use of FORCE, even in the last resort!

★　★　★

Laval was not disposed to approach Russia in the firm spirit of Barthou. But in France there was now an urgent need. It seemed, above all, necessary to those concerned with the life of France to obtain national unity on the two years' military service which had been approved by a narrow majority in March. Only the Soviet Government could give permission to the important section of Frenchmen whose allegiance they commanded. Besides this, there was a general desire in France for a revival of the old alliance of 1895, or something like it. On May 2 the French Government put their signature to a Franco-Soviet pact. This was a nebulous document guaranteeing mutual assistance in the face of aggression over a period of five years.

To obtain tangible results in the French political field M. Laval now went on a three days' visit to Moscow, where he was welcomed by Stalin. There were lengthy discussions, of which a fragment not hitherto published may be recorded. Stalin and Molotov were of course anxious to know above all else what was to be the strength of the French Army on the Western Front: how many divisions? what period of service? After this field had been explored Laval said: "Can't you do something to encourage religion and the Catholics in Russia? It would help me so much with the Pope." "Oho!" said Stalin. "The Pope! How many divisions has *he* got?" Laval's answer was not reported to me; but he might certainly have mentioned a number of legions not always visible on parade. Laval had never intended to commit France to any of the specific obligations which it is the habit of the Soviet to demand. Nevertheless he obtained a public declaration from Stalin on May 15 approving the policy of national defence carried out by France in order to maintain her armed forces at the level of security. On these instructions the French Communists immediately turned about and gave vociferous support to the defence programme and the two years' service. As a factor in European security the Franco-Soviet Pact, which contained no engagements binding on either party in the event of German aggression, had only limited advantages. No real confederacy was achieved with Russia. Moreover, on his return journey the French Foreign Minister stopped at Cracow to attend the funeral of Marshal Pilsudski. Here he met Goering, with whom he talked with much cordiality. His expressions of distrust and dislike of the Soviets were duly reported through German channels to Moscow.

Mr. MacDonald's health and capacity had declined to a point which made his continuance as Prime Minister impossible. He had never been popular with the Conservative Party, who regarded him, on account of his political and war records and Socialist faith, with long-bred prejudice, softened in later years by pity. No man was more hated, or with better reason, by the Labour-Socialist Party, which he had so largely created and then laid low by what they viewed as his treacherous desertion in 1931. In the massive majority of the Government he had but seven party followers. The disarmament policy to which he had given his utmost personal efforts had now proved a disastrous failure. A General Election could not be far distant, in which he could play no helpful part. In these circumstances there was no surprise when, on June 7, it was announced that he and Mr. Baldwin had changed places and offices and that Mr. Baldwin had become Prime Minister for the third time. The Foreign Office also passed to another hand. Sir Samuel Hoare's labours at the India Office had been crowned by the passing of the Government of India Bill, and he was now free to turn to a more immediately important sphere. For some time past Sir John Simon had been bitterly attacked for his foreign policy by influential Conservatives closely associated with the Government. He now moved to the Home Office, with which he was well acquainted, and Sir Samuel Hoare became Secretary of State for Foreign Affairs.

At the same time Mr. Baldwin adopted a novel expedient. He appointed Mr. Eden, whose prestige was steadily growing and whose health was now restored, to be Minister for League of Nations Affairs. Mr. Eden was to work in the Foreign Office with equal status to the Foreign Secretary and with full access to the dispatches and the departmental staff. Mr. Baldwin's object was no doubt to conciliate the strong tide of public opinion associated with the League of Nations Union by showing the importance which he attached to the League and to the conduct of our affairs at Geneva. When about a month later I had the opportunity of commenting on what I described as "the new plan of having two equal Foreign Secretaries", I drew attention to its defects:

I was very glad indeed that the Prime Minister said yesterday that this was only a temporary experiment. I cannot feel that it will last long or ever be renewed. . . . We need the integral thought of a single man responsible for Foreign Affairs, ranging over the entire field and making every factor and every incident contribute to the general purpose upon which Parliament has agreed. The Foreign Secretary, whoever he is, whichever he is, must be supreme in his department, and everyone in that great office ought to look to him, and to him alone. I remember that we had a discussion in the war about unity of command, and that Mr. Lloyd George said, "It is not a question of one General being better than another, but of one General being better than two." There is no reason why a strong Cabinet Committee should not sit with the Foreign Secretary every day in these difficult times, or why the Prime Minister should not see him or his officials at any time; but when the topic is so complicated and vast, when it is in such continued flux, it seems to me that confusion will only be made worse confounded by dual allegiances and equal dual responsibilities.

All this was certainly borne out by events.

* * *

While men and matters were in this posture a most surprising act was committed by the British Government. Some at least of its impulse came from the Admiralty. It is always dangerous for soldiers, sailors, or airmen to play at politics. They enter a sphere in which the values are quite different from those to which they have hitherto been accustomed. Of course they were following the inclination or even the direction of the First Lord and the Cabinet, who alone bore the responsibility. But there was a strong favourable Admiralty breeze. There had been for some time conversations between the British and German Admiralties about the proportions of the two Navies. By the Treaty of Versailles the Germans were not entitled to build more than six armoured ships of 10,000 tons, in addition to six light cruisers not exceeding 6,000 tons. The British Admiralty had recently found out that the last two pocket-battleships being constructed, the *Scharnhorst* and the *Gneisenau*, were of a far larger size than the Treaty allowed, and of a quite different type. In fact, they turned out to be 26,000-ton light battle-cruisers, or commerce-destroyers of the highest class.

In the face of this brazen and fraudulent violation of the Peace Treaty, carefully planned and begun at least two years earlier (1933), the Admiralty actually thought it was worth while making an Anglo-German Naval Agreement. His Majesty's Government did this without consulting their French ally or informing the League of Nations. At the very time when they themselves were appealing to the League and enlisting the support of its members to protest against Hitler's violation of the military clauses of the Treaty they proceeded by a private agreement to sweep away the naval clauses of the same Treaty.

The main feature of the agreement was that the German Navy should not exceed one-third of the British. This greatly attracted the Admiralty, who looked back to the days before the Great War when we had been content with a ratio of sixteen to ten. For the sake of that prospect, taking German assurances at their face value, they proceeded to concede to Germany the right to build U-boats, explicitly denied to her in the Peace Treaty. Germany might build 60 per cent. of the British submarine strength, and if she decided that the circumstances were exceptional she might build to 100 per cent. The Germans, of course, gave assurances that their U-boats would never be used against merchant ships. Why, then, were they needed? For, clearly, if the rest of the agreement was kept, they could not influence the naval decision, so far as warships were concerned.

The limitation of the German Fleet to a third of the British allowed Germany a programme of new construction which would set her yards to work at maximum activity for at least ten years. There was therefore no practical limitation or restraint of any kind imposed upon German naval expansion. They could build as fast as was physically possible. The quota of ships assigned to Germany by the British project was, in fact, far more lavish than Germany found it expedient to use, having regard partly no doubt to the competition for armour-plate arising between warship and tank construction. They were authorised to build five capital ships, two aircraft-carriers, twenty-one cruisers, and sixty-four destroyers. In fact however all they had ready or approaching completion by the outbreak of war was two capital ships, no aircraft-carriers, eleven cruisers, and twenty-five destroyers, or considerably less than half what we had so complacently accorded them. By concentrating their available resources on cruisers and destroyers at the expense of battleships, they could have put themselves in a more advantageous position for a war with Britain in 1939 or 1940. Hitler, as we now know, informed Admiral Raeder that war with England would not be likely till 1944-45. The development of the German Navy was therefore planned on a long-term basis. In U-boats alone did they build to the full paper limits allowed. As soon as they were able to pass the 60 per cent. limit they invoked the provision allowing them to build to 100 per cent., and fifty-seven were actually constructed when war began.

In the design of new battleships the Germans had the further advantage of not being parties to the provisions of the Washington Naval Agreement or the London Conference. They immediately laid down the *Bismarck* and *Tirpitz*, and, while Britain, France, and the United States were all bound by the 35,000 tons limitation, these two great vessels were being designed with a displacement of over 45,000 tons, which made them, when completed, certainly the strongest vessels afloat in the world.

It was also at this moment a great diplomatic advantage to Hitler to divide the Allies, to have one of them ready to condone breaches of the Treaty of Versailles, and to invest the regaining of full freedom to rearm with the sanction of agreement with Britain. The effect of the announcement was another blow at the League of Nations. The French had every right to complain that their vital interests were affected by the permission accorded by Great Britain for the building of U-boats. Mussolini saw in this episode evidence that Great Britain was not acting in good faith with her other allies, and that, so long as her special naval interests were secured, she would apparently go to any length in accommodation with Germany, regardless of the detriment to friendly Powers menaced by the growth of the German land forces. He was encouraged by what seemed the cynical and selfish attitude of Great Britain to press on with his plans against Abyssinia. The Scandinavian Powers, who only a fortnight before had courageously sustained the protest against Hitler's introduction of compulsory service in the German Army, now found that Great Britain had behind the scenes agreed to a German Navy which, though only a third of the British, would within this limit be master of the Baltic.

Great play was made by British Ministers with the German offer to co-operate with us in abolishing the submarine. Considering that the condition attached to it was that all other countries should agree at the same time, and that it was well known there was not the slightest chance of other countries agreeing, this was a very safe offer for the Germans to make. This also applied to the German agreement to restrict the use of submarines so as to strip submarine warfare against commerce of inhumanity. Who could suppose that the Germans, possessing a great fleet of U-boats and watching their women and children being starved by a British blockade, would abstain from the fullest use of that arm? I described this view as "the acme of gullibility".

Far from being a step towards disarmament, the agreement, had it been carried out over a period of years, would inevitably have provoked a world-wide development of new warship-building. The French Navy, except for its latest vessels, would require reconstruction. This again would react upon Italy. For ourselves, it was evident that we should have to rebuild the British Fleet on a very large scale in order to maintain our three to one superiority in modern ships. It may be that the idea of the German Navy being one-third of the British also presented itself to our Admiralty as the British Navy being three times the German. This perhaps might clear the path to a reasonable and overdue rebuilding of our Fleet. But where were the statesmen?

This agreement was announced to Parliament by the First Lord of the Admiralty, Sir Bolton Eyres-Monsell, on June 21, 1935. On the first opportunity, July 11, and again on July 22, I condemned it:

I do not believe that this isolated action by Great Britain will be found to work for the cause of peace. The immediate reaction is that every day the German Fleet approaches a tonnage which gives it absolute command of the Baltic, and very soon one of the deterrents of a European war will gradually fade away. So far as the position in the Mediterranean is concerned, it seems to me that we are in for very great difficulties. Certainly a large addition of new shipbuilding must come when the French have to modernise their Fleet to meet German construction and the Italians follow suit, and we shall have pressure upon us to rebuild from that point of view, or else our position in the

The Rise of Hitler and the Growth of Fascism

15 One of the first clandestine meetings of the Hitler Party in the cellars of Kalkberge.
16 A Nazi demonstration in front of the house of a Jew, Karl Liebknecht, in Berlin, January 1933.

17 An attitude typical of Hitler, during a speech, 1935.

18 Hitler marching in the streets of Weimar on the occasion of the first meeting of the National Socialist (Nazi) Party, 5th July, 1926.
19 On board the battleship "Cavour", 7th May, 1938. From left to right: von Ribbentrop, Mussolini, Count Ciano, Hitler.

20 Munich, 1937: SS men swearing an oath of allegiance to Hitler.

Mediterranean will be affected. But worst of all is the effect upon our position at the other end of the world, in China and in the Far East. What a windfall this has been to Japan! Observe what the consequences are. The First Lord said, "Face the facts." The British Fleet, when this programme is completed, will be largely anchored to the North Sea. That means to say that the whole position in the Far East has been very gravely altered, to the detriment of the United States and of Great Britain and to the detriment of China. . . .

I regret that we are not dealing with this problem of the resuscitation of German naval power with the Concert of Europe on our side, and in conjunction with many other nations whose fortunes are affected and whose fears are aroused equally with our own by the enormous developments of German armaments. What those developments are no one can accurately measure. We have seen that powerful vessels, much more powerful than we expected, can be constructed unknown even to the Admiralty. We have seen what has been done in the air. I believe that if the figures of the expenditure of Germany during the current financial year could be ascertained the House and the country would be staggered and appalled by the enormous expenditure upon war preparations which is being poured out all over that country, converting the whole mighty nation and empire of Germany into an arsenal virtually on the threshold of mobilisation.

*   *   *

It is only right to state here the contrary argument as put forward by Sir Samuel Hoare in his first speech as Foreign Secretary on July 11, 1935, in response to many domestic and European criticisms:

The Anglo-German Naval Agreement is in no sense a selfish agreement. On no account could we have made an agreement that was not manifestly in our view to the advantage of the other naval Powers. On no account could we have made an agreement that we did not think, so far from hindering general agreement, would actually further it. The question of naval disarmament has always been treated distinctively from the question of land and air disarmament. The naval question has always been treated apart, and it was always the intention, so far as I know, of the naval Powers to treat it apart.

Apart however from the juridical position, there seemed to us to be, in the interests of peace—which is the main objective of the British Government—overwhelming reasons why we should conclude the agreement. In the opinion of our naval experts, we were advised to accept the agreement as a safe agreement for the British Empire. Here again we saw a chance that might not recur of eliminating one of the causes that chiefly led to the embitterment before the Great War—the race of German naval armaments. Incidentally, out of that discussion arose the very important statement of the German Government that henceforth, so far as they were concerned, they would eliminate one of the causes that made the war so terrible, namely, the unrestricted use of submarines against merchant ships. Thirdly, we came definitely to the view that there was a chance of making an agreement that seemed on naval grounds manifestly to the advantage of other naval Powers, including France. . . . With the French Fleet at approximately its present level as compared with our own Fleet, the agreement gives France a permanent superiority over the German Fleet of 43 per cent., as compared with an inferiority of about 30 per cent. before the war. . . . I am therefore bold enough to believe that, when the world looks more dispassionately at these results, the overwhelming majority of those who stand for peace and a restriction of armaments will say that the British Government took not only a wise course but the only course that in the circumstances was open to them.

What had in fact been done was to authorise Germany to build to her utmost capacity for five or six years to come.

★ ★ ★

Meanwhile in the military sphere the formal establishment of conscription in Germany on March 16, 1935, marked the fundamental challenge to Versailles. But the steps by which the German Army was now magnified and reorganised are not of technical interest only. The whole function of the Army in the National-Socialist State required definition. The purpose of the Law of May 21, 1935, was to expand the technical *élite* of secretly-trained specialists into the armed expression of the whole nation. The name Reichswehr was changed to that of Wehrmacht. The Army was to be subordinated to the supreme leadership of the Fuehrer. Every soldier took the oath, not, as formerly, to the Constitution, but to the person of Adolf Hitler. The War Ministry was directly subordinated to the orders of the Fuehrer. Military service was an essential civic duty, and it was the responsibility of the Army to educate and to unify once and for all the population of the Reich. The second clause of the Law reads: "The Wehrmacht is the armed force and the school of military education of the German people."

Here indeed was the formal and legal embodiment of Hitler's words in *Mein Kampf*:

The coming National-Socialist State should not fall into the error of the past and assign to the Army a task which it does not and should not have. The German Army is not to be a school for the maintenance of tribal peculiarities, but rather a school for the mutual understanding and adjustment of all Germans. Whatever may have a disruptive effect in national life should be given a unifying effect through the Army. It should furthermore raise the individual youth above the narrow horizon of his little countryside and place him in the German nation. He must learn to respect, not the boundaries of his birthplace, but the boundaries of his Fatherland; for it is these which he too must some day defend.

Upon these ideological bases the Law also established a new territorial organisation. The Army was now organised in three commands, with headquarters at Berlin, Cassel, and Dresden, subdivided into ten (later twelve) Wehrkreise (military districts). Each Wehrkreis contained an Army Corps of three divisions. In addition a new kind of formation was planned—the Armoured Division, of which three were soon in being.

Detailed arrangements were also made regarding military service. The regimentation of German youth was the prime task of the new *régime*. Starting in the ranks of the Hitler Youth, the boyhood of Germany passed at the age of eighteen on a voluntary basis into the S.A. for two years. By a Law of June 26, 1935, service in the Work Battalions or Arbeitsdienst became a compulsory duty on every male German reaching the age of twenty. For six months he would have to serve his country, constructing roads, building barracks, or draining marshes, thus fitting him physically and morally for the crowning duty of a German citizen, service with the armed forces. In the Work Battalions the emphasis lay upon the abolition of class and the stressing of the social unity of the German people; in the Army it was put upon discipline and the territorial unity of the nation.

The gigantic task of training the new body and of expanding the cadres prescribed by the technical conception of Seeckt now began. On October 15, 1935, again in defiance of the clauses of Versailles, the German Staff College was reopened with formal ceremony by Hitler, accompanied by the chiefs of the armed services. Here was the apex of the pyramid, whose base was now already constituted by the myriad formations of the Work Battalions. On November 7, 1935, the first class, born in 1914, was called up for service: 596,000 young men to be trained in the profession of arms. Thus at one stroke, on paper at least, the German Army was raised to nearly 700,000 effectives.

With the task of training came the problems of financing rearmament and expanding German industry to meet the needs of the new national Army. By secret decrees Dr. Schacht had been made virtual Economic Dictator of Germany. Seeckt's pioneer work was now put to its supreme test. The two major difficulties were, first, the expansion of the Officers Corps, and, secondly, the organisation of the specialised units, the Artillery, the Engineers, and the Signals. By October 1935 ten Army Corps were forming. Two more followed a year later, and a thirteenth in October 1937. The police formations were also incorporated in the armed forces.

It was realised that after the first call-up of the 1914 class, in Germany as in France, the succeeding years would bring a diminishing number of recruits, owing to the decline in births during the period of the World War. Therefore in August 1936 the period of active military service in Germany was raised to two years. The 1915 class numbered 464,000, and with the retention of the 1914 class for another year the number of Germans under regular military training in 1936 was 1,511,000 men, excluding the para-military formations of the party and the Work Battalions. The effective strength of the French Army, apart from reserves, in the same year was 623,000 men, of whom only 407,000 were in France.

The following figures, which actuaries could foresee with some precision, tell their tale:

TABLE OF THE COMPARATIVE FRENCH AND GERMAN FIGURES FOR THE CLASSES BORN FROM 1914 TO 1920, AND CALLED UP FROM 1934 TO 1940

Class	German	French
1914	596,000 men	279,000 men
1915	464,000 ,,	184,000 ,,
1916	351,000 ,,	165,000 ,,
1917	314,000 ,,	171,000 ,,
1918	326,000 ,,	197,000 ,,
1919	485,000 ,,	218,000 ,,
1920	636,000 ,,	360,000 ,,
	3,172,000 men	1,574,000 men

Until these figures became facts as the years unfolded they were still but warning shadows. All that was done up to 1935 fell far short of the strength and power of the French Army and its vast reserves, apart from its numerous and vigorous allies. Even at this time a resolute decision upon the authority, which could easily have been obtained, of the League of Nations might have arrested the whole process. Germany could either have been brought to the bar at Geneva and invited to give a full explanation and allow inter-Allied missions of inquiry to examine the state of her armaments and military formations in breach of the Treaty, or, in the event of refusal, the Rhine bridgeheads could have been reoccupied until compliance with the Treaty had been secured, without there being any possibility of effective resistance or much likelihood of bloodshed. In this way the Second World War could have been at least delayed indefinitely. Many of the facts and their whole general tendency were well known to the French and British Staffs, and were to a lesser extent realised by the Governments. The French Government, which was in ceaseless flux in the fascinating game of party politics, and the British Government, which arrived at the same vices by the opposite process of general agreement to keep things quiet, were equally incapable of any drastic or clear-cut action, however justifiable both by treaty and by common prudence. The French Government had not accepted all the reductions of their own forces pressed upon them by their ally; but, like their British colleagues, they lacked the quality to resist in any effective manner what Seeckt in his day had called "the Resurrection of German Military Power".

CHAPTER IX

PROBLEMS OF AIR AND SEA

1935-1939

A Technical Interlude – German Power to Blackmail – Approaches to Mr. Baldwin and the Prime Minister – The Earth v. the Air – Mr. Baldwin's Invitation – The Air Defence Research Committee – Some General Principles – Progress of Our Work – The Development of Radar – Professor Watson-Watt and Radio Echoes – The Tizard Report – The Chain of Coastal Stations – Air-Marshal Dowding's Network of Telephonic Communications – The Graf Zeppelin Flies Up Our East Coast: Spring of 1939 *– I.F.F. – A Visit to Martlesham,* 1939 *– My Admiralty Contacts – The Fleet Air Arm – The Question of Building New Battleships – Calibre of Guns – Weight of Broadsides – Number of Turrets – My Letter to Sir Samuel Hoare of August* 1, 1936 *– The Admiralty Case – Quadruple Turrets – An Unfortunate Sequel – A Visit to Portland: the "Asdics".*

*T*ECHNICAL decisions of high consequence affecting our future safety now require to be mentioned, and it will be convenient in this chapter to cover the whole four years which lay between us and the outbreak of war.

After the loss of air parity we were liable to be blackmailed by Hitler. If we had taken steps betimes to create an Air Force half as strong again, or twice as strong, as any that Germany could produce in breach of her treaty we should have kept control of the future. But even air parity, which no one could say was aggressive, would have given us a solid measure of defensive confidence in these critical years, and a broad basis from which to conduct our diplomacy or expand our Air Force. But we had lost air parity. And such attempts as were made to recover it were vain. We had entered a period when the weapon which had played a considerable part in the previous war had become obsessive in men's minds, and also a prime military factor. Ministers had to imagine the most frightful scenes of ruin and slaughter in London if we quarrelled with the German Dictator. Although these considerations were not special to Great Britain they affected our policy, and by consequence all the world.

During the summer of 1934 Professor Lindemann wrote to the *Times* newspaper pointing out the possibility of decisive scientific results being obtained in air defence research. In August we tried to bring the subject to the attention not merely of the officials at the Air Ministry, who were already on the move, but of their masters in the Government. In September we journeyed from Cannes to Aix-les-Bains, and had an agreeable conversation with Mr. Baldwin, who appeared deeply interested. Our request was for an inquiry on a high level. When we came back to London departmental difficulties arose, and the matter hung in suspense. Early in 1935 an Air Ministry committee composed of scientists was set up and instructed to explore the future. We remembered that it was upon the advice of the Air Ministry that Mr. Baldwin had made the speech which produced so great an impression in 1932, when he said that there was really no defence. "The bomber will always get through." We had therefore no confidence in any Air Ministry departmental committee, and thought the subject should be transferred from the Air Ministry to the Committee of Imperial Defence, where the heads of the Government, the most powerful politicians in the country, would be able to supervise and superintend its actions and also to make sure that the necessary funds were not denied. At this stage we were joined by Sir Austen Chamberlain, and we continued at intervals to address Ministers on the subject.

In February we were received by Mr. MacDonald personally, and we laid our case before him. No difference of principle at all existed between us. The Prime Minister was most sympathetic when I pointed out the peace aspect of the argument. Nothing, I said, could lessen the terrors and anxieties which overclouded the world so much as the removal of the idea of surprise attacks upon the civil populations. Mr. MacDonald seemed at this time greatly troubled with his eyesight. He gazed blankly out of the windows on to Palace Yard, and assured us he was hardening his heart to overcome departmental resistance. The Air Ministry, for their part, resented the idea of any outside or superior body interfering in their special affairs, and for a while nothing happened.

I therefore raised the matter in the House on June 7, 1935.

The point [I said] is limited, and largely scientific in its character. It is concerned with the methods which can be invented or adopted or discovered to enable the Earth to control the Air, to enable defence from the ground to exercise control—indeed domination—upon aeroplanes high above its surface. . . . My experience is that in these matters, when the need is fully explained by military and political authorities, science is always able to provide something. We were told that it was impossible to grapple with submarines, but methods were found which enabled us to strangle the submarines below the surface of the water, a problem not necessarily harder than that of clawing down marauding aeroplanes. Many things were adopted in the war which we were told were technically impossible, but patience, perseverance, and above all the spur of necessity under war conditions, made men's brains act with greater vigour, and science responded to the demands. . . .

It is only in the twentieth century that this hateful conception of inducing nations to surrender by terrorising the helpless civil population by massacring the women and children has gained acceptance and countenance among men. This is not the cause of any one nation. Every country would feel safer if once it were found that the bombing aeroplane was at the mercy of appliances directed from the earth, and the haunting fears and suspicions which are leading nations nearer and nearer to another catastrophe would be abated. . . . We have not only to fear attacks upon our civil population in our great cities, in respect of which we are more vulnerable than any other country in the world, but also attacks upon the dockyards and other technical establishments without which our Fleet, still an essential factor in our defence, might be paralysed or even destroyed. Therefore it is not only for the sake of a world effort to eliminate one of the worst causes of suspicion and of war, but as a means of restoring to us here in Great Britain the old security of our Island, that this matter should receive and command the most vigorous thought of the greatest men in our country and our Government, and should be pressed forward by every resource that the science of Britain can apply and the wealth of the country can liberate.

On the very next day the Ministerial changes recorded in the previous chapter took place, and Mr. Baldwin became Prime Minister. Sir Philip Cunliffe-Lister—Lord Swinton as he soon afterwards became—succeeded Lord Londonderry as Air Minister. One afternoon a month later I was in the smoking-room of the

House of Commons when Mr. Baldwin came in. He sat down next to me and said at once: "I have a proposal to make to you. Philip is very anxious that you should join the newly-formed Committee of Imperial Defence on Air Defence Research, and I hope you will." I said I was a critic of our air preparations and must reserve my freedom of action. He said: "That is quite understood. Of course you will be perfectly free except upon the secret matters you learn only at the Committee."

I made it a condition that Professor Lindemann should at least be a member of the Technical Sub-Committee, because I depended upon his aid. A few days later the Prime Minister wrote:

July 8, 1935

I am glad you have seen Hankey, and I take your letter as an expression of your willingness to serve on that Committee.

I am glad, and I think you may be of real help in a most important investigation.

Of course, you are free as air (the correct expression in this case!) to debate the general issues of policy, programmes, and all else connected with the Air Services.

My invitation was not intended as a muzzle, but as a gesture of friendliness to an old colleague.

Accordingly for the next four years I attended these meetings, and thus obtained a full view of this vital sphere of our air defence, and built up my ideas upon it year by year in close and constant discussion with Lindemann. I immediately prepared a memorandum for the Committee which embodied the thought and knowledge I had already gathered, without official information, in my talks and studies with Lindemann and from my own military conceptions. This paper is of interest because of the light which it throws on the position in July 1935. No one at that time had considered the use of radio beams for guiding bombers. The difficulties of training large numbers of individual pilots were obvious, and it was generally held that at night large fleets of aircraft would be led by a few master-bombers. Great advances into new fields were made in the four years which were to pass before the life of the nation was to be at stake; and meanwhile the adoption of bombing guided by radio beams caused profound tactical changes. Hence much that was written then was superseded, but a good deal was tried by me when I had power—not all with success.

July 23, 1935

The following notes are submitted with much diffidence, and in haste on account of our early meeting, in the hopes that they may be a contribution to our combined thought.

General tactical conceptions and what is technically feasible act and react upon one another. Thus the scientist should be told what facilities the Air Force would like to have, and aeroplane design be made to fit into and implement a definite scheme of warfare.

At this stage we must assume a reasonable war hypothesis, namely, that Great Britain, France, and Belgium are allies attacked by Germany.

After the outbreak of such a war the dominating event will be the mobilisation of the great Continental armies. This will take at least a fortnight, diversified and hampered by mechanised and motorised inroads. The French and German General Staff's minds will be riveted upon the assembly and deployment of the armies. Neither could afford to be markedly behindhand at the first main shock. It may be hoped that Germany will not be ready for a war in which the Army and Navy are to play an important part for two or three years. Their Navy is at the moment exiguous; they have not yet obtained the command of the Baltic; and it would appear that their heavy artillery is still inadequate. To build a navy and to produce heavy artillery and train the men will take a time measured in years rather than in months.

A large part of German munitions production is concentrated in the Ruhr, which is easily accessible to enemy bombing. She must realise that she would be cut off from foreign supplies of many essential war materials (copper, tungsten, cobalt, vanadium, petrol, rubber, wool, etc.), and *even her iron supply will be reduced unless she dominates the Baltic*, so that she is scarcely yet in a position to undertake a war of long duration. Great efforts are of course being made to overcome these handicaps, such as the removal of certain factories from the frontier to Central Germany, the synthetic production of substances such as petrol and rubber, and the accumulation of large stocks. But it seems unlikely that Germany will be in a position before 1937 or 1938 to begin with any hope of success a war of the three Services, which might last for years, and in which she would have scarcely any allies.

It would appear in such a war the first task of the Anglo-French Air Force should be the breaking down of enemy communications, their railways, motor roads, Rhine bridges, viaducts, etc., and the maximum disturbance of their assembly zones and munition dumps. Next in priority come the most accessible factories for their war industry in all its forms. It seems fairly certain that if our efforts from zero hour were concentrated on these vital targets *we should impose a similar policy on the enemy.* Otherwise the French would have an unobstructed mobilisation and command the initiative in the great land battle. Thus any German aircraft used to commit acts of terror upon the British and French civil populations will be grudged and sparingly diverted.

Nevertheless we must expect that even in a three-Service war attempts will be made to burn down London, or other great cities within easy reach, in order to test the resisting will-power of the Government and people under these terrible ordeals. Secondly, the Port of London, and the dockyards upon which the life of the Fleet depends, are also military targets of the highest possible consequence.

There is however always the ugly possibility that those in authority in Germany may believe that it would be possible to beat a nation to its knees in a very few months, or even weeks, by violent aerial mass attack. The conception of psychological shock tactics has a great attraction for the German mind. Whether they are right or wrong is beside the point. If the German Government believes that it can force a country to sue for peace by destroying its great cities and slaughtering the civilian population from the air before the Allied armies have mobilised and advanced materially, this might well lead it to commence hostilities with the air arm alone. It need scarcely be added that England, if she could be separated from France, would be a particularly apt victim for this form of aggression. For her main form of counter-attack, apart from aerial reprisals, namely, a naval blockade, only makes itself felt after a considerable time.

If the aerial bombardment of our cities can be restricted or prevented, the chance (which may in any case be illusory) that our morale could be broken by "frightfulness" will vanish, and the decision will remain in the long run with the armies and navies. The more our defences are respected the greater will be the deterrent upon a purely air war.

* * *

I had some ideas to contribute. It must be remembered that in 1935 we had still more than four years to run before any radio-detection method came into play.

* * *

The Committee worked in secret, and no statement was ever made of my association with the Government, whom I continued to criticise and attack with increasing severity in other parts of the field. It is often possible in England for experienced politicians to reconcile functions of this kind, in the same way as the sharpest political differences are sometimes found not incompatible with personal friendship. Scientists are however a far more jealous society. In 1937 a considerable difference on the Technical Sub-Committee grew between them and Professor Lindemann. His colleagues resented the fact that he was in constant touch with me, and that I pressed his points on the main Committee, to which they considered Sir Henry Tizard, Rector of the Imperial College of Science and Technology, should alone explain their collective view. Lindemann was therefore asked to retire. He was perfectly right in arming me with the facts on which to argue; indeed this was the basis on which we had both joined in the work. Nevertheless, in the public interest, in spite of his departure, I continued, with his full agreement, to remain a member; and in 1938, as will presently be described, I was able to procure his reinstatement.

★　　★　　★

The possibility of using radio waves scattered back from aircraft and other metal objects seems to have occurred to a very large number of people in England, America, Germany, and France in the nineteen-thirties. We talked of them as R.D.F. (Radio Direction Finding), or later as "Radar". The practical aim was to discern the approach of hostile aircraft, not by human senses, by eye or ear, but by the echo which they sent back from radio waves. About seventy miles up there is a reflecting canopy (ionosphere), the existence of which prevents ordinary wireless waves from wandering off into space, and thus makes long-range wireless communication possible. The technique of sending up very short pulses and observing their echo had been actively developed for some years by our scientists, notably by Professor Appleton.

In February 1935 a Government research scientist, Professor Watson-Watt, had first explained to the Technical Sub-Committee that the detection of aircraft by radio echoes might be feasible and had proposed that it should be tested. The Committee was impressed. It was assumed that it would take five years to detect aircraft up to a range of fifty miles. On July 25, 1935, at the fourth meeting of the Air Defence Research Committee, and the first which I attended, Tizard made his report upon radio-location. The preliminary experiments were held to justify further executive action. The Service departments were invited to formulate plans. A special organisation was set up, and a chain of stations established in the Dover-Orfordness area for experimental purposes. The possibility of radio-location of ships was also to be explored.

By March 1936 stations were being erected and equipped along the south coast, and it was hoped to carry out experimental exercises in the autumn. During the summer there were considerable delays in construction, and the problem of hostile jamming appeared. In July 1937 plans were brought forward by the Air Ministry, and approved by the Air Defence Research Committee, to create a chain of twenty stations from the Isle of Wight to the Tees by the end of 1939 at the cost of over a million pounds. Experiments were now tried for finding hostile aircraft after they had come inland. By the end of the year we could track them up to a distance of thirty-five miles at ten thousand feet. Progress was also being made about ships. It had been proved possible to fix vessels from the air at a range of nine miles. Two ships of the Home Fleet were already equipped with apparatus for aircraft detection, and experiments were taking place for range-finding on aircraft, for fire control of anti-aircraft guns, and for the direction of searchlights. Work proceeded. By December 1938 fourteen of the twenty new stations planned were operating with temporary equipment. Location of ships from the air was now possible at thirty miles.

By 1939 the Air Ministry, using comparatively long-wave radio (ten metres), had constructed the so-called coastal chain, which enabled us to detect aircraft approaching over the sea at distances up to about sixty miles. An elaborate network of telephonic communication had been installed under Air-Marshal Dowding, of Fighter Command, linking all these stations with a central command station at Uxbridge, where the movements of all aircraft observed could be plotted on large maps and thus the control in action of all our own air forces be maintained. Apparatus called I.F.F.* had also been devised which enabled our coastal chain Radar stations to distinguish British aircraft which carried it from enemy aircraft. It was found that these long-wave stations did not detect aircraft approaching at low heights over the sea, and as a counter to this danger a supplementary set of

* Identification Friend or Foe.

stations called C.H.L.* was constructed, using much shorter waves (one and a half metres), but only effective over a shorter range.

To follow enemy aircraft once they had come inland we had meanwhile to rely upon the Royal Observer Corps, which only operated by ear and eye, but which when linked up with all the telephone exchanges proved of high value, and in the early part of the Battle of Britain was our main foundation. It was not enough to detect approaching enemy aircraft over the sea, though that gave at least fifteen to twenty minutes' warning. We must seek to guide our own aircraft towards the attackers and intercept them over the land. For this purpose a number of stations with what were called G.C.I.† were being erected. But all this was still embryonic at the outbreak of war.

* * *

The Germans were also busy, and in the spring of 1939 the "Graf Zeppelin" flew up the East Coast of Britain. General Martini, Director-General of Signals in the Luftwaffe, had arranged that she carried special listening equipment to discover the existence of British Radar transmissions, if any. The attempt failed, but had her listening equipment been working properly the "Graf Zeppelin" ought certainly to have been able to carry back to Germany the information that we had Radar, for our Radar stations were not only operating at the time, but also detected her movements and divined her intention. The Germans would not have been surprised to hear our Radar pulses, for they had developed a technically efficient Radar system which was in some respects ahead of our own. What would have surprised them however was the extent to which we had turned our discoveries to practical effect, and woven all into our general air defence system. In this we led the world, and it was operational efficiency rather than novelty of equipment that was the British achievement.

The final meeting of the Air Defence Research Committee took place on July 11, 1939. Twenty Radar stations were at that time in existence between Portsmouth and Scapa Flow, able to detect aircraft flying above ten thousand feet, with ranges varying

* Chain Stations Home Service Low Cover.
† Ground Control of Interception.

from fifty to a hundred and twenty miles. A satisfactory anti-jamming device and a simplified method of I.F.F. were now actually in production. Flight trials were taking place with experimental sets in aircraft to try to "home" on enemy machines. The experimental sets for the location of ships from the air had proved too bulky for air-service purposes, and were passed to the Admiralty for possible use by ships.

*   *   *

I add a final note. In June 1939 Sir Henry Tizard, at the desire of the Secretary of State, conducted me in a rather disreputable aeroplane to see the establishments which had been developed on the East Coast. We flew around all day. I sent my impressions to the Air Minister, and I print them here because they give a glimpse of where we were in this Radar field on the eve of the task.

Mr. Churchill to Sir Kingsley Wood

. . . I found my visit to Martlesham and Bawdsey under Tizard's guidance profoundly interesting, and also encouraging. It may be useful if I put down a few points which rest in my mind.

These vital R.D.F. stations require immediate protection. We thought at first of erecting dummy duplicates and triplicates of them at little expense; but on reflection it seems to me that here is a case for using the smoke-cloud. . . .

A weak point in this wonderful development is of course that when the raider crosses the coast it leaves the R.D.F., and we become dependent upon the Observer Corps. This would seem transition from the middle of the twentieth century to the Early Stone Age. Although I hear that good results are obtained from the Observer Corps, we must regard following the raider inland by some application of R.D.F. as most urgently needed. It will be some time before the R.D.F. stations can look back inland, and then only upon a crowded and confused air theatre. . . .

The progress in R.D.F. especially applied to range-finding must surely be of high consequence to the Navy. It would give power to engage an enemy irrespective of visibility. How different would have been the fate of the German battle-cruisers when they attacked Scarborough and Hartlepool in 1914 if we could have pierced the mist! I cannot conceive why the Admiralty are not now hot upon this trail. Tizard also pointed out the enormous value to destroyers and submarines of directing torpedoes accurately, irrespective of visibility by night or day. I should have thought this was one of the biggest things that had happened for a long time, and all for our benefit.

141

The method of discrimination between friend and foe is also of the highest consequence to the Navy, and should entirely supersede recognition signals, with all their peril. I presume the Admiralty knows all about it.

Finally, let me congratulate you upon the progress that has been made. We are on the threshold of immense securities for our Island. Unfortunately we want to go farther than the threshold, and time is short.

I shall in a later volume explain the way in which, by these and other processes known only to a very small circle, the German attack on Great Britain was to a large extent parried in the autumn and winter of 1940. There is no doubt that the work of the Air Ministry and the Air Defence Research Committee, both under Lord Swinton and his successor, played the decisive part in procuring this precious reinforcement to our fighter aircraft. When in 1940 the chief responsibility fell upon me and our national survival depended upon victory in the air, I had the advantage of a layman's insight into the problems of air warfare resulting from four long years of study and thought based upon the fullest official and technical information. Although I have never tried to be learned in technical matters, this mental field was well lit for me. I knew the various pieces and the moves on the board, and could understand anything I was told about the game.

* * *

My contacts with the Admiralty during these years were also constant and intimate. In the summer of 1936 Sir Samuel Hoare became First Lord, and he authorised his officers to discuss Admiralty matters freely with me; and as I took a keen interest in the Navy I availed myself fully of these opportunities. I had known the First Sea Lord, Admiral Chatfield, from the Beatty days of 1914, and my correspondence with him on naval problems began in 1936. I also had a long-standing acquaintance with Admiral Henderson, the Controller of the Navy and Third Sea Lord, who dealt with all questions of construction and design. He was one of our finest gunnery experts in 1912, and as I used when First Lord often to go out and see the initial firings of battleships before their gun-mountings were accepted from the contractors I was able to form a very high opinion of his work. Both these officers at the summit of their careers treated me with the utmost confidence, and although I differed from them and criticised severely much that was done or not done, no complaint or personal reproaches ever disturbed our association.

The question of whether the Fleet Air Arm should be under the Admiralty or the Air Ministry was hotly disputed between the two departments and services. I took the Navy view, and my advocacy of it in Parliament drew a cordial letter of thanks from the First Sea Lord, in which he entered upon the whole question of naval policy. Sir Thomas Inskip came down to see me at Chartwell, and asked for my advice on this nicely-balanced issue. I drew up for him a memorandum which was eventually adopted almost word for word by His Majesty's Government.*

$$\star \quad \star \quad \star$$

When at last it was decided to begin building battleships again, the question of their design caused me great concern. Up to this moment practically all the capital ships of the Royal Navy had been built or designed during my administration of the Admiralty from 1911 to 1915. Only the *Nelson* and the *Rodney* were created after the First World War. I have in *The World Crisis* described all the process of rebuilding the Navy and the designing of the *Queen Elizabeth* class of fast battleships in my first tenure of the Admiralty, when I had at my disposal so much of the genius and inspiration of Lord Fisher. To this I was always able to apply my own thought, gathered from many other naval expert sources, and I still held strong opinions.

As soon as I heard that a battleship programme had been agreed to by the Cabinet, I was at once sure that our new ships should continue to mount the 16-inch gun, and that this could be achieved within 35,000 tons displacement—the Treaty limit, which we alone rigidly respected—by three triple 16-inch-gun turrets. I had several talks and some correspondence with Sir Samuel Hoare, and as I was not convinced by the arguments I heard I began to ask questions in the House about the relative weight of broadsides from 14-inch- and 16-inch-gunned ships. For my private information the following figures were given:

14-inch 9-gun broadside	6.38 tons
16-inch 9-gun broadside	9.55 tons

The figure for the 16-inch gun is based, not on the existing 16-inch

* See Appendix B.

gun of H.M.S. *Nelson*, but on a hypothetical 16-inch gun of the type which the Americans have in mind for their new capital ships.

I was deeply impressed by the superior weight of the 16-inch broadside. I therefore wrote to Sir Samuel Hoare:

Sir,   1.VIII.36
It is very civil of you to attach any importance to my opinion, and *prima facie* there is a case. I cannot answer the argument about the long delay involved. Once again we alone are injured by treaties. I cannot doubt that a far stronger ship could be built with three triple 16-inch-gun turrets in a 35,000-ton hull, than any combination of 14-inch. Not only would she be a better ship, but she would be rated a better ship and a more powerful token of naval power by everyone, including those who serve in her. Remember the Germans get far better results out of their guns per calibre than we do. They throw a heavier shell farther and more accurately. The answer is a big punch. Not only is there an enormous increase in the weight of broadside, but in addition the explosive charge of a 16-inch shell must be far larger than that of a 14-inch. If you can get through the armour it is worth while doing something inside with the explosion.

Another aspect is the number of turrets. What a waste to have four turrets, which I suppose weigh 2,000 tons each, when three will give a bigger punch! With three turrets the centralisation of armour against gunfire and torpedoes can be much more intense, and the decks all the more clear for the anti-aircraft batteries. If you ask your people to give you a legend for a 16-inch-gun ship, I am persuaded they would show you decidedly better proportions than could be achieved at 14-inch. Of course, there may be an argument about gunnery control, the spread of shot, etc., with which I am not familiar. Still, I should have thought that the optimum gunnery effect could be reached with salvos of four and five alternately.

Nothing would induce me to succumb to 14-inch if I were in your shoes. The Admiralty will look rather silly if they are committed to two 14-inch-gun ships and both Japan and the United States go in for 16-inch a few months later. I should have thought it was quite possible to lie back and save six months in construction. It is terrible deliberately to build British battleships costing £7,000,000 apiece that are not the strongest in the world! As old Fisher used to say, "The British Navy always travels first class."

However, these are only vaticinations! I went through all this in bygone years, or I would not venture to obtrude it on you. I will get in touch with Chatfield as you suggest.

The First Lord in no way resented my arguments and a considerable correspondence took place between us; and I also had several conversations with him and the First Sea Lord. Before leaving the Admiralty at the end of May 1937 Sir Samuel Hoare sent me two memoranda prepared by the Naval Staff, one dealing with battleships and the other with cruisers. The Admiralty case about battleship design was that since the Washington Treaty Great Britain had continually pressed for a reduction in displacement and size of guns on grounds of economy. It had not been possible when the new British battleships were at last sanctioned in 1936 to throw over the Treaty limitations of the 14-inch gun or the 35,000-ton ship. The design of the battleships of the *King George V* class had to be started before it could become known whether other Powers would accept these limits as governing the immediate future. The turrets of the *King George V* class had in fact been ordered in May 1936. Had the Admiralty delayed decision upon design until April 1937 only two ships would be available by 1941, instead of five. Should foreign countries go beyond the Washington limits the designs for the 1938 programme ships, which would be complete in 1942, could take a larger scope.

If however we should eventually be forced to go to fully-balanced 16-inch-gun ships and not sacrifice any of the structural strength and other characteristics of the *King George V* class, there would be considerable increase in displacement. The resultant vessels could not pass through the Panama Canal, and we should have to enlarge our docks as well as add to the cost of each ship. The Admiralty concurred with my preference for a ship of nine 16-inch guns in three turrets, rather than one with ten 14-inch guns in four turrets. All their battleship designs were of ships having three "multi-gun turrets".

After studying this long and massive paper I recognised that we could not face the delay involved in putting larger guns in the first five battleships. The decision was irrevocable. I urged however that the designs for the larger guns and turrets should be completed as a precaution, and that the tools and appliances necessary to adapt the gun-plants, etc., to the larger calibre should actually be made, even at considerable expense.

In my discussions with the Admiralty about battleship design I had not appreciated the fact that they had designed and were in process of drawing out quadruple turrets for the 14-inch gun, thus achieving a total of twelve guns. Had I realised this I should have been forced to reconsider my view. The expression "multi-gun turrets" led to this misunderstanding on my part. Three quadruple turrets would have avoided many of the evils which I saw in a four-turret ship, and twelve 14-inch guns, though not the equal of nine 16-inch, were a considerable improvement in weight of metal.

However, the sequel of the Admiralty policy was unfortunate. Serious delays took place in the designing of the entirely novel quadruple turret for the 14-inch gun. No sooner had work been started upon this than the Admiralty Board decided to change the third turret superposed forward for a two-gun turret. This of course meant redesigning the two or three thousand parts which composed these amazing pieces of mechanism, and a further delay of at least a year in the completion of the *King George V* and *Prince of Wales* was caused by this change of plan. Moreover, our new ships were now reduced to ten guns, and all my arguments about the inferiority of their broadsides compared with 16-inch-gun ships resumed their force. Meanwhile the Americans got round the problem of putting three triple 16-inch turrets into a 35,000-ton hull. The French and the Germans chose the 15-inch gun, the French mounting eight guns in two quadruple turrets, and the Germans eight in four twin turrets. The Germans, however, like the Japanese, had no intention of being bound by any treaty limitations, and the *Bismarck's* displacement exceeded 45,000 tons, with all the advantages which thus accrued. We alone, having after all these years at last decided to build five battleships, on which the life of the Navy and the maintenance of sea-power were judged to depend, went back from the 16-inch gun to the 14-inch, while others increased their calibres. We therefore produced a series of vessels, each taking five years to build, which might well have carried heavier gun-power.

* * *

On June 15, 1938, the First Sea Lord took me down to Portland to show me the Asdics. This was the name which described the system of groping for submarines below the surface by means of sound waves through the water which echoed back from any steel structure they met. From this echo the position of the submarine could be fixed with some accuracy. We were on the threshold of this development at the end of the First World War.

We slept on board the flagship, and had a long talk with Sir Charles Forbes, the Commander-in-Chief. All the morning was spent at the Anti-Submarine School, and in about four hours I received a very full account. We then went to sea in a destroyer, and during the afternoon and evening an exercise of great interest was conducted for my benefit. A number of submarines were scattered about in the offing. Standing on the bridge of the destroyer which was using the Asdic, with another destroyer half a mile away, in constant intercourse, I could see and hear the whole process, which was the Sacred Treasure of the Admiralty, and in the culture of which for a whole generation they had faithfully persevered. Often I had criticised their policy. No doubt on this occasion I overrated, as they did, the magnitude of their achievement, and forgot for a moment how broad are the seas. Nevertheless, if this twenty years' study had not been pursued with large annual expenditure and thousands of highly-skilled officers and men employed and trained with nothing to show for it—all quite unmentionable—our problem in dealing with the U-boat, grievous though it proved, might well have found no answer but defeat.

To Chatfield I wrote:

I have reflected constantly on all that you showed me, and I am sure the nation owes the Admiralty, and those who have guided it, an inestimable debt for the faithful effort sustained over so many years, which has, as I feel convinced, relieved us of one of our great dangers.

What surprised me was the clarity and force of the [Asdic] indications. I had imagined something almost imperceptible, certainly vague and doubtful. I never imagined that I should hear one of those creatures asking to be destroyed. It is a marvellous system and achievement.

The Asdics did not conquer the U-boat; but without the Asdics the U-boat would not have been conquered.

CHAPTER X

SANCTIONS AGAINST ITALY

1935

A Second Heavy Stroke – Adowa Memories – A Time of Caution – A Talk at the Foreign Office – The Peace Ballot – British Naval Strength in the Mediterranean – Sir Samuel Hoare's Speech at Geneva and British Naval Movements – My Speech to the City Carlton Club – Mussolini Invades Abyssinia – Strong Reaction in Britain; Mr. Lansbury Resigns the Leadership of the Labour Parliamentary Party – Sham Sanctions – Mr. Baldwin Resolved on Peace – The Conservative Party Conference – His Conduct of the Election – His Great Majority – The Hoare-Laval Agreement – The Parliamentary Convulsion – I Stay Abroad – The Effect upon Europe of Mussolini's Conquest of Abyssinia.

WORLD peace now suffered its second heavy stroke. The loss by Britain of air parity was followed by the transference of Italy to the German side. The two events combined enabled Hitler to advance along his predetermined deadly course. We have seen how helpful Mussolini had been in the protection of Austrian independence, with all that it implied in Central and South-eastern Europe. Now he was to march over to the opposite camp. Nazi Germany was no longer to be alone. One of the principal Allies of the First World War would soon join her. The gravity of this downward turn in the balance of safety oppressed my mind.

Mussolini's designs upon Abyssinia were unsuited to the ethics of the twentieth century. They belonged to those dark ages when white men felt themselves entitled to conquer yellow, brown, black, or red men, and subjugate them by their superior strength and weapons. In our enlightened days, when crimes and cruelties have been committed from which the savages of former times would have recoiled, or of which they would at least have been incapable, such conduct was at once obsolete and reprehensible. Moreover, Abyssinia was a member of the League of Nations. By a curious inversion it was Italy who had in 1923 pressed for her inclusion, and Britain who had opposed it. The British view was that the character of the Ethiopian Government and the conditions prevailing in that wild land of tyranny, slavery, and tribal war were not consonant with membership of the League. But the Italians had had their way, and Abyssinia was a member of the League, with all its rights and such securities as it could offer. Here indeed was a testing case for the instrument of world government upon which the hopes of all good men were founded.

The Italian Dictator was not actuated solely by desire for territorial gains. His rule, his safety, depended upon prestige. The humiliating defeat which Italy had suffered forty years before at Adowa, and the mockery of the world when an Italian army had not only been destroyed or captured but shamefully mutilated, rankled in the minds of all Italians. They had seen how Britain had after the passage of years avenged both Khartoum and Majuba. To proclaim their manhood by avenging Adowa meant almost as much in Italy as the recovery of Alsace-Lorraine in France. There seemed no way in which Mussolini could more easily or at less risk and cost consolidate his own power or, as he saw it, raise the authority of Italy in Europe than by wiping out the stain of bygone years and adding Abyssinia to the recently-built Italian Empire. All such thoughts were wrong and evil, but since it is always wise to try to understand another country's point of view they may be recorded.

In the fearful struggle against rearming Nazi Germany which I could feel approaching with inexorable strides, I was most reluctant to see Italy estranged, and even driven into the opposite camp. There was no doubt that the attack by one member of the League of Nations upon another at this juncture, if not resented, would be finally destructive of the League as a factor for welding together the forces which could alone control the might of resurgent Germany and the awful Hitler menace. More could perhaps be got out of the vindicated majesty of the League than Italy could ever give, withhold, or transfer. If therefore the League were prepared to use the united strength of all its members to curb

Mussolini's policy, it was our bounden duty to take our share and play a faithful part. There seemed in all the circumstances no obligation upon Britain to take the lead herself. She had a duty to take account of her own weakness caused by the loss of air parity, and even more of the military position of France, in the face of German rearmament. One thing was clear and certain. Half-measures were useless for the League, and pernicious to Britain if she assumed its leadership. If we thought it right and necessary for the law and welfare of Europe to quarrel mortally with Mussolini's Italy, we must also strike him down. The fall of the lesser Dictator might combine and bring into action all the forces—and they were still overwhelming—which would enable us to restrain the greater Dictator, and thus prevent a second German war.

These general reflections are a prelude to the narrative of this chapter.

*　　*　　*

Ever since the Stresa Conference Mussolini's preparations for the conquest of Abyssinia had been apparent. It was evident that British opinion would be hostile to such an act of Italian aggression. Those of us who saw in Hitler's Germany a danger not only to peace but to survival dreaded this movement of a first-class Power, as Italy was then rated, from our side to the other. I remember a dinner at which Sir Robert Vansittart and Mr. Duff Cooper, then only an Under-Secretary, were present, at which this adverse change in the balance of Europe was clearly foreseen. The project was mooted of some of us going out to see Mussolini in order to explain to him the inevitable effects which would be produced in Great Britain. Nothing came of this; nor would it have been of any good. Mussolini, like Hitler, regarded Britannia as a frightened, flabby old woman, who at the worst would only bluster, and was anyhow incapable of making war. Lord Lloyd, who was on friendly terms with him, noted how he had been struck by the Joad resolution of the Oxford undergraduates in 1933 refusing to "fight for King and Country".

*　　*　　*

In Parliament I expressed my misgivings on July 11:

We seem to have allowed the impression to be created that we were ourselves coming forward as a sort of bell-wether or fugleman

150

to lead opinion in Europe against Italy's Abyssinian designs. It was even suggested that we would act individually and independently. I am glad to hear from the Foreign Secretary that there is no foundation for that. We must do our duty, but we must do it with other nations only in accordance with the obligations which others recognise as well. We are not strong enough to be the law-giver and the spokesman of the world. We will do our part, but we cannot be asked to do more than our part in these matters. . . .

As we stand to-day there is no doubt that a cloud has come over the old friendship between Great Britain and Italy, a cloud which, it seems to me, may very easily not pass away, although undoubtedly it is everyone's desire that it should. It is an old friendship, and we must not forget, what is a little-known fact, that at the time Italy entered into the Triple Alliance in the last century she stipulated particularly that in no circumstances would the obligations under the Alliance bring her into armed conflict with Great Britain.

*　　*　　*

In August the Foreign Secretary invited me and also the Opposition Party leaders to visit him separately at the Foreign Office, and the fact of these consultations was made public by the Government. Sir Samuel Hoare told me of this growing anxiety about Italian aggression against Abyssinia, and asked me how far I should be prepared to go against it. Wishing to know more about the internal and personal situation at the Foreign Office under diarchy before replying, I asked about Eden's view. "I will get him to come," said Hoare, and in a few minutes Anthony arrived, smiling and in the best of tempers. We had an easy talk. I said I thought the Foreign Secretary was *justified in going as far with the League of Nations against Italy as he could carry France*; but I added that he ought not to put any pressure upon France, because of her military convention with Italy and her German preoccupation; and that in the circumstances I did not expect France would go very far. I then spoke of the Italian divisions on the Brenner Pass, of the unguarded southern front of France, and other military aspects.

Generally I strongly advised the Ministers not to try to take a leading part or to put themselves forward too prominently. In this I was of course oppressed by my German fears and the conditions to which our defences had been reduced.

*　　*　　*

In the early months of 1935 there was organised a Peace Ballot for collective security and for upholding the Covenant of the League of Nations. This scheme received the blessing of the League of Nations Union, but was sponsored by a separate organisation largely supported by the Labour and Liberal Parties. The following were the questions put:

THE PEACE BALLOT

1. Should Great Britain remain a member of the League of Nations?
2. Are you in favour of an all-round reduction of armaments by international agreement?
3. Are you in favour of the all-round abolition of national military and naval aircraft by international agreement?
4. Should the manufacture and sale of armaments for private profit be prohibited by international agreement?
5. Do you consider that if a nation insists on attacking another the other nations should combine to compel it to stop by:
   (a) economic and non-military measures,
   (b) if necessary military measures?

It was announced on June 27 that over eleven million persons had subscribed their names affirmatively to this. The Peace Ballot seemed at first to be misunderstood by Ministers. Its name overshadowed its purpose. It of course combined the contradictory propositions of reduction of armaments and forcible resistance to aggression. It was regarded in many quarters as a part of the Pacifist campaign. On the contrary, Clause 5 affirmed a positive and courageous policy which could at this time have been followed with an overwhelming measure of national support. Lord Cecil and other leaders of the League of Nations Union were, as this clause declared, and as events soon showed, willing, and indeed resolved, to go to war in a righteous cause, provided that all necessary action was taken under the auspices of the League of Nations. Their evaluation of the facts underwent considerable changes in the next few months. Indeed, within a year I was working with them in harmony upon the policy which I described as "Arms and the Covenant".

*　　*　　*

As the summer drew on the movement of Italian troopships through the Suez Canal was continuous, and considerable forces

and supplies were assembled along the eastern Abyssinian frontier. Suddenly an extraordinary and to me, after my talks at the
Foreign Office, a quite unexpected event occurred. On August
24 the Cabinet resolved and declared that Britain would uphold
its obligation under its treaties and under the Covenant of the
League. This produced an immediate crisis in the Mediterranean,
and I thought it right, since I had been so recently consulted, to
ask the Foreign Secretary to reassure me about the naval situation.

Mr. Churchill to Sir Samuel Hoare   *August 25, 1935*
   I am sure you will be on your guard against the capital fault of
letting diplomacy get ahead of naval preparedness. We took care
about this in 1914.
   Where are the fleets? Are they in good order? Are they adequate?
Are they capable of rapid and complete concentration? Are they safe?
Have they been formally warned to take precautions? Remember
you are putting extreme pressure upon a Dictator who may get into
desperate straits. He may well measure your corn by his bushel. He
may at any moment in the next fortnight credit you with designs far
beyond what the Cabinet at present harbour. While you are talking
judicious, nicely-graded formulas he may act with violence. Far
better put temptation out of his way.
   I see by the newspapers that the Mediterranean Fleet is leaving Malta
for the Levant. Certainly it is wise [for the Fleet] to quit Malta,
which, I understand, is totally unprovided with anti-aircraft defence.
The Mediterranean Fleet based at Alexandria, etc., is on paper—that is
all we are justified in going by—far weaker than the Italian Navy.
I spent some time to-day looking up the cruiser and flotilla construction of the two countries since the war. It seems to me that you have
not half the strength of Italy in modern cruisers and destroyers, and
still less in modern submarines. Therefore it seems to me that very
searching questions should be asked of the Admiralty *now* as to the
position of this British Fleet in the Levant. It is enough to do us
grievous loss. Is it enough to defend itself? It is more than three
thousand miles from reinforcement by the Atlantic and Home Fleets.
Much might happen before these could effect a junction. I do not,
indeed I dare not, doubt but that the Admiralty have studied the
dispositions with vigilance. I hope you will satisfy yourself that their
answers to these suggestions are adequate.
   I heard some time ago talk about a plan for evacuating the Mediterranean in the event of a war with Italy and holding only the Straits of
Gibraltar and the Red Sea. The movement of the Mediterranean
Fleet to the Levant looks like a piece of this policy. If so I hope it has

been thought out. If we abandon the Mediterranean while in a state of war or quasi-war with Italy there is nothing to prevent Mussolini landing in Egypt in force and seizing the Canal. Nothing but France. Is the Admiralty sure of France in such a contingency?

George Lloyd, who is with me, thinks I ought to send you this letter in view of the hazards of the situation. I do not ask you for a detailed answer; but we should like your assurance that you have been satisfied with the Admiralty dispositions.

The Foreign Secretary replied on August 27:

You may rest assured that all the points you have mentioned have been, and are being, actively discussed. I am fully alive to the kind of risks that you mention, and I will do my best to see that they are not ignored. Please have no hesitation in sending me any suggestions or warnings that you think necessary. You know as well as anyone the risks of a situation such as this, and you also know as well as anyone, at least outside the Government, the present state of our Imperial defences.

* * *

Mr. Eden, Minister for League of Nations Affairs and almost co-equal of the Foreign Secretary, had already been for some weeks at Geneva, where he had rallied the Assembly to a policy of "Sanctions" against Italy if she invaded Abyssinia. The peculiar office to which he had been appointed made him by its very nature concentrate upon the Abyssinian question with an emphasis which outweighed other aspects. "Sanctions" meant the cutting off from Italy of all financial aid and of economic supplies, and the giving of all such assistance to Abyssinia. To a country like Italy, dependent for so many commodities needed in war upon unhampered imports from overseas, this was indeed a formidable deterrent. Eden's zeal and address and ʰhe principles which he proclaimed dominated the Assembly. On September 11 the Foreign Secretary, Sir Samuel Hoare, having arrived at Geneva, himself addressed them:

I will begin by reaffirming the support of the League by the Government I represent and the interest of the British people in collective security.... The ideas enshrined in the Covenant and in particular the aspiration to establish the rule of law in international affairs have become a part of our national conscience. It is to the principles of the League and not to any particular manifestation that the British nation has demonstrated its adherence. Any other view is at once an underestimation of our good faith and an imputation upon our sincerity. In conformity with its precise and explicit obligations the League stands, and my country stands with it, for the collective maintenance of the Covenant in its entirety, and particularly for steady and collective resistance to all acts of unprovoked aggression.

In spite of my anxieties about Germany, and little as I liked the way our affairs were handled, I remember being stirred by this speech when I read it in Riviera sunshine. It aroused everyone, and reverberated throughout the United States. It united all those forces in Britain which stood for a fearless combination of righteousness and strength. Here at least was a policy. If only the orator had realised what tremendous powers he held unleashed in his hand at that moment he might indeed for a while have led the world.

These declarations gathered their validity from the fact that they had behind them, like many causes which in the past have proved vital to human progress and freedom, the British Navy. For the first and the last time the League of Nations seemed to have at its disposal a secular arm. Here was the international police force upon the ultimate authority of which all kinds of diplomatic and economic pressures and persuasion could be employed. When on September 12, the very next day, the battle-cruisers *Hood* and *Renown*, accompanied by the Second Cruiser Squadron and a destroyer flotilla, arrived at Gibraltar, it was assumed on all sides that Britain would back her words with deeds. Policy and action alike gained immediate and overwhelming support at home. It was taken for granted, not unnaturally, that neither the declaration nor the movement of warships would have been made without careful expert calculation by the Admiralty of the fleet or fleets required in the Mediterranean to make our undertakings good.

At the end of September I had to make a speech at the City Carlton Club, an orthodox body of some influence. I tried to convey a warning to Mussolini, which I believe he read:

To cast an army of nearly a quarter of a million men, embodying the flower of Italian manhood, upon a barren shore two thousand miles from home, against the goodwill of the whole world and without command of the sea, and then in this position embark upon what may well be a series of campaigns against a people and in regions which no conqueror in four thousand years ever thought it worth

155

while to subdue, is to give hostages to fortune unparalleled in all history.*

Sir Austen Chamberlain wrote to me agreeing with this speech, and I replied:

October 1, 1935

I am glad you approve the line I took about Abyssinia; but I am very unhappy. It would be a terrible deed to smash up Italy, and it will cost us dear. How strange it is that after all these years of begging France to make it up with Italy we are now forcing her to choose between Italy and ourselves! I do not think we ought to have taken the lead in such a vehement way. If we had felt so strongly on the subject we should have warned Mussolini two months before. The sensible course would have been gradually to strengthen the Fleet in the Mediterranean during the early summer, and so let him see how grave the matter was. Now what can he do? I expect a very serious rise of temperature when the fighting [in Abyssinia] begins.

* * *

In October Mussolini, undeterred by belated British naval movements, launched the Italian armies upon the invasion of Abyssinia. On the 10th, by the votes of fifty sovereign States to one, the Assembly of the League resolved to take collective measures against Italy, and a Committee of Eighteen was appointed to make further efforts for a peaceful solution. Mussolini, thus confronted, made a clear-cut statement marked by deep shrewdness. Instead of saying, "Italy will meet sanctions with war," he said, "Italy will meet them with discipline, with frugality, and with sacrifice." At the same time however he intimated that *he would not tolerate the imposition of any sanctions which hampered his invasion of Abyssinia.* If that enterprise were endangered he would go to war with whoever stood in his path. "Fifty nations!" he said. "Fifty nations, led by one!" Such was the position in the weeks which preceded the Dissolution of Parliament in Britain and the General Election, which was now constitutionally due.

* * *

Bloodshed in Abyssinia, hatred of Fascism, the invocation of Sanctions by the League, produced a convulsion within the British Labour Party. Trade unionists, among whom Mr. Ernest Bevin

* See also my conversation with Count Grandi, Appendix A.

was outstanding, were by no means pacifist by temperament. A very strong desire to fight the Italian Dictator, to enforce Sanctions of a decisive character, and to use the British Fleet, if need be, surged through the sturdy wage-earners. Rough and harsh words were spoken at excited meetings. On one occasion Mr. Bevin complained that "he was tired of having George Lansbury's conscience carted about from conference to conference". Many members of the Parliamentary Labour Party shared the trade union mood. In a far wider sphere, all the leaders of the League of Nations Union felt themselves bound to the cause of the League. Clause 5 of their Peace Ballot was plainly involved. Here were principles in obedience to which lifelong humanitarians were ready to die, and if to die, also to kill. On October 8 Mr. Lansbury resigned his leadership of the Labour Parliamentary Party, and Major Attlee, who had a fine war record, reigned in his stead.

* * *

But this national awakening was not in accord with Mr. Baldwin's outlook or intentions. It was not till several months after the election that I began to understand the principles upon which Sanctions were founded. The Prime Minister had declared that Sanctions meant war; secondly, he was resolved there must be no war; and, thirdly, he decided upon Sanctions. It was evidently impossible to reconcile these three conditions. Under the guidance of Britain and the pressures of Laval the League of Nations Committee, charged with devising Sanctions, kept clear of any that would provoke war. A large number of commodities, some of which were war materials, were prohibited from entering Italy, and an imposing schedule was drawn up. But oil, without which the campaign in Abyssinia could not have been maintained, continued to enter freely, because it was understood that to stop it meant war. Here the attitude of the United States, not a member of the League of Nations, and the world's main oil supplier, though benevolent, was uncertain. Moreover, to stop it to Italy involved also stopping it to Germany. The export of aluminium to Italy was strictly forbidden; but aluminium was almost the only metal that Italy produced in quantities beyond her own needs. The importation of scrap iron and iron ore into Italy was sternly vetoed in the name of public justice. But as the Italian metallurgical industry made but little use of them, and as steel billets and pig iron were not interfered with, Italy suffered no hindrance. Thus the measures pressed with so great a parade were not real sanctions to paralyse the aggressor, but merely such half-hearted sanctions as the aggressor would tolerate, because in fact, though onerous, they stimulated Italian war spirit. The League of Nations therefore proceeded to the rescue of Abyssinia on the basis that nothing must be done to hamper the invading Italian armies. These facts were not known to the British public at the time of the election. They earnestly supported the policy of Sanctions, and believed that this was a sure way of bringing the Italian assault upon Abyssinia to an end.

Still less did His Majesty's Government contemplate the use of the Fleet. All kinds of tales were told of Italian suicide squadrons of dive-bombers which would hurl themselves upon the decks of our ships and blow them to pieces. The British fleet which was lying at Alexandria had now been reinforced. It could by a gesture have turned back Italian transports from the Suez Canal, and would as a consequence have had to offer battle to the Italian Navy. We were told that it was not capable of meeting such an antagonist. I had raised the question at the outset, but had been reassured. Our battleships of course were old, and it now appeared that we had no aircraft cover and very little anti-aircraft ammunition. It transpired however that the Admiral commanding resented the suggestion attributed to him that he was not strong enough to fight a fleet action. It would seem that before taking their first decision to oppose the Italian aggression His Majesty's Government should carefully have examined ways and means, and also made up their minds.

There is no doubt, on our present knowledge, that a bold decision would have cut the Italian communications with Ethiopia, and that we should have been successful in any naval battle which might have followed. I was never in favour of isolated action by Great Britain, but having gone so far it was a grievous deed to recoil. Moreover, Mussolini would never have dared to come to grips with a resolute British Government. Nearly the whole of the world was against him, and he would have had to risk his *régime* upon a single-handed war with Britain, in which a fleet action in the Mediterranean would be the early and decisive test. How could Italy have fought this war? Apart from a limited advantage in modern light cruisers, her Navy

The Reorganization of the German Army

21 Training the German Army with tanks made of tin and cardboard. The Treaty of Versailles did not permit the German Army to use tanks.
22 Hindenburg and General von Seeckt reviewing the German Army in front of the Reichstag.

23 General von Seeckt, 1923, the man who reshaped and reorganized the German Army.

24 A parade by the German Army, about 1930.
25 German soldiers in front of the Munich Memorial, 1935.

26 A march-past by the German Army at the Congress of Nuremberg.
Parading the flags before Hitler, 16th September, 1935.

was but a fourth the size of the British. Her numerous conscript Army, which was vaunted in millions, could not come into action. Her air-power was in quantity and quality far below even our modest establishments. She would instantly have been blockaded. The Italian armies in Abyssinia would have famished for supplies and ammunition. Germany could as yet give no effective help. If ever there was an opportunity of striking a decisive blow in a generous cause with the minimum of risk, it was here and now. The fact that the nerve of the British Government was not equal to the occasion can be excused only by their sincere love of peace. Actually it played a part in leading to an infinitely more terrible war. Mussolini's bluff succeeded, and an important spectator drew far-reaching conclusions from the fact. Hitler had long resolved on war for German aggrandisement. He now formed a view of Great Britain's degeneracy, which was only to be changed too late for peace and too late for him. In Japan also there were pensive spectators.

* * *

The two opposite processes of gathering national unity on the burning issue of the hour and the clash of party interests inseparable from a General Election moved forward together. This was greatly to the advantage of Mr. Baldwin and his supporters. "The League of Nations would remain as heretofore the keystone of British foreign policy": so ran the Government's election manifesto. "The prevention of war and the establishment of peace in the world must always be the most vital interest of the British people, and the League is the instrument which has been framed and to which we look for the attainment of these objects. We shall therefore continue to do all in our power to uphold the Covenant and to maintain and increase the efficiency of the League. In the present unhappy dispute between Italy and Abyssinia *there will be no wavering in the policy we have hitherto pursued.*"

The Labour Party, on the other hand, was much divided. The majority was pacifist, but Mr. Bevin's active campaign commanded many supporters among the masses. The official leaders therefore tried to give general satisfaction by pointing opposite ways at once. On the one hand they clamoured for decisive action against the Italian Dictator; on the other they denounced the policy of rearmament. Thus Mr. Attlee in the House of Commons on October 22: "We want effective sanctions, effectively applied.

FROM WAR TO WAR

We support economic sanctions. We support the League system." But then, later in the same speech: "We are not persuaded that the way to safety is by piling up armaments. We do not believe that in this [time] there is such a thing as national defence. We think that you have to go forward to disarmament and not to the piling up of armaments." Neither side usually has much to be proud of at election times. The Prime Minister himself was no doubt conscious of the growing strength behind the Government's foreign policy. He was however determined not to be drawn into war on any account. It seemed to me, viewing the proceedings from outside, that he was anxious to gather as much support as possible and use it to begin British rearmament on a modest scale.

★　　★　　★

The Conservative Party Conference was held at Bournemouth on the very day when Mussolini began his attack on Abyssinia and his bombs were falling on Adowa. In view of this, and not less of the now imminent General Election, we all closed our ranks as party men.

I supported a resolution which was carried unanimously:

(1) To repair the serious deficiencies in the defence forces of the Crown, and in particular, first, to organise our industry for speedy conversion to defence purposes, if need be.

(2) To make a renewed effort to establish equality in the air with the strongest foreign Air Force within striking distance of our shores.

(3) To rebuild the British Fleet and strengthen the Royal Navy, so as to safeguard our food and livelihood and preserve the coherence of the British Empire.

Hitherto in these years I had not desired office, having had so much of it, and being opposed to the Government on their Indian policy. But with the passage of the India Bill, which was to take some years to come into force, this barrier had fallen away. The growing German menace made me anxious to lay my hands upon our military machine. I could now feel very keenly what was coming. Distracted France and timid, peace-loving Britain would soon be confronted with the challenge of the European Dictators. I was in sympathy with the changing temper of the Labour Party. Here was the chance of a true National Government. It was understood that the Admiralty would be vacant, and I wished very much to go there should the Conservatives be returned to power. I was of course well aware that this desire was not shared by several of Mr. Baldwin's principal colleagues. I represented a policy, and it was known that I should strive for it whether from without or from within. If they could do without me they would certainly be very glad. To some extent this depended upon their majority.

★ ★ ★

At the General Election the Prime Minister spoke in strong terms of the need for rearmament, and his principal speech was devoted to the unsatisfactory condition of the Navy. However, having gained all that there was in sight upon a programme of Sanctions and rearmament, he became very anxious to comfort the professional peace-loving elements in the nation and allay any fears in their breasts which his talk about naval requirements might have caused. On October 1, six weeks before the poll, he made a speech to the Peace Society at the Guildhall. In the course of this he said: "I give you my word there will be no great armaments." In the light of the knowledge which the Government had of strenuous German preparations, this was a singular promise. Thus the votes both of those who sought to see the nation prepare itself against the dangers of the future and of those who believed that peace could be preserved by praising its virtues were gained.

★ ★ ★

I fought my contest in the Epping Division upon the need for rearmament and upon a severe and *bona fide* policy of Sanctions. Generally speaking I supported the Government, and although many of my Conservative friends had been offended by my almost ceaseless criticism of Government measures I was returned by an ample majority. Upon the declaration of the poll I thought it right to safeguard my own position. "I take it from your vote, in view of the speeches I have made, that you desire me to exercise my independent judgment as a Member of Parliament, and, in accordance with the highest traditions of that House, to give the fruits of my knowledge and experience freely and without fear." The result of the General Election was a triumph for Mr. Baldwin. The electors accorded him a majority of two hundred and forty-seven over all other parties combined, and after five years of office he reached a position of personal power unequalled by any Prime Minister since the close of the Great War. All who had opposed him, whether on India or on the neglect of our defences, were stultified by this renewed vote of confidence, which he had gained by his skilful and fortunate tactics in home politics and by the esteem so widely felt for his personal character. Thus an Administration more disastrous than any in our history saw all its errors and shortcomings acclaimed by the nation. There was however a bill to be paid, and it took the new House of Commons nearly ten years to pay it.

★　★　★

It had been widely bruited that I should join the Government as First Lord of the Admiralty. But after the figures of his victory had been proclaimed Mr. Baldwin lost no time in announcing through the Central Office that there was no intention to include me in the Government. In this way he paid some of his debt to the pacifist deputation which he had received in the last days of the election. There was much mocking in the Press about my exclusion. But now one can see how lucky I was. Over me beat the invisible wings.

And I had agreeable consolations. I set out with my paint-box for more genial climes without waiting for the meeting of Parliament.

★　★　★

There was an awkward sequel to Mr. Baldwin's triumph, for the sake of which we may sacrifice chronology. His Foreign Secretary, Sir Samuel Hoare, travelling through Paris to Switzerland on a well-earned skating holiday, had a talk with M. Laval, still French Foreign Minister. The result of this was the Hoare-Laval pact of December 9. It is worth while to look a little into the background of this celebrated incident.

The idea of Britain leading the League of Nations against Mussolini's Fascist invasion of Abyssinia had carried the nation in one of its big swings. But once the election was over and the Ministers found themselves in possession of a majority which might give them for five years the guidance of the State many tiresome consequences had to be considered. At the root of them all lay Mr. Baldwin's "There must be no war", and also "There must be no large rearmaments". This remarkable Party Manager,

162

having won the election on world leadership against aggression, was profoundly convinced that we must keep peace at any price.

Moreover, now from the Foreign Office came a very powerful thrust. Sir Robert Vansittart never removed his eyes for one moment from the Hitler peril. He and I were of one mind on that point. And now British policy had forced Mussolini to change sides. Germany was no longer isolated. The four Western Powers were divided two against two instead of three against one. This marked deterioration in our affairs aggravated the anxiety in France. The French Government had already made the Franco-Italian agreement of January. Following thereupon had come the military convention with Italy. It was calculated that this convention saved eighteen French divisions from the Italian front for transference to the front against Germany. In his negotiations it is certain that M. Laval had given more than a hint to Mussolini that France would not trouble herself about anything that might happen to Abyssinia. The French had a considerable case to argue with British Ministers. First, for several years we had tried to make them reduce their army, which was all they had to live upon. Secondly, the British had had a very good run in the leadership of the League of Nations against Mussolini. They had even won an election upon it; and in democracies elections are very important. Thirdly, we had made a naval agreement, supposed to be very good for ourselves, which made us quite comfortable upon the seas, apart from submarine warfare.

But what about the French front? How was it to be manned against the ever-growing German military power? Two divisions, to be sent only under many reservations, was all the British could offer for the first six months, so really they should not talk too much. Now the British Government, in a fine flow of martial, moral, and world sentiment, "fifty nations led by one", were making a mortal feud with Italy. France had much to worry about, and only very silly people, of whom there are extremely large numbers in every country, could ignore all this. If Britain had used her naval power, closed the Suez Canal, and defeated the Italian Navy in a general engagement, she would have had the right to call the tune in Europe. But, on the contrary, she had definitely declared that whatever happened she would not go to war over Abyssinia. Honest Mr. Baldwin: a triumphant vote in the constituencies; a solid Tory majority for five more years;

every aspect of righteous indignation, but no war, no war! The French therefore felt very strongly that they should not be drawn into permanent estrangement from Italy because of all the strong feeling which had suddenly surged up in England against Mussolini. Especially did they feel this when they remembered that Britain had bowed before the Italian naval challenge in the Mediterranean, and when two divisions of troops were all we could send at the outset to help France if she were invaded by Germany. One can certainly understand Monsieur Laval's point of view at this time.

Now in December a new set of arguments marched upon the scene. Mussolini, hard pressed by Sanctions, and under the very heavy threat of "fifty nations led by one", would, it was whispered, welcome a compromise on Abyssinia. Poison gas, though effective against the native Ethiopians, would certainly not elevate the name of Italy in the world. The Abyssinians were being defeated. They were not, it was said, prepared to make large concessions and wide surrenders of territory. Could not a peace be made which gave Italy what she had aggressively demanded and left Abyssinia four-fifths of her entire empire? Vansittart, who happened to be in Paris at the time the Foreign Secretary passed through, and was thus drawn into the affair, should not be misjudged because he thought continuously of the German threat and wished to have Britain and France organised at their strongest to face this major danger, with Italy in their rear a friend and not a foe.

But the British nation from time to time gives way to waves of crusading sentiment. More than any other country in the world, it is at rare intervals ready to fight for a cause or a theme, just because it is convinced in its heart and soul that it will not get any material advantage out of the conflict. Baldwin and his Ministers had given a great uplift to Britain in their resistance to Mussolini at Geneva. They had gone so far that their only salvation before history was to go all lengths. Unless they were prepared to back words and gestures by action, it might have been better to keep out of it all, like the United States, and let things rip and see what happened. Here was an arguable plan. But it was not the plan they had adopted. They had appealed to the millions, and the unarmed, and hitherto unconcerned, millions had answered with a loud shout, overpowering all other cries,

"Yes, we will march against evil, and we will march now. Give us the weapons."

The new House of Commons was a spirited body. With all that lay before them in the next ten years, they had need to be. It was therefore with a horrible shock that, while tingling from the election, they received the news that a compromise had been made between Sir Samuel Hoare and M. Laval about Abyssinia. This crisis nearly cost Mr. Baldwin his political life. It shook Parliament and the nation to its base. Mr. Baldwin fell almost overnight from his pinnacle of acclaimed national leadership to a depth where he was derided and despised. His position in the House during these days was pitiful. He had never understood why people should worry about all these bothersome foreign affairs. They had a Conservative majority and no war. What more could they want? But the experienced pilot felt and measured the full force of the storm.

The Cabinet, on December 9, had approved the Hoare-Laval plan to partition Abyssinia between Italy and the Emperor. On the 13th the full text of the Hoare-Laval proposals was laid before the League. On the 18th the Cabinet abandoned the Hoare-Laval proposals, thus entailing the resignation of Sir Samuel Hoare. In the debate on the 19th Mr. Baldwin said:

I felt that these proposals went too far. I was not at all surprised at the expression of feeling in that direction. I was not expecting that deeper feeling that was manifest in many parts of the country on what I may call the grounds of conscience and of honour. The moment I am confronted with that, I know that something has happened that has appealed to the deepest feelings of our countrymen, that some note has been struck that brings back from them a response from the depths. I examined again all that I had done, and I felt that . . . there could not be support in this country behind those proposals even as terms of negotiation. It is perfectly obvious now that the proposals are absolutely and completely dead. This Government is certainly going to make no attempt to resurrect them. If there arose a storm when I knew I was in the right, I would let it break on me, and I would either survive it or break. If I felt after examination of myself that there was in that storm something which showed me that I had done something that was not wise or right, then I would bow to it.

The House accepted this apologia. The crisis passed. On his return from Geneva Mr. Eden was summoned to 10 Downing

Street by the Prime Minister to discuss the situation following Sir Samuel Hoare's resignation. Mr. Eden at once suggested that Sir Austen Chamberlain should be invited to take over the Foreign Office, and added that if desired he was prepared to serve under him in any capacity. Mr. Baldwin replied that he had already considered this and had informed Sir Austen himself that he did not feel able to offer the Foreign Office to him. This may have been due to Sir Austen's health. On December 22 Mr. Eden became Foreign Secretary.

★   ★   ★

My wife and I passed this exciting week at Barcelona. Several of my best friends advised me not to return. They said I should only do myself harm if I were mixed up in this violent conflict. Our comfortable Barcelona hotel was the rendezvous of the Spanish Left. In the excellent restaurant where we lunched and dined were always several groups of eager-faced, black-coated young men purring together with glistening eyes about Spanish politics, in which quite soon a million Spaniards were to die. Looking back, I think I ought to have come home. I might have brought an element of decision and combination to the anti-Government gatherings which would have ended the Baldwin *régime*. Perhaps a Government under Sir Austen Chamberlain might have been established at this moment. On the other hand, my friends cried, "Better stay away. Your return will only be regarded as a personal challenge to the Government." I did not relish the advice, which was certainly not flattering; but I yielded to the impression that I could do no good, and stayed on at Barcelona daubing canvases in the sunshine. Thereafter Frederick Lindemann joined me, and we cruised in a nice steam-ship around the eastern coasts of Spain and landed at Tangier. Here I found Lord Rothermere with a pleasant circle. He told me that Mr. Lloyd George was at Marrakesh, where the weather was lovely. We all motored thither. I lingered painting in delightful Morocco, and did not return till the sudden death of King George V on January 20.

★   ★   ★

The collapse of Abyssinian resistance and the annexation of the whole country by Italy produced unhelpful effects in German public opinion. Even those elements which did not approve of

Mussolini's policy or action admired the swift, efficient, and ruthless manner in which, as it seemed, the campaign had been conducted. The general view was that Great Britain had emerged thoroughly weakened. She had earned the undying hatred of Italy; she had wrecked the Stresa front once and for all; and her loss of prestige in the world contrasted agreeably with the growing strength and repute of the new Germany. "I am impressed," wrote one of our representatives in Bavaria, "by the note of contempt in references to Great Britain in many quarters. . . . It is to be feared that Germany's attitude in the negotiations for a settlement in Western Europe and for a more general settlement of European and extra-European questions will be found to have stiffened."

An article in the *Muenchener Zeitung* (May 16, 1936) contains some illuminating passages:

The English like a comfortable life compared with our German standards. This does not indeed mean that they are incapable of sustained efforts, but they avoid them so far as they can, without impairing their personal and national security. They also control means and wealth which have enabled them, in contrast with us, for a century or so, to increase their capital more or less automatically. . . . After the war, in which the English after some preliminary hesitation showed certainly an amazing energy, the British masters of the world thought they had at last earned a little rest. They disarmed along the whole line—in civil life even more than on land and sea. They reconciled themselves to abandoning the two-Power [naval] standard and accepted parity with America. . . . How about the Army? How about the Air Force? . . . For the land and air defence forces England needs above all men, not merely money, but also the lives of her citizens for Empire defence. Indeed, of the eleven thousand men needed for the new air programme seven thousand are lacking. Again, the small Regular Army shows a large deficiency, about one whole division, and the Territorial Army (a sort of Sunday school for amateur soldiers) is so far below its authorised numbers that it cannot in any way be considered an effective combatant force. Mr. Baldwin himself said a short time ago that he had no intention of changing the system of recruiting by the introduction of conscription.

A policy which seeks to achieve success by postponing decisions can to-day hardly hope to resist the whirlwind which is shaking Europe, and indeed the whole world. Few are the men who, upon national and not upon party grounds, rage against the spineless and ambiguous attitude of the Government, and hold them responsible for the dangers into which the Empire is being driven all unaware. The masses seem to agree with the Government that the situation will improve by marking time, and that by means of small adjustments and carefully-thought-out manœuvres the balance can once again be rectified. . . .

To-day all Abyssinia is irrevocably, fully, and finally Italian alone. This being so, neither Geneva nor London can have any doubt that only the use of extraordinary force can drive the Italians out of Abyssinia. But neither the power nor the courage to use force is at hand.

All this was only too true. His Majesty's Government had imprudently advanced to champion a great world cause. They had led fifty nations forward with much brave language. Confronted with brute facts Mr. Baldwin had recoiled. Their policy had for a long time been designed to give satisfaction to powerful elements of opinion at home rather than to seek the realities of the European situation. By estranging Italy they had upset the whole balance of Europe and gained nothing for Abyssinia. They had led the League of Nations into an utter fiasco, most damaging if not fatally injurious to its effective life as an institution.

CHAPTER XI

HITLER STRIKES

1936

A New Atmosphere in Britain – Hitler Free to Strike – Ratification of the Franco-Soviet Pact – The Rhineland and the Treaties of Versailles and Locarno – Hitler Reoccupies the Rhineland, March 7 – French Hesitation – Flandin's Visit to London – British Pacifism – Flandin and Baldwin – Ralph Wigram's Grief – Hitler's Vindication and Triumph – A Minister of Co-ordination of Defence – Sir Thomas Inskip Chosen – A Blessing in Disguise – My Hopes of the League – Eden Insists on Staff Conversations with France – German Fortification of the Rhineland – My Warnings in Parliament – Mr. Bullitt's Post-War Revelations – Hitler's Pledge to Austria, July 11.

WHEN I returned at the end of January 1936 I was conscious of a new atmosphere in England. Mussolini's conquest of Ethiopia and the brutal methods by which it had been accomplished, the shock of the Hoare-Laval negotiations, the discomfiture of the League of Nations, the obvious breakdown of "Collective Security", had altered the mood not only of the Labour and Liberal Parties, but of that great body of well-meaning but hitherto futile opinion represented by the eleven million votes cast in the Peace Ballot only seven months before. All these forces were now prepared to contemplate war against Fascist or Nazi tyranny. Far from being excluded from lawful thought, the use of force gradually became a decisive point in the minds of a vast mass of peace-loving people, and even of many who had hitherto been proud to be called pacifists. But force, according to the principles which they served, could only be used on the initiative and under the authority of the League of Nations. Although both the Opposition parties continued to oppose all measures of rearmament, there was an immense measure of agreement open, and had His Majesty's Government risen to the occasion they could have led a united people forward into the whole business of preparation in an emergency spirit.

The Government adhered to their policy of moderation, half-measures, and keeping things quiet. It was astonishing to me that they did not seek to utilise all the growing harmonies that now existed in the nation. By this means they would enormously have strengthened themselves and have gained the power to strengthen the country. Mr. Baldwin had no such inclinations. He was ageing fast. He rested upon the great majority which the election had given him, and the Conservative Party lay tranquil in his hand.

★   ★   ★

Once Hitler's Germany had been allowed to rearm without active interference by the Allies and former associated Powers, a second World War was almost certain. The longer a decisive trial of strength was put off the worse would be our chances, at first of stopping Hitler without serious fighting, and as a second stage of being victorious after a terrible ordeal. In the summer of 1935 Germany had reinstituted conscription in breach of the treaties. Great Britain had condoned this, and by a separate agreement her rebuilding of a Navy, if desired with U-boats on the British scale. Nazi Germany had secretly and unlawfully created a military Air Force which, by the spring of 1935, openly claimed to be equal to the British. She was now in the second year of active munitions production after long covert preparations. Great Britain and all Europe, and what was then thought distant America, were faced with the organised might and will-to-war of seventy millions of the most efficient race in Europe, longing to regain their national glory, and driven, in case they faltered, by a merciless military, social, and party régime.

Hitler was now free to strike. The successive steps which he took encountered no effective resistance from the two liberal democracies of Europe, and, apart from their far-seeing President, only gradually excited the attention of the United States. The battle for peace which could during 1935 have been won was now almost lost. Mussolini had triumphed in Abyssinia, and had successfully defied the League of Nations and especially Great

Britain. He was now bitterly estranged from us, and had joined hands with Hitler. The Berlin-Rome Axis was in being. There was now, as it turned out, little hope of averting war, or of postponing it by a trial of strength equivalent to war. Almost all that remained open to France and Britain was to await the moment of the challenge and do the best they could.

There was, perhaps, still time for an assertion of Collective Security, based upon the avowed readiness of all members concerned to enforce the decisions of the League of Nations by the sword. The democracies and their dependent States were still actually and potentially far stronger than the dictatorships, but their position relatively to their opponents was less than half as good as it had been twelve months before. Virtuous motives, trammelled by inertia and timidity, are no match for armed and resolute wickedness. A sincere love of peace is no excuse for muddling hundreds of millions of humble folk into total war. The cheers of weak, well-meaning assemblies soon cease to echo, and their votes soon cease to count. Doom marches on.

★   ★   ★

Germany had, during the course of 1935, repulsed and sabotaged the efforts of the Western Powers to negotiate an Eastern Locarno. The new Reich at this moment declared itself a bulwark against Bolshevism, and for them, they said, there could be no question of working with the Soviets. Hitler told the Polish Ambassador in Berlin on December 18 that "he was resolutely opposed to any co-operation of the West with Russia". It was in this mood that he sought to hinder and undermine the French attempts to reach direct agreement with Moscow. The Franco-Soviet Pact had been signed in May, but not ratified by either party. It became a major object of German diplomacy to prevent such a ratification. Laval was warned from Berlin that if this move took place there could be no hope of any further Franco-German rapprochement. His reluctance to persevere thereafter became marked, but did not affect the event.

In January 1936, M. Flandin, the new French Foreign Minister, came to London for the funeral of King George V. On the evening of his visit he dined at Downing Street with Mr. Baldwin and Mr. Eden. The conversation turned to the future attitude of France and Britain in the event of a violation of the Locarno

Treaty by Germany. Such a step by Hitler was considered probable, as the French Government now intended to proceed with the ratification of the Franco-Soviet Pact. Flandin undertook to seek the official views of the French Cabinet and General Staff. In February at Geneva, according to his account, he informed Mr. Eden that the armed forces of France would be put at the disposal of the League in the event of a Treaty violation by Germany, and asked the British Minister for the eventual assistance of Great Britain in conformity with the clauses of Locarno.

On February 27 the French Chamber ratified the Franco-Soviet Pact, and the following day the French Ambassador in Berlin was instructed to approach the German Government and inquire upon what basis general negotiations for a Franco-German understanding could be initiated. Hitler, in reply, asked for a few days in which to reflect. At 10 o'clock on the morning of March 7 Herr von Neurath, the German Foreign Minister, summoned the British, French, Belgian, and Italian Ambassadors to the Wilhelmstrasse to announce to them a proposal for a twenty-five-year pact, a demilitarisation on both sides of the Rhine frontier, a pact limiting air forces, and non-aggression pacts to be negotiated with Eastern and Western neighbours.

*   *   *

The "demilitarised zone" in the Rhineland had been established by Articles 42, 43, and 44 of the Treaty of Versailles. These articles declared that Germany should not have or establish fortifications on the left bank of the Rhine or within fifty kilometres of its right bank. Neither should Germany have in this zone any military forces, nor hold at any time any military manœuvres, nor maintain any facilities for military mobilisation. On top of this lay the Treaty of Locarno, freely negotiated by both sides. In this treaty the signatory Powers guaranteed individually and collectively the permanence of the frontiers of Germany and Belgium and of Germany and France. Article 2 of the Treaty of Locarno promised that Germany, France, and Belgium would never invade or attack across these frontiers. Should, however, Articles 42 or 43 of the Treaty of Versailles be infringed, such a violation would constitute "an unprovoked act of aggression", and immediate action would be required from the offended signatories because of the assembling of armed forces in the demilitarised zone. Such a violation should be brought at once before the League of Nations, and the League, having established the fact of violation, must then advise the signatory Powers that they were bound to give their military aid to the Power against whom the offence had been perpetrated.

*　*　*

At noon on this same March 7, 1936, two hours after his proposal for a twenty-five-years pact, Hitler announced to the Reichstag that he intended to reoccupy the Rhineland, and even while he spoke German columns streamed across the boundary and entered all the main German towns. They were everywhere received with rejoicing, tempered by the fear of Allied action. Simultaneously, in order to baffle British and American public opinion, Hitler declared that the occupation was purely symbolic. The German Ambassador in London handed Mr. Eden similar proposals to those which Neurath in Berlin had given to the Ambassadors of the other Locarno Powers in the morning. This provided comfort for everyone on both sides of the Atlantic who wished to be humbugged. Mr. Eden made a stern reply to the Ambassador. We now know of course that Hitler was merely using these conciliatory proposals as part of his design and as a cover for the violent act he had committed, the success of which was vital to his prestige and thus to the next step in his programme.

It was not only a breach of an obligation exacted by force of arms in war, and of the Treaty of Locarno, signed freely in full peace, but the taking advantage of the friendly evacuation by the Allies of the Rhineland several years before it was due. This news caused a world-wide sensation. The French Government, under M. Sarraut, in which M. Flandin was Foreign Minister, uprose in vociferous wrath and appealed to all its allies and to the League. At this time France commanded the loyalty of the "Little Entente", namely, Czechoslovakia, Yugoslavia, and Roumania. The Baltic States and Poland were also associated with the French system. Above all France also had a right to look to Great Britain, having regard to the guarantee we had given for the French frontier against German aggression, and the pressure we had put upon France for the earlier evacuation of the Rhineland. Here if ever was the violation, not only of the Peace Treaty, but of the

Treaty of Locarno, and an obligation binding upon all the Powers concerned.

*   *   *

In France there was a hideous shock. MM. Sarraut and Flandin had the impulse to act at once by general mobilisation. If they had been equal to their task they would have done so, and thus compelled all others to come into line. It was a vital issue for France. But they appeared unable to move without the concurrence of Britain. This is an explanation, but no excuse. The issue was vital to France, and any French Government worthy of the name should have made up its own mind and trusted to the Treaty obligations. More than once in these fluid years French Ministers in their ever-changing Governments were content to find in British pacifism an excuse for their own. Be this as it may, they did not meet with any encouragement to resist the German aggression from the British. On the contrary, if they hesitated to act, their British allies did not hesitate to dissuade them. During the whole of Sunday there were agitated telephonic conversations between London and Paris. His Majesty's Government exhorted the French to wait in order that both countries might act jointly and after full consideration. A velvet carpet for retreat!

The unofficial responses from London were chilling. Mr. Lloyd George hastened to say, "In my judgment Herr Hitler's greatest crime was not the breach of a treaty, because there was provocation." He added that "he hoped we should keep our heads". The provocation was presumably the failure of the Allies to disarm themselves more than they had done. Lord Snowden concentrated upon the proposed Non-Aggression Pact, and said that Hitler's previous peace overtures had been ignored, but the peoples would not permit *this* peace offer to be neglected. These utterances may have expressed misguided British public opinion at the moment, but will not be deemed creditable to their authors. The British Cabinet, seeking the line of least resistance, felt that the easiest way out was to press France into another appeal to the League of Nations.

*   *   *

There was also great division in France. On the whole it was the politicians who wished to mobilise the Army and send an ultimatum to Hitler, and the generals who, like their German

174

counterparts, pleaded for calm, patience, and delay. We now know of the conflicts of opinion which arose at this time between Hitler and the German High Command. If the French Government had mobilised the French Army, with nearly a hundred divisions, and its Air Force (then still falsely believed to be the strongest in Europe), there is no doubt that Hitler would have been compelled by his own General Staff to withdraw, and a check would have been given to his pretensions which might well have proved fatal to his rule. It must be remembered that France alone was at this time quite strong enough to drive the Germans out of the Rhineland, even without the aid which her own action, once begun, and the invocation of the Locarno Treaty would certainly have drawn from Great Britain. In fact she remained completely inert and paralysed, and thus lost irretrievably the last chance of arresting Hitler's ambitions without a serious war. Instead, the French Government were urged by Britain to cast their burden upon the League of Nations, already weakened and disheartened by the fiasco of Sanctions and the Anglo-German Naval Agreement of the previous year.

On Monday, March 9, Mr. Eden went to Paris, accompanied by Lord Halifax and Ralph Wigram. The first plan had been to convene a meeting of the League in Paris, but presently Wigram, on Eden's authority, was sent to tell Flandin to come to London to have the meeting of the League in England, as he would thus get more effective support from Britain. This was an unwelcome mission for the faithful official. Immediately on his return to London on March 11 he came to see me, and told me the story. Flandin himself arrived late the same night, and at about 8.30 on Thursday morning he came to my flat in Morpeth Mansions. He told me that he proposed to demand from the British Government simultaneous mobilisation of the land, sea, and air forces of both countries, and that he had received assurances of support from all the nations of the "Little Entente" and from other States. He read out an impressive list of the replies received. There was no doubt that superior strength still lay with the Allies of the former war. They had only to act to win. Although we did not know what was passing between Hitler and his generals, it was evident that overwhelming force lay on our side. There was little I could do in my detached private position, but I wished our visitor all success in bringing matters to a head and promised any assistance that was in my power. I gathered my principal associates at dinner that night to hear M. Flandin's exhortations.

Mr. Chamberlain was at this time, as Chancellor of the Exchequer, the most effective Member of the Government. His able biographer, Mr. Keith Feiling, gives the following extract from his diary: "March 12, talked to Flandin, emphasising that public opinion would not support us in sanctions of any kind. His view is that if a firm front is maintained Germany will yield without war. We cannot accept this as a reliable estimate of a mad Dictator's reaction." When Flandin urged at least an economic boycott Chamberlain replied by suggesting an international force during negotiations, agreed to a pact for mutual assistance, and declared that if by giving up a colony we could secure lasting peace he would consider it.*

Meanwhile most of the British Press, with the *Times* and the *Daily Herald* in the van, expressed their belief in the sincerity of Hitler's offers of a non-aggression pact. Austen Chamberlain, in a speech at Cambridge, proclaimed the opposite view. Wigram thought it was within the compass of his duty to bring Flandin into touch with everyone he could think of from the City, from the Press, and from the Government, and also with Lord Lothian. To all whom Flandin met at the Wigrams' he spoke in the following terms: "The whole world and especially the small nations to-day turn their eyes towards England. If England will act now she can lead Europe. You will have a policy, all the world will follow you, and thus you will prevent war. It is your last chance. If you do not stop Germany now, all is over. France cannot guarantee Czechoslovakia any more, because that will become geographically impossible. If you do not maintain the Treaty of Locarno all that will remain to you is to await a re-armament by Germany, against which France can do nothing. If you do not stop Germany by force to-day war is inevitable, even if you make a temporary friendship with Germany. As for myself, I do not believe that friendship is possible between France and Germany; the two countries will always be in tension, Nevertheless, if you abandon Locarno I shall change my policy, for there will be nothing else to do." These were brave words; but action would have spoken louder.

Lord Lothian's contribution was: "After all, they are only going

* Keith Feiling, *Life of Neville Chamberlain.*

into their own back-garden." This was a representative British view.

★ ★ ★

When I heard how ill things were going, and after a talk with Wigram, I advised M. Flandin to demand an interview with Mr. Baldwin before he left. This took place at Downing Street. The Prime Minister received M. Flandin with the utmost courtesy. Mr. Baldwin explained that although he knew little of foreign affairs he was able to interpret accurately the feelings of the British people. And they wanted peace. M. Flandin says that he rejoined that the only way to ensure this was to stop Hitlerite aggression while such action was still possible. France had no wish to drag Great Britain into war; she asked for no practical aid, and she would herself undertake what would be a simple police operation, as, according to French information, the German troops in the Rhineland had orders to withdraw if opposed in a forcible manner. Flandin asserts that he said that all that France asked of her Ally was a free hand. This is certainly not true. How could Britain have restrained France from action to which, under the Locarno Treaty, she was legally entitled? The British Prime Minister repeated that his country could not accept the risk of war. He asked what the French Government had resolved to do. To this no plain answer was returned. According to Flandin,* Mr. Baldwin then said: "You may be right, but if there is *even one chance in a hundred* that war would follow from your police operation I have not the right to commit England." And after a pause he added: "England is not in a state to go to war." There is no confirmation of this. M. Flandin returned to France convinced, first that his own divided country could not be united except in the presence of a strong will-power in Britain, and secondly that, so far from this being forthcoming, no strong impulse could be expected from her. Quite wrongly he plunged into the dismal conclusion that the only hope for France was in an arrangement with an ever more aggressive Germany.

Nevertheless, in view of what I saw of Flandin's attitude during these anxious days, I felt it my duty, in spite of his subsequent lapses, to come to his aid, so far as I was able, in later years. I used my power in the winter of 1943–44 to protect him when he was

* Pierre-Etienne Flandin, *Politique Française*, 1919-40, pp. 207-8.

arrested in Algeria by the de Gaulle Administration. In this I invoked and received active help from President Roosevelt. When after the war Flandin was brought to trial, my son Randolph, who had seen much of Flandin during the African campaign, was summoned as a witness, and I am glad to think that his advocacy, and also a letter which I wrote for Flandin to use in his defence, were not without influence in procuring the acquittal which he received from the French tribunal. Weakness is not treason, though it may be equally disastrous. Nothing however can relieve the French Government of their prime responsibility. Clemenceau or Poincaré would have left Mr. Baldwin no option.

★   ★   ★

The British and French submission to the violations of the Treaties of Versailles and Locarno involved in Hitler's seizure of the Rhineland was a mortal blow to Wigram. "After the French delegation had left," wrote his wife to me, "Ralph came back, and sat down in a corner of the room where he had never sat before, and said to me, 'War is now *inevitable*, and it will be the most terrible war there has ever been. I don't think I shall see it, but you will. Wait now for bombs on this little house.'★ I was frightened at his words, and he went on, 'All my work these many years has been no use. I am a failure. I have failed to make the people here realise what is at stake. I am not strong enough, I suppose. I have not been able to make them understand. Winston has always, always understood, and he is strong and will go on to the end.'"

My friend never seemed to recover from this shock. He took it too much to heart. After all, one can always go on doing what one believes to be his duty, and running ever greater risks till knocked out. Wigram's profound comprehension reacted on his sensitive nature unduly. His untimely death in December 1936 was an irreparable loss to the Foreign Office, and played its part in the miserable decline of our fortunes.

★   ★   ★

When Hitler met his generals after the successful reoccupation of the Rhineland he was able to confront them with the falsity of their fears and prove to them how superior his judgment or

★ It was actually smitten.

"intuition" was to that of ordinary military men. The generals bowed. As good Germans they were glad to see their country gaining ground so rapidly in Europe and its former adversaries so divided and tame. Undoubtedly Hitler's prestige and authority in the supreme circle of German power was sufficiently enhanced by this episode to encourage and enable him to march forward to greater tests. To the world he said: "All Germany's territorial ambitions have now been satisfied."

France was thrown into incoherency, amid which fear of war, and relief that it had been avoided, predominated. The simple English were taught by their simple Press to comfort themselves with the reflection, "After all, the Germans are only going back to their own country. How should we feel if we had been kept out of, say, Yorkshire for ten or fifteen years?" No one stopped to note that the detrainment points from which the German Army could invade France had been advanced by one hundred miles. No one worried about the proof given to all the Powers of the "Little Entente" and to Europe that France would not fight, and that England would hold her back even if she would. This episode confirmed Hitler's power over the Reich, and stultified, in a manner ignominious and slurring upon their patriotism, the generals who had hitherto sought to restrain him.

★ ★ ★

During this exciting period my own personal fortunes were, it now appears, discussed in high quarters. The Prime Minister, under constant pressure, had decided at last to create a new Ministry—not of Defence, but of the Co-ordination of Defence. Neville Chamberlain's biographer has given some account of this. Austen Chamberlain, whose influence with the Government stood high, thought and said that it was an "immense mistake" to exclude me. Sir Samuel Hoare had returned from convalescence, and in view of the docility with which he had accepted his dismissal after the Hoare-Laval crisis he evidently had strong claims for re-employment. The Prime Minister thought it would be best for Neville Chamberlain to take the new office, and for Austen to go back to the Exchequer. Neville, who was certain to succeed Baldwin in the immediate future, declined this proposal. "The party," says Mr. Feiling, "would not have the immediate return of Hoare. If the new Ministry went to

Churchill it would alarm those Liberal and Central elements who had taken his exclusion as a pledge against militarism,* it would be against the advice of those responsible for interpreting the party's general will, and would it not when Baldwin disappeared raise a disputed succession?" For a whole month, we are told, "these niceties and gravities were well weighed".

I was naturally aware that this process was going on. In the debate of March 9 I was careful not to derogate in the slightest degree from my attitude of severe though friendly criticism of Government policy, and I was held to have made a successful speech. I did not consider the constitution of the new office and its powers satisfactory. But I would gladly have accepted the post, being confident that knowledge and experience would prevail. Apparently (according to Mr. Feiling) the German entry into the Rhineland on March 7 was decisive against my appointment. It was certainly obvious that Hitler would not like it. On the 9th Mr. Baldwin selected Sir Thomas Inskip, an able lawyer, who had the advantages of being little known himself and knowing nothing about military subjects. The Prime Minister's choice was received with astonishment by Press and public. To me this definite and as it seemed final exclusion from all share in our preparations for defence was a heavy blow.

I had to be very careful not to lose my poise in the great discussions and debates which crowded upon us, and in which I was often prominent. I had to control my feelings and appear serene, indifferent, detached. In this endeavour continuous recurrence to the safety of the country was a good and simple rule. In order to steady and absorb my mind I planned in outline a history of what had happened since the Treaty of Versailles down to the date we had reached. I even began the opening chapter, and part of what I wrote then finds its place without the need of alteration in this present book. I did not however carry this project very far because of the press of events, and also of the current literary work by which I earned my pleasant life at Chartwell. Moreover, by the end of 1936 I became absorbed in my *History of the English-Speaking Peoples*, which I actually finished before the outbreak of war and which will some day be published. Writing a long and substantial book is like having a friend and companion at your side,

---

* This was the reverse of the truth at this time. The signers of the Peace Ballot were at one with me upon armed collective security.

to whom you can always turn for comfort and amusement, and whose society becomes more attractive as a new and widening field of interest is lighted in the mind.

Mr. Baldwin certainly had good reason to use the last flickers of his power against one who had exposed his mistakes so severely and so often. Moreover, as a profoundly astute party manager, thinking in majorities and aiming at a quiet life between elections, he did not wish to have my disturbing aid. He thought, no doubt, that he had dealt me a politically fatal stroke, and I felt he might well be right. How little can we foresee the consequences either of wise or unwise action, of virtue or of malice! Without this measureless and perpetual uncertainty the drama of human life would be destroyed. Mr. Baldwin knew no more than I how great was the service he was doing me in preventing me from becoming involved in all the Cabinet compromises and shortcomings of the next three years, and from having, if I had remained a Minister, to enter upon a war bearing direct responsibility for conditions of national defence bound to prove fearfully inadequate.

This was not the first time—or indeed the last—that I have received a blessing in what was at the time a very effective disguise.

*　　*　　*

I still had the hope that the appeal which France had made to the League of Nations would result in bringing into being an international pressure upon Germany to carry out the decisions of the League.

France [I wrote on March 13, 1936] has taken her case before the Court, and she asks for justice there. If the Court finds that her case is just but is unable to offer her any satisfaction, the Covenant of the League of Nations will have been proved a fraud, and Collective Security a sham. If no means of lawful redress can be offered to the aggrieved party, the whole doctrine of international law and cooperation upon which the hopes of the future are based would lapse ignominiously. It would be replaced immediately by a system of alliances and groups of nations deprived of all guarantees but their own right arm. On the other hand, if the League of Nations were able to enforce its decree upon one of the most powerful countries in the world found to be an aggressor, then the authority of the League would be set upon so majestic a pedestal that it must henceforth be the accepted sovereign authority by which all the quarrels of people can be determined and controlled. Thus we might upon this occasion reach by one single bound the realisation of our most cherished dreams.

But the risk! No one must ignore it. How can it be minimised? There is a simple method: the assembly of an overwhelming force, moral and physical, in support of international law. If the relative strengths are narrowly balanced war may break out in a few weeks, and no one can measure what the course of war may be, or who will be drawn into its whirlpools, or how, if ever, they will emerge. But if the forces at the disposal of the League of Nations are four or five times as strong as those which the aggressor can as yet command the chances of a peaceful and friendly solution are very good. Therefore every nation, great or small, should play its part according to the Covenant of the League.

Upon what force can the League of Nations count at this cardinal moment? Has she sheriffs and constables with whom to sustain her judgments, or is she left alone, impotent, a hollow mockery amid the lip-serving platitudes of irresolute or cynical devotees? Strangely enough for the destiny of the world, there was never a moment or occasion when the League of Nations could command such over-whelming force. The Constabulary of the world is at hand. On every side of Geneva stand great nations, armed and ready, whose interests as well as whose obligations bind them to uphold, and in the last resort enforce, the public law. This may never come to pass again. The fateful moment has arrived for choice between the New Age and the Old.

All this language was agreeable to the Liberal and Labour forces with whom I and several of my Conservative friends were at this time working. It united Conservatives alarmed about national safety with trade unionists, with Liberals, and with the immense body of peace-minded men and women who had signed the Peace Ballot of a year before. There is no doubt that had His Majesty's Government chosen to act with firmness and resolve through the League of Nations they could have led a united Britain forward on a final quest to avert war.

★ ★ ★

The violation of the Rhineland was not debated till March 26. The interval was partly filled by a meeting of the Council of the League of Nations in London. As the result Germany was invited to submit to the Hague Court her case against the Franco-Soviet Pact, about which Hitler had complained, and to undertake not to increase her troops in the Rhineland pending further negotiations. If Germany refused this latter request, the British and Italian Governments undertook to carry out the steps entailed by their obligations under the Treaty of Locarno. Not much value could be assigned to the Italian promise. Mussolini was already in close contact with Hitler. Germany felt strong enough to decline any conditions limiting her forces in the Rhineland. Mr. Eden therefore insisted that Staff conversations should take place between Great Britain, France, and Belgium to enable any joint action which might at some future time become necessary under the Treaty of Locarno to be studied and prepared in advance. The youthful Foreign Secretary made a courageous speech, and carried the House with him. Austen Chamberlain and I both spoke at length in his support. The Cabinet was lukewarm, and it was no easy task for Eden even to procure the institution of Staff conversations. Usually such conversations do not play any part as diplomatic counters, and take place secretly or even informally. Now they were the only practical outcome of three weeks' parleyings and protestations, and the only Allied reply to Hitler's breach of the Treaty and solid gain of the Rhineland.

In the course of my speech I said:

We cannot look back with much pleasure on our foreign policy in the last five years. They certainly have been disastrous years. God forbid that I should lay on the Government of my own country the charge of responsibility for the evils which have come upon the world in that period. ... But certainly we have seen the most depressing and alarming change in the outlook of mankind which has ever taken place in so short a period. Five years ago all felt safe; five years ago all were looking forward to peace, to a period in which mankind would rejoice in the treasures which science can spread to all classes if conditions of peace and justice prevail. Five years ago to talk of war would have been regarded not only as a folly and a crime, but almost as a sign of lunacy. ...

The violation of the Rhineland is serious because of the menace to which it exposes Holland, Belgium, and France. I listened with apprehension to what the Secretary of State said about the Germans declining even to refrain from entrenching themselves during the period of negotiations. When there is a line of fortifications, as I suppose there will be in a very short time, it will produce reactions on the European situation. *It will be a barrier across Germany's front door which will leave her free to sally out eastwards and southwards by the other doors.*

The far-reaching consequences of the fortification of the Rhineland were only gradually comprehended in Britain and the United States. On April 6, when the Government asked for a Vote of Confidence in their foreign policy, I recurred to this subject:

Herr Hitler has torn up the treaties and has garrisoned the Rhineland. His troops are there, and there they are going to stay. All this means that the Nazi *régime* has gained a new prestige in Germany and in all the neighbouring countries. But more than that, Germany is now fortifying the Rhine zone or is about to fortify it. No doubt it will take some time. We are told that in the first instance only field entrenchments will be erected, but those who know to what perfection the Germans can carry field entrenchments, like the Hindenburg Line, with all the masses of concrete and the underground chambers there included, will realise that field entrenchments differ only in degree from permanent fortifications, and work steadily up from the first cutting of the sods to their final and perfect form.
I do not doubt that the whole of the German frontier opposite to France is to be fortified as strongly and as speedily as possible. Three, four, or six months will certainly see a barrier of enormous strength. What will be the diplomatic and strategic consequences of that? . . . *The creation of a line of forts opposite to the French frontier will enable the German troops to be economised on that line, and will enable the main forces to swing round through Belgium and Holland. . . .* Then look East. There the consequences of the Rhineland fortification may be more immediate. That is to us a less direct danger, but it is a more imminent danger. The moment those fortifications are completed, and in proportion as they are completed, the whole aspect of Middle Europe is changed. *The Baltic States, Poland, and Czechoslovakia, with which must be associated Yugoslavia, Roumania, Austria, and some other countries, are all affected very decisively the moment that this great work of construction has been completed.*

Every word of this warning was successively and swiftly proved true.

★   ★   ★

After the occupation of the Rhineland and the development of the line of fortifications against France, the incorporation of Austria in the German Reich was evidently to be the next step. The story that had opened with the murder of Chancellor Dollfuss in July 1934 had soon another and a consequential chapter to unfold. With illuminating candour, as we now know, the German Foreign Minister Neurath told the American Ambassador in Moscow, Mr. Bullitt, on May 18, 1936, that it was the policy of the German Government to do nothing active in foreign affairs until the Rhineland had been digested. He explained that *until the German defences had been built on the French and Belgian frontiers* the German Government would do everything to prevent rather than encourage an outbreak by the Nazis in Austria, and that they would pursue a quiet line with regard to Czechoslovakia. *"As soon as our fortifications are constructed,"* he said, *"and the countries in Central Europe realise that France cannot enter German territory, all these countries will begin to feel very differently about their foreign policies, and a new constellation will develop."* Neurath further informed Mr. Bullitt that the youth of Austria was turning more and more towards the Nazis, and the dominance of the Nazi Party in Austria was inevitable and only a question of time. *But the governing factor was the completion of the German fortifications on the French frontier*, for otherwise a German quarrel with Italy might lead to a French attack on Germany.

On May 21, 1936, Hitler in a speech to the Reichstag declared that "Germany neither intends nor wishes to interfere in the internal affairs of Austria, to annex Austria, or to conclude an Anschluss". On July 11, 1936, he signed a pact with the Austrian Government agreeing not to influence in any way the internal affairs of Austria, and especially not to give any active support to the Austrian National-Socialist movement. Within five days of this agreement secret instructions were sent to the National-Socialist Party in Austria to extend and intensify their activities. Meanwhile the German General Staff, under Hitler's orders, were set to draw up military plans for the occupation of Austria when the hour should strike.

CHAPTER XII

THE LOADED PAUSE. SPAIN

1936-1937

The Foreign Policy of England – The New Dominator – The League of Nations – Two Years' Interlude – My Memorandum on Supply Organisation, June 6, 1936 – The Civil War in Spain – Non-Intervention – The Anti-Comintern Pact – Mr. Baldwin's "Frankness" Speech – Arms and the Covenant – The Albert Hall Meeting – The Abdication of King Edward VIII – Mr. Baldwin's Wisdom – The Coronation of King George VI – A Letter from the King – Mr. Baldwin's Retirement – Mr. Chamberlain Prime Minister – Ministerial Changes – Baldwin and Chamberlain – A Talk with Ribbentrop.

ERE is the place to set forth the principles of British policy towards Europe which I had followed for many years and follow still. I cannot better express them than in the words which I used to the Conservative Members' Committee on Foreign Affairs, who invited me to address them in private at the end of March 1936.

"For four hundred years the foreign policy of England has been to oppose the strongest, most aggressive, most dominating Power on the Continent, and particularly to prevent the Low Countries falling into the hands of such a Power. Viewed in the light of history, these four centuries of consistent purpose amid so many changes of names and facts, of circumstances and conditions, must rank as one of the most remarkable episodes which the records of any race, nation, State, or people can show. Moreover, on all occasions England took the more difficult course. Faced by Philip II of Spain, against Louis XIV under William III and Marlborough, against Napoleon, against William II of Germany, it would have been easy and must have been very tempting to

186

join with the stronger and share the fruits of his conquest. However, we always took the harder course, joined with the less strong Powers, made a combination among them, and thus defeated and frustrated the Continental military tyrant, whoever he was, whatever nation he led. Thus we preserved the liberties of Europe, protected the growth of its vivacious and varied society, and emerged after four terrible struggles with an ever-growing fame and widening Empire, and with the Low Countries safely protected in their independence. Here is the wonderful unconscious tradition of British Foreign Policy. All our thoughts rest in that tradition to-day. I know of nothing which has occurred to alter or weaken the justice, wisdom, valour, and prudence upon which our ancestors acted. I know of nothing that has happened to human nature which in the slightest degree alters the validity of their conclusions. I know of nothing in military, political, economic, or scientific fact which makes me feel that we are less capable. I know of nothing which makes me feel that we might not, or cannot, march along the same road. I venture to put this very general proposition before you because it seems to me that if it is accepted everything else becomes much more simple.

"Observe that the policy of England takes no account of which nation it is that seeks the overlordship of Europe. The question is not whether it is Spain, or the French Monarchy, or the French Empire, or the German Empire, or the Hitler *régime*. It has nothing to do with rulers or nations; it is concerned solely with whoever is the strongest or the potentially dominating tyrant. Therefore we should not be afraid of being accused of being pro-French or anti-German. If the circumstances were reversed, we could equally be pro-German and anti-French. It is a law of public policy which we are following, and not a mere expedient dictated by accidental circumstances, or likes and dislikes, or any other sentiment.

"The question therefore arises which is to-day the Power in Europe which is the strongest, and which seeks in a dangerous and oppressive sense to dominate. To-day, for this year, probably for part of 1937, the French Army is the strongest in Europe. But no one is afraid of France. Everyone knows that France wants to be let alone, and that with her it is only a case of self-preservation. Everyone knows that the French are peaceful and overhung by fear. They are at once brave, resolute, peace-loving, and weighed down by anxiety. They are a liberal nation with free Parliamentary institutions.

"Germany, on the other hand, fears no one. She is arming in a manner which has never been seen in German history. She is led by a handful of triumphant desperadoes. The money is running short, discontents are arising beneath these despotic rulers. Very soon they will have to choose on the one hand between economic and financial collapse or internal upheaval, and on the other a war which could have no other object, and which if successful can have no other result, than a Germanised Europe under Nazi control. Therefore it seems to me that all the old conditions present themselves again, and that our national salvation depends upon our gathering once again all the forces of Europe to contain, to restrain, and if necessary to frustrate German domination. For, believe me, if any of those other Powers, Spain, Louis XIV, Napoleon, Kaiser Wilhelm II, had with our aid become the absolute masters of Europe, they could have despoiled us, reduced us to insignificance and penury on the morrow of their victory. We ought to set the life and endurance of the British Empire and the greatness of this Island very high in our duty, and not be led astray by illusions about an ideal world, which only means that other and worse controls will step into our place, and that the future direction will belong to them.

"It is at this stage that the spacious conception and extremely vital organisation of the League of Nations presents itself as a prime factor. The League of Nations is, in a practical sense, a British conception, and it harmonises perfectly with all our past methods and actions. Moreover, it harmonises with those broad ideas of right and wrong, and of peace based upon controlling the major aggressor, which we have always followed. We wish for the reign of law and freedom among nations and within nations, and it was for that, and nothing less than that, that those bygone architects of our repute, magnitude, and civilisation fought, toiled, and won. The dream of a reign of International Law and of the settlement of disputes by patient discussion, but still in accordance with what is lawful and just, is very dear to the British people. You must not underrate the force which these ideals exert upon the modern British democracy. One does not know how these seeds are planted by the winds of the centuries in the hearts of the working people. They are there, and just as strong as their love of liberty. We should not neglect them, because they are the essence of the genius of this Island. Therefore we believe that in the fostering and fortifying of the League of Nations will be found the best means of defending our island security, as well as maintaining grand universal causes with which we have very often found our own interests in natural accord.

"My three main propositions are: first, that we must oppose the would-be dominator or potential aggressor; secondly, that Germany, under its present Nazi *régime*, and with its prodigious armaments, so swiftly developing, fills unmistakably that part; thirdly, that the League of Nations rallies many countries, and unites our own people here at home in the most effective way to control the would-be aggressor. I venture most respectfully to submit these main themes to your consideration. Everything else will follow from them.

"It is always more easy to discover and proclaim general principles than to apply them. First, we ought to count our effective association with France. That does not mean that we should develop a needlessly hostile mood against Germany. It is a part of our duty and our interest to keep the temperature low between these two countries. We shall not have any difficulty in this so far as France is concerned. Like us, they are a Parliamentary democracy with tremendous inhibitions against war, and, like us, under considerable drawbacks in preparing their defence. Therefore I say we ought to regard our defensive association with France as fundamental. Everything else must be viewed in proper subordination now that the times have become so sharp and perilous. Those who are possessed of a definite body of doctrine and of deeply-rooted convictions upon it will be in a much better position to deal with the shifts and surprises of daily affairs than those who are merely taking short views, and indulging their natural impulses as they are evoked by what they read from day to day. The first thing is to decide where you want to go. For myself, I am for the armed League of all Nations, or as many as you can get, against the potential aggressor, with England and France as the core of it. Let us neglect nothing in our power to establish the great international framework. If that should prove to be beyond our strength, or if it breaks down through the weakness or wrongdoing of others, then at least let us make sure that England and France, the two surviving free great countries of Europe, can together ride out any storm that may blow with good and reasonable hopes of once again coming safely into port."

If we add the United States to Britain and France; if we change the name of the potential aggressor; if we substitute the United Nations Organisation for the League of Nations, the Atlantic Ocean for the English Channel, and the world for Europe, the argument is not necessarily without its application to-day.

★   ★   ★

Two whole years passed between Hitler's seizure of the Rhineland in March 1936 and his rape of Austria in March 1938. This was a longer interval than I had expected. Everything happened in the order foreseen and stated, but the spacing between the successive blows was longer. During this period no time was wasted by Germany. The fortification of the Rhineland, or "the West Wall", proceeded apace, and an immense line of permanent and semi-permanent fortifications grew continually. The German Army, now on the full methodical basis of compulsory service and reinforced by ardent volunteering, grew stronger month by month, both in numbers and in the maturity and quality of its formations. The German Air Force held and steadily improved the lead it had obtained over Great Britain. The German munitions plants were working at high pressure. The wheels revolved and the hammers descended day and night in Germany, making its whole industry an arsenal, and welding all its population into one disciplined war machine. At home in the autumn of 1936 Hitler inaugurated a Four Years' Plan to reorganise German economy for greater self-sufficiency in war. Abroad he obtained that "strong alliance" which he had stated in *Mein Kampf* would be necessary for Germany's foreign policy. He came to terms with Mussolini, and the Rome-Berlin Axis was formed.

Up till the middle of 1936 Hitler's aggressive policy and treaty-breaking had rested, not upon Germany's strength, but upon the disunion and timidity of France and Britain and the isolation of the United States. Each of his preliminary steps had been gambles in which he knew he could not afford to be seriously challenged. The seizure of the Rhineland and its subsequent fortification was the greatest gamble of all. It had succeeded brilliantly. His opponents were too irresolute to call his bluff. When next he moved in 1938 his bluff was bluff no more. Aggression was backed by force, and it might well be by superior force. When the Governments of France and Britain realised the terrible transformation which had taken place it was too late.

★   ★   ★

I continued to give the closest attention to our military preparations. My relations with Sir Thomas Inskip, Minister for Co-ordination of Defence, were friendly, and I did my best to help him privately. At his request I wrote and sent him a memorandum about the much-needed Ministry of Supply, which is dated June 6, 1936. See Appendix C. No effective action was however taken to create a Ministry of Supply until the spring of 1939, nearly three years later, nor was any attempt made to introduce emergency conditions into our munitions production.

★   ★   ★

At the end of July 1936 the increasing degeneration of the Parliamentary *régime* in Spain, and the growing strength of the movements for a Communist, or alternatively an anarchist revolution, led to a military revolt which had long been preparing. It is part of the Communist doctrine and drill-book, laid down by Lenin himself, that Communists should aid all movements towards the Left and help into office weak Constitutional, Radical, or Socialist Governments. These they should undermine, and from their falling hands snatch absolute power, and found the Marxist State. In fact, a perfect reproduction of the Kerensky period in Russia was taking place in Spain. But the strength of Spain had not been shattered by foreign war. The Army still maintained a measure of cohesion. Side by side with the Communist conspiracy there was elaborated in secret a deep military counterplot. Neither side could claim with justice the title-deeds of legality, and Spaniards of all classes were bound to consider the life of Spain.

Many of the ordinary guarantees of civilised society had been already liquidated by the Communist pervasion of the decayed Parliamentary Government. Murders began on both sides, and the Communist pestilence had reached a point where it could take political opponents in the streets or from their beds and kill them.

191

Already a large number of these assassinations had taken place in and around Madrid. The climax was the murder of Señor Sotelo, the Conservative leader, who corresponded somewhat to the type of Sir Edward Carson in British politics before the 1914 war. This crime was the signal for the generals of the Army to act. General Franco had a month before written a letter to the Spanish War Minister, making it clear that if the Spanish Government could not maintain the normal securities of law in daily life the Army would have to intervene. Spain had seen many *pronunciamientos* by military chiefs in the past. When, after General Sanjurjo had perished in an air crash, General Franco raised the standard of revolt, he was supported by the Army, including the rank and file. The Church, with the noteworthy exception of the Dominicans, and nearly all the elements of the Right and Centre adhered to him, and he became immediately the master of several important provinces. The Spanish sailors killed their officers and joined what soon became the Communist side. In the collapse of civilised government the Communist sect obtained control, and acted in accordance with their drill. Bitter civil war now began. Wholesale cold-blooded massacres of their political opponents, and of the well-to-do, were perpetrated by the Communists who had seized power. These were repaid with interest by the forces under Franco. All Spaniards went to their deaths with remarkable composure, and great numbers on both sides were shot. The military cadets defended their college at the Alcazar in Toledo with the utmost tenacity, and Franco's troops, forcing their way up from the south, leaving a trail of vengeance behind them in every Communist village, presently achieved their relief. This episode deserves the notice of historians.

In this quarrel I was neutral. Naturally I was not in favour of the Communists. How could I be, when if I had been a Spaniard they would have murdered me and my family and friends? I was sure however that with all the rest they had on their hands the British Government were right to keep out of Spain. France proposed a plan of Non-Intervention, whereby both sides would be left to fight it out without any external aid. The British, German, Italian, and Russian Governments subscribed to this. In consequence the Spanish Government, now in the hands of the most extreme revolutionaries, found itself deprived of the right even to buy the arms ordered with the gold it physically possessed. It would have been more reasonable to follow the normal course and to have recognised the belligerency of both sides, as was done in the American Civil War of 1861–65. Instead, however, the policy of Non-Intervention was adopted and formally agreed to by all the Great Powers. This agreement was strictly observed by Great Britain; but Italy and Germany on the one side, and Soviet Russia on the other, broke their engagement constantly and threw their weight into the struggle one against the other. Germany in particular used her air-power to commit such experimental horrors as the bombing of the defenceless little township of Guernica.

The Government of M. Léon Blum, which had succeeded the Ministry of M. Albert Sarraut on June 4, was under pressure from its Communist supporters in the Chamber to support the Spanish Government with war material. The Air Minister, M. Cot, without too much regard for the strength of the French Air Force, then in a state of decay, was secretly delivering planes and equipment to the Republican armies. I was perturbed at such developments, and on July 31, 1936, I wrote to M. Corbin, the French Ambassador:

One of the greatest difficulties I meet with in trying to hold on to the old position is the German talk that the anti-Communist countries should stand together. I am sure if France sent aeroplanes, etc., to the present Madrid Government, and the Germans and Italians pushed in from the other angle, the dominant forces here would be pleased with Germany and Italy, and estranged from France. I hope you will not mind my writing this, which I do of course entirely on my own account. I do not like to hear people talking of England, Germany, and Italy forming up against European Communism. It is too easy to be good.

I am sure that an absolutely rigid neutrality, with the strongest protest against any breach of it, is the only correct and safe course at the present time. A day may come, if there is a stalemate, when the League of Nations may intervene to wind up the horrors. But even that is very doubtful.

* * *

There is another event which must be recorded here. On November 25, 1936, the Ambassadors of all the Powers represented in Berlin were summoned to the Foreign Office, where Herr von Neurath disclosed the details of the Anti-Comintern

Pact, which had been negotiated with the Japanese Government. The purpose of the pact was to take common action against the international activities of the Comintern, either within the boundaries of the contracting States or beyond them.

* * *

During the whole of 1936 the anxiety of the nation and Parliament continued to mount, and was concentrated in particular upon our air defences. In the Debate on the Address on November 12 I severely reproached Mr. Baldwin for having failed to keep his pledge that "any Government of this country—a National Government more than any, and this Government—will see to it that in air strength and air power this country shall no longer be in a position inferior to any country within striking distance of its shores". I said: "The Government simply cannot make up their minds, or they cannot get the Prime Minister to make up his mind. So they go on in strange paradox, decided only to be undecided, resolved to be irresolute, adamant for drift, solid for fluidity, all-powerful to be impotent. So we go on preparing more months and years—precious, perhaps vital, to the greatness of Britain—for the locusts to eat."

Mr. Baldwin replied to me in a remarkable speech, in which he said:

I want to speak to the House with the utmost frankness. . . . The difference of opinion between Mr. Churchill and myself is in the years 1933 onwards. In 1931-32, although it is not admitted by the Opposition, there was a period of financial crisis. But there was another reason. I would remind the House that not once but on many occasions in speeches and in various places, when I have been speaking and advocating as far as I am able the democratic principle, I have stated that *a democracy is always two years behind the dictator*. I believe that to be true. It has been true in this case. I put before the whole House my own views with an appalling frankness. You will remember at that time the Disarmament Conference was sitting in Geneva. You will remember at that time there was probably a stronger pacifist feeling running through this country than at any time since the war. You will remember *the election at Fulham in the autumn of 1933, when a seat which the National Government held was lost by about 7,000 votes on no issue but the pacifist*. . . . My position as the leader of a great party was not altogether a comfortable one. I asked myself what chance was there—when that feeling that was given expression to in Fulham was common throughout the country—what chance was there within the next year or two of that feeling being so changed that the country would give a mandate for rearmament? Supposing I had gone to the country and said that Germany was rearming, and that we must rearm, does anybody think that this pacific democracy would have rallied to that cry at that moment? *I cannot think of anything that would have made the loss of the election from my point of view more certain.*

This was indeed appalling frankness. It carried naked truth about his motives into indecency. That a Prime Minister should avow that he had not done his duty in regard to national safety because he was afraid of losing the election was an incident without parallel in our Parliamentary history. Mr. Baldwin was of course not moved by any ignoble wish to remain in office. He was in fact in 1936 earnestly desirous of retiring. His policy was dictated by the fear that if the Socialists came into power even less would be done than his Government intended. All their declarations and votes against defence measures are upon record. But this was no complete defence, and less than justice to the spirit of the British people. The success which had attended the naïve confession of miscalculation in air parity the previous year was not repeated on this occasion. The House was shocked. Indeed, the impression produced was so painful that it might well have been fatal to Mr. Baldwin, who was also at that time in failing health, had not the unexpected intervened.

*   *   *

At this time there was a great drawing together of men and women of all parties in England who saw the perils of the future, and were resolute upon practical measures to secure our safety and the cause of freedom, equally menaced by both the totalitarian impulsions and our Government's complacency. Our plan was the most rapid large-scale rearmament of Britain, combined with the complete acceptance and employment of the authority of the League of Nations. I called this policy "Arms and the Covenant". Mr. Baldwin's performance in the House of Commons was viewed among us all with disdain. The culmination of this campaign was to be a meeting at the Albert Hall. Here on December 3 we gathered many of the leading men in all the parties—strong Tories of the Right Wing earnestly convinced of the national peril; the leaders of the League of Nations Peace

Ballot; the representatives of many great trade unions, including in the chair my old opponent of the General Strike, Sir Walter Citrine; the Liberal Party and its leader, Sir Archibald Sinclair. We had the feeling that we were upon the threshold of not only gaining respect for our views, but of making them dominant. It was at this moment that the King's passion to marry the woman he loved caused the casting of all else into the background. The Abdication crisis was at hand.

Before I replied to the Vote of Thanks there was a cry, "God Save the King," and this excited prolonged cheering. I explained therefore on the spur of the moment my personal position.

There is another grave matter which overshadows our minds to-night. In a few minutes we are going to sing "God Save the King". I shall sing it with more heartfelt fervour than I have ever sung it in my life. I hope and pray that no irrevocable decision will be taken in haste, but that time and public opinion will be allowed to play their part, and that a cherished and unique personality may not be incontinently severed from the people he loves so well. I hope that Parliament will be allowed to discharge its function in these high constitutional questions. I trust that our King may be guided by the opinions that are now for the first time being expressed by the British nation and the British Empire, and that the British people will not in their turn be found wanting in generous consideration for the occupant of the Throne.

It is not relevant to this account to describe the brief but intensely violent controversy that followed. I had known King Edward VIII since he was a child, and had in 1910 as Home Secretary read out to a wonderful assembly the Proclamation creating him Prince of Wales at Carnarvon Castle. I felt bound to place my personal loyalty to him upon the highest plane. Although during the summer I had been made fully aware of what was going forward, I in no way interfered or communicated with him at any time. However, presently in his distress he asked the Prime Minister for permission to consult me. Mr. Baldwin gave formal consent, and on this being conveyed to me I went to the King at Fort Belvedere. I remained in contact with him till his abdication, and did my utmost to plead both to the King and to the public for patience and delay. I have never repented of this—indeed, I could do no other.

The Prime Minister proved himself to be a shrewd judge of

British national feeling. Undoubtedly he perceived and expressed the profound will of the nation. His deft and skilful handling of the Abdication issue raised him in a fortnight from the depths to the pinnacle. There were several moments when I seemed to be entirely alone against a wrathful House of Commons. I am not, when in action, unduly affected by hostile currents of feeling; but it was on more than one occasion almost physically impossible to make myself heard. All the forces I had gathered together on "Arms and the Covenant", of which I conceived myself to be the mainspring, were estranged or dissolved, and I was myself so smitten in public opinion that it was the almost universal view that my political life was at last ended. How strange it is that this very House of Commons which had regarded me with so much hostility should have been the same instrument which hearkened to my guidance and upheld me through the long adverse years of war till victory over all our foes was gained! What a proof is here offered that the only wise and safe course is to act from day to day in accordance with what one's own conscience seems to decree!

From the Abdication of one King we passed to the Coronation of another, and until the end of May 1937 the ceremonial and pageantry of a solemn national act of allegiance and the consecration of British loyalties at home and throughout the Empire to the new Sovereign filled all minds. Foreign affairs and the state of our defences lost all claim upon the public mood. Our Island might have been ten thousand miles away from Europe. However, I am permitted to record that on May 18, 1937, on the morrow of the Coronation, I received from the new King, His present Majesty, a letter in his own handwriting:

THE ROYAL LODGE,
THE GREAT PARK,
WINDSOR, BERKS.
18.V.37

My dear Mr. Churchill,
I am writing to thank you for your very nice letter to me. I know how devoted you have been, and still are, to my dear brother, and I feel touched beyond words by your sympathy and understanding in the very difficult problems that have arisen since he left us in December. I fully realise the great responsibilities and cares that I have taken on as King, and I feel most encouraged to receive your good wishes, as

one of our great statesmen, and from one who has served his country so faithfully. I can only hope and trust that the good feeling and hope that exists in the Country and Empire now will prove a good example to other Nations in the world.

Believe me,

Yours very sincerely,

GEORGE R.I.

This gesture of magnanimity towards one whose influence at that time had fallen to zero will ever be a cherished experience in my life.

★　　★　　★

On May 28, 1937, after King George VI had been crowned, Mr. Baldwin retired. His long public services were suitably rewarded by an Earldom and the Garter. He laid down the wide authority he had gathered and carefully maintained, but had used as little as possible. He departed in a glow of public gratitude and esteem. There was no doubt who his successor should be. Mr. Neville Chamberlain had, as Chancellor of the Exchequer, not only done the main work of the Government for five years past, but was the ablest and most forceful Minister, with high abilities and an historic name. I had described him a year earlier at Birmingham in Shakespeare's words as the "packhorse in our great affairs", and he had accepted this description as a compliment. I had no expectation that he would wish to work with me, nor would he have been wise to do so at such a time. His ideas were far different from mine on the treatment of the dominant issues of the day. But I welcomed the accession to power of a live, competent, executive figure. While still Chancellor of the Exchequer he had involved himself in a fiscal proposal for a small-scale national defence contribution which had been ill-received by the Conservative Party and was of course criticised by the Opposition. I was able, in the first days of his Premiership, to make a speech upon this subject which helped him to withdraw, without any loss of dignity, from a position which had become untenable. Our relations continued to be cool, easy, and polite both in public and in private.

Mr. Chamberlain made few changes in the Government. He had had disagreements with Mr. Duff Cooper about War Office administration, and much surprised him by offering him advancement to the great key office of the Admiralty. The Prime

198

Minister evidently did not know the eyes through which his new First Lord, whose early career had been in the Foreign Office, viewed the European scene. In my turn I was astonished that Sir Samuel Hoare, who had just secured a large expansion of the naval programme, should wish to leave the Admiralty for the Home Office. Hoare seems to have believed that prison reform in a broad humanitarian sense would become the prevailing topic in the immediate future; and since his family was connected with the famous Elizabeth Fry, he had a strong personal sentiment about it.

* * *

I may here set down a comparative appreciation of these two Prime Ministers, Baldwin and Chamberlain, whom I had known so long and under whom I had served or was to serve. Stanley Baldwin was the wiser, more comprehending personality, but without detailed executive capacity. He was largely detached from foreign and military affairs. He knew little of Europe, and disliked what he knew. He had a deep knowledge of British party politics, and represented in a broad way some of the strengths and many of the infirmities of our Island race. He had fought five General Elections as leader of the Conservative Party and had won three of them. He had a genius for waiting upon events and an imperturbability under adverse criticism. He was singularly adroit in letting events work for him, and capable of seizing the ripe moment when it came. He seemed to me to revive the impressions history gives us of Sir Robert Walpole, without of course the eighteenth-century corruption, and he was master of British politics for nearly as long.

Neville Chamberlain, on the other hand, was alert, businesslike, opinionated and self-confident in a very high degree. Unlike Baldwin, he conceived himself able to comprehend the whole field of Europe, and indeed the world. Instead of a vague but none the less deep-seated intuition, we had now a narrow, sharp-edged efficiency within the limits of the policy in which he believed. Both as Chancellor of the Exchequer and as Prime Minister he kept the tightest and most rigid control upon military expenditure. He was throughout this period the masterful opponent of all emergency measures. He had formed decided judgments about all the political figures of the day, both at home and abroad, and felt himself capable of dealing with them. His all-pervading hope was to go down to history as the great Peace-maker, and for this he was prepared to strive continually in the teeth of facts, and face great risks for himself and his country. Unhappily he ran into tides the force of which he could not measure, and met hurricanes from which he did not flinch, but with which he could not cope. In these closing years before the war I should have found it easier to work with Baldwin, as I knew him, than with Chamberlain; but neither of them had any wish to work with me except in the last resort.

★   ★   ★

One day in 1937 I had a meeting with Herr von Ribbentrop, German Ambassador to Britain. In one of my fortnightly articles I had noted that he had been misrepresented in some speech he had made. I had of course met him several times in society. He now asked me whether I would come to see him and have a talk. He received me in the large upstairs room at the German Embassy. We had a conversation lasting for more than two hours. Ribbentrop was most polite, and we ranged over the European scene, both in respect of armaments and policy. The gist of his statement to me was that Germany sought the friendship of England (on the Continent we are still often called "England"). He said he could have been Foreign Minister of Germany, but he had asked Hitler to let him come over to London in order to make the full case for an Anglo-German entente or even alliance. Germany would stand guard for the British Empire in all its greatness and extent. They might ask for the return of the German colonies, but this was evidently not cardinal. What was required was that Britain should give Germany a free hand in the East of Europe. She must have her Lebensraum, or living-space, for her increasing population. Therefore Poland and the Danzig Corridor must be absorbed. White Russia and the Ukraine were indispensable to the future life of the German Reich of some seventy million souls. Nothing less would suffice. All that was asked of the British Commonwealth and Empire was not to interfere. There was a large map on the wall, and the Ambassador several times led me to it to illustrate his projects.

After hearing all this I said at once that I was sure the British Government would not agree to give Germany a free hand in Eastern Europe. It was true we were on bad terms with Soviet

Russia and that we hated Communism as much as Hitler did, but he might be sure that even if France were safeguarded Great Britain would never disinterest herself in the fortunes of the Continent to an extent which would enable Germany to gain the domination of Central and Eastern Europe. We were actually standing before the map when I said this. Ribbentrop turned abruptly away. He then said, "In that case, war is inevitable. There is no way out. The Fuehrer is resolved. Nothing will stop him and nothing will stop us." We then returned to our chairs. I was only a private Member of Parliament, but of some prominence. I thought it right to say to the German Ambassador —in fact, I remember the words well, "When you talk of war, which no doubt would be general war, you must not underrate England. She is a curious country, and few foreigners can understand her mind. Do not judge by the attitude of the present Administration. Once a great cause is presented to the people all kinds of unexpected actions might be taken by this very Government and by the British nation." And I repeated, "Do not underrate England. She is very clever. If you plunge us all into another Great War she will bring the whole world against you, like last time." At this the Ambassador rose in heat and said, "Ah, England may be very clever, but this time she will not bring the world against Germany." We turned the conversation on to easier lines, and nothing more of note occurred. The incident however remains in my memory, and as I reported it at the time to the Foreign Office I feel it right to put it on record.

When he was on his trial for his life by the conquerors Ribbentrop gave a distorted version of this conversation and claimed that I should be summoned as a witness. What I have set down about it is what I should have said had I been called.

CHAPTER XIII

GERMANY ARMED

1936-1938

*The "Overall Strategic Objective" – German Expenditure on Arma-
ments – Independent Inquiries – The Conservative Deputation to the
Prime Minister, July 28, 1936 – My Statement of the Case – General
Conclusions – My Fear – Our Second Meeting, November 23, 1936 –
Lord Swinton Leaves the Air Ministry, May 12, 1938 – Debate in
Parliament – Lindemann Rejoins the Air Defence Research Com-
mittee – My Correspondence with M. Daladier – The French Estimate
of German Air Strength, 1938 – My Estimate of the German Army,
June 1938 – M. Daladier Concurs – The Decay of the French Air
Force – The Careless Islanders.*

ADVANTAGE is gained in war and also in foreign policy
and other things by selecting from many attractive or
unpleasant alternatives the dominating point. American
military thought has coined the expression "Overall Strategic
Objective". When our officers first heard this they laughed; but
later on its wisdom became apparent and accepted. Evidently
this should be the rule, and other great business be set in subordinate relationship to it. Failure to adhere to this simple principle
produces confusion and futility of action, and nearly always makes
things much worse later on.

Personally I had no difficulty in conforming to the rule long
before I heard it proclaimed. My mind was obsessed by the
impression of the terrific Germany I had seen and felt in action
during the years of 1914 to 1918 suddenly becoming again possessed of all her martial power, while the Allies, who had so
narrowly survived, gaped idle and bewildered. Therefore I continued by every means and on every occasion to use what in-

fluence I had with the House of Commons and also with individual Ministers to urge forward our military preparations and to procure Allies and associates for what would before long become again the Common Cause.

One day a friend of mine in a high confidential position under the Government came over to Chartwell to swim with me in my pool when the sun shone bright and the water was fairly warm. We talked of nothing but the coming war, of the certainty of which he was not entirely convinced. As I saw him off he suddenly on an impulse turned and said to me, "The Germans are spending a thousand million pounds sterling a year on their armaments." I thought Parliament and the British public ought to know the facts. I therefore set to work to examine German finance. Budgets were produced and still published every year in Germany; but from their wealth of figures it was very difficult to tell what was happening. However, in April 1936 I privately instituted two separate lines of scrutiny. The first rested upon two German refugees of high ability and inflexible purpose. They understood all the details of the presentation of German budgets, the value of the mark, and so forth. At the same time I asked my friend Sir Henry Strakosch whether he could not find out what was actually happening. Strakosch was the head of the firm called Union Corporation, with great resources, and a highly-skilled, devoted personnel. The brains of this City company were turned for several weeks on to the problem. Presently they reported with precise and lengthy detail that the German war expenditure was certainly round about a thousand million pounds sterling a year. At the same time the German refugees, by a totally different series of arguments, arrived independently at the same conclusion. One thousand million pounds sterling per annum at the money values of 1936!

I had therefore two separate structures of fact on which to base a public assertion. So I accosted Mr. Neville Chamberlain, still Chancellor of the Exchequer, in the Lobby the day before a debate and said to him, "To-morrow I shall ask you whether it is not a fact that the Germans are spending a thousand million pounds a year on warlike preparations, and I shall ask you to confirm or deny." Chamberlain said, "I cannot deny it, and if you put the point I shall confirm it." I must quote my words:

Taking the figures from German official sources, the expenditure on capital account from the end of March 1933 to the end of June 1935 has been as follows: in 1933 nearly five milliards of marks; in 1934 nearly eight milliards; and in 1935 nearly eleven milliards—a total of twenty-four milliards, or roughly £2,000,000,000. Look at these figures, 5, 8, and 11 for the three years. They give you exactly the kind of progression which a properly-developing munitions industry would make.

Specifically I asked the Chancellor:

Whether he is aware that the expenditure by Germany upon purposes directly and indirectly concerned with military preparations, including strategic roads, may well have amounted to the equivalent of £800 millions during the calendar year 1935; and whether this rate of expenditure seems to be continuing in the current calendar year.

Mr. Chamberlain: The Government have no official figures, but from such information as they have I see no reason to think that the figure mentioned in my right hon. friend's question is necessarily excessive as applied to either year, although, as he himself would agree, there are elements of conjecture.

I substituted the figure of £800 millions for £1,000 millions to cover my secret information, and also to be on the safe side.

* * *

I sought by several means to bring the relative state of British and German armaments to a clear-cut issue. I asked for a debate in Secret Session. This was refused. "It would cause needless alarm." I got little support. All Secret Sessions are unpopular with the Press. Then on July 20, 1936, I asked the Prime Minister whether he would receive a deputation of Privy Councillors and a few others who would lay before him the facts so far as they knew them. Lord Salisbury requested that a similar deputation from the House of Lords should also come. This was agreed. Although I made personal appeals both to Mr. Attlee and Sir Archibald Sinclair, the Labour and Liberal Parties declined to be represented. Accordingly, on July 28 we were received in the Prime Minister's House of Commons room by Mr. Baldwin, Lord Halifax, and Sir Thomas Inskip. The following Conservative and non-party notables came with me. Sir Austen Chamberlain introduced us.

The Deputation

House of Commons	*House of Lords*
Sir Austen Chamberlain.	The Marquess of Salisbury.
Mr. Churchill.	Viscount Fitzalan.
Sir Robert Horne.	Viscount Trenchard.
Mr. Amery.	Lord Lloyd.
Sir John Gilmour.	Lord Milne.
Captain Guest.	
Admiral Sir Roger Keyes.	
Earl Winterton.	
Sir Henry Croft.	
Sir Edward Grigg.	
Viscount Wolmer.	
Lieut.-Col. Moore-Brabazon.	
Sir Hugh O'Neill.	

This was a great occasion. I cannot recall anything like it in what I have seen of British public life. The group of eminent men, with no thought of personal advantage, but whose lives had been centred upon public affairs, represented a weight of Conservative opinion which could not easily be disregarded. If the leaders of the Labour and Liberal Oppositions had come with us there might have been a political situation so tense as to enforce remedial action. The proceedings occupied three or four hours on each of two successive days. I have always said Mr. Baldwin was a good listener. He certainly seemed to listen with the greatest interest and attention. With him were various members of the staff of the Committee of Imperial Defence. On the first day I opened the case in a statement of an hour and a quarter, of which some extracts, given in Appendix D, throw a true light on the scene.

I ended as follows:

First, we are facing the greatest danger and emergency of our history. Second, we have no hope of solving our problem except in conjunction with the French Republic. The union of the British Fleet and the French Army, together with their combined Air Forces operating from close behind the French and Belgian frontiers, together with all that Britain and France stand for, constitutes a deterrent in which salvation may reside. Anyhow it is the best hope. Coming down to detail, we must lay aside every impediment in raising our own strength. We cannot possibly provide against all possible dangers.

We must concentrate upon what is vital and take our punishment elsewhere. Coming to still more definite propositions, we must increase the development of our air-power in priority over every other consideration. At all costs we must draw the flower of our youth into piloting aeroplanes. Never mind what inducements must be offered; we must draw from every source, by every means. We must accelerate and simplify our aeroplane production and push it to the largest scale, and not hesitate to make contracts with the United States and elsewhere for the largest possible quantities of aviation material and equipment of all kinds. We are in danger, as we have never been in danger before—no, not even at the height of the submarine campaign [1917].

This thought preys upon me: *The months slip by rapidly. If we delay too long in repairing our defences we may be forbidden by superior power to complete the process.*

★ ★ ★

We were much disappointed that the Chancellor of the Exchequer could not be present. It was evident that Mr. Baldwin's health was failing, and it was well known that he would soon seek rest from his burdens. There could be no doubt who would be his successor. Unhappily, Mr. Neville Chamberlain was absent upon a well-deserved holiday, and did not have the opportunity of this direct confrontation with the facts from members of the Conservative Party, who included his brother and so many of his most valued personal friends.

Most earnest consideration was given by Ministers to our formidable representations, but it was not till after the Recess, on November 23, 1936, that we were all invited by Mr. Baldwin to receive a more fully considered statement on the whole position. Sir Thomas Inskip then gave a frank and able account, in which he did not conceal from us the gravity of the plight into which we had come. In substance this was to the effect that our estimates, and in particular my statements, took a too gloomy view of our prospects; that great efforts were being made (as indeed they were) to recover the lost ground; but that no case existed which would justify the Government in adopting emergency measures; that these would necessarily be of a character to upset the whole industrial life of this country, would cause widespread alarm, and advertise any deficiencies that existed, and that within these limits everything possible was being done. On this Sir Austen Chamberlain recorded our general impression that our anxieties were not relieved and that we were by no means satisfied. Thus we took our leave.

I cannot contend that at this date, the end of 1936, the position could have been retrieved. Much more however could and ought to have been done by an intense convulsive effort. And of course the fact and proof of this effort must have had its immeasurable effect on Germany, if not on Hitler. But the paramount fact remained that the Germans had the lead of us in the air, and also over the whole field of munitions production, even making allowance for our smaller military needs, and for the fact that we had a right also to count upon France and the French Army and Air Force. It was no longer in our power to forestall Hitler or to regain air parity. Nothing could now prevent the German Army and the German Air Force from becoming the strongest in Europe. By extraordinary and disturbing exertions we could improve our position. We could not cure it.

These sombre conclusions, which were not seriously disputed by the Government, no doubt influenced their foreign policy; and full account must be taken of them when we try to form a judgment upon the decision which Mr. Chamberlain, when he became Prime Minister, took before and during the Munich crisis. I was at this time only a private Member of Parliament, and I bore no official responsibility. I strove my utmost to galvanise the Government into vehemence and extraordinary preparation, even at the cost of world alarm. In these endeavours no doubt I painted the picture even darker than it was. The emphasis which I had put upon the two years' lag which afflicted us may well be judged inconsistent with my desire to come to grips with Hitler in October 1938. I remain convinced however that it was right to spur the Government by every means, and that it would have been better in all the circumstances, which will presently be described, to fight Hitler in 1938 than it was when we finally had to do so in September 1939. Of this more later.

★   ★   ★

Presently Mr. Baldwin, as we have seen, gave place to Mr. Neville Chamberlain; and we must now move on to 1938. Lord Swinton was a very keen and efficient Air Minister, and for a long time had great influence in the Cabinet in procuring the necessary facilities and funds. The anxiety about our air defences continued to grow, and reached its climax in May. The many great and valuable expansions and improvements which Lord Swinton had made could not become apparent quickly, and in any case the whole policy of the Government lacked both magnitude and urgency. I continued to press for an inquiry into the state of our air programme, and found increasing support. Swinton had made the mistake of accepting a peerage. He was not therefore able to defend himself and his department in the House of Commons. The spokesman who was chosen from the Government Front Bench was utterly unable to stem the rising tide of alarm and dissatisfaction. After one most unfortunate debate it became obvious that the Air Minister should be in the House of Commons.

One morning (May 12) at the Air Defence Research Committee we were all busily engaged—scientists, politicians, and officials—on technical problems, when a note was brought in to the Air Minister asking him to go to Downing Street. He desired us to continue our discussions, and left at once. He never returned. He had been dismissed by Mr. Chamberlain.

In the agitated debate which followed on the 25th I tried to distinguish between the exertions and capacity of the fallen Minister and the general complaint against the Government:

The credit of Government statements has been compromised by what has occurred. The House has been consistently misled about the air position. The Prime Minister himself has been misled. He was misled right up to the last moment, apparently. Look at the statement which he made in March, when he spoke about our armaments:

"The sight of this enormous, this almost terrifying, power which Britain is building up has a sobering effect, a steadying effect, on the opinion of the world."

I have often warned the House that the air programmes were falling into arrear. But I have never attacked Lord Swinton. I have never thought that he was the one to blame—certainly not the only one to blame. It is usual for the critics of a Government to discover hitherto unnoticed virtues in any Minister who is forced to resign. But perhaps I may quote what I said three months ago: "It would be unfair to throw the blame on any one Minister, or upon Lord Swinton, for our deficiency. He certainly represents an extremely able and whole-hearted effort to do the best he possibly could to expand our air-power, and the results which he achieved would be bright if they were not darkened by the time-table, and if they were not outshone by other relative facts occurring elsewhere." . . .

The hard responsibility for the failure to fulfil the promises made to us rests upon those who have governed and guided this Island for the last five years, that is to say, from the date when German rearmament in real earnest became apparent and known. I certainly did not attempt to join in a man-hunt of Lord Swinton. I was very glad to-day to hear the Prime Minister's tribute to him. Certainly he deserves our sympathy. He had the confidence and friendship of the Prime Minister, he had the support of an enormous Parliamentary majority; yet he has been taken from his post at what, I think, is the worst moment in the story of air expansion. It may be that in a few months there will be a considerable flow of aircraft arriving; yet he has had to answer for his record at this particularly dark moment for him. I was reading the other day a letter of the great Duke of Marlborough, in which he said: "To remove a General in the midst of a campaign—that is the mortal stroke."

I turned to other aspects of our defences:

We are now in the third year of openly avowed rearmament. Why is it, if all is going well, there are so many deficiencies? Why, for instance, are the Guards drilling with flags instead of machine-guns? Why is it that our small Territorial Army is in a rudimentary condition? Is that all according to schedule? Why, when you consider how small are our forces, should it be impossible to equip the Territorial Army simultaneously with the Regular Army? It would have been a paltry task for British industry, which is more flexible and more fertile than German industry in every sphere except munitions. . . .

The other day the Secretary of State for War was asked about the anti-aircraft artillery. The old 3-inch guns of the Great War, he said, had been modernised, and deliveries of the newer guns—and there is more than one type of newer gun—were proceeding "in advance of schedule". But what is the schedule? If your schedule prescribes a delivery of half a dozen, ten, a dozen, twenty, or whatever it may be, guns per month, no doubt that may easily be up to schedule, and easily be in advance of it. But what is the adequacy of such a schedule to our needs? A year ago I reminded the House of the published progress of Germany in anti-aircraft artillery—thirty regiments of twelve batteries each of mobile artillery alone, aggregating something between twelve and thirteen hundred guns, in addition to three or four thousand guns in fixed positions. These are all modern guns, not guns of 1915, but all guns made since the year 1933.

Does not that give the House an idea of the tremendous scale of these transactions? We do not need to have a gigantic army like Continental countries; but in the matter of anti-aircraft defence we are on equal terms. We are just as vulnerable, and perhaps more vulnerable. Here is the Government thinking of anti-aircraft artillery in terms of hundreds where the Germans have it to-day in terms of thousands. . . .

We are thinking at the present time in terms of production for three separate armed forces. In fact and in truth, the supply of arms for all fighting forces resolves itself into a common problem of the provision and distribution of skilled labour, raw materials, plant, machinery, and technical appliances. That problem can only be dealt with comprehensively, harmoniously, and economically through one central dominating control. At the present time there is inefficiency and over-lapping, and there is certainly waste. Why is it that this skilful aircraft industry of Britain requires ninety thousand men, and that it produces only one-half to one-third of what is being produced by about one hundred and ten thousand men in Germany? Is that not an extra-ordinary fact? It is incredible that we have not been able to produce a greater supply of aeroplanes at this time. Given a plain office table, an empty field, money, and labour, we should receive a flow of aero-planes by eighteen months; yet this is the thirty-fourth month since Lord Baldwin decided that the Air Force must be tripled.

*　　*　　*

The new Secretary of State for Air, Sir Kingsley Wood, invited me to remain on the Air Defence Research Committee. The skies had now grown much darker, and I felt keenly the need of Lindemann's interpretation of the technical aspects and of his advice and aid. I therefore wrote to him saying that unless he was associated with me I would not continue. After some tussling behind the scenes Lindemann was placed on the main Committee, and we resumed our joint work.

*　　*　　*

Always, up till the armistice of June 1940, whether in peace or war, in a private station or as head of the Government, I enjoyed confidential relations with the often-changing Premiers of the French Republic and with many of its leading Ministers. I was most anxious to find out the truth about German rearmament and to cross-check my own calculations by theirs.

I therefore wrote to M. Daladier, with whom I was personally acquainted.

Mr. Churchill to M. Daladier   *May* 3, 1938
  Your predecessors, MM. Blum and Flandin, were both kind enough
to give me the French estimates of the German air strength at particular
periods in recent years. I should be much obliged if you could let me
know what your view is now. I have several sources of information
which have proved accurate in the past, but am anxious to have a
cross-check from an independent source.
  I am so glad that your visit here was so successful, and I hope now
that all those staff arrangements will be made, the need for which I
have pressed upon our Ministers.

  In response M. Daladier sent me a document of seventeen pages
dated May 11, 1938, which "had been deeply thought out by
the French Air Staff". I showed this important paper to my
friends in the British department concerned, who examined it
searchingly and reported that "it agreed in every essential with
the independent opinions formed by the British Air Staff on the
basis of their own information". The French estimate of the size
of the German Air Force was slightly higher than the British.
Early in June I was in a position to write to M. Daladier with a
considerable amount of authoritative opinion behind me.

Mr. Churchill to M. Daladier   *June* 6, 1938
  I am very much obliged to you for the invaluable information which
I have received through the French Military Attaché. You may be
sure I shall use it only with the greatest discretion, and in our common
interests.
  The general estimate of the German Air Force at the present time
agrees with the private views I have been able to form. I am inclined
to think however that the German aircraft industry is turning out aircraft at a somewhat higher rate than is allowed, and that the figure
given is that for the actual deliveries of aircraft of military types to
the German Air Force, excluding deliveries for export, and to General
Franco. It is probable that the German Air Force will consist of three
hundred squadrons by April 1, 1939, and four hundred squadrons
by April 1, 1940.

  I was also most anxious to cross-check my own estimates of the
German Army with those which I had been able to form from
English sources. Accordingly I added the following:

I venture to enclose a very short note of the information I have been able to gather from various sources about the present and prospective strength of the German Army. It would be a convenience to me to know whether this agrees broadly with your estimates. It would be quite sufficient if the figures, as you understand them, could be pencilled in in any case where you think I am in error.

NOTE

The German Army at this date, June 1, consists of 36 regular divisions, and 4 armoured divisions, the whole at full war-strength. The non-armoured divisions are rapidly acquiring the power to triple themselves, and can at the present time be doubled. The artillery beyond 70 divisions is markedly incomplete. The Officer Corps is thin over the whole force. Nevertheless by October 1, 1938, we cannot expect less than 56 plus 4 armoured, equals 60 fully equipped and armed divisional formations. Behind these will stand a reservoir of trained men equal in man-power to about another 36 divisions, for which skeleton formations have been devised and for which armaments, small arms, and a very low complement of artillery would be available if a lower standard were accepted for part of the active army. This takes no account of the man-power of Austria, which at the extreme computation could provide 12 divisions without arms but ready to draw on the general pool of German munitions industry. In addition there are a number of men and formations of an unbrigaded nature—frontier defence force, Landwehr divisions, and so on, who are relatively unarmed.

On June 18, 1938, M. Daladier wrote:

I am particularly pleased to learn that the information enclosed in my letter of May 16 corresponds to yours.

I am entirely in accord with you in the facts relating to the German Army contained in the note annexed to your letter of June 6. It should be pointed out however that of the 36 ordinary divisions of which Germany actually disposes 4 are entirely motorised and 2 are in the course of becoming so soon.

In fact, according to our post-war information from German sources, this epitome of the German Army in the summer of 1938 was remarkably accurate, considering that it was produced by a private person. It shows that in my long series of campaigns for British rearmament I was by no means ill-informed.

* * *

References have been made at various points in this tale to the French air-power. At one time it was double our own and

Germany was not supposed to have an Air Force at all. Until 1933 France had held a high place among the air fleets of Europe. But in the very year in which Hitler came into power a fateful lack of interest and support began to be displayed. Money was grudged; the productive capacity of the factories was allowed to dwindle; modern types were not developed. The French forty-hour week could not rival the output of a Germany working harsh hours under war-time conditions. All this happened about the same time as the loss of air parity in Britain which has been so fully described. In fact the Western Allies, who had the right to create whatever Air Forces they thought necessary for their safety, neglected this vital weapon, while the Germans, who were prohibited by treaty from touching it, made it the spear-point of their diplomacy and eventual attack.

The French "Popular Front" Government of 1936 and later took many substantial measures to prepare the French Army and Navy for war. No corresponding exertion was made in the air. There is an ugly graph in Appendix E which shows in a decisive fashion the downward streak of French air-power and its inter-section in 1935 by the line of ever-rising German achievement. It was not until January 1938, when M. Guy La Chambre became Air Minister, that vigorous steps were taken to revive the French Air Force. But then only eighteen months remained. Nothing that the French could do could prevent the German Army grow-ing and ripening as each year passed and thus overtaking their own Army. But it is astonishing that their air-power should have been allowed to fall by the wayside. It is not for me to apportion responsibility and blame to the Ministers of friendly and Allied foreign countries, but when in France they are looking out for "guilty men" it would seem that here is a field which might well be searchingly explored.

*   *   *

The spirit of the British nation and of the Parliament they had newly elected gradually rose as consciousness of the German, and soon of the German-Italian, menace slowly and fitfully dawned upon them. They became willing, and even eager, for all kinds of steps which, taken two or three years earlier, would have prevented their troubles. But as their mood improved the power of their opponents and also the difficulty of their task increased.

Many say that nothing except war could have stopped Hitler after we had submitted to the seizure of the Rhineland. This may indeed be the verdict of future generations. Much however could have been done to make us better prepared and thus lessen our hazards. And who shall say what could not have happened?

CHAPTER XIV

MR. EDEN AT THE FOREIGN OFFICE.
HIS RESIGNATION

Foreign Secretary and Prime Minister – Eden and Chamberlain – Sir Robert Vansittart – My Contacts with the Foreign Secretary about Spain – The Nyon Conference – Our Correspondence – A British Success – Divergence between Prime Minister and Foreign Secretary – Lord Halifax Visits Germany and Hitler – I Decline an Invitation – Eden Feels Isolated – President Roosevelt's Overture – The Prime Minister's Reply – The President Rebuffed and Discouraged – Mr. Chamberlain's Grave Responsibility – Final Breach between Eden and Chamberlain about Conversations in Rome – A Sleepless Night at Chartwell.

THE Foreign Secretary has a special position in a British Cabinet. He is treated with marked respect in his high and responsible office, but he usually conducts his affairs under the continuous scrutiny, if not of the whole Cabinet, at least of its principal members. He is under an obligation to keep them informed. He circulates to his colleagues, as a matter of custom and routine, all his executive telegrams, the reports from our Embassies abroad, the records of his interviews with foreign Ambassadors or other notables. At least this has been the case during my experience of Cabinet life. This supervision is of course especially maintained by the Prime Minister, who personally or through his Cabinet is responsible for controlling, and has the power to control, the main course of foreign policy. From him at least there must be no secrets. No Foreign Secretary can do his work unless he is supported constantly by his chief. To make things go smoothly, there must not only be agreement between them on fundamentals, but also a harmony of outlook and even to some extent of temperament. This is all the more important if the Prime Minister himself devotes special attention to foreign affairs.

Eden was the Foreign Secretary of Mr. Baldwin, who, apart from his main well-known desire for peace and a quiet life, took no active share in foreign policy. Mr. Chamberlain, on the other hand, sought to exercise a masterful control in many departments. He had strong views about foreign affairs, and from the beginning asserted his undoubted right to discuss them with foreign Ambassadors. His assumption of the Premiership therefore implied a delicate but perceptible change in the position of the Foreign Secretary.

To this was added a profound, though at first latent, difference of spirit and opinion. The Prime Minister wished to get on good terms with the two European Dictators, and believed that conciliation and the avoidance of anything likely to offend them was the best method. Eden, on the other hand, had won his reputation at Geneva by rallying the nations of Europe against one Dictator; and, left to himself, might well have carried Sanctions to the verge of war, and perhaps beyond. He was a devoted adherent of the French Entente. He had just insisted upon "Staff conversations". He was anxious to have more intimate relations with Soviet Russia. He felt and feared the Hitler peril. He was alarmed by the weakness of our armaments, and its reaction on foreign affairs. It might almost be said that there was not much difference of view between him and me, except of course that he was in harness. It seemed therefore to me from the beginning that differences would be likely to arise between these two leading Ministerial figures as the world situation became more acute.

Moreover, in Lord Halifax the Prime Minister had a colleague who seemed to share his views on foreign affairs with sympathy and conviction. My long and intimate associations with Edward Halifax dated from 1922, when, in the days of Lloyd George, he became my Under-Secretary at the Dominions and Colonial Office. Political differences—even as serious and prolonged as those which arose between us about his policy as Viceroy of India—had never destroyed our personal relations. I thought I knew him very well, and I was sure that there was a gulf between us. I felt also that this same gulf, or one like it, was open between him and Anthony Eden. It would have been wiser, on the whole, for Mr. Chamberlain to have made Lord Halifax his Foreign

Secretary when he formed his Government. Eden would have been far more happily placed in the War Office or the Admiralty, and the Prime Minister would have had a kindred spirit and his own man at the Foreign Office. This inauspicious situation developed steadily during the year that Eden and Chamberlain worked together.

* * *

Up to this time and during many anxious years Sir Robert Vansittart had been the official head of the Foreign Office. His fortuitous connection with the Hoare-Laval pact had affected his position both with the new Foreign Secretary, Mr. Eden, and in wide political circles. The Prime Minister, who leaned more and more upon his Chief Industrial Adviser, Sir Horace Wilson, and consulted him a great deal on matters entirely outside his province or compass, regarded Vansittart as hostile to Germany. This was indeed true, for no one more clearly realised or foresaw the growth of the German danger or was more ready to subordinate other considerations to meeting it. The Foreign Secretary felt he could work more easily with Sir Alexander Cadogan, a Foreign Office official also of the highest character and ability. Therefore, at the end of 1937 Vansittart was apprised of his impending dismissal, and on January 1, 1938, was appointed to the special post of "Chief Diplomatic Adviser to His Majesty's Government". This was represented to the public as promotion, and might well indeed appear to be so. In fact however the whole responsibility for managing the Foreign Office passed out of his hands. He kept his old traditional room, but he saw the Foreign Office telegrams only after they had reached the Foreign Secretary with the minutes of the department upon them. Vansittart, who refused the Embassy in Paris, continued in this detached position for some time.

* * *

Between the summer of 1937 and the end of that year divergence, both in method and aim, grew between the Prime Minister and his Foreign Secretary. The sequence of events which led to Mr. Eden's resignation in February 1938 followed a logical course.

The original points of difference arose about our relations with Germany and Italy. Mr. Chamberlain was determined to press his suit with the two Dictators. In July 1937 he invited the Italian

Ambassador, Count Grandi, to Downing Street. The conversation took place with the knowledge but not in the presence of Mr. Eden. Mr. Chamberlain spoke of his desire for an improvement in Anglo-Italian relations. Count Grandi suggested to him that as a preliminary move it might be well if the Prime Minister were to write a personal appeal to Mussolini. Mr. Chamberlain sat down and wrote such a letter during the interview. It was dispatched without reference to the Foreign Secretary, who was in the Foreign Office a few yards away. The letter produced no apparent results, and our relations with Italy, because of the increasing Italian intervention in Spain, got steadily worse.

Mr. Chamberlain was imbued with a sense of a special and personal mission to come to friendly terms with the Dictators of Italy and Germany, and he conceived himself capable of achieving this relationship. To Mussolini he wished to accord recognition of the Italian conquest of Abyssinia as a prelude to a general settlement of differences. To Hitler he was prepared to offer colonial concessions. At the same time he was disinclined to consider in a conspicuous manner the improvements of British armaments or the necessity of close collaboration with France, both on the Staff and political levels. Mr. Eden, on the other hand, was convinced that any arrangement with Italy must be part of a general Mediterranean settlement, which must include Spain, and be reached in close understanding with France. In the negotiation of such a settlement our recognition of Italy's position in Abyssinia would clearly be an important bargaining counter. To throw this away in the prelude and appear eager to initiate negotiations was, in the Foreign Secretary's view, unwise.

During the autumn of 1937 these differences became more severe. Mr. Chamberlain considered that the Foreign Office was obstructing his attempts to open discussions with Germany and Italy, and Mr. Eden felt that his chief was displaying immoderate haste in approaching the Dictators, particularly while British armaments were so weak. There was in fact a profound practical and psychological divergence of view.

* * *

In spite of my differences with the Government, I was in close sympathy with their Foreign Secretary. He seemed to me the most resolute and courageous figure in the Administration, and although as a Private Secretary and later as an Under-Secretary of State in the Foreign Office he had had to adapt himself to many things I had attacked and still condemn, I felt sure his heart was in the right place and that he had the root of the matter in him. For his part, he made a point of inviting me to Foreign Office functions, and we corresponded freely. There was of course no impropriety in this practice, and Mr. Eden held to the well-established precedent whereby the Foreign Secretary is accustomed to keep in contact with the prominent political figures of the day on all broad international issues.

On August 7, 1937, I wrote to him:

This Spanish business cuts across my thoughts. It seems to me most important to make Blum stay with us strictly neutral, even if Germany and Italy continue to back the rebels and Russia sends money to the Government. If the French Government takes sides against the rebels it will be a godsend to the Germans and pro-Germans. In case you have a spare moment look at my article in the *Evening Standard* on Monday.

In this article I had written:

The worst quarrels only arise when both sides are equally in the right and in the wrong. Here, on the one hand, the passions of a poverty-stricken and backward proletariat demand the overthrow of Church, State, and property, and the inauguration of a Communist *régime*. On the other hand, the patriotic, religious, and *bourgeois* forces, under the leadership of the Army, and sustained by the countryside in many provinces, are marching to re-establish order by setting up a military dictatorship. The cruelties and ruthless executions extorted by the desperation of both sides, the appalling hatreds unloosed, the clash of creed and interest, make it only too probable that victory will be followed by the merciless extermination of the active elements of the vanquished and by a prolonged period of iron rule.

In the autumn of 1937 Eden and I had reached, though by somewhat different paths, a similar standpoint against active Axis intervention in the Spanish Civil War. I always supported him in the House when he took resolute action, even though it was upon a very limited scale. I knew well what his difficulties were with some of his senior colleagues in the Cabinet and with his chief, and that he would act more boldly if he were not enmeshed. We saw a good deal of each other at the end of August at Cannes, and one day I gave him and Mr. Lloyd George luncheon at a restaurant half-way between Cannes and Nice. Our conversation ran over the whole field—the Spanish struggle, Mussolini's persistent bad faith and intervention in Spain, and finally of course the dark background of ever-growing German power. I thought we were all three pretty well agreed. The Foreign Secretary was naturally most guarded about his relations with his chief and colleagues, and no reference was made to this delicate topic. Nothing could have been more correct than his demeanour. Nevertheless I was sure he was not a happy man in his great office.

* * *

Soon in the Mediterranean a crisis arose which he handled with firmness and skill, and which was accordingly solved in a manner reflecting a gleam of credit upon our course. A number of merchant ships had been sunk by so-called Spanish submarines. Actually there was no doubt that they were not Spanish but Italian. This was sheer piracy, and it stirred all who knew about it to action. A Conference of the Mediterranean Powers was convened at Nyon for September 10. To this the Foreign Secretary, accompanied by Vansittart and Lord Chatfield, the First Sea Lord, proceeded.

Mr. Churchill to Mr. Eden   9.IX.37

In your last letter you said that you would be very glad to see Lloyd George and me before you left for Geneva. We have met to-day, and I venture to let you know our views.

This is the moment to rally Italy to her international duty. Submarine piracy in the Mediterranean and the sinking of ships of many countries without any care for the lives of their crews must be suppressed. For this purpose all Mediterranean Powers should agree to keep their own submarines away from certain defined routes for commerce. In these routes the French and British Navies should search for all submarines, and any found by the detector apparatus should be pursued and sunk as pirates. Italy should be asked in the most courteous manner to participate in this. If however she will not do so, she should be told "that is what we are going to do".

At the same time, as it is very important to have the friendly concurrence of Italy, France should say that unless this concurrence is obtained she will open the Pyrenees frontier to the import of munitions of all kinds. Thus, on the one hand, Italy would be faced by the fact that the sea routes through the Mediterranean are going to be cleared of pirate submarines whatever happens, while at the same time she will gain nothing by not joining in, because the French frontier will be open. This point we consider essential. This combination of pressure upon Italy to join with the other Mediterranean Powers, coupled with the fact that she would risk much and gain nothing by standing out, would almost certainly be effective provided Mussolini knows that France and England are in earnest.

It is not believed that Germany is ready for a major war this year, and if it is hoped to have good relations with Italy in the future matters should be brought to a head now. The danger from which we suffer is that Mussolini thinks all can be carried off by bluff and bullying, and that in the end we shall only blether and withdraw. It is in the interests of European peace that a firm front should be shown now, and if you feel able to act in this sense we wish to assure you of our support upon such a policy in the House of Commons and in the country however matters may turn.

Speaking personally, I feel that this is as important a moment for you as when you insisted upon the Staff conversations with France after the violation of the Rhineland. The bold path is the path of safety.

Pray make any use of this letter privately or publicly that you may consider helpful to British interests and to the interests of peace.

P.S.—I have read this letter to Mr. Lloyd George, who declares himself in full agreement with it.

The Conference at Nyon was brief and successful. It was agreed to establish British and French anti-submarine patrols, with orders which left no doubt as to the fate of any submarine encountered. This was acquiesced in by Italy, and the outrages stopped at once.

Mr. Eden to Mr. Churchill   14.IX.37

You will now have seen the line which we have taken at Nyon, which in part at least coincides with that suggested in your letter. I hope you will agree that the results of the Conference are satisfactory. They seem so as viewed from here. The really important political fact is that we have emphasised that co-operation between Britain and France can be effective, and that the two Western Democracies can still play a decisive part in European affairs. The programme upon which we eventually agreed was worked out jointly by the French and ourselves. I must say that they could not have co-operated more sincerely, and we have been surprised at the extent of the naval co-operation which they have been ready to offer. It is fair to say that if we include their help in the air we shall be working on a fifty-fifty basis.

I agree that what we have done here only deals with one aspect of the Spanish problem. But it has much increased our authority among the nations at a time when we needed such an increase badly. The attitude of the smaller Powers of the Mediterranean was no less satisfactory. They played up well under the almost effusively friendly lead of Turkey. Chatfield has been a great success with everyone, and I feel that the Nyon Conference, by its brevity and success, has done something to put us on the map again. I hope that this may be your feeling too.

At least it has heartened the French and ourselves to tackle our immensely formidable task together.

Mr. Churchill to Mr. Eden   20.IX.37

It was very good of you, when so busy, to write to me. Indeed I congratulate you on a very considerable achievement. It is only rarely that an opportunity comes when stern and effective measures can be brought to bear upon an evildoer without incurring the risk of war. I have no doubt that the House of Commons will be very much pleased with the result.

I was very glad to see that Neville has been backing you up, and not, as represented by the Popular Press, holding you back by the coat-tails. My hope is that the advantages you have gained will be firmly held on to. Mussolini only understands superior force, such as he is now confronted with in the Mediterranean. The whole naval position there is transformed from the moment that the French bases are at our disposal. Italy cannot resist an effective Anglo-French combination. I hope therefore that Mussolini will be left to find his own way out of the diplomatic ditch into which he has blundered. The crystal-lisation against him for an unassailable purpose which has taken place in the Mediterranean is the one thing above all that he should have laboured to avoid. He has brought it about. I hope that the Anglo-French naval co-operation which has now begun will be continued indefinitely, and that both Navies and Air Forces will continue to use each other's facilities. This will be needed to prevent trouble arising about the Balearic Islands. The continued fortification of the Mediterranean by Italy against us will have to be dealt with in the future, as it is a capital danger to the British Empire. The more permanent the present arrangement becomes the less loaded with danger will this situation be.

Bernard Baruch telegraphs he is writing the results of his interview with the President [after our talks in London]. I have little doubt that the President's speech against dictatorships has been largely influenced by our talk, and I trust that the ground on the tariff and currency side is also being explored.

27 British artillery.
28 British "Tommies".

29 French infantrymen.
30 Russian riflemen.

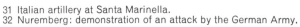
31 Italian artillery at Santa Marinella.
32 Nuremberg: demonstration of an attack by the German Army.

33 A parade by the Chinese Army.
34 A march-past by Japanese troops, led by Prince Chichibu, brother of the Emperor.

Mr. Eden to Mr. Churchill   25.IX.37

Thank you so much for your letter of September 20, and for the generous things you have written about Nyon, which I much appreciate I thought your summing up of the position at Nyon, "It is only rarely that an opportunity comes when stern and effective measures can be brought to bear upon an evildoer without incurring the risk of war," effectively described the position. Mussolini has been unwise enough to overstep the limits, and he has had to pay the penalty. There is no doubt that the spectacle of eighty Anglo-French destroyers patrolling the Mediterranean assisted by a considerable force of aircraft has made a profound impression on opinion in Europe. From reports which I have received, Germany herself has not been slow to take note of this fact. It was a great relief, both to Delbos and me, to be able to assert the position of our respective countries in this way in the autumn of a year in which we have inevitably had to be so much on the defensive. There is plenty of trouble ahead, and we are not yet of course anything like as strong in the military sense as I would wish, but Nyon has enabled us to improve our position and to gain more time.

I also cordially agree with you on the importance of the Anglo-French co-operation which we have now created in the Mediterranean. The whole French attitude was of course fundamentally different from that which prevailed when Laval was in command. The French Naval Staff could not have been more helpful, and they really made a great effort to make an important contribution to the joint force. Our Admiralty were, I am sure, impressed. Moreover, the mutual advantages to which you refer in respect of the use of each other's bases are very valuable. Nor will Italian participation, whatever its ultimate form, be able to affect the realities of the situation.

The Nyon Conference, although an incident, is a proof of how powerful the combined influence of Britain and France, if expressed with conviction and a readiness to use force, would have been upon the mood and policy of the Dictators. That such a policy would have prevented war at this stage cannot be asserted. It might easily have delayed it. It is the fact that whereas "appeasement" in all its forms only encouraged their aggression and gave the Dictators more power with their own peoples, any sign of a positive counter-offensive by the Western Democracies immediately produced an abatement of tension. This rule prevailed during the whole of 1937. After that the scene and conditions were different.

★　　★　　★

Early in October 1937 I was invited to a dinner at the Foreign Office for the Yugoslav Premier, M. Stoyadinovitch. Afterwards, when we were all standing about and I was talking to Eden, Lord Halifax came up and said in a genial way that Goering had invited him to Germany on a sports visit, and the hope was held out that he would certainly be able to see Hitler. He said that he had spoken about it to the Prime Minister, who thought it would be a very good thing, and therefore he had accepted. I had the impression that Eden was surprised and did not like it; but everything passed off pleasantly. Halifax therefore visited Germany in his capacity as a Master of Foxhounds. The Nazi Press welcomed him as *Lord Halalifax*, "*Halali!*" being a Continental hunting-cry, and after some sporting entertainment he was in fact bidden to Berchtesgaden and had an informal and none too ceremonious interview with the Fuehrer. This did not go very well. One could hardly conceive two personalities less able to comprehend one another. This High Church Yorkshire aristocrat and ardent peace-lover, reared in all the smiling goodwill of former English life, who had taken his part in the war as a good officer, met on the other side the demon-genius sprung from the abyss of poverty, inflamed by defeat, devoured by hatred and revenge, and convulsed by his design to make the German race masters of Europe or maybe the world. Nothing came of all this but chatter and bewilderment.

*   *   *

I may mention here that Ribbentrop twice tendered me an invitation to visit Herr Hitler. Long before, as Colonial Under-Secretary and a major in the Oxfordshire Yeomanry, I had been the guest of the Kaiser at the German Manœuvres in 1907 and in 1909. But now there was a different tune. Mortal quarrels were afoot, and I had my station in them. I would gladly have met Hitler with the authority of Britain behind me. But as a private individual I should have placed myself and my country at a disadvantage. If I had agreed with the Dictator-host I should have misled him. If I had disagreed he would have been offended, and I should have been accused of spoiling Anglo-German relations. Therefore I declined, or rather let lapse, both invitations. All those Englishmen who visited the German Fuehrer in these years were embarrassed or compromised. No one was more completely misled than Mr. Lloyd George, whose rapturous accounts of his conversations make odd reading to-day. There is no doubt that Hitler had a power of fascinating men, and the sense of force and authority is apt to assert itself unduly upon the tourist. Unless the terms are equal it is better to keep away.

*   *   *

During these November days Eden became increasingly concerned about our slow rearmament. On the 11th he had an interview with the Prime Minister and tried to convey his misgivings. Mr. Neville Chamberlain after a while refused to listen to him. He advised him to "go home and take an aspirin". When Halifax returned from Berlin he reported that Hitler had told him the colonial question was the only outstanding issue between Britain and Germany. He believed the Germans were in no hurry. There was no immediate prospect of a peace deal. His conclusions were negative and his mood passive.

In February 1938 the Foreign Secretary conceived himself to be almost isolated in the Cabinet. The Prime Minister had strong support against him and his outlook. A whole band of important Ministers thought the Foreign Office policy dangerous and even provocative. On the other hand, a number of the younger Ministers were very ready to understand his point of view. Some of them later complained that he did not take them into his confidence. He did not however contemplate anything like forming a group against his leader. The Chiefs of Staff could give him no help. Indeed, they enjoined caution and dwelt upon the dangers of the situation. They were reluctant to draw too close to the French lest we should enter into engagements beyond our power to fulfil. They took a gloomy view of Russian military strength after the purge. They believed it necessary to deal with our problems as though we had three enemies—Germany, Italy, and Japan—who might all attack us together, and few to help us. We might ask for air bases in France, but we were not able to send an army in the first instance. Even this modest suggestion encountered strong resistance in the Cabinet.

*   *   *

But the actual breach came over a new and separate issue. On the evening of January 11, 1938, Mr. Sumner Welles, the American Under-Secretary of State, called upon the British Ambassador in Washington. He was the bearer of a secret and confidential message from President Roosevelt to Mr. Chamberlain. The President was deeply anxious at the deterioration of the international situation, and proposed to take the initiative by inviting the representatives of certain Governments to Washington to discuss the underlying causes of present difficulties. Before taking this step however he wished to consult the British Government on their view of such a plan, and stipulated that no other Government should be informed either of the nature or the existence of such a proposal. He asked that not later than January 17 he should be given a reply to his message, and intimated that only if his suggestion met with "the cordial approval and whole-hearted support of His Majesty's Government" would he then approach the Governments of France, Germany, and Italy. Here was a formidable and measureless step.

In forwarding this most secret message to London the British Ambassador, Sir Ronald Lindsay, commented that in his view the President's plan was a genuine effort to relax international tension, and that if His Majesty's Government withheld their support the progress which had been made in Anglo-American co-operation during the previous two years would be destroyed. He urged in the most earnest manner acceptance of the proposal by the British Government. The Foreign Office received the Washington telegram on January 12, and copies were sent to the Prime Minister in the country that evening. On the following morning he came to London, and on his instructions a reply was sent to the President's message. Mr. Eden was at this time on a brief holiday in the South of France. Mr. Chamberlain's reply was to the effect that he appreciated the confidence of President Roosevelt in consulting him in this fashion upon his proposed plan to alleviate the existing tension in Europe, but he wished to explain the position of his own efforts to reach agreement with Germany and Italy, particularly in the case of the latter. "His Majesty's Government would be prepared, for their part, if possible with the authority of the League of Nations, to recognise *de jure* the Italian occupation of Abyssinia, if they found that the Italian Government on their side were ready to give evidence of their desire to contribute to the restoration of confidence and friendly relations." The Prime Minister mentioned these facts, the message continued, so that the President might consider whether his present proposal might not cut across the British efforts. Would it not therefore be wiser to postpone the launching of the American plan?

This reply was received by the President with some disappointment. He intimated that he would reply by letter to Mr. Chamberlain on January 17. On the evening of January 15 the Foreign Secretary returned to England. He had been urged to come back, not by his chief, who was content to act without him, but by his devoted officials at the Foreign Office. The vigilant Alexander Cadogan awaited him upon the pier at Dover. Mr. Eden, who had worked long and hard to improve Anglo-American relations, was deeply perturbed. He immediately sent a telegram to Sir Ronald Lindsay attempting to minimise the effects of Mr. Chamberlain's chilling answer. The President's letter reached London on the morning of January 18. In it he agreed to postpone making his proposal in view of the fact that the British Government were contemplating direct negotiations, but he added that he was gravely concerned at the suggestion that His Majesty's Government might accord recognition to the Italian position in Abyssinia. He thought that this would have a most harmful effect upon Japanese policy in the Far East and upon American public opinion. Mr. Cordell Hull, in delivering this letter to the British Ambassador in Washington, expressed himself even more emphatically. He said that such a recognition would "rouse a feeling of disgust, would revive and multiply all fears of pulling the chestnuts out of the fire; it would be represented as a corrupt bargain completed in Europe at the expense of interests in the Far East in which America was intimately concerned".

The President's letter was considered at a series of meetings of the Foreign Affairs Committee of the Cabinet. Mr. Eden succeeded in procuring a considerable modification of the previous attitude. Most of the Ministers thought he was satisfied. He did not make it clear to them that he was not. Following these discussions two messages were sent to Washington on the evening of January 21. The substance of these replies was that the Prime Minister warmly welcomed the President's initiative, but was not anxious to bear any responsibility for its failure if American overtures were badly received. Mr. Chamberlain wished to point out that we did not accept in an unqualified manner the

President's suggested procedure, which would clearly irritate both the Dictators and Japan. Nor did His Majesty's Government feel that the President had fully understood our position in regard to *de jure* recognition. The second message was in fact an explanation of our attitude in this matter. We intended to accord such recognition only as part of a general settlement with Italy.

The British Ambassador reported his conversation with Mr. Sumner Welles when he handed these messages to the President on January 22. He stated that Mr. Welles told him that "the President regarded recognition as an unpleasant pill which we should both have to swallow, and he wished that we should both swallow it together".

Thus it was that President Roosevelt's proposal to use American influence for the purpose of bringing together the leading European Powers to discuss the chances of a general settlement, this of course involving however tentatively the mighty power of the United States, was rebuffed by Mr. Chamberlain. This attitude defined in a decisive manner the difference of view between the British Prime Minister and his Foreign Secretary. Their disagreements were still confined to the circle of the Cabinet for a little time longer; but the split was fundamental. The comments of Mr. Chamberlain's biographer, Professor Feiling, upon this episode, are not without interest. "While Chamberlain feared the Dictators would pay no heed or else *would use this line-up of the Democracies as a pretext for a break*, it was found on Eden's return that he would rather risk that calamity than the loss of American goodwill. There was the first breath of resignation. But a compromise was beaten out. . . ." Poor England! Leading her free, careless life from day to day, amid endless good-tempered Parliamentary babble, she followed, wondering, along the downward path which led to all she wanted to avoid. She was continually reassured by the leading articles of the most influential newspapers, with some honourable exceptions, and behaved as if all the world were as easy, uncalculating, and well-meaning as herself.

★　★　★

It was plain that no resignation by the Foreign Secretary could be founded upon the rebuff administered by Mr. Chamberlain to the President's overture. Mr. Roosevelt was indeed running great risks in his own domestic politics by deliberately involving the United States in the darkening European scene. All the forces of Isolationism would have been aroused if any part of these interchanges had transpired. On the other hand, no event could have been more likely to stave off, or even prevent, war than the arrival of the United States in the circle of European hates and fears. To Britain it was a matter almost of life and death. No one can measure in retrospect its effect upon the course of events in Austria and later at Munich. We must regard its rejection—for such it was—as the loss of the last frail chance to save the world from tyranny otherwise than by war. That Mr. Chamberlain, with his limited outlook and inexperience of the European scene, should have possessed the self-sufficiency to wave away the proffered hand stretched out across the Atlantic leaves one, even at this date, breathless with amazement. The lack of all sense of proportion, and even of self-preservation, which this episode reveals in an upright, competent, well-meaning man, charged with the destinies of our country and all who depended upon it, is appalling. One cannot to-day even reconstruct the state of mind which would render such gestures possible.

* * *

I have yet to unfold the story of the treatment of the Russian offers of collaboration in the advent of Munich. If only the British people could have known and realised that, having neglected our defences and sought to diminish the defences of France, we were now disengaging ourselves, one after the other, from the two mighty nations whose extreme efforts were needed to save our lives and their own, history might have taken a different turn. But all seemed so easy from day to day. Now ten years later let the lessons of the past be a guide.

* * *

It must have been with declining confidence in the future that Mr. Eden went to Paris on January 25 to consult with the French. Everything now turned upon the success of the approach to Italy, of which we had made such a point in our replies to the President. The French Ministers impressed upon Mr. Eden the necessity of the inclusion of Spain in any general settlement with the Italians; on this he needed little convincing. On February 10 the Prime Minister and the Foreign Secretary met Count Grandi, who declared that the Italians were ready in principle to open the conversations.

On February 15 the news came of the submission of the Austrian Chancellor, Schuschnigg, to the German demand for the introduction into the Austrian Cabinet of the chief Nazi agent, Seyss-Inquart, as Minister of the Interior and Head of the Austrian Police. This grave event did not avert the personal crisis between Mr. Chamberlain and Mr. Eden. On February 18 they saw Count Grandi again. This was the last business they conducted together. The Ambassador refused either to discuss the Italian position towards Austria, or to consider the British plan for the withdrawal of volunteers, or so-called volunteers—in this case five divisions of the regular Italian Army—from Spain. Grandi asked however for general conversations to be opened in Rome. The Prime Minister wished for these, and the Foreign Secretary was strongly opposed to such a step.

There were prolonged parleyings and Cabinet meetings. Of these the only authoritative account yet disclosed is in Mr. Chamberlain's biography. Professor Feiling says that the Prime Minister "let the Cabinet see that the alternative to Eden's resignation might be his own". He quotes from some diary or private letter, to which he was given access, the following statement by the Prime Minister: "I thought it necessary to say clearly that I could not accept any decision in the opposite sense." "The Cabinet," says Mr. Feiling, "were unanimous, though with a few reserves." We have no knowledge of how and when these statements were made during the protracted discussions. But at the end Mr. Eden briefly tendered his resignation on the issue of the Italian conversations taking place at this stage and in these circumstances. At this his colleagues were astonished. Mr. Feiling says they were "much shaken". They had not realised that the differences between the Foreign Secretary and the Prime Minister had reached breaking-point. Evidently if Mr. Eden's resignation was involved a new question raising larger and more general issues was raised. However, they had all committed themselves on the merits of the matter in dispute. The rest of the long day was spent in efforts to induce the Foreign Secretary to change his mind. Mr. Chamberlain was impressed by the distress of the Cabinet. "Seeing how my colleagues had been taken aback, I proposed an adjournment until next day." But Eden saw no use in continuing a search for formulas, and by midnight, on the 20th, his resignation became final. "Greatly to his credit, as I see it," noted the Prime Minister. Lord Halifax was at once appointed Foreign Secretary in his place.*

It had of course become known that there were serious differences in the Cabinet, though the cause was obscure. I had heard something of this, but carefully abstained from any communication with Mr. Eden. I hoped that he would not on any account resign without building up his case beforehand, and giving his many friends in Parliament a chance to draw out the issues. But the Government at this time was so powerful and aloof that the struggle was fought out inside the Ministerial conclave, and mainly between the two men.

★ ★ ★

Late in the night of February 20 a telephone message reached me as I sat in my old room at Chartwell (as I often sit now) that Eden had resigned. I must confess that my heart sank, and for a while the dark waters of despair overwhelmed me. In a long life I have had many ups and downs. During all the war soon to come and in its darkest times I never had any trouble in sleeping. In the crisis of 1940, when so much responsibility lay upon me, and also at many very anxious, awkward moments in the following five years, I could always flop into bed and go to sleep after the day's work was done—subject of course to any emergency call. I slept sound and awoke refreshed, and had no feelings except appetite to grapple with whatever the morning's boxes might bring. But now on this night of February 20, 1938, and on this occasion only, sleep deserted me. From midnight till dawn I lay in my bed consumed by emotions of sorrow and fear. There seemed one strong young figure standing up against long, dismal, drawling tides of drift and surrender, of wrong measurements and feeble impulses. My conduct of affairs would have been different from his in various ways; but he seemed to me at this moment to embody the life-hope of the British nation, the grand old British race that had done so much for men, and had yet some more to give. Now he was gone. I watched the daylight slowly creep in through the windows, and saw before me in mental gaze the vision of Death.

* Feiling, *op. cit.*, p. 338.

CHAPTER XV

THE RAPE OF AUSTRIA
February 1938

"Case Otto" – Hitler Assumes Supreme Command – The Austrian Chancellor Summoned to Berchtesgaden – His Ordeal – Schuschnigg's Collapse – Hitler's Speech to the Reichstag, February 20 – Debate on Mr. Eden's Resignation – Hitler and Mussolini in Combination – The Austrian Plebiscite – The Invasion of Austria – Hitler's Debt to Mussolini – The Triumphal Entry into Vienna and its Background – A Farewell Luncheon to Ribbentrop – The Debate of March 12 – Consequences of the Fall of Vienna – Danger to Czechoslovakia – Mr. Chamberlain and the Soviet Overture – A Side Blow – Negotiation with Mr. de Valera – Surrender of the Irish Ports – A Major Injury to Britain – Irish Neutrality – My Vain Protest.

USUALLY in modern times when States have been defeated in war they have preserved their structure, their identity, and the secrecy of their archives. On this occasion, the war being fought to an utter finish, we have come into full possession of the inside story of the enemy. From this we can check up with some exactness our own information and performances. We have seen how in July 1936 Hitler had instructed the German General Staff to draw up military plans for the occupation of Austria when the hour should strike. This operation was labelled "Case Otto". Now, a year later, on June 24, 1937, he crystallised these plans by a special directive. On November 5 he unfolded his future designs to the chiefs of his armed forces. Germany must have more "living space". This could best be found in Eastern Europe—Poland, White Russia, and the Ukraine. To obtain this would involve a major war, and incidentally the extermination of the people then living in those parts. Germany would have to reckon with her two "hateful enemies", England and France, to whom "a German Colossus in the centre of Europe would be intolerable". In order to profit by the lead she had gained in munitions production and by the patriotic fervour aroused and represented by the Nazi Party, she must therefore make war at the first promising opportunity, and deal with her two obvious opponents before they were ready to fight.

Neurath, Fritsch, and even Blomberg, all of them influenced by the views of the German Foreign Office, General Staff, and Officer Corps, were alarmed by this policy. They thought that the risks to be run were too high. They recognised that by the audacity of the Fuehrer they were definitely ahead of the Allies in every form of rearmament. The Army was maturing month by month; the internal decay of France and the lack of will-power in Britain were favourable factors which might well run their full course. What was a year or two when all was moving so well? They must have time to complete the war machine, and a conciliatory speech now and again from the Fuehrer would keep these futile and degenerate democracies chattering. But Hitler was not sure of this. His genius taught him that victory would not be achieved by processes of certainty. Risks had to be run. The leap had to be made. He was flushed with his successes, first in rearmament, second in conscription, third in the Rhineland, fourth by the accession of Mussolini's Italy. To wait till everything was ready was probably to wait till all was too late. It is very easy for historians and other people, who do not have to live and act from day to day, to say that he would have had the whole fortunes of the world in his hand if he had gone on growing in strength for another two or three years before striking. However, this does not follow. There are no certainties in human life or in the life of States. Hitler was resolved to hurry, and have the war while he was in his prime.

Blomberg, weakened with the Officer Corps by an inappropriate marriage, was first removed; and then, on February 4, 1938, Hitler dismissed Fritsch, and himself assumed supreme command of the armed forces. So far as it is possible for one man, however gifted and powerful, however terrible the penalties he can inflict, to make his will effective over spheres so vast, the Fuehrer assumed direct control, not only of the policy of the

State, but of the military machine. He had at this time something like the power of Napoleon after Austerlitz and Jena, without of course the glory of winning great battles by his personal direction on horseback, but with triumphs in the political and diplomatic field which all his circle and followers knew were due alone to him and to his judgment and daring.

*　　*　　*

Apart from his resolve, so plainly described in *Mein Kampf*, to bring all Teutonic races into the Reich, Hitler had two reasons for wishing to absorb the Austrian Republic. It opened to Germany both the door of Czechoslovakia and the more spacious portals of South-eastern Europe. Since the murder of Chancellor Dollfuss in July 1934 by the Austrian section of the Nazi Party the process of subverting the independent Austrian Government by money, intrigue, and force had never ceased. The Nazi movement in Austria grew with every success that Hitler reaped elsewhere, whether inside Germany or against the Allies. It had been necessary to proceed step by step. Officially Papen was instructed to maintain the most cordial relations with the Austrian Government, and to procure the official recognition by them of the Austrian Nazi Party as a legal body. At that time the attitude of Mussolini had imposed restraint. After the murder of Dr. Dollfuss the Italian Dictator had flown to Venice to receive and comfort the widow, who had taken refuge there, and considerable Italian forces had been concentrated on the southern frontier of Austria. But now in the dawn of 1938 decisive changes in European groupings and values had taken place. The Siegfried Line confronted France with a growing barrier of steel and concrete, requiring as it seemed an enormous sacrifice of French manhood to pierce. The door from the West was shut. Mussolini had been driven into the German system by sanctions so ineffectual that they had angered him without weakening his power. He might well have pondered with relish on Machiavelli's celebrated remark, "Men avenge slight injuries, but not grave ones." Above all the Western Democracies had seemed to give repeated proofs that they would bow to violence so long as they were not themselves directly assailed. Papen was working skilfully inside the Austrian political structure. Many Austrian notables had yielded to his pressure and intrigues. The tourist trade, so important to Vienna, was impeded by the prevailing uncertainty. In the background terrorist activity and bomb outrages shook the frail life of the Austrian Republic.

It was thought that the hour had now come to obtain control of Austrian policy by procuring the entry into the Vienna Cabinet of the leaders of the lately legalised Austrian Nazi Party. On February 12, 1938, eight days after assuming the supreme command, Hitler had summoned the Austrian Chancellor, Herr von Schuschnigg, to Berchtesgaden. He had obeyed, and was accompanied by his Foreign Minister, Guido Schmidt. We now have Schuschnigg's record, in which the following dialogue occurs.* Hitler had mentioned the defences of the Austrian frontier. These were no more than might be required to make a military operation necessary to overcome them, and thus raise major issues of peace and war.

Hitler: "I only need to give an order, and overnight all the ridiculous scarecrows on the frontier will vanish. You don't really believe that you could hold me up for half an hour? Who knows—perhaps I shall be suddenly overnight in Vienna: like a spring storm. Then you will really experience something. I would willingly spare the Austrians this; it will cost many victims. *After the troops will follow the S.A. and the Legion!* No one will be able to hinder their vengeance, not even myself. Do you want to turn Austria into another Spain? All this I would like if possible to avoid."

Schuschnigg: "I will obtain the necessary information and put a stop to the building of any defence works on the German frontier. Naturally I realise that you can march into Austria, but, Mr. Chancellor, whether we wish it or not, that would lead to the shedding of blood. We are not alone in the world. That probably means war."

Hitler: "That is very easy to say at this moment as we sit here in club armchairs, but behind it all there lies a sum of suffering and blood. Will you take the responsibility for that, Herr Schuschnigg? Don't believe that anyone in the world will hinder me in my decisions! Italy? I am quite clear with Mussolini: with Italy I am on the closest possible terms. England? England will not lift a finger for Austria. . . . And France? Well, two years ago when we marched into the Rhineland with a handful of

* Schuschnigg, *Ein Requiem in Rot-Weiss-Rot*, p. 37 ff.

battalions—at that moment I risked a great deal. If France had marched then we should have been forced to withdraw. . . . But for France it is now too late!"

This first interview took place at eleven in the morning. After a formal lunch the Austrians were summoned into a small room, and there confronted by Ribbentrop and Papen with a written ultimatum. The terms were not open to discussion. They included the appointment of the Austrian Nazi Seyss-Inquart as Minister of Security in the Austrian Cabinet, a general amnesty for all Austrian Nazis under detention, and the official incorporation of the Austrian Nazi Party in the Government-sponsored Fatherland Front.

Later Hitler received the Austrian Chancellor. "I repeat to you, this is the very last chance. Within three days I expect the execution of this agreement." In Jodl's diary the entry reads, "Von Schuschnigg together with Guido Schmidt are again being put under heaviest political and military pressure. At 11 p.m. Schuschnigg signs the 'protocol'."[*] As Papen drove back with Schuschnigg in the sledge which conveyed them over the snow-covered roads to Salzburg he commented, "Yes, that is how the Fuehrer can be; now you have experienced it for yourself. But when you next come you will have a much easier time. The Fuehrer can be really charming."[†]

On February 20 Hitler spoke to the Reichstag:

I am happy to be able to tell you, gentlemen, that during the past few days a further understanding has been reached with a country that is particularly close to us for many reasons. The Reich and German Austria are bound together not only because they are the same people, but also because they share a long history and a common culture. The difficulties which had been experienced in carrying out the Agreement of July 11, 1936, compelled us to make an attempt to clear out of the way misunderstandings and hindrances to a final conciliation. Had this not been done, it is clear that an intolerable situation might one day have developed, whether intentionally or otherwise, which might have brought about a very serious catastrophe. I am glad to be able to assure you that these considerations corresponded with the views of the Austrian Chancellor, whom I invited to come to visit me. The idea and the intention were to bring about a relaxation of the strain in our relations with one another by giving

* *Nuremberg Documents* (H.M. Stationery Office), Pt. I, p. 249
† Schuschnigg, *op. cit.*, pp. 51–2.

under the existing legislation the same legal rights to citizens holding National-Socialist views as are enjoyed by the other citizens of German Austria. In conjunction with this there should be a practical contribution towards peace by granting a general amnesty, and by creating a better understanding between the two States through a still closer friendly co-operation in as many different fields as possible—political, personal, and economic—all complementary to and within the framework of the Agreement of July 11. I express in this connection before the German people my sincere thanks to the Austrian Chancellor for his great understanding and the warm-hearted willingness with which he accepted my invitation and worked with me, so that we might discover a way of serving the best interests of the two countries; for, after all, it is the interest of the whole German people, whose sons we all are, wherever we may have been born.*

One can hardly find a more perfect specimen of humbug and hypocrisy for British and American benefit. I only print it because of its unique quality in these respects. What is astounding is that it should have been regarded with anything but scorn by men and women of intelligence in any free country.

* * *

For a moment we must return to the serious British event which the previous chapter has described. On the next day, February 21, there was an imposing debate in the House of Commons on the resignation of the Foreign Secretary and his Under-Secretary, Lord Cranborne—a man in whom "still waters ran deep"—who acted with him in loyalty and conviction. Eden could of course make no open reference to President Roosevelt's overture and its discouragement. The differences about Italy were on a minor plane. Eden said:

I have spoken of the immediate difference which has divided me from my colleagues, and I should not be frank if I were to pretend that it is an isolated issue. It is not. *Within the last few weeks upon one most important decision of foreign policy which did not concern Italy at all the difference was fundamental.*

He concluded:

I do not believe that we can make progress in European appeasement if we allow the impression to gain currency abroad that we yield to constant pressure. . . . I am certain in my own mind that progress

---

* *Hitler's Speeches* (ed. N. H. Baynes), II, 1407–8.

depends above all on the temper of the nation, and that temper must find expression in a firm spirit. That spirit I am confident is there. Not to give voice to it is, I believe, fair neither to this country nor to the world.

Mr. Attlee made a searching point. The resignation of Mr. Eden was being proclaimed in Italy as "another great victory for the Duce". "All over the world we hear the story, 'You see how great is the power of our Leader; the British Foreign Secretary has gone.'"

I did not speak till the second day, when I paid my tribute to both the resigning Ministers. I also sustained Mr. Attlee's accusation:

This last week has been a good week for the Dictators—one of the best they have ever had. The German Dictator has laid his heavy hand upon a small but historic country, and the Italian Dictator has carried his vendetta against Mr. Eden to a victorious conclusion. The conflict between them has been long. There can be no doubt whatever that Signor Mussolini has won. All the majesty, power, and dominion of the British Empire have not been able to secure the success of the causes which were entrusted to the late Foreign Secretary by the general will of Parliament and of the country. . . . So that is the end of this part of the story, namely, the departure from power of the Englishman whom the British nation and the British Parliament entrusted with a certain task, and the complete triumph of the Italian Dictator, at a moment when he desperately needed success for domestic reasons. All over the world, in every land, under every sky and every system of government, wherever they may be, the friends of England are dismayed and the foes of England are exultant. . . .

The resignation of the late Foreign Secretary may well be a milestone in history. Great quarrels, it has been well said, arise from small occasions but seldom from small causes. The late Foreign Secretary adhered to the old policy which we have all forgotten for so long. The Prime Minister and his colleagues have entered upon another and a new policy. The old policy was an effort to establish the rule of law in Europe, and build up through the League of Nations effective deterrents against the aggressor. Is it the new policy to come to terms with the totalitarian Powers in the hope that by great and far-reaching acts of submission, not merely in sentiment and pride, but in material factors, peace may be preserved?

The other day Lord Halifax said that Europe was confused. The part of Europe which is confused is that part ruled by Parliamentary Governments. I know of no confusion on the side of the great

Dictators. They know what they want, and no one can deny that up to the present at every step they are getting what they want. The grave and largely irreparable injury to world security took place in the years 1932 to 1935. . . . The next opportunity when the Sibylline books were presented to us was the reoccupation of the Rhineland at the beginning of 1936. Now we know that a firm stand by France and Britain, under the authority of the League of Nations, would have been followed by the immediate evacuation of the Rhineland without the shedding of a drop of blood; and the effects of that *might have enabled the more prudent elements in the German Army to regain their proper position,* and would not have given to the political head of Germany that enormous ascendancy which has enabled him to move forward. Now we are at a moment when a third move is made, but when that opportunity does not present itself in the same favourable manner. Austria has been laid in thrall, *and we do not know whether Czechoslovakia will not suffer a similar attack.*

* * *

The Continental drama ran its course. Mussolini now sent a verbal message to Schuschnigg saying that he considered the Austrian attitude at Berchtesgaden to be both right and adroit. He assured him both of the unalterable attitude of Italy towards the Austrian question and of his personal friendship. On February 24 the Austrian Chancellor himself spoke to the Austrian Parliament, welcoming the settlement with Germany, but emphasising, with some sharpness, that beyond the specific terms of the agreement Austria would never go. On March 3 he sent a confidential message to Mussolini through the Austrian Military Attaché in Rome informing the Duce that he intended to strengthen the political position in Austria by holding a plebiscite. Twenty-four hours later he received a message from the Austrian Military Attaché in Rome describing his interview with Mussolini. In this the Duce expressed himself optimistically. The situation would improve. An imminent *détente* between Rome and London would ensure a lightening of the existing pressure. . . . As to the plebiscite Mussolini uttered a warning: *"E un errore"* (It's a mistake). "If the result is satisfactory, people will say that it is not genuine. If it is bad, the situation of the Government will be unbearable; and if it is indecisive, then it is worthless." But Schuschnigg was determined. On March 9 he announced officially that a plebiscite would be held throughout Austria on the following Sunday, March 13.

At first nothing happened. Seyss-Inquart seemed to accept the idea without demur. At 5.30 a.m. however on the morning of March 11 Schuschnigg was rung up on the telephone from Police Headquarters in Vienna. He was told: "The German frontier at Salzburg was closed an hour ago. The German customs officials have been withdrawn. Railway communications have been cut." The next message to reach the Austrian Chancellor was from his Consul-General in Munich saying that the German Army Corps there had been mobilised: supposed destination—Austria!

Later in the morning Seyss-Inquart came to announce that Goering had just telephoned to him that the plebiscite must be called off within an hour. If no reply was received within that time Goering would assume that Seyss-Inquart had been hindered from telephoning, and would act accordingly. After being informed by responsible officials that the police and Army were not entirely reliable, Schuschnigg informed Seyss-Inquart that the plebiscite would be postponed. A quarter of an hour later the latter returned with a reply from Goering scribbled on a message-pad:

The situation can only be saved if the Chancellor resigns immediately and if within two hours Dr. Seyss-Inquart is nominated Chancellor. If nothing is done within this period the German invasion of Austria will follow.*

Schuschnigg waited on President Miklas to tender his resignation. While in the President's room he received a deciphered message from the Italian Government that they could offer no counsel. The old President was obstinate: "So in the decisive hour I am left alone." He steadfastly refused to nominate a Nazi Chancellor. He was determined to force the Germans into a shameful and violent deed. But for this they were well prepared.

A vivid account of the German reaction is found again in Jodl's diary for March 10:

By surprise and without consulting his Ministers, von Schuschnigg ordered a plebiscite for Sunday, March 13, which should bring a strong majority for the legitimate party *in the absence of plan or preparation*. The Fuehrer is determined not to tolerate it. This very night, March 9–10, he calls for Goering. General von Reichenau is called back from the Cairo Olympic Committee; General von Schubert is

---

* Schuschnigg, *op. cit.*, pp. 66, 72.

ordered to come, as well as Minister Glaise-Horstenau, who is with the District Leader [Gauleiter Burckel] in the Palatinate. General Keitel communicates the facts at 1.45. He drives to the Reichskanzlei at ten o'clock. I follow at 10.15 to give him the old draft "Prepare Case Otto". 13.00 hours, General K. [Keitel] informs Chief of Operational Staff and Admiral Canaris; Ribbentrop is detained in London. Neurath takes over the Foreign Office. Fuehrer wants to transmit ultimatum to the Austrian Cabinet. A personal letter is dispatched to Mussolini, and the reasons are developed which forced the Fuehrer to take action.*

On the following day, March 11, orders were issued by Hitler to the German armed forces for the military occupation of Austria. Operation "Otto", so long studied, so carefully prepared, began. President Miklas confronted Seyss-Inquart and the Austrian Nazi leaders in Vienna with firmness throughout a hectic day. The telephone conversation between Hitler and Prince Philip of Hesse, his special envoy to the Duce, was quoted in evidence at Nuremberg, and is of interest:

Hesse: I have just come back from the Palazzo Venezia. The Duce accepted the whole thing in a very friendly manner. He sends you his regards. He had been informed from Austria; von Schuschnigg gave him the news. He had then said it [*i.e.*, Italian intervention] would be a complete impossibility; it would be a bluff; such a thing could not be done. So he [Schuschnigg] was told that it was unfortunately arranged thus, and it could not be changed any more. Then Mussolini said that Austria would be immaterial to him.

Hitler: Then please tell Mussolini I will never forget him for this.

Hesse: Yes.

Hitler: Never, never, never, whatever happens. I am still ready to make a quite different agreement with him.

Hesse: Yes, I told him that too.

Hitler: As soon as the Austrian affair has been settled I shall be ready to go with him through thick and thin; nothing matters.

Hesse: Yes, my Fuehrer.

Hitler: Listen. I will make any agreement—I am no longer in fear of the terrible position which would have existed militarily in case we had become involved in a conflict. You may tell him that I do thank him ever so much; never, never shall I forget that.

Hesse: Yes, my Fuehrer.

Hitler: I will never forget it, whatever may happen. If he should ever need any help or be in any danger he can be convinced that I shall

* *Nuremberg Documents,* I, p. 251.

stick to him whatever might happen, even if the whole world were against him.

Hesse: Yes, my Fuehrer.*

Certainly when he rescued Mussolini from the Italian Provisional Government in 1943 Hitler kept his word.

* * *

A triumphal entry into Vienna had been the Austrian Corporal's dream. On the night of Saturday, March 12, the Nazi Party in the capital had planned a torchlight procession to welcome the conquering hero. But nobody arrived. Three bewildered Bavarians of the supply services who had come by train to make billeting arrangements for the invading army had therefore to be carried shoulder-high through the streets. The cause of this hitch leaked out slowly. The German war machine had lumbered falteringly over the frontier and come to a standstill near Linz. In spite of perfect weather and road conditions the majority of the tanks broke down. Defects appeared in the motorised heavy artillery. The road from Linz to Vienna was blocked with heavy vehicles at a standstill. General von Reichenau, Hitler's special favourite, Commander of Army Group IV, was deemed responsible for a breakdown which exposed the unripe condition of the German Army at this stage in its reconstruction.

Hitler himself, motoring through Linz, saw the traffic jam, and was infuriated. The light tanks were disengaged from confusion and straggled into Vienna in the early hours of Sunday morning. The armoured vehicles and motorised heavy artillery were loaded on to the railway trucks, and only thus arrived in time for the ceremony. The pictures of Hitler driving through Vienna amid exultant or terrified crowds are well known. But this moment of mystic glory had an unquiet background. The Fuehrer was in fact convulsed with anger at the obvious shortcomings of his military machine. He rated his generals, and they answered back. They reminded him of his refusal to listen to Fritsch and his warnings that Germany was not in a position to undertake the risk of a major conflict. Appearances were preserved. The official celebrations and parades took place. On the Sunday, after large numbers of German troops and Austrian Nazis had taken possession of Vienna, Hitler declared the dissolu-

---

* Schuschnigg, *op. cit.*, pp. 102–3, and *Nuremberg Documents*, I, pp. 258–9.

tion of the Austrian Republic and the annexation of its territory to the German Reich.

* * *

Herr von Ribbentrop was at this time about to leave London to take up his duties as Foreign Secretary in Germany. Mr. Chamberlain gave a farewell luncheon in his honour at No. 10 Downing Street. My wife and I accepted the Prime Minister's invitation to attend. There were perhaps sixteen people present. My wife sat next to Sir Alexander Cadogan, near one end of the table. About half-way through the meal a Foreign Office messenger brought him an envelope. He opened it and was absorbed in the contents. Then he got up, walked round to where the Prime Minister was sitting, and gave him the message. Although Cadogan's demeanour would not have indicated that anything had happened, I could not help noticing the Prime Minister's evident preoccupation. Presently Cadogan came back with the paper and resumed his seat. Later I was told its contents. It said that Hitler had invaded Austria and that the German mechanised forces were advancing fast upon Vienna. The meal proceeded without the slightest interruption, but quite soon Mrs. Chamberlain, who had received some signal from her husband, got up, saying, "Let us *all* have coffee in the drawing-room." We trooped in there, and it was evident to me and perhaps to some others that Mr. and Mrs. Chamberlain wished to bring the proceedings to an end. A kind of general restlessness pervaded the company, and everyone stood about ready to say good-bye to the guests of honour.

However, Herr von Ribbentrop and his wife did not seem at all conscious of this atmosphere. On the contrary, they tarried for nearly half an hour engaging their host and hostess in voluble conversation. At one moment I came in contact with Frau von Ribbentrop, and in a valedictory vein I said, "I hope England and Germany will preserve their friendship." "Be careful you don't spoil it," was her graceful rejoinder. I am sure they both knew perfectly well what had happened, but thought it was a good manœuvre to keep the Prime Minister away from his work and the telephone. At length Mr. Chamberlain said to the Ambassador, "I am sorry I have to go now to attend to urgent business," and without more ado he left the room. The Ribbentrops lingered on, so that most of us made our excuses and our way home. Eventually I suppose they left. This was the last time I saw Herr von Ribbentrop before he was hanged.

*   *   *

The outrage against Austria and the subjugation of beautiful Vienna, with all its fame, culture, and contribution to the story of Europe, hit me hard. On the morrow of these events, March 14, I said in the House of Commons:

The gravity of the event of March 12 cannot be exaggerated. Europe is confronted with a programme of aggression, nicely calculated and timed, unfolding stage by stage, and there is only one choice open, not only to us but to other countries, either to submit like Austria, or else take effective measures while time remains to ward off the danger, and if it cannot be warded off to cope with it. . . . If we go on waiting upon events, how much shall we throw away of resources now available for our security and the maintenance of peace? How many friends will be alienated, how many potential allies shall we see go one by one down the grisly gulf? How many times will bluff succeed until behind bluff ever gathering forces have accumulated reality? . . . *Where are we going to be two years hence, for instance, when the German Army will certainly be much larger than the French Army*, and when all the small nations will have fled from Geneva to pay homage to the ever-waxing power of the Nazi system, and to make the best terms that they can for themselves?

And further:

Vienna is the centre of the communications of all the countries which formed the old Austro-Hungarian Empire, and of the countries lying to the south-east of Europe. A long stretch of the Danube is now in German hands. This mastery of Vienna gives to Nazi Germany military and economic control of the whole of the communications of South-eastern Europe, by road, by river, and by rail. What is the effect of this on the structure of Europe? What is the effect of it upon what is called the balance of power, such as it is—upon what is called the Little Entente? I must say a word about this group of Powers called the Little Entente. Taken singly, the three countries of the Little Entente may be called Powers of the second rank, but they are very powerful and vigorous States, and united they are a great Power. They have hitherto been, and are still, united by the closest military agreement. Together they make the complement of a great Power and of the military machinery of a great Power. Roumania has the oil, Yugoslavia has the minerals and raw materials. Both have large armies, both are mainly supplied with munitions from Czechoslovakia.

To English ears the name of Czechoslovakia sounds outlandish. No doubt they are only a small democratic State, no doubt they have an army only two or three times as large as ours, no doubt they have a munitions supply only three times as great as that of Italy, but still they are a virile people, they have their rights, they have their treaty rights, they have a line of fortresses, and they have a strongly-manifested will to live, a will to live freely.

Czechoslovakia is at this moment isolated, both in the economic and in the military sense. Her trade outlet through Hamburg, which is based upon the Peace Treaty, can of course be closed at any moment. Now her communications by rail and river to the south, and beyond the south to the south-east, are liable to be severed at any moment. Her trade may be subjected to tolls of a destructive character, of an absolutely strangling character. Here is a country which was once the greatest manufacturing area in the old Austro-Hungarian Empire. It is now cut off, or may be cut off at once, unless out of these discussions which must follow arrangements are made securing the communications of Czechoslovakia. She may be cut off at once from the sources of her raw materials in Yugoslavia and from the natural markets which she has established there. The economic life of this small State may be very largely strangled as a result of the act of violence which was perpetrated last Friday night. A wedge has been driven into the heart of what is called the Little Entente, this group of countries which have as much right to live in Europe unmolested as any of us have the right to live unmolested in our native land.

* * *

It was the Russians who now sounded the alarm, and on March 18 proposed a conference on the situation. They wished to discuss, if only in outline, ways and means of implementing the Franco-Soviet pact within the frame of League action in the event of a major threat to peace by Germany. This met with little warmth in Paris and London. The French Government was distracted by other preoccupations. There were serious strikes in the aircraft factories. Franco's armies were driving deep into the territory of Communist Spain. Chamberlain was both sceptical and depressed. He profoundly disagreed with my interpretation of the dangers ahead and the means of combating them. I had been urging the prospects of a Franco-British-Russian alliance as the only hope of checking the Nazi onrush.

Mr. Feiling tells us that the Prime Minister expressed his mood in a letter to his sister on March 20:

The plan of the "Grand Alliance", as Winston calls it, had occurred to me long before he mentioned it. . . . I talked about it to Halifax, and we submitted it to the Chiefs of Staff and F.O. experts. It is a very attractive idea; indeed, there is almost everything to be said for it until you come to examine its practicability. From that moment its attraction vanishes. You have only to look at the map to see that nothing that France or we could do could possibly save Czechoslovakia from being overrun by the Germans, if they wanted to do it. I have therefore abandoned any idea of giving guarantees to Czechoslovakia, or to the French in connection with her obligations to that country.*

Here was at any rate a decision. It was taken on wrong arguments. In modern wars of great nations or alliances particular areas are not defended only by local exertions. The whole vast balance of the war-front is involved. This is still more true of policy before war begins and while it may still be averted. It surely did not take much thought from the "Chiefs of Staff and F.O. experts" to tell the Prime Minister that the British Navy and the French Army could not be deployed on the Bohemian mountain front to stand between the Czechoslovak Republic and Hitler's invading army. This was indeed evident from the map. But the certainty that the crossing of the Bohemian frontier line would have involved a general European war might well even at that date have deterred or delayed Hitler's next assault. How erroneous Mr. Chamberlain's private and earnest reasoning appears when we cast our minds forward to the guarantee he was to give to Poland *within a year*, after all the strategic value of Czechoslovakia had been cast away, and Hitler's power and prestige had almost doubled!

* * *

On March 24, 1938, in the House of Commons, the Prime Minister gave us his view about the Russian move:

His Majesty's Government are of the opinion that the indirect but none the less inevitable consequence of such action as is proposed by the Soviet Government would be to aggravate the tendency towards the establishment of exclusive groups of nations, which must in the view of His Majesty's Government be inimical to the prospects of European peace.

Nevertheless the Prime Minister could not avoid facing the

* Feiling, *op. cit.*, pp. 347-8.

brutal fact that there existed a "profound disturbance of international confidence", and that the Government would have sooner or later to decide upon a definition of Great Britain's obligations in Europe. What would be our obligations in Central Europe? "If war broke out it would be unlikely to be confined to those who have assumed legal obligations. It would be quite impossible to say where it would end and what Governments might be involved." It must further be observed that the argument about the evils of "exclusive groups of nations" loses its validity if the alternative is being mopped up one by one by the aggressor. Moreover, it overlooks all questions of right and wrong in international relationships. There was after all in existence the League of Nations and its Charter.

The Prime Minister's course was now marked out: simultaneous diplomatic pressure on Berlin and Prague, appeasement in regard to Italy, a strictly restrained definition of our obligations to France. To carry out the first two moves, it was essential to be careful and precise about the last.

★　　★　　★

The reader is now invited to move westward to the Emerald Isle. "It's a long way to Tipperary," but a visit there is sometimes irresistible. In the interval between Hitler's seizure of Austria and his unfolding design upon Czechoslovakia we must turn to a wholly different kind of misfortune which befell us.

Since the beginning of 1938 there had been negotiations between the British Government and that of Mr. de Valera in Southern Ireland, and on April 25 an agreement was signed whereby, among other matters, Great Britain renounced all rights to occupy for naval purposes the two Southern Irish ports of Queenstown and Berehaven, and the base in Lough Swilly. The two southern ports were a vital feature in the naval defence of our food supply. When in 1922 as Colonial and Dominions Secretary I had dealt with the details of the Irish Settlement which the Cabinet of those days had made, I brought Admiral Beatty to the Colonial Office to explain to Michael Collins the importance of these ports to our whole system of bringing supplies into Britain. Collins was immediately convinced. "Of course you must have the ports," he said; "they are necessary for your life." Thus the matter was arranged, and everything had worked smoothly in the sixteen years that had passed. The reason why Queenstown and Berehaven were necessary to our safety is easy to understand. They were the fuelling bases from which our destroyer flotillas ranged westward into the Atlantic to hunt U-boats and protect incoming convoys as they reached the throat of the narrow seas. Lough Swilly was similarly needed to protect the approaches to the Clyde and Mersey. To abandon these meant that our flotillas would have to start in the north from Lamlash and in the south from Pembroke Dock or Falmouth, thus decreasing their radius of action and the protection they could afford by more than 400 miles out and home.

It was incredible to me that the Chiefs of Staff should have agreed to throw away this major security, and to the last moment I thought that at least we had safeguarded our right to occupy these Irish ports in the event of war. However, Mr. de Valera announced in the Dail that no conditions of any kind were attached to the cession. I was later assured that Mr. de Valera was surprised at the readiness with which the British Government had deferred to his request. He had included it in his proposals as a bargaining counter which could be dispensed with when other points were satisfactorily settled.

Lord Chatfield has in his last book devoted a chapter to explaining the course he and the other Chiefs of Staff took.* This should certainly be read by those who wish to pursue the subject. Personally I remain convinced that the gratuitous surrender of our right to use the Irish ports in war was a major injury to British national life and safety. A more feckless act can hardly be imagined—and at such a time. It is true that in the end we survived without the ports. It is also true that if we had not been able to do without them we should have retaken them by force rather than perish by famine. But this is no excuse. Many a ship and many a life were soon to be lost as the result of this improvident example of appeasement.

The whole Conservative Party, except the handful of Ulster Members, supported the Prime Minister, and of course a step like this was meat and drink to the Labour and Liberal Opposition. I was therefore almost entirely alone when on May 5 I rose to make my protest. I was listened to with a patient air of scepticism. There was even a kind of sympathetic wonder that anyone

* Lord Chatfield, *It Might Happen Again*, Chapter XVIII.

of my standing should attempt to plead so hopeless a case. I never saw the House of Commons more completely misled. It was but fifteen months to the declaration of war. The Members were to feel very differently about it when our existence hung in the balance during the Battle of the Atlantic. As my speech has been fully published in *Into Battle* I do not quote it here save on one point. The issue of Southern Irish neutrality in time of war was not faced.

What guarantee [I asked] have you that Southern Ireland, or the Irish Republic as they claim to be, will not declare neutrality if we are engaged in war with some powerful nation? The first step certainly which such an enemy would take would be to offer complete immunity of every kind to Southern Ireland if she would remain neutral. . . . You cannot exclude this possibility of neutrality as being one which may come within the immediate sphere of our experience. The ports may be denied us in the hour of need, and we may be hampered in the gravest manner in protecting the British population from privation and even starvation. Who would wish to put his head in such a noose? Is there any other country in the world where such a step would even have been contemplated? It would be an easy step for a Dublin Government to deny the ports to us once we have gone. The cannon are there, the mines will be there. But more important for this purpose, the juridical right will be there. You had the rights; you have ceded them; you hope in their place to have goodwill strong enough to endure tribulation for your sake. Suppose you have it not. It will be no use saying, "Then we will retake the ports." You will have no right to do so. To violate Irish neutrality should it be declared at the moment of a Great War may put you out of court in the opinion of the world, and may vitiate the cause by which you may be involved in war. . . . You are casting away real and important means of security and survival for vain shadows and for ease.

The comment of the *Times* newspaper was illuminating.

The agreement on defence . . . releases the Government of the United Kingdom from the articles of the Anglo-Irish Treaty of 1921, by which they assumed the onerous and delicate task of defending the fortified harbours of Cork, Berehaven, and Lough Swilly in the event of war.

Further releases might have been obtained by handing over Gibraltar to Spain and Malta to Italy. Neither touched the actual existence of our population more directly.

With that I leave this lamentable and amazing episode.

CHAPTER XVI

CZECHOSLOVAKIA

An Unlikely Historical Controversy – Hitler's Next Objective – "No Evil Intentions towards Czechoslovakia" – M. Blum's Pledge – My Visit to Paris, March 1938 – M. Daladier succeeds M. Blum – The Anglo-Italian Pact – An Interview with the Sudeten Leader – Misgivings and Reluctance of the German Generals – The Relations of Soviet Russia with Czechoslovakia – Stalin and Beneš – Plot and Purge in Russia – M. Daladier's Declaration of June 12 – Hitler's Promise to Keitel – Captain Wiedemann's Mission to London – I Address My Constituents at Theydon Bois, August 27 – My Letter to Lord Halifax of August 31 – The Soviet Ambassador's Visit to Chartwell – My Report to the Foreign Office – The "Times" Leading Article of September 7 – M. Bonnet's Question and the British Answer – Hitler's Crisis Speech at Nuremberg.

*F*OR SOME YEARS it seemed that the question whether Britain and France were wise or foolish in the Munich episode would become a matter of long historical controversy. However, the revelations which have been made from German sources, and particularly at the Nuremberg Trials, have rendered this unlikely. The two main issues in dispute were: first, whether decisive action by Britain and France would have forced Hitler to recede or have led to his overthrow by a military conspiracy; secondly, whether the year that intervened between Munich and the outbreak of war placed the Western Powers relatively in a better or worse position, compared with Germany, than in September 1938.

Many volumes have been written, and will be written, upon the crisis that was ended at Munich by the sacrifice of Czechoslovakia, and it is only intended here to give a few of the cardinal facts and establish the main proportions of events. These follow inexorably from Hitler's resolve to reunite all Germans in a Greater Reich and to expand eastwards, and his conviction that the men at the head of France and Britain would not fight owing to their love of peace and failure to rearm. The usual technique was employed against Czechoslovakia. The grievances, which were not unreal, of the Sudeten Germans were magnified and exploited. The public case was opened against Czechoslovakia by Hitler in his speech to the Reichstag on February 20, 1938. "Over ten million Germans," he said, "live in two of the States adjoining our frontier." It was the duty of Germany to protect those fellow-Germans and secure to them "general freedom, personal, political, and ideological."

This public announcement of the intention of the German Government to interest themselves in the position of the German inhabitants of Austria and Czechoslovakia was intimately related to the secret planning of Germany's political offensive in Europe. The declared objectives of the Nazi German Government were twofold—the absorption by the Reich of all German minorities living beyond her frontiers, and thereby the extension of her living space in the East. The less publicised purpose of German policy was military in character—the liquidation of Czechoslovakia with its potentialities both as a Russian air-base and as an Anglo-French military make-weight in the event of war. As early as June 1937 the German General Staff had been, on Hitler's instructions, busy at work drafting plans for the invasion and destruction of the Czechoslovak State.

One draft reads:

The aim and object of this surprise attack by the German armed forces should be to eliminate from the very beginning and for the duration of the war the threat from Czechoslovakia to the rear of the operations in the West, and to take from the Russian Air Force the most substantial portion of its operational base in Czechoslovakia.*

The acceptance by the Western Democracies of the German subjugation of Austria encouraged Hitler to pursue his designs more sharply against Czechoslovakia. The military control of Austrian territory was in fact intended to be the indispensable preliminary to the assault on the Bohemian bastion. While the invasion of Austria was in full swing Hitler said in the motor-car

* *Nuremberg Documents*, II, p. 4.

to General von Halder, "This will be very inconvenient to the Czechs." Halder saw immediately the significance of this remark. To him it lighted up the future. It showed him Hitler's intentions, and at the same time, as he viewed it, Hitler's military ignorance. "It was practically impossible," he has explained, "for a German army to attack Czechoslovakia from the south. The single railway line through Linz was completely exposed, and surprise was out of the question." But Hitler's main political strategic conception was correct. The West Wall was growing, and, although far from complete, already confronted the French Army with horrible memories of the Somme and Passchendaele. He was convinced that neither France nor Britain would fight.

On the day of the march of the German armies into Austria the French Ambassador in Berlin reported that Goering had given a solemn assurance to the Czech Minister in Berlin that Germany had *"no evil intentions towards Czechoslovakia"*. On March 14 the French Premier, M. Blum, solemnly declared to the Czech Minister in Paris that France would unreservedly honour her engagement to Czechoslovakia. These diplomatic reassurances could not conceal the grim reality. The whole strategic position on the Continent had changed. The German arguments and armies could now concentrate directly upon the western frontiers of Czechoslovakia, whose border districts were German in racial character, with an aggressive and active German Nationalist Party eager to act as a fifth column in the event of trouble.

At the end of March I went to Paris and had searching conversations with the French leaders. The Government were agreeable to my going to vivify my French contacts. I stayed at our Embassy, and saw in a continued succession many of the principal French figures—Premier Léon Blum, Flandin, General Gamelin, Paul Reynaud, Pierre Cot, Herriot, Louis Marin, and others. To Blum I said at one moment, "The German field howitzer is believed to be superior in range and of course in striking power to the *soixante-quinze* even when relined." He replied, "Is it from you that I am to learn the state of the French artillery?" I said, "No, but ask your École Polytechnique, who are by no means convinced by the exposition lately given to them of the relative power of the modernised *soixante-quinze*." He was immediately genial and friendly. Reynaud said to me, "We quite understand that England will never have conscription. Why do you not therefore go in for a mechanical army? If you had six armoured divisions you would indeed be an effective Continental force," or words to that effect. It seemed that a Colonel de Gaulle had written a much-criticised book about the offensive power of modern armoured vehicles.

The Ambassador and I had a long luncheon alone with Flandin. He was quite a different man from the one I had known in 1936: then responsible and agitated; now out of office, cool, massive, and completely convinced that there was no hope for France except in an arrangement with Germany. We argued for two hours. Gamelin, who also visited me, was rightly confident in the strength of the French Army at the moment, but none too comfortable when I questioned him upon the artillery, about which he had precise knowledge. He was always trying his best within the limits of the French political system. But the attention of the French Government to the dangers of the European scene was distracted by the ceaseless whirlpool of internal politics at the moment and by the imminent fall of the Blum Government. It was all the more essential that our common and mutual obligations in the event of a general crisis should be established without any trace of misunderstanding. On April 10 the French Government was re-formed with M. Daladier as Premier and M. Bonnet as Minister for Foreign Affairs. These two men were to bear the responsibility for French policy in the critical months ahead.

In the hope of deterring Germany from a further aggression the British Government, in accordance with Mr. Chamberlain's resolve, sought a settlement with Italy in the Mediterranean. This would strengthen the position of France, and would enable both the French and British to concentrate upon events in Central Europe. Mussolini, to some extent placated by the fall of Eden, and feeling himself in a strong bargaining position, did not repulse the British repentance. On April 16, 1938, an Anglo-Italian agreement was signed, giving Italy in effect a free hand in Abyssinia and Spain in return for the imponderable value of Italian goodwill in Central Europe. The Foreign Office was sceptical of this transaction. Mr. Chamberlain's biographer tells us that he wrote in a personal and private letter, "You should have seen the draft put up to me by the F.O.; it would have frozen a Polar bear."[*]

* Feiling, *op. cit.*, p. 350.

I shared the misgivings of the Foreign Office at this move:

Mr. Churchill to Mr. Eden   18.IV.38

The Italian pact is of course a complete triumph for Mussolini, who gains our cordial acceptance for his fortification of the Mediterranean against us, for his conquest of Abyssinia, and for his violence in Spain. The fact that we are not to fortify Cyprus without "previous consultation" is highly detrimental. The rest of it is to my mind only padding.

Nevertheless I feel that considerable caution is necessary in opposing the agreement bluntly. It is a done thing. It is called a move towards peace. It undoubtedly makes it less likely that sparks from the Mediterranean should light a European conflagration. France will have to follow suit for her own protection, in order not to be divided from Britain. Finally, there is the possibility that Mussolini may be drawn by his interests to discourage German interference in the Danube basin.

Before making up my mind, I should like to know your views and intentions. I think the Anglo-Italian pact is only the first step, and that the second will be an attempt to patch up something even more specious with Germany, which will lull the British public while letting the German armed strength grow and German designs in the East of Europe develop.

Chamberlain last week told the Executive of the National Union [of Conservative Associations] in secret that he "had not abandoned hopes of similar arrangements with Germany". They took this rather coldly.

Meanwhile our progress in the air is increasingly disappointing. . . .

Mr. Eden to Mr. Churchill   28.IV.38

. . . With regard to the Italian pact, I agree with what you write. Mussolini gives us nothing more than the repetition of promises previously made and broken by him, except for the withdrawal of troops from Libya, troops which were probably originally sent there for their nuisance value. It has now become clear that, as I expected, Mussolini continued his intervention in Spain after the conversations in Rome had opened. He must be an optimist indeed who believes that Mussolini will cease increasing that intervention now, should it be required to secure Franco's victory.

As a diplomatic instrument the pact embodies a machinery which is likely to be found very troublesome to work. It is not to come into force until after the Italians leave Spain. It is almost certain however that many months will elapse before that occurs, and since what is important is not the presence of Italian infantry, but the assertions of their experts and the Germans, it will be difficult to establish with

35 Winston Churchill reviewing the Home Fleet at Spithead.

37 Stalin and von Ribbentrop.

38 Konrad Henlein, leader of the Sudetenland.

certainty that the withdrawal has taken place. But maybe some do not mind much about that.

Then there is the Italian position in Abyssinia, which, from what I hear, so far from improving grows steadily worse. I am afraid that the moment we are choosing for its recognition will not benefit our authority among the many millions of the King's coloured subjects.

None the less I equally agree as to the need for caution in any attitude taken up towards the agreement. After all it is not an Agreement yet, and it would be wrong certainly for me to say anything which could be considered as making its fruition more difficult. After all, this is precisely what I promised I would not do in my resignation speech and at Leamington.

The most anxious feature of the international situation, as I see it, is that temporary relaxation of tension may be taken as a pretext for the relaxation of national effort, which is already inadequate to the gravity of the times. . . .

Hitler was watching the scene with vigilance. To him also the ultimate alignment of Italy in a European crisis was important. In conference with his Chiefs of Staff at the end of April he was considering how to force the pace. Mussolini wanted a free hand in Abyssinia. In spite of the acquiescence of the British Government, he might ultimately need German support in this venture. If so, he should accept German action against Czechoslovakia. This issue must be brought to a head, and in the settling of the Czech question Italy would be involved on Germany's side. The declarations of British and French statesmen were of course studied in Berlin. The intention of these Western Powers to persuade the Czechs to be reasonable in the interests of European peace was noted with satisfaction. The Nazi Party of the Sudetenland, led by Henlein, now formulated their demands for autonomy in the German-border regions of that country. Their programme had been announced in Henlein's speech at Carlsbad on April 24. The British and French Ministers in Prague called on the Czech Foreign Minister shortly after this to "express the hope that the Czech Government will go to the furthest limit in order to settle the question".

During May the Germans in Czechoslovakia were ordered to increase their agitation. On May 12 Henlein visited London to acquaint the British Government with the wrongs inflicted upo his followers. He expressed a wish to see me. I therefore arranged a talk at Morpeth Mansions the next day, at which Sir Archibald

Sinclair was present, and Professor Lindemann was our interpreter.

Henlein's solution, as he described it, may be summed up as follows:

There should be a central Parliament in Prague, which should have control of foreign policy, defence, finance, and communications. All parties should be entitled to express their views there, and the Government would act on majority decisions. The frontier fortresses could be manned by Czech troops, who would of course have unhindered access thereto. The Sudeten German regions, and possibly the other minority districts, should enjoy local autonomy; that is to say, they should have their own town and county councils, and a Diet in which matters of common regional concern could be debated within definitely delimited frontiers. He would be prepared to submit questions of fact, *e.g.*, the tracing of the boundary, to an impartial tribunal, perhaps even appointed by the League of Nations. All parties would be free to organise and offer themselves for election, and impartial courts of justice would function in autonomous districts. The officials—*i.e.*, postal, railway, and police officers—in the German-speaking region would of course be German-speaking, and a reasonable proportion of the total taxes collected should be returned to these regions for their administration.

M. Masaryk, the Czech Minister in London, who was afterwards informed of this conversation, professed himself contented with a settlement on these lines. A peaceful solution of admitted racial and minority quarrels compatible with the independence of the Czech Republic was by no means impossible, if there were German good faith and goodwill. But on this condition I had no illusions.

On May 17 negotiations about the Sudeten question began between Henlein, who had visited Hitler on his return journey, and the Czech Government. Municipal elections were due in Czechoslovakia, and the German Government began a calculated war of nerves in preparation for them. Persistent rumours already circulated of German troop movements towards the Czech frontier. On May 20 Sir Nevile Henderson was requested to make inquiries in Berlin on this matter. German denials did not reassure the Czechs, who on the night of May 20–21 decreed a partial mobilisation of their Army.

★　★　★

It is important at this stage to consider the German intentions. Hitler had for some time been convinced that neither France nor Britain would fight for Czechoslovakia. On May 28 he called a meeting of his principal advisers and gave instructions for the preparations to attack Czechoslovakia. He declared this later in public in a speech to the Reichstag on January 30, 1939:

> In view of this intolerable provocation . . . I resolved to settle once and for all, and this time radically, the Sudeten-German question. On May 28 I ordered (1) that preparations should be made for military action against this State by October 2; and (2) the immense and accelerated expansion of our defensive front in the West.*

His Service advisers, however, did not share unanimously his overwhelming confidence. The German generals could not be persuaded, considering the still enormous preponderance of Allied strength except in the air, that France and Britain would submit to the Fuehrer's challenge. To break the Czech Army and pierce or turn the Bohemian fortress line would require practically the whole of thirty-five divisions. The German Chiefs of Staff informed Hitler that the Czech Army must be considered efficient and up-to-date in arms and equipment. The fortifications of the West Wall or Siegfried Line, though already in existence as field works, were far from completed. Thus at the moment of attacking the Czechs only five effective and eight Reserve divisions would be available to protect the whole of Germany's western frontier against the French Army, which could mobilise a hundred divisions. The generals were aghast at running such risks, when by waiting a few years the German Army would again be master. Although Hitler's political judgment had been proved correct by the pacifism and weakness of the Allies about conscription, the Rhineland, and Austria, the German High Command could not believe that Hitler's bluff would succeed a fourth time. It seemed so much beyond the bounds of reason that great victorious nations, possessing evident military superiority, would once again abandon the path of duty and honour, which was also for them the path of common sense and prudence. Besides all this there was Russia, with her Slav affinities with Czechoslovakia, and whose attitude towards Germany at this juncture was full of menace.

* _Hitler's Speeches_, II, 1571.

The relations of Soviet Russia with Czechoslovakia as a State, and personally with President Beneš, were those of intimate and solid friendship. The roots of this lay in a certain racial affinity, and also in comparatively recent events which require a brief digression. When President Beneš visited me at Marrakesh in January 1944 he told me this story. In 1935 he had received an offer from Hitler to respect in all circumstances the integrity of Czechoslovakia in return for a guarantee that she would remain neutral in the event of a Franco-German war. When Beneš pointed to his treaty obliging him to act with France in such a case, the German Ambassador replied that there was no need to denounce the treaty. It would be sufficient to break it, if and when the time came, by simply failing to mobilise or march. The small republic was not in a position to indulge in indignation at such a suggestion. Their fear of Germany was already very grave, more especially as the question of the Sudeten Germans might at any time be raised and fomented by Germany, to their extreme embarrassment and growing peril. They therefore let the matter drop without comment or commitment, and it did not stir for more than a year. In the autumn of 1936 a message from a high military source in Germany was conveyed to President Beneš to the effect that if he wanted to take advantage of the Fuehrer's offer he had better be quick, because events would shortly take place in Russia rendering any help he could give to Germany insignificant.

While Beneš was pondering over this disturbing hint he became aware that communications were passing through the Soviet Embassy in Prague between important personages in Russia and the German Government. This was a part of the so-called military and Old-Guard-Communist conspiracy to overthrow Stalin and introduce a new *régime* based on a pro-German policy. President Beneš lost no time in communicating all he could find out to Stalin.* Thereafter there followed the merciless, but perhaps not needless, military and political purge in Soviet Russia, and the series of trials in January 1937, in which Vyshinsky, the Public Prosecutor, played so masterful a part.

Although it is highly improbable that the Old-Guard Com-

* There is however some evidence that Beneš's information had previously been imparted to the Czech police by the Ogpu, who wished it to reach Stalin from a friendly foreign source. This did not detract from Beneš's service to Stalin, and is therefore irrelevant.

munists had made common cause with the military leaders, or
vice versa, they were certainly filled with jealousy of Stalin, who
had ousted them. It may therefore have been convenient to get
rid of them at the same time, according to the standards maintained in a totalitarian State. Zinoviev, Bukharin, and others of
the original leaders of the Revolution, Marshal Tukhachevsky,
who had been invited to represent the Soviet Union at the
Coronation of King George VI, and many other high officers of
the Army, were shot. In all not less than five thousand officers
and officials above the rank of Captain were "liquidated". The
Russian Army was purged of its pro-German elements at a heavy
cost to its military efficiency. The bias of the Soviet Government
was turned in a marked manner against Germany. Stalin was
conscious of a personal debt to President Beneš, and a very strong
desire to help him and his threatened country against the Nazi
peril animated the Soviet Government. The situation was of
course thoroughly understood by Hitler; but I am not aware that
the British and French Governments were equally enlightened.
To Mr. Chamberlain and the British and French General Staffs
the purge of 1937 presented itself mainly as a tearing to pieces
internally of the Russian Army, and a picture of the Soviet
Union as riven asunder by ferocious hatreds and vengeance. This
was perhaps an excessive view; for a system of government
founded on terror may well be strengthened by a ruthless and
successful assertion of its power. The salient fact for the purposes
of this account is the close association of Russia and Czechoslovakia, and of Stalin and Beneš.

But neither the internal stresses in Germany nor the ties between
Beneš and Stalin were known to the outside world, or appreciated
by the British and French Ministers. The Siegfried Line, albeit
unperfected, seemed a fearful deterrent. The exact strength and
fighting power of the German Army, new though it was, could
not be accurately estimated and was certainly exaggerated. There
were also the unmeasured dangers of air attack on undefended
cities. Above all there was the hatred of war in the hearts of the
Democracies.

Nevertheless on June 12 M. Daladier renewed his predecessor's
pledge of March 14, and declared that France's engagements
towards Czechoslovakia "are sacred, and cannot be evaded".
This considerable statement sweeps away all chatter about the

Treaty of Locarno thirteen years before having by implication left everything in the East vague pending an Eastern Locarno. There can be no doubt before history that the treaty between France and Czechoslovakia of 1924 had complete validity not only in law but in fact, and that this was reaffirmed by successive heads of the French Government in all the circumstances of 1938.

But on this subject Hitler was convinced that his judgment alone was sound, and on June 18 he issued a final directive for the attack on Czechoslovakia, in the course of which he sought to reassure his anxious generals.

Hitler to Keitel

I will decide to take action against Czechoslovakia only if I am firmly convinced, as in the case of the demilitarised zone and the entry into Austria, that France will not march, and that therefore England will not intervene.*

With the object of confusing the issue Hitler at the beginning of July sent his personal aide, Captain Wiedemann, to London. This envoy was received by Lord Halifax on July 18, ostensibly without the knowledge of the German Embassy. The Fuehrer was, it was suggested, hurt at our lack of response to his overtures in the past. Perhaps the British Government would receive Goering in London for fuller discussions. The Germans might, in certain circumstances, be prepared to delay action against the Czechs for a year. A few days later Chamberlain took up this possibility with the German Ambassador. To clear the ground in Prague the British Prime Minister had already suggested to the Czechs the sending of an investigator to Czechoslovakia to promote a friendly compromise. The Royal visit to Paris on July 20 gave Halifax the opportunity of discussing this proposal with the French Government, and in a brief interchange of views both Governments agreed to make this effort at mediation.

On July 26, 1938, Chamberlain announced to Parliament the mission of Lord Runciman to Prague with the object of seeking a solution there by arrangements between the Czech Government and Herr Henlein. On the following day the Czechs issued a draft statute for national minorities to form a basis of negotiations. On the same day Lord Halifax stated in Parliament: "*I do not believe that those responsible for the Government of any country in*

---

* *Nuremberg Documents*, Pt. II, No. 10.

Europe to-day want war." On August 3 Lord Runciman reached Prague, and a series of interminable and complicated discussions took place with the various interested parties. Within a fortnight these negotiations broke down, and from this point events moved rapidly.

On August 27 Ribbentrop, now Foreign Minister, reported a visit which he had received from the Italian Ambassador in Berlin, who "had received another written instruction from Mussolini asking that Germany would communicate in time the probable date of action against Czechoslovakia". Mussolini asked for such notification in order "to be able to take in due time the necessary measures on the French frontier".

* * *

Anxiety grew steadily during August. To my constituents I said on the 27th:

It is difficult for us in this ancient forest of Theydon Bois, the very name of which carries us back to Norman days—here, in the heart of peaceful, law-abiding England—to realise the ferocious passions which are rife in Europe. During this anxious month you have no doubt seen reports in the newspapers, one week good, another week bad; one week better, another week worse. But I must tell you that the whole state of Europe and of the world is moving steadily towards a climax which cannot be long delayed.

War is certainly not inevitable. But the danger to peace will not be removed until the vast German armies which have been called from their homes into the ranks have been dispersed. For a country which is itself not menaced by anyone, in no fear of anyone, to place over fifteen hundred thousand soldiers upon a war footing is a very grave step. . . . It seems to me, and I must tell it to you plainly, that these great forces have not been placed upon a war footing without an intention to reach a conclusion within a very limited space of time. . . .

We are all in full agreement with the course our Government have taken in sending Lord Runciman to Prague. We hope—indeed, we pray—that his mission of conciliation will be successful, and certainly it looks as if the Government of Czechoslovakia were doing their utmost to put their house in order, and to meet every demand which is not designed to compass their ruin as a State. . . . But larger and fiercer ambitions may prevent a settlement, and then Europe and the civilised world will have to face the demands of Nazi Germany, or perhaps be confronted with some sudden violent action on the part of the German Nazi Party, carrying with it the invasion of a small country and its subjugation. Such an episode would not be simply an attack upon Czechoslovakia; it would be an outrage against the civilisation and freedom of the whole world. . . .

Whatever may happen, foreign countries should know—and the Government are right to let them know—that Great Britain and the British Empire must not be deemed incapable of playing their part and doing their duty as they have done on other great occasions which have not yet been forgotten by history.

I was in these days in some contact with Ministers. My relations with Lord Halifax were of course marked by the grave political differences which existed between me and His Majesty's Government, both in defence and foreign policy. In the main Eden and I meant the same thing. I could not feel the same about his successor. None the less, whenever there was any occasion we met as friends and former colleagues of many years' standing, and I wrote to him from time to time. Now and then he asked me to go to see him.

Mr. Churchill to Lord Halifax   31.VIII.38

If Beneš makes good, and Runciman thinks it a fair offer, yet nevertheless it is turned down, it seems to me there are two things which might have been done this week to increase the deterrents against violent action by Hitler, neither of which would commit you to the dread guarantee.

First, would it not be possible to frame a Joint Note between Britain, France, and Russia stating: (a) their desire for peace and friendly relations; (b) their deep anxiety at the military preparations of Germany; (c) their joint interest in a peaceful solution of the Czechoslovak controversy; and (d) that an invasion by Germany of Czechoslovakia would raise capital issues for all three Powers? This Note, when drafted, should be formally shown to Roosevelt by the Ambassadors of the three Powers, and we should use every effort to induce him to do his utmost upon it. It seems to me not impossible that he would then himself address Hitler, emphasising the gravity of the situation, and saying that it seemed to him that a world war would inevitably follow from an invasion of Czechoslovakia, and that he earnestly counselled a friendly settlement.

It seems to me that this process would give the best chance to the peaceful elements in German official circles to make a stand, and that Hitler might find a way out for himself by parleying with Roosevelt. However, none of these developments can be predicted; one only sees them as hopes. *The important thing is the Joint Note.*

The second step which might save the situation would be fleet movements, and the placing of the reserve flotillas and cruiser squadrons into full commission. I do not suggest calling out the Royal Fleet Reserve or mobilisation, but there are, I believe, five or six flotillas which could be raised to First Fleet scale, and also there are about two hundred trawlers which could be used for anti-submarine work. The taking of these and other measures would make a great stir in the naval ports, the effect of which could only be beneficial as a deterrent, and a timely precaution if the worst happened.

I venture to hope that you will not resent these suggestions from one who has lived through such days before. It is clear that speed is vital.

*　　*　　*

In the afternoon of September 2 I received a message from the Soviet Ambassador that he would like to come down to Chartwell and see me at once upon a matter of urgency. I had for some time had friendly personal relations with M. Maisky, who also saw a good deal of my son Randolph. I thereupon received the Ambassador, and after a few preliminaries he told me in precise and formal detail the story set out below. Before he had got very far I realised that he was making a declaration to me, a private person, because the Soviet Government preferred this channel to a direct offer to the Foreign Office, which might have encountered a rebuff. It was clearly intended that I should report what I was told to His Majesty's Government. This was not actually stated by the Ambassador, but it was implied by the fact that no request for secrecy was made. As the matter struck me at once as being of the first importance, I was careful not to prejudice its consideration by Halifax and Chamberlain by proceeding to commit myself in any way, or use language which would excite controversy between us.

Mr. Churchill to Lord Halifax　　　　　　　　　　　　　　　　3.IX.38

I have received privately from an absolutely sure source the following information, which I feel it my duty to report to you, although I was not asked to do so.

Yesterday, September 2, the French Chargé d'Affaires in Moscow (the Ambassador being on leave) called upon M. Litvinov and, in the name of the French Government, asked him what aid Russia would give to Czechoslovakia against a German attack, having regard particularly to the difficulties which might be created by the neutrality of Poland or Roumania. Litvinov asked in reply what the French would do themselves, pointing out that the French had a direct obligation, whereas the Russian obligation was dependent on the action of France. The French Chargé d'Affaires did not reply to this question. Nevertheless, Litvinov stated to him, first, that the Russian Soviet Union had resolved to fulfil their obligations. He recognised the difficulties created by the attitude of Poland and Roumania, but he thought that in the case of Roumania these could be overcome.

In the last few months the policy of the Roumanian Government had been markedly friendly to Russia, and their relations had greatly improved. M. Litvinov thought that the best way to overcome the reluctance of Roumania would be through the agency of the League of Nations. If, for instance, the League decided that Czechoslovakia was the victim of aggression and that Germany was the aggressor, that would probably determine the action of Roumania in regard to allowing Russian troops and air forces to pass through her territory.

The French Chargé d'Affaires raised the point that the Council might not be unanimous, and was answered that M. Litvinov thought a majority decision would be sufficient, and that Roumania would probably associate herself with the majority in the vote of the Council. M. Litvinov therefore advised that the Council of the League should be invoked under Article 11, on the ground that there was danger of war, and that the League Powers should consult together. He thought the sooner this was done the better, as time might be very short. He next proceeded to tell the French Chargé d'Affaires that Staff conversations ought immediately to take place between Russia, France, and Czechoslovakia as to the means and measures of giving assistance. The Soviet Union was ready to join in such Staff conversations at once.

Fourthly, he recurred to his interview of March 17, of which you no doubt have a copy in the Foreign Office, advocating consultation among the peaceful Powers about the best method of preserving peace, with a view, perhaps, to a joint declaration including the three Great Powers concerned, France, Russia, and Great Britain. He believed that the United States would give moral support to such a declaration. All these statements were made on behalf of the Russian Government as what they think may be the best way of stopping a war.

I pointed out that the news to-day seemed to indicate a more peaceful attitude on the part of Herr Hitler, and that I thought it was unlikely that the British Government would consider any further steps until or unless there was a fresh breakdown in the Henlein-Beneš negotiations, in which the fault could not on any account be attributed to the Government of Czechoslovakia. We should not want to irritate Herr Hitler, if his mind was really turning towards a peaceful solution.

All this may of course have reached you through other channels,

THE HITLERITE AGGRESSIONS

but I considered the declarations of M. Litvinov so important that I ought not to leave this to chance.

I sent the report to Lord Halifax as soon as I had dictated it, and he replied on September 5 in a guarded manner, that he did not at present feel that action of the kind proposed under Article 11 would be helpful, but that he would keep it in his mind. "For the present, I think, as you indicated, we must review the situation in the light of the report with which Henlein has returned from Berchtesgaden." He added that the situation remained very anxious.

*　*　*

In its leading article of September 7 the *Times* stated:

If the Sudetens now ask for more than the Czech Government are ready to give in their latest set of proposals, it can only be inferred that the Germans are going beyond the mere removal of disabilities for those who do not find themselves at ease within the Czechoslovak Republic. In that case it might be worth while for the Czechoslovak Government to consider whether they should exclude altogether the project, which has found favour in some quarters, of making Czechoslovakia a more homogeneous state by the cession of that fringe of alien populations who are contiguous to the nation to which they are united by race.

This of course involved the surrender of the whole of the Bohemian fortress line. Although the British Government stated at once that this *Times* article did not represent their views, public opinion abroad, particularly in France, was far from reassured. During the course of the same day—September 7—the French Ambassador in London called on Lord Halifax on behalf of his Government to ask for a clarification of the British position in the event of a German attack on Czechoslovakia.

M. Bonnet, then French Foreign Minister, declares that on September 10, 1938, he put the following question to our Ambassador in Paris, Sir Eric Phipps: "To-morrow Hitler may attack Czechoslovakia. If he does France will mobilise at once. She will turn to you, saying, 'We march: do you march with us?' What will be the answer of Great Britain?"

The following was the answer approved by the Cabinet, sent by Lord Halifax through Sir Eric Phipps on the 12th:

I naturally recognise of what importance it would be to the French

Government to have a plain answer to such a question. But, as you pointed out to Bonnet, the question itself, though plain in form, cannot be dissociated from the circumstances in which it might be posed, which are necessarily at this stage completely hypothetical.

Moreover, in this matter it is impossible for His Majesty's Government to have regard only to their own position, inasmuch as in any decision they may reach or action they may take they would, in fact, be committing the Dominions. Their Governments would quite certainly be unwilling to have their position in any way decided for them in advance of the actual circumstances, of which they would desire themselves to judge.

So far therefore as I am in a position to give any answer at this stage to M. Bonnet's question, it would have to be that while His Majesty's Government would never allow the security of France to be threatened, they are unable to make precise statements of the character of their future action, or the time at which it would be taken, in circumstances that they cannot at present foresee.*

Upon the statement that "His Majesty's Government would never allow the security of France to be threatened" the French asked what aid they could expect if it were. The reply from London was, according to Bonnet, two divisions, not motorised, and 150 aeroplanes during the first six months of the war. If M. Bonnet was seeking for an excuse for leaving the Czechs to their fate, it must be admitted that his search had met with some success.

On September 12 also Hitler delivered at a Nuremberg Party rally a violent attack on the Czechs, who replied on the following day by the establishment of martial law in certain districts of the republic. On September 14 negotiations with Henlein were definitely broken off, and on the 15th the Sudeten leader fled to Germany.

The summit of the crisis was now reached.

* Printed in Georges Bonnet, *De Washington au Quai d'Orsay*, pp. 360-1.

CHAPTER XVII

THE TRAGEDY OF MUNICH

Chamberlain in Control – He Visits Berchtesgaden – His Meeting with Hitler – The End of the Runciman Mission – Anglo-French Pressure upon Czechoslovakia – President Beneš's Submission – General Faucher Renounces French Citizenship – My Statement of September 21 – Litvinov's Formidable Declaration at the League Assembly – Soviet Power Ignored – The Vultures Gather Round the Doomed State – Chamberlain and Hitler at Godesberg – Hitler's Ultimatum – Rejection by the British and French Cabinets – Sir Horace Wilson's Mission to Berlin – My Visit to Downing Street on September 26 – Lord Halifax's Communiqué – Mobilisation of the British Navy – Behind the German Front – Dismissal of General von Beck – Hitler's Struggle with His Own Army Staff – General von Halder's Plot – Alleged Reason for its Collapse, September 14 – Memorial of the German General Staff to Hitler, September 26 – Admiral Raeder's Remonstrance – Hitler Wavers – Mr. Chamberlain's Broadcast of September 27 – His Third Offer to Visit Hitler – His Appeal to Mussolini – Drama in the House of Commons, September 28 – Conference at Munich – A Scrap of Paper – Chamberlain's Triumphant Return – "Peace with Honour!" – Marshal Keitel's Evidence at Nuremberg – Hitler's Judgment Again Vindicated – Some General Principles of Morals and Action – A Fatal Course for France and Britain.

MR. CHAMBERLAIN was now in complete control of British foreign policy, and Sir Horace Wilson was his principal confidant and agent. Lord Halifax, in spite of increasing doubts derived from the atmosphere of his department, followed the guidance of his chief. The Cabinet was deeply perturbed, but obeyed. The Government majority in the House of Commons was skilfully handled by the Whips. One man and one man only conducted our affairs. He did not shrink either from the responsibility which he incurred or from the personal exertions required.

During the night of September 13–14 M. Daladier got in touch with Mr. Chamberlain. The French Government were of the opinion that a joint approach to Hitler on a personal basis by the French and British leaders might be of value. Chamberlain however had been communing with himself. On his own initiative he telegraphed to Hitler proposing to come to see him. He informed the Cabinet of his action the next day, and in the afternoon received Hitler's reply inviting him to Berchtesgaden. Accordingly on the morning of September 15 the British Prime Minister flew to the Munich airfield. The moment was not in all respects well chosen. When the news reached Prague the Czech leaders could not believe it was true. They were astonished that at the very moment when for the first time they had the internal situation in the Sudeten areas in hand the British Prime Minister should himself pay a direct visit to Hitler. This, they felt, would weaken their position with Germany. Hitler's provocative speech of September 12, and the German-sponsored revolt of Henlein's adherents which had followed, had failed to gain local support. Henlein had fled to Germany, and the Sudeten German Party, bereft of his leadership, was clearly opposed to direct action. The Czech Government in the so-called "Fourth Plan" had officially proposed to the Sudeten German leaders administrative schemes for regional autonomy which not only exceeded Henlein's Carlsbad requests of April, but also fully met Chamberlain's view expressed in his speech of March 24, and Sir John Simon's statements in his speech of August 27. But even Lord Runciman realised that the last thing the Germans wanted was a satisfactory bargain between the Sudeten leaders and the Czech Government. Chamberlain's journeys gave them an opportunity to increase their demands; and on instructions from Berlin the extremists in the Sudeten Party now openly claimed union with the Reich.

★　　★　　★

The Prime Minister's plane arrived at Munich Airport in the afternoon of September 15; he travelled by train to Berchtesgaden. Meanwhile all the radio stations of Germany broadcast a proclamation by Henlein demanding the annexation of the

Sudeten areas to the Reich. This was the first news that reached Mr. Chamberlain when he landed. It was no doubt planned that he should know it before meeting Hitler. The question of *ANNEXATION* had never yet been raised either by the German Government or by Henlein; and a few days earlier the Foreign Office had stated that it was not the accepted policy of the British Government.

Mr. Feiling has already published such records as are extant of the conversations between Chamberlain and Hitler. The salient point we may derive from his account is this:

> In spite of the hardness and ruthlessness I thought I saw in his face, I got the impression that *here was a man who could be relied upon when he had given his word.*★

In fact Hitler had for months past, as we have seen, resolved and prepared for the invasion of Czechoslovakia, which awaited only the final signal. When the Prime Minister reached London on Saturday, September 17, he summoned the Cabinet. Lord Runciman had now returned, and his report was assured of attention. He had all this time been failing in health, and the violent stress to which he had been exposed in his mission had reduced him to modest dimensions. He now recommended "a policy for immediate and drastic action", namely "the transfer of predominantly German districts to Germany." This at least had the merit of simplicity.

Both the Prime Minister and Lord Runciman were convinced that only the cession of the Sudeten areas to Germany would dissuade Hitler from ordering the invasion of Czechoslovakia. Mr. Chamberlain had been strongly impressed at his meeting with Hitler that he was "in a fighting mood". His Cabinet were also of the opinion that the French had no fight in them. There could therefore be no question of resisting Hitler's demands upon the Czech State. Some Ministers found consolation in such phrases as "the rights of self-determination", "the claims of a national minority to just treatment"; and even the mood appeared of "championing the small man against the Czech bully".

It was now necessary to keep in backward step with the French Government. On September 18 Daladier and Bonnet came to London. Chamberlain had already decided in principle to accept

★ Feiling, *op. cit.*, p. 367.

Hitler's demands as explained to him at Berchtesgaden. There only remained the business of drafting the proposals to be presented to the Czech Government by the British and French representatives in Prague. The French Ministers brought with them a set of draft proposals which were certainly more skilfully conceived. They did not favour a plebiscite, because, they observed, there might be demands for further plebiscites in the Slovak and Ruthene areas. They favoured an outright cession of the Sudetenland to Germany. They added however that the British Government, with France *and with Russia*, whom they had not consulted, should guarantee the new frontiers of the mutilated Czechoslovakia.

Many of us, even outside Cabinet circles, had the sensation that Bonnet represented the quintessence of defeatism, and that all his clever verbal manœuvres had the aim of "peace at any price". In his book, written after the war, he labours naturally to thrust the whole burden upon Chamberlain and Halifax. There can be no doubt of what he had in his own mind. At all costs he wished to avoid having to fulfil the solemn, precise, and so recently renewed obligations of France to go to war in defence of Czechoslovakia. The British and French Cabinets at this time presented a front of two over-ripe melons crushed together; whereas what was needed was a gleam of steel. On one thing they were all agreed: there should be no consultation with the Czechs. These should be confronted with the decision of their guardians. The Babes in the Wood had no worse treatment.

In presenting their decision or ultimatum to the Czechs England and France said: "Both the French and British Governments recognise how great is the sacrifice thus required of Czechoslovakia. They have felt it their duty jointly to set forth frankly the conditions essential to security. . . . The Prime Minister must resume conversations with Herr Hitler not later than Wednesday, or sooner if possible. We therefore feel we must ask for your reply at the earliest possible moment." Proposals involving the immediate cession to Germany of all areas in Czechoslovakia containing over 50 per cent. of German inhabitants were therefore handed to the Czech Government in the afternoon of September 19.

Great Britain after all had no treaty obligation to defend Czechoslovakia, nor was she pledged in any informal way. But

France had definitely bound herself by treaty to make war upon Germany if she attacked Czechoslovakia. For twenty years President Beneš had been the faithful ally and almost vassal of France, always supporting French policies and French interests on the League of Nations and elsewhere. If ever there was a case of solemn obligation it was here and now. Fresh and vivid were the declarations of MM. Blum and Daladier. It was a portent of doom when a French Government failed to keep the word of France. I have always believed that Beneš was wrong to yield. He should have defended his fortress line. Once fighting had begun, in my opinion at that time, France would have moved to his aid in a surge of national passion, and Britain would have rallied to France almost immediately. At the height of this crisis (on September 20) I visited Paris for two days in order to see my friends in the French Government, Reynaud and Mandel. Both these Ministers were in lively distress and on the verge of resigning from the Daladier Cabinet. I was against this, as their sacrifice could not alter the course of events, and would only leave the French Government weakened by the loss of its two most capable and resolute men. I ventured even to speak to them in this sense. After this painful visit I returned to London.

★   ★   ★

At 2 a.m. on the night of September 20–21 the British and French Ministers in Prague called on President Beneš to inform him in effect that there was no hope of arbitration on the basis of the German Czechoslovak Treaty of 1925, and to urge upon him the acceptance of the Anglo-French proposals *"before producing a situation for which France and Britain could take no responsibility"*. The French Government at least was sufficiently ashamed of this communication to instruct its Minister to make it only verbally. Under this pressure on September 21 the Czech Government bowed to the Anglo-French proposals. There was in Prague at this moment a general of the French Army named Faucher. He had been in Czechoslovakia with the French Military Mission since 1919, and had been its chief since 1926. He now requested the French Government to relieve him of his duties, and placed himself at the disposal of the Czechoslovak Army. He also adopted Czech citizenship.

The following French defence has been made, and it cannot be lightly dismissed. If Czechoslovakia had refused to submit, and war had resulted, France would have fulfilled her obligations; but if the Czechs chose to give in under whatever pressures were administered French honour was saved. We must leave this to the judgment of history.

* * *

On the same day, September 21, I issued a statement on the crisis to the Press in London:

The partition of Czechoslovakia under pressure from England and France amounts to the complete surrender of the Western Democracies to the Nazi threat of force. Such a collapse will bring peace or security neither to England nor to France. On the contrary, it will place these two nations in an ever weaker and more dangerous situation. The mere neutralisation of Czechoslovakia means the liberation of twenty-five German divisions, which will threaten the Western front; in addition to which it will open up for the triumphant Nazis the road to the Black Sea. It is not Czechoslovakia alone which is menaced, but also the freedom and the democracy of all nations. The belief that security can be obtained by throwing a small State to the wolves is a fatal delusion. The war potential of Germany will increase in a short time more rapidly than it will be possible for France and Great Britain to complete the measures necessary for their defence.

* * *

At the Assembly of the League of Nations on September 21 an official warning was given by Litvinov:

... At the present time Czechoslovakia is suffering interference in its internal affairs at the hands of a neighbouring State, and is publicly and loudly menaced with attack. One of the oldest, most cultured, most hard-working of European peoples, who acquired their independence after centuries of oppression, to-day or to-morrow may decide to take up arms in defence of that independence. ...

Such an event as the disappearance of Austria passed unnoticed by the League of Nations. Realising the significance of this event for the fate of the whole of Europe, and particularly of Czechoslovakia, the Soviet Government, immediately after the Anschluss, officially approached the other European Great Powers with a proposal for an immediate collective deliberation on the possible consequences of that event, in order to adopt collective preventive measures. To our regret, this proposal, which if carried out could have saved us from the alarm which all the world now feels for the fate of Czechoslovakia, did not receive its just appreciation. . . . When, a few days before I left for Geneva, the French Government for the first time inquired as to our attitude in the event of an attack on Czechoslovakia, I gave in the name of my Government the following perfectly clear and unambiguous reply:

"We intend to fulfil our obligations under the Pact, and together with France to afford assistance to Czechoslovakia by the ways open to us. Our War Department is ready immediately to participate in a conference with representatives of the French and Czechoslovak War Departments, in order to discuss the measures appropriate to the moment. . . ." It was only two days ago that the Czechoslovak Government addressed a formal inquiry to my Government as to whether the Soviet Union is prepared, in accordance with the Soviet-Czech Pact, to render Czechoslovakia immediate and effective aid if France, loyal to her obligations, will render similar assistance, to which my Government gave a clear answer in the affirmative.

It is indeed astonishing that this public, and unqualified, declaration by one of the greatest Powers concerned should not have played its part in Mr. Chamberlain's negotiations, or in the French conduct of the crisis. I have heard it suggested that it was geographically impossible for Russia to send troops into Czechoslovakia and that Russian aid in the event of war would have been limited to modest air support. The assent of Roumania, and also to a lesser extent of Hungary, to allow Russian forces to pass through their territory was of course necessary. This might well have been obtained from Roumania at least, as indicated to me by M. Maisky, through the pressures and guarantees of a Grand Alliance acting under the ægis of the League of Nations. There were two railways from Russia into Czechoslovakia through the Carpathian Mountains, the northerly from Czernowitz through the Bukovina, the southerly through Hungary by Debreczen. These two railways alone, which avoid both Bucharest and Budapest by good margins, might well have supported Russian armies of thirty divisions. As a counter for keeping the peace these possibilities would have been a substantial deterrent upon Hitler, and would almost certainly have led to far greater developments in the event of war. Stress has also been laid upon Soviet duplicity and bad faith. Anyhow, the Soviet offer was in effect ignored. They were not brought into the scale against Hitler, and were treated with an indifference—not to say disdain—which left a mark in Stalin's mind. Events took their course as if Soviet Russia did not exist. For this we afterwards paid dearly.

★ ★ ★

Mussolini, speaking at Treviso on September 21, said—not without some pith—"If Czechoslovakia finds herself to-day in what might be called a 'delicate situation', it is because she was— one may already say 'was', and I shall tell you why immediately— not just Czechoslovakia, but 'Czecho - Germano - Polono - Magyaro - Rutheno - Roumano-Slovakia', and I would emphasise that now that this problem is being faced it is essential it should be solved in a general manner."★

Under the humiliation of the Anglo-French proposals the Czech Government resigned, and a non-party Administration was formed under General Syrovy, the commander of the Czechoslovak legions in Siberia during the World War. On September 22 President Beneš broadcast to the Czech nation a dignified appeal for calm. While Beneš was preparing his broadcast Chamberlain had been flying to his second meeting with Hitler, this time at the Rhineland town of Godesberg. The British Prime Minister carried with him, as a basis for final discussion with the Fuehrer, the details of the Anglo-French proposals accepted by the Czech Government. The two men met in the hotel at Godesberg which Hitler had quitted in haste four years earlier for the Roehm purge. From the first Chamberlain realised that he was confronted with what he called in his own words "a totally unexpected situation". He described the scene in the House of Commons on his return:

> I had been told at Berchtesgaden that if the principle of self-determination were accepted Herr Hitler would discuss with me the ways and means of carrying it out. He told me afterwards that he never for one moment supposed that I should be able to come back and say that the principle was accepted. I do not want the House to think that he was deliberately deceiving me—I do not think so for one moment—but, for me, I expected that when I got back to Godesberg I had only to discuss quietly with him the proposals that I had brought with me; and it was a profound shock to me when I was told at the beginning of the conversation that these proposals were not acceptable, and that they were to be replaced by other proposals of a kind which I had not contemplated at all.

★ Quoted in Ripka, *Munich and After*, p. 117.

275

I felt that I must have a little time to consider what I was to do. Consequently I withdrew, my mind full of foreboding as to the success of my mission. I first however obtained from Herr Hitler an extension of his previous assurance that he would not move his troops pending the results of the negotiations. I, on my side, undertook to appeal to the Czech Government to avoid any action which might provoke incidents.

Discussions were broken off until the next day. Throughout the morning of September 23 Chamberlain paced the balcony of his hotel. He sent a written message to Hitler after breakfast stating that he was ready to convey the new German proposals to the Czech Government, but pointing out grave difficulties. Hitler's reply in the afternoon showed little signs of yielding, and Chamberlain asked that a formal memorandum accompanied by maps should be handed to him at a final meeting that evening. The Czechs were now mobilising, and both the British and French Governments officially stated to their representatives in Prague that they could no longer take the responsibility of advising them not to. At 10.30 that night Chamberlain again met Hitler. The description of the meeting is best told in his own words:

The memorandum and the map were handed to me at my final interview with the Chancellor, which began at half-past ten that night and lasted into the small hours of the morning, an interview at which the German Foreign Secretary was present, as well as Sir Nevile Henderson and Sir Horace Wilson; and, for the first time, I found in the memorandum a time limit. Accordingly, on this occasion I spoke very frankly. I dwelt with all the emphasis at my command on the risks which would be incurred by insisting on such terms, and on the terrible consequences of a war, if war ensued. I declared that the language and the manner of the documents, which I described as an ultimatum rather than a memorandum, would profoundly shock public opinion in neutral countries, and I bitterly reproached the Chancellor for his failure to respond in any way to the efforts which I had made to secure peace.

I should add that Hitler repeated to me with great earnestness what he had said already at Berchtesgaden, namely, that this was the last of his territorial ambitions in Europe and that he had no wish to include in the Reich people of other races than Germans. In the second place he said, again very earnestly, that he wanted to be friends with England, and that if only this Sudeten question could be got out of the way in peace *he would gladly resume conversations*. It is true he said, "There is one awkward question, the Colonies; but that is not a matter for war."

On the afternoon of September 24 Mr. Chamberlain returned to London, and on the following day three meetings of the Cabinet were held. There was a noticeable stiffening of opinion both in London and in Paris. It was decided to reject the Godesberg terms, and this information was conveyed to the German Government. The French Cabinet agreed, and a partial French mobilisation was carried out promptly and with more efficiency than was expected. On the evening of September 25 the French Ministers came again to London and reluctantly accepted their obligations to the Czechs. During the course of the following afternoon Sir Horace Wilson was sent with a personal letter to Hitler in Berlin three hours before the latter was to speak in the Sports Palace. The only answer Sir Horace was able to obtain was that Hitler would not depart from the time limit set by the Godesberg ultimatum, namely, Saturday, October 1, on which day he would march into the territories concerned unless he received Czech acquiescence by 2 p.m. on Wednesday the 28th.

That evening Hitler spoke in Berlin. He referred to England and France in accommodating phrases, launching at the same time a coarse and brutal attack on Beneš and the Czechs. He said categorically that the Czechs must clear out of the Sudetenland by the 26th, but once this was settled he had no more interest in what happened to Czechoslovakia. "*This is the last territorial claim I have to make in Europe.*"

★　★　★

As on similar occasions, my contacts with His Majesty's Government became more frequent and intimate with the mounting of the crisis. On September 10 I had visited the Prime Minister at Downing Street for a long talk. Again on September 26 he either invited me or readily accorded me an interview. At 3.30 in the afternoon of this critical day I was received by him and Lord Halifax in the Cabinet Room. I pressed upon them the policy set forth in my letter to Lord Halifax of August 31, namely, a declaration showing the unity of sentiment and purpose between Britain, France, *and* Russia against Hitlerite aggression. We discussed at length and in detail a communiqué, and we seemed to be in complete agreement. Lord Halifax and I were at one, and

I certainly thought the Prime Minister was in full accord. There was present a high official of the Foreign Office, who built up the draft. When we separated I was satisfied and relieved.

About 8 o'clock that night Mr. Leeper, then Head of the Foreign Office Press Department, now Sir Reginald Leeper, presented to the Foreign Secretary a communiqué of which the following is the pith:

If, in spite of the efforts made by the British Prime Minister, a German attack is made upon Czechoslovakia, the immediate result must be that France will be bound to come to her assistance, and Great Britain *and Russia* will certainly stand by France.

This was approved by Lord Halifax and immediately issued.

When earlier I returned to my flat at Morpeth Mansions I found about fifteen gentlemen assembled. They were all Conservatives: Lord Cecil, Lord Lloyd, Sir Edward Grigg, Sir Robert Horne, Mr. Boothby, Mr. Bracken, and Mr. Law. The feeling was passionate. It all focused on the point, "We must get Russia in". I was impressed and indeed surprised by this intensity of view in Tory circles, showing how completely they had cast away all thoughts of class, party, or ideological interests, and to what a pitch their mood had come. I reported to them what had happened at Downing Street and described the character of the communiqué. They were all greatly reassured.

The French Right Press treated this communiqué with suspicion and disdain. The *Matin* called it "a clever lie". M. Bonnet, who is now very busy showing how forward in action he was, told several Deputies that he had no confirmation of it, leaving on them the impression that this was not the British pledge he was looking for. This was no doubt not difficult for him to convey.

I dined that night with Mr. Duff Cooper at the Admiralty. He told me that he was demanding from the Prime Minister the immediate mobilisation of the Fleet. I recalled my own experiences a quarter of a century before, when similar circumstances had presented themselves.

* * *

It seemed that the moment of clash had arrived and that the opposing forces were aligned. The Czechs had a million and a half men armed behind the strongest fortress line in Europe, and equipped by a highly organised and powerful industrial machine. The French Army was partly mobilised, and, albeit reluctantly, the French Ministers were prepared to honour their obligations to Czechoslovakia. Just before midnight on September 27 the warning telegram was sent out from the Admiralty ordering the mobilisation of the Fleet for the following day. This information was given to the British Press almost simultaneously (at 11.38 p.m.). At 11.20 a.m. on September 28 the actual orders to the British Fleet to mobilise were issued from the Admiralty.

★   ★   ★

We may now look behind the brazen front which Hitler presented to the British and French Governments. General Beck, the Chief of the Army General Staff, had become profoundly alarmed about Hitler's schemes. He entirely disapproved of them, and was prepared to resist. After the invasion of Austria in March he had sent a memorandum to Hitler arguing by detailed facts that the continuance of a programme of conquest must lead to world-wide catastrophe and the ruin of the now reviving Reich. To this Hitler did not reply. There was a pause. Beck refused to share the responsibility before history for the war plunge which the Fuehrer was resolved to make. In July a personal confrontation took place. When the imminence of an attack on Czechoslovakia became clear Beck demanded an assurance against further military adventures. Here was a crunch. Hitler rejoined that the Army was the instrument of the State, that he was the Head of the State, and that the Army and other forces owed unquestioning obedience to his will. On this Beck resigned. His request to be relieved of his post remained unanswered. But the General's decision was irrevocable. Henceforth he absented himself from the War Ministry. Hitler was therefore forced to dismiss him, and appointed Halder as his successor. For Beck there remained only a tragic but honourable fate.

All this was kept within a secret circle; but there now began an intense, unceasing struggle between the Fuehrer and his expert advisers. Beck was universally trusted and respected by the Army Staff, who were united not only in professional opinion but in resentment of civilian and party dictation. The September crisis seemed to provide all the circumstances which the German generals dreaded. Between thirty and forty Czech divisions were deploying upon Germany's eastern frontiers, and the weight of the French Army, at odds of nearly eight to one, began to lie heavy on the Western Wall. A hostile Russia might operate from Czech airfields, and Soviet armies might wend their way forward through Poland or Roumania. Finally, in the last stage the British Navy was said to be mobilising. As all this developed passions rose to fever-heat.

First we have the account, given by General Halder, of a definite plot to arrest Hitler and his principal associates. The evidence for this does not rest only on Halder's detailed statements. Plans were certainly made, but how far they were at the time backed by resolve cannot be judged precisely. The generals were repeatedly planning revolts, and as often drew back at the last moment for one reason or another. It was to the interest of the parties concerned after they were the prisoners of the Allies to dwell upon their efforts for peace. There can be no doubt however of the existence of the plot at this moment, and of serious measures taken to make it effective.

By the beginning of September [Halder says] we had taken the necessary steps to immunize Germany from this madman. At this time the prospect of war filled the great majority of the German people with horror. We did not intend to kill the Nazi leaders—merely to arrest them, establish a military Government, and issue a proclamation to the people that we had taken this action only because we were convinced they were being led to certain disaster.

The following were in the plot: Generals Halder, Beck, Stuelpnagel, Witzleben (Commander of the Berlin Garrison), Thomas (Controller of Armaments), Brockdorff (Commander of the Potsdam Garrison), and Graf von Helldorf, who was in charge of the Berlin police. The Commander-in-Chief, General von Brauchitsch, was informed, and approved.

It was easy, as a part of the troop movements against Czechoslovakia, and of ordinary military routine, to hold one Panzer division so near to Berlin that it could reach the capital by a night's march. The evidence is clear that the Third Panzer Division, commanded by General Hoeppner, was at the time of the Munich crisis stationed south of Berlin. General Hoeppner's secret mission was to occupy the capital, the Chancellery, and the important Nazi Ministries and offices at a given signal. For this purpose it was added to General Witzleben's command. According to Halder's account, Helldorf, Chief of the Berlin Police, then made meticulous arrangements to arrest Hitler, Goering, Goebbels, and Himmler. "There was no possibility of a hitch. All that was required for a completely successful *coup* was Hitler's presence in Berlin." He arrived there from Berchtesgaden on the morning of September 14. Halder heard of this at midday, and immediately went over to see Witzleben and complete the plans. It was decided to strike at 8 p.m. that same evening. At 4 p.m., according to Halder, a message was received in Witzleben's office that Mr. Chamberlain was going to fly to see the Fuehrer at Berchtesgaden. A meeting was at once held, at which he, Halder, told Witzleben that "if Hitler had succeeded in his bluff, he would not be justified, as Chief of Staff, in calling it." It was accordingly decided to defer action and await events.

Such is the tale, which historians should probe, of this internal crisis in Berlin as told by General Halder, at that time Chief of the Staff. It has since been confirmed by General Mueller-Hillebrandt, and has been accepted as genuine by various authorities who have examined it. If it should eventually be accepted as historical truth, it will be another example of the very small accidents upon which the fortunes of mankind turn.

Of other less violent but earnest efforts of the General Staff.to restrain Hitler there can be no doubt. On September 26 a deputation, consisting of General von Hanneken, Ritter von Leeb, and Colonel Bodenschatz, called at the Chancellery of the Reich and requested to be received by Herr Hitler. They were sent away. At noon on the following day the principal generals held a meeting at the War Office. They agreed upon a memorial, which they left at the Chancellery. This document was published in France in November 1938.* It consisted of eighteen pages, divided into five chapters and three appendices. Chapter I stresses the divergences between the political and military leadership of the Third Reich, and declares that the low morale of the German population renders it incapable of sustaining a European war. It states that in the event of war breaking out exceptional powers must be given to the military authorities. Chapter II describes the bad

---

* Published by Professor Bernard Lavergne in *L'Année Politique Française et Étrangère* in November 1938. Quoted in Ripka, *op. cit.*, pp. 212 ff.

condition of the Reichswehr and mentions that the military authorities have felt obliged "to shut their eyes in many serious cases to the absence of discipline". Chapter III enumerates the various deficiencies in German armaments, dwelling upon the defects in the Siegfried Line, so hurriedly constructed, and the lack of fortifications in the Aix-la-Chapelle and Saarbruck areas. Fear is expressed of an incursion into Belgium by the French troops concentrated around Givet. Finally, emphasis is laid on the shortage of officers. No fewer than forty-eight thousand officers and a hundred thousand N.C.O.s were necessary to bring the Army up to war strength, and in the event of a general mobilisation no fewer than eighteen divisions would find themselves devoid of trained subordinate commanders.

The document presents the reasons why defeat must be expected in any but a strictly local war, and affirms that less than a fifth of the officers of the Reichswehr believed in the possibility of a victory for Germany. A military appreciation about Czechoslovakia in the Appendix states that the Czechoslovak Army, even if fighting without allies, could hold out for three months, and that Germany would need to retain covering forces on the Polish and French frontiers as well as on the Baltic and North Sea coasts, and to keep a force of at least a quarter of a million troops in Austria to guard against popular risings and a possible Czechoslovak offensive. Finally, the General Staff believed that it was highly improbable that hostilities would remain localised during the three-month period.

The warnings of the soldiers were finally reinforced by Admiral Raeder, Chief of the German Admiralty. At 10 p.m. on September 27 Raeder was received by the Fuehrer. He made a vehement appeal, which was emphasised a few hours later by the news that the British Fleet was being mobilised. Hitler now wavered. At 2 a.m. the German radio broadcast an official denial that Germany intended to mobilise on the 29th, and at 11.45 a.m. the same morning a statement of the German official news agency was given to the British Press again denying the reports of the intended German mobilisation. The strain upon this one man and upon his astounding will-power must at this moment have been most severe. Evidently he had brought himself to the brink of a general war. Could he take the plunge in the face of an unfavourable public opinion and of the solemn warning of the chiefs of his Army,

Navy, and Air Force? Could he, on the other hand, afford to retreat after living so long upon prestige?

*   *   *

While the Fuehrer was at grips with his generals Mr. Chamberlain himself was preparing to broadcast to the English nation. On the evening of September 27 he spoke as follows:

How horrible, fantastic, incredible, it is that we should be digging trenches and trying on gas-masks here because of a quarrel in a far-away country between people of whom we know nothing! . . . I would not hesitate to pay even a third visit to Germany if I thought it would do any good. . . . I am myself a man of peace to the depths of my soul. Armed conflict between nations is a nightmare to me; but if I were convinced that any nation had made up its mind to dominate the world by fear of its force I should feel that it must be resisted. Under such a domination life for people who believe in liberty would not be worth living; but war is a fearful thing, and we must be very clear, before we embark on it, that it is really the great issues that are at stake.

After delivering this balancing broadcast he received Hitler's reply to the letter he had sent through Sir Horace Wilson. This letter opened a chink of hope. Hitler offered to join in a guarantee of the new frontiers of Czechoslovakia, and was willing to give further assurances about the manner of carrying out the new plebiscite. There was little time to lose. The German ultimatum contained in the Godesberg memorandum was due to expire at 2 p.m. on the following day, Wednesday, September 28. Chamberlain therefore drafted a personal message to Hitler: "After reading your letter I feel certain that you can get all essentials without war, and without delay. I am ready to come to Berlin myself at once to discuss arrangements for transfer with you and representatives of the Czech Government, together with representatives of France and Italy, if you desire. I feel convinced that we could reach agreement in a week."* At the same time he telegraphed to Mussolini informing him of this last appeal to Hitler: "I trust your Excellency will inform the German Chancellor that you are willing to be represented, and urge him to agree to my proposal, which will keep our peoples out of war."

It is one of the remarkable features of this crisis that no close and

* Feiling, *op. cit.*, p. 372.

confidential consultation seems to have existed between London and Paris. There was a broad coincidence of view, but little or no personal contact. While Mr. Chamberlain, without consulting either the French Government or his own Cabinet colleagues, was drafting these two letters, the French Ministers were taking their own separate measures along parallel lines. We have seen the strength of the forces opposed to standing up to Germany in the French Press, and how the firm British communiqué, naming Russia, was suggested in Paris newspapers inspired by the French Foreign Office to be a forgery. The French Ambassador in Berlin was instructed on the night of the 27th to make yet further proposals extending the territory in the Sudetenland to be handed over for immediate German occupation. While M. François-Poncet was with Hitler a message arrived from Mussolini advising that Chamberlain's idea of a conference should be accepted and that Italy should take part.[1] At 3 o'clock on the afternoon of September 28 Hitler sent messages to Chamberlain and Daladier proposing a meeting at Munich on the following day together with Mussolini. At that hour Mr. Chamberlain was addressing the House of Commons, giving them a general view of recent events. As he neared the end of his speech the message inviting him to Munich was passed down to him by Lord Halifax, who was sitting in the Peers' Gallery. Mr. Chamberlain was at that moment describing the letter which he had sent to Mussolini and the results of his move:

In reply to my message to Signor Mussolini, I was informed that instructions had been sent by the Duce . . . that while Italy would fulfil completely her pledges to stand by Germany, yet, in view of the great importance of the request made by His Majesty's Government to Signor Mussolini, the latter hoped Herr Hitler would see his way to postpone action which the Chancellor had told Sir Horace Wilson was to be taken at 2 p.m. to-day for at least twenty-four hours, so as to allow Signor Mussolini time to re-examine the situation and endeavour to find a peaceful settlement. In response, Herr Hitler has agreed to postpone mobilisation for twenty-four hours. . . . That is not all. I have something further to say to the House yet. I have now been informed by Herr Hitler that he invites me to meet him at Munich to-morrow morning. He has also invited Signor Mussolini and M. Daladier. Signor Mussolini has accepted, and I have no doubt M. Daladier will also accept. I need not say what my answer will be.

. . . I am sure that the House will be ready to release me now to go and see what I can make of this last effort.

Thus for the third time Mr. Chamberlain flew to Germany.

*   *   *

Many accounts have been written of this memorable meeting, and it is not possible here to do more than emphasise some special features. No invitation was extended to Russia. Nor were the Czechs themselves allowed to be present at the meetings. The Czech Government had been informed in bald terms on the evening of the 28th that a conference of the representatives of the four European Powers would take place the following day. Agreement was reached between "the Big Four" with speed. The conversations began at noon and lasted till two o'clock the next morning. A memorandum was drawn up and signed at 2 a.m. on September 30. It was in essentials the acceptance of the Godesberg ultimatum. The Sudetenland was to be evacuated in five stages beginning on October 1, and to be completed within ten days. An International Commission was to determine the final frontiers. The document was placed before the Czech delegates who had been allowed to come to Munich to receive the decisions.

While the four statesmen were waiting for the experts to draft the final document the Prime Minister asked Hitler whether he would care for a private talk. Hitler "jumped at the idea."* The two leaders met in Hitler's Munich flat on the morning of September 30, and were alone except for the interpreter. Chamberlain produced a draft declaration which he had prepared, as follows:

We, the German Fuehrer and Chancellor, and the British Prime Minister, have had a further meeting to-day, and are agreed in recognising that the question of Anglo-German relations is of the first importance for the two countries and for Europe.

We regard the Agreement signed last night, and the Anglo-German Naval Agreement, as symbolic of the desire of our two peoples never to go to war with one another again.

We are resolved that the method of consultation shall be the method adopted to deal with any other questions that may concern our two countries, and we are determined to continue our efforts to remove

* See Feiling, op. cit., p. 376.

possible sources of difference, and thus to contribute to assure the peace of Europe.

Hitler read this Note and signed it without demur.

Chamberlain returned to England. At Heston, where he landed, he waved the joint declaration which he had got Hitler to sign, and read it to the crowd of notables and others who welcomed him. As his car drove through cheering crowds from the airport, he said to Halifax, sitting beside him, "All this will be over in three months"; but from the windows of Downing Street he waved his piece of paper again and used these words, "This is the second time in our history that there has come back from Germany to Downing Street peace with honour. I believe it is peace for our time."*

* * *

We have now also Marshal von Keitel's answer to the specific question put to him by the Czech representative at the Nuremberg trials:

Colonel Eger, representing Czechoslovakia, asked Marshal Keitel:
"Would the Reich have attacked Czechoslovakia in 1938 if the Western Powers had stood by Prague?"
Marshal Keitel answered:
"Certainly not. We were not strong enough militarily. The object of Munich [i.e., reaching an agreement at Munich] was to get Russia out of Europe, to gain time, and to complete the German armaments."†

* * *

Hitler's judgment had been once more decisively vindicated. The German General Staff was utterly abashed. Once again the Fuehrer had been right after all. He with his genius and intuition alone had truly measured all the circumstances, military and political. Once again, as in the Rhineland, the Fuehrer's leadership had triumphed over the obstruction of the German military chiefs. All these generals were patriotic men. They longed to see the Fatherland regain its position in the world. They were devoting themselves night and day to every process that could strengthen the German forces. They therefore felt smitten in their hearts at having been found so much below the level of the event,

---

* Feiling, *op. cit.*, p. 381.
† Quoted in Paul Reynaud's *La France a Sauvé l'Europe*, I, 561 n.

39 The Spanish Civil War: a machine-gun nest on the Madrid front.
40 The Spanish Civil War: inhabitants of the village of Villanova held under close
   guard by soldiers of Franco.

41 The Spanish Civil War: the evils of war; the bullet-ridden body of a young girl.
42 The Spanish Civil War: Barcelona in ruins, March 1938.

43 The Sino-Japanese War: Chinese Communist soldiers with American sten guns.
44 The Sino-Japanese War: Japanese tanks entering Nankin, January 1938.

45 The Ethiopian War: the arrival of an Italian expeditionary force.
46 The Ethiopian War: the capture of Lake Tana by the Italian Army, 24th April, 1936.

and in many cases their dislike and their distrust of Hitler were overpowered by admiration for his commanding gifts and miraculous luck. Surely here was a star to follow, surely here was a guide to obey. Thus did Hitler finally become the undisputed master of Germany, and the path was clear for the great design. The conspirators lay low, and were not betrayed by their military comrades.

★   ★   ★

It may be well here to set down some principles of morals and action which may be a guide in the future. No case of this kind can be judged apart from its circumstances. The facts may be unknown at the time, and estimates of them must be largely guesswork, coloured by the general feeling and aims of whoever is trying to pronounce. Those who are prone by temperament and character to seek sharp and clear-cut solutions of difficult and obscure problems, who are ready to fight whenever some challenge comes from a foreign Power, have not always been right. On the other hand, those whose inclination is to bow their heads, to seek patiently and faithfully for peaceful compromise, are not always wrong. On the contrary, in the majority of instances they may be right, not only morally but from a practical standpoint. How many wars have been averted by patience and persisting goodwill! Religion and virtue alike lend their sanctions to meekness and humility, not only between men but between nations. How many wars have been precipitated by firebrands! How many misunderstandings which led to wars could have been removed by temporising! How often have countries fought cruel wars and then after a few years of peace found themselves not only friends but allies!

The Sermon on the Mount is the last word in Christian ethics. Everyone respects the Quakers. Still, it is not on these terms that Ministers assume their responsibilities of guiding States. Their duty is first so to deal with other nations as to avoid strife and war and to eschew aggression in all its forms, whether for nationalistic or ideological objects. But the safety of the State, the lives and freedom of their own fellow-countrymen, to whom they owe their position, make it right and imperative in the last resort, or when a final and definite conviction has been reached, that the use of force should not be excluded. If the circumstances are such as to warrant it, force may be used. And if this be so it should be used under the conditions which are most favourable. There is no merit in putting off a war for a year if, when it comes, it is a far worse war or one much harder to win. These are the tormenting dilemmas upon which mankind has throughout its history been so frequently impaled. Final judgment upon them can only be recorded by history in relation to the facts of the case as known to the parties at the time, and also as subsequently proved.

There is however one helpful guide, namely, for a nation to keep its word and to act in accordance with its treaty obligations to allies. This guide is called honour. It is baffling to reflect that what men call honour does not correspond always to Christian ethics. Honour is often influenced by that element of pride which plays so large a part in its inspiration. An exaggerated code of honour leading to the performance of utterly vain and unreasonable deeds could not be defended, however fine it might look. Here however the moment came when honour pointed the path of duty, and when also the right judgment of the facts at that time would have reinforced its dictates.

For the French Government to leave her faithful ally Czechoslovakia to her fate was a melancholy lapse from which flowed terrible consequences. Not only wise and fair policy, but chivalry, honour, and sympathy for a small threatened people made an overwhelming concentration. Great Britain, who would certainly have fought if bound by treaty obligations, was nevertheless now deeply involved, and it must be recorded with regret that the British Government not only acquiesced but encouraged the French Government in a fatal course.

CHAPTER XVIII

MUNICH WINTER

Poland and Hungary: Beasts of Prey – Stresses in English Life – Mr. Duff Cooper's Resignation Speech – The Munich Debate – Hitler's Speech of October 9 – The British Cabinet Dilemma: Rearmament or Peace – The Question of a General Election – Correspondence with Mr. Duff Cooper – The Mutilation of Czechoslovakia – The Prime Minister's Power and Responsibility – His Approaches to Italy and Visit to Paris, November 1938 – M. Bonnet's Addresses to Germany – Consequences of Munich – Decline, Actual and Prospective, in the Relative Strength of the Anglo-French Combination – Improvement in the British Air Position – British and German Air-Power, 1938– 1940 – Germany's Population Increased by Ten Millions in 1938.

O N SEPTEMBER 30 Czechoslovakia bowed to the decisions of Munich. "They wished," they said, "to register their protest before the world against a decision in which they had no part." President Beneš resigned because "he might now prove a hindrance to the developments to which our new State must adapt itself". He departed from Czechoslovakia and found shelter in England. The dismemberment of the Czechoslovak State proceeded in accordance with the Agreement. But the Germans were not the only vultures upon the carcass. Immediately after the Munich Agreement on September 30 the Polish Government sent a twenty-four-hour ultimatum to the Czechs demanding the immediate handing over of the frontier district of Teschen. There was no means of resisting this harsh demand.

The heroic characteristics of the Polish race must not blind us to their errors, which over centuries have led them through measureless suffering. We see them in 1919, a people restored by the victory of the Western Allies after long generations of partition and servitude to be an independent republic and one of the main Powers in Europe. Now, in 1938, over a question so minor as Teschen, they sundered themselves from all those friends in France, Britain, and the United States who had lifted them once again to a national, coherent life, and whom they were soon to need so sorely. We see them hurrying, while the might of Germany glowered up against them, to grasp their share of the pillage and ruin of Czechoslovakia. During the crisis the door was shut in the face of the British and French Ambassadors, who were denied even access to the Foreign Secretary of the Polish State. It is a mystery and tragedy of European history that a people capable of every heroic virtue, gifted, valiant, charming, as individuals, should repeatedly show such inveterate faults in almost every aspect of their governmental life. All our hearts are with the Polish people in their new subjugation, and we are sure that we shall never seek in vain for their perennial impulse to strike against tyranny, and to suffer with invincible fortitude all the agonies which befall them. We all look forward to the dawn.

* * *

The Hungarians had also been on the fringe of the Munich discussions. Horthy had visited Germany at the end of August 1938, but Hitler had been very reserved in his attitude. Although he talked long with the Hungarian Regent on the afternoon of August 23, he did not reveal to him the date of his intended move against Czechoslovakia. "He himself did not know the time. Whoever wanted to join the meal would have to share in the cooking as well." But the hour of the meal had not been disclosed. Now however the Hungarians arrived with their claims.

* * *

It is not easy in these latter days, when we have all passed through years of intense moral and physical stress and exertion, to portray for another generation the passions which raged in Britain about the Munich Agreement. Among the Conservatives families and friends in intimate contact were divided to a degree the like of which I have never seen. Men and women, long bound together by party ties, social amenities, and family connections, glared upon one another in scorn and anger. The issue was not one to be settled by the cheering crowds which had welcomed Mr. Chamberlain back from the airport or blocked Downing

Street and its approaches, nor by the redoubtable exertions of the Ministerial Whips and partisans. We who were in a minority at the moment cared nothing for the jokes or scowls of the Government supporters. The Cabinet was shaken to its foundations, but the event had happened and they held together. One Minister alone stood forth. The First Lord of the Admiralty, Mr. Duff Cooper, resigned his great office, which he had dignified by the mobilisation of the Fleet. At the moment of Mr. Chamberlain's overwhelming mastery of public opinion he thrust his way through the exulting throng to declare his total disagreement with its leader.

At the opening of the three days' debate on Munich he made his resignation speech. This was a vivid incident in our Parliamentary life. Speaking with ease and without a note, for forty minutes he held the hostile majority of his party under his spell. It was easy for Labour men and Liberals in hot opposition to the Government of the day to applaud him. This was a rending quarrel within the Tory Party. Some of the truths he uttered must be recorded here:

> I besought my colleagues not to see this problem always in terms of Czechoslovakia, not to review it always from the difficult strategic position of that small country, but rather to say to themselves, "A moment may come when, owing to the invasion of Czechoslovakia, a European war will begin, and when that moment comes we must take part in that war, we cannot keep out of it, and there is no doubt upon which side we shall fight." Let the world know that, and it will give those who are prepared to disturb the peace reason to hold their hand. . . .
>
> Then came the last appeal from the Prime Minister on Wednesday morning. For the first time from the beginning to the end of the four weeks of negotiations Herr Hitler was prepared to yield an inch, an ell perhaps, but to yield some measure to the representations of Great Britain. But I would remind the House that the message from the Prime Minister was not the first news that he had received that morning. At dawn he had learned of the mobilisation of the British Fleet. It is impossible to know what are the motives of man, and we shall probably never be satisfied as to which of these two sources of inspiration moved him most when he agreed to go to Munich; but we do know that never before had he given in, and that then he did. I had been urging the mobilisation of the Fleet for many days. I had thought that this was the kind of language which would be easier for Herr

Hitler to understand than the guarded language of diplomacy or the conditional clauses of the Civil Service. I had urged that something in that direction might be done at the end of August and before the Prime Minister went to Berchtesgaden. I had suggested that it should accompany the mission of Sir Horace Wilson. I remember the Prime Minister stating it was the one thing that would ruin that mission, and I said it was the one thing that would lead it to success.

That is the deep difference between the Prime Minister and myself throughout these days. The Prime Minister has believed in addressing Herr Hitler through the language of sweet reasonableness. I have believed that he was more open to the language of the mailed fist. . . .

The Prime Minister has confidence in the goodwill and in the word of Herr Hitler, although when Herr Hitler broke the Treaty of Versailles he undertook to keep the Treaty of Locarno, and when he broke the Treaty of Locarno he undertook not to interfere further, or to have further territorial claims in Europe. When he entered Austria by force he authorised his henchmen to give an authoritative assurance that he would not interfere with Czechoslovakia. That was less than six months ago. Still the Prime Minister believes that he can rely upon the good faith of Hitler.

★   ★   ★

The long debate was not unworthy of the emotions aroused and the issues at stake. I well remember that when I said "We have sustained a total and unmitigated defeat" the storm which met me made it necessary to pause for a while before resuming. There was widespread and sincere admiration for Mr. Chamberlain's persevering and unflinching efforts to maintain peace, and for the personal exertions which he had made. It is impossible in this account to avoid marking the long series of miscalculations, and misjudgments of men and facts, on which he based himself; but the motives which inspired him have never been impugned, and the course he followed required the highest degree of moral courage. To this I paid tribute two years later in my speech after his death. The differences which arose between leading Conservatives, fierce though they were, carried with them no lack of mutual respect, nor in most cases did they sever, except temporarily, personal relations. It was common ground between us that the Labour and Liberal Oppositions, now so vehement for action, had never missed an opportunity of gaining popularity by resisting and denouncing even the half-measures for defence which the Government had taken.

There was also a serious and practical line of argument, albeit not to their credit, on which the Government could rest themselves. No one could deny that we were hideously unprepared for war. Who had been more forward in proving this than I and my friends? Great Britain had allowed herself to be far surpassed by the strength of the German Air Force. All our vulnerable points were unprotected. Barely a hundred anti-aircraft guns could be found for the defence of the largest city and centre of population in the world; and these were largely in the hands of untrained men. If Hitler was honest and lasting peace had in fact been achieved, Chamberlain was right. If, unhappily, he had been deceived, at least we should gain a breathing-space to repair the worst of our neglects. These considerations, and the general relief and rejoicing that the horrors of war had been temporarily averted, commanded the loyal assent of the mass of Government supporters. The House approved the policy of His Majesty's Government "by which war was averted in the recent crisis" by 366 to 144. The thirty or forty dissentient Conservatives could do no more than register their disapproval by abstention. This we did as a formal and united act.

In the course of my speech I said:

We really must not waste time after all this long debate upon the difference between the positions reached at Berchtesgaden, at Godesberg, and at Munich. They can be very simply epitomised, if the House will permit me to vary the metaphor. £1 was demanded at the pistol's point. When it was given, £2 were demanded at the pistol's point. Finally the Dictator consented to take £1 17s. 6d. and the rest in promises of goodwill for the future.

No one has been a more resolute and uncompromising struggler for peace than the Prime Minister. Everyone knows that. Never has there been such intense and undaunted determination to maintain and secure peace. Nevertheless, I am not quite clear why there was so much danger of Great Britain or France being involved in a war with Germany at this juncture if in fact they were ready all along to sacrifice Czechoslovakia The terms which the Prime Minister brought back with him could easily have been agreed, I believe, through the ordinary diplomatic channels at any time during the summer. And I will say this, that I believe the Czechs, left to themselves, and told they were going to get no help from the Western Powers, would have been able to make better terms than they have got after all this tremendous perturbation. They could hardly have had worse.

All is over. Silent, mournful, abandoned, broken, Czechoslovakia recedes into the darkness. She has suffered in every respect by her associations with France, under whose guidance and policy she has been actuated for so long. . . .

I find unendurable the sense of our country falling into the power, into the orbit and influence of Nazi Germany, and of our existence becoming dependent upon their goodwill or pleasure. It is to prevent that that I have tried my best to urge the maintenance of every bulwark of defence—first, the timely creation of an Air Force superior to anything within striking distance of our shores; secondly, the gathering together of the collective strength of many nations; and, thirdly, the making of alliances and military conventions, all within the Covenant, in order to gather together forces at any rate to restrain the onward movement of this power. It has all been in vain. Every position has been successively undermined and abandoned on specious and plausible excuses.

I do not grudge our loyal, brave people, who were ready to do their duty no matter what the cost, who never flinched under the strain of last week, the natural, spontaneous outburst of joy and relief when they learned that the hard ordeal would no longer be required of them at the moment; but they should know the truth. They should know that there has been gross neglect and deficiency in our defences; they should know that we have sustained a defeat without a war, the consequences of which will travel far with us along our road; they should know that we have passed an awful milestone in our history, when the whole equilibrium of Europe has been deranged, and that the terrible words have for the time being been pronounced against the Western democracies: "Thou art weighed in the balance and found wanting." And do not suppose that this is the end. This is only the beginning of the reckoning. This is only the first sip, the first foretaste of a bitter cup which will be proffered to us year by year unless, by a supreme recovery of moral health and martial vigour, we arise again and take our stand for freedom as in the olden time.

★   ★   ★

Hitler's gratitude for British goodwill and for the sincere rejoicings that peace with Germany had been preserved at Munich found only frigid expression. On October 9, less than a fortnight after he had signed the declaration of mutual friendship which Mr. Chamberlain had pressed upon him, he said in a speech at Saarbrucken:

The statesmen who are opposed to us wish for peace . . . but they govern in countries whose domestic organisation makes it possible that at any time they may lose their position to make way for others who are not anxious for peace. And those others are there. It only needs that in England instead of Chamberlain Mr. Duff Cooper or Mr. Eden or Mr. Churchill should come to power, and then we know quite well that it would be the aim of these men immediately to begin a new World War. They make no secret of the fact: they admit it openly. We know further that now, as in the past, there lurks in the background the menacing figure of that Jewish-international foe who has found a basis and a form for himself in a State turned Bolshevist. And we know further the power of a certain international Press which lives only on lies and slander. That obliges us to be watchful and to remember the protection of the Reich. At any time ready for peace, but at every hour also ready to defend ourselves.

I have therefore decided, as I announced in my speech at Nuremberg, to continue the construction of our fortifications in the West with increased energy. I shall now also bring within the line of these forti-fications the two large areas which up to the present lay in front of our fortifications—the district of Aachen [Aix-la-Chapelle] and the district of Saarbrucken.

He added:

It would be a good thing if in Great Britain people would gradually drop certain airs which they have inherited from the Versailles epoch. We cannot tolerate any longer *the tutelage of governesses*. Inquiries of British politicians concerning the fate of Germans within the frontiers of the Reich, or of others belonging to the Reich, are not in place. We for our part do not trouble ourselves about similar things in England. The outside world might often have reason enough to concern itself with its own national affairs, or, for instance, with affairs in Palestine.

After the sense of relief springing from the Munich agreement had worn off Mr. Chamberlain and his Government found them-selves confronted by a sharp dilemma. The Prime Minister had said, "I believe it is peace for our time." But the majority of his colleagues wished to utilise "our time" to rearm as rapidly as possible. Here a division arose in the Cabinet. The sensations of alarm which the Munich crisis had aroused, the flagrant ex-posure of our deficiencies, especially in anti-aircraft guns, dictated vehement rearmament. Hitler, on the other hand, was shocked at such a mood. "Is this the trust and friendship," he might have pretended, "of our Munich pact? If we are friends and you trust us, why is it necessary for you to rearm? Let me have the arms, and you show the trust." But this view, though it would have been thoroughly justified on the data presented to Parliament, carried no conviction. There was a strong forward surge for invigorated rearmament. And this of course was criticised by the German Government and its inspired Press. However, there was no doubt of the opinion of the British nation. While rejoicing at being delivered from war by the Prime Minister and cheering peace slogans to the echo, they felt the need of weapons acutely All the Service departments put in their claims and referred to the alarming shortages which the crisis had exposed. The Cabinet reached an agreeable compromise on the basis of all possible preparations without disturbing the trade of the country or irritating the Germans and Italians by large-scale measures.

*　*　*

It was to Mr. Chamberlain's credit that he did not yield to temptation and pressures to seek a General Election on the morrow of Munich. This could only have led to greater confusion. Nevertheless the winter months were anxious and depressing to those Conservatives who had criticised and refused to vote for the Munich settlement. Each of us was attacked in his constituency by the Conservative Party machine, and many there were who a year later were our ardent supporters who agitated against us. In my own constituency, the Epping Division, matters came to such a pass that I had to make it clear that if a resolution of censure were carried against me in my local association I should immediately resign my seat and fight a by-election. However, my ever-faithful and tireless champion and chairman, Sir James Hawkey, with a strong circle of determined men and women, fought the ground inch by inch and stood by me, and at the decisive meeting of the association I received in this murky hour a vote of confidence of three to two. But it was a gloomy winter.

In November we had another debate on national defence in which I spoke at length.

Mr. Duff Cooper to Mr. Churchill　　　　　　　　　19.XI.38

I am very distressed to hear that you resented the reference that I made to you in my speech in the House last Thursday. I cannot see why you should. I merely said that I thought that all the P.M. meant by his reference to 1914 was that any inquiry after mobilisation would always show up gaps and deficiencies, and that therefore he had hardly merited the rebuke you delivered to him. I might of course have omitted all reference to you, but I think it is always a good thing in debate to hang one's arguments on to previous speeches. Nor was my position on Thursday quite simple. Your great philippic, which I enjoyed immensely and admired still more, was an onslaught on the Government's record over a period of three years, during the whole of which, except the last six weeks, I was a member of the Government. You could hardly expect me therefore to say that I entirely agreed with you and to vote accordingly. However, I am not the less sorry to have hurt you, whether your reasons for feeling hurt are good or bad, and I hope you will forgive me, because your friendship, your companionship, and your advice are very, very precious to me.

Mr. Churchill to Mr. Duff Cooper   22.XI.38

Thank you so much for your letter, which I was very glad to get. In the position in which our small band of friends now is it is a great mistake ever to take points off one another. The only rule is: Help each other when you can, but never harm.—Never help the Bear. With your facility of speech it ought to be quite easy to make your position clear without showing differences from me. I will always observe this rule. Although there was nothing in what you said to which I could possibly object, yet the fact that you went out of your way to answer me led several of my friends to wonder whether there was not some purpose behind it; for instance, the desire to isolate me as much as possible from the other Conservatives who disagree with the Government. I did not credit this myself, and I am entirely reassured by your charming letter. We are so few, enemies so many, the cause so great, that we cannot afford to weaken each other in any way.

I thought the parts of your speech which I heard very fine indeed, especially the catalogue of disasters which we have sustained in the last three years. I don't know how you remembered them all without a note.

I am of course sorry about the debate. Chamberlain has now got away with everything. Munich is dead, the unpreparedness is forgotten, and there is to be no real, earnest, new effort to arm the nation. Even the breathing-space, purchased at a hideous cost, is to be wasted. It was my distress at these public matters that made me grumpy when you suggested supper, for I did not then know what you had said in the early part of your speech.

But anyway count always upon your sincere friend.

★   ★   ★

On November 1 a nonentity, Dr. Hacha, was elected to the vacant Presidency of the remnants of Czechoslovakia. A new Government took office in Prague. "Conditions in Europe and the world in general," said the Foreign Minister of this forlorn Administration, "are not such that we should hope for a period of calm in the near future." Hitler thought so too. A formal division of the spoils was made by Germany at the beginning of November. Poland was not disturbed in her occupation of Teschen. The Slovaks, who had been used as a pawn by Germany, obtained a precarious autonomy. Hungary received a piece of flesh at the expense of Slovakia. When these consequences of Munich were raised in the House of Commons Mr. Chamberlain explained that the French and British offer of an international guarantee to Czechoslovakia which had been given after the Munich Pact did not affect the existing frontiers of that State, but referred only to the hypothetical question of unprovoked aggression. "What we are doing now," he said, with much detachment, "is witnessing the readjustment of frontiers laid down in the Treaty of Versailles. I do not know whether the people who were responsible for those frontiers thought they would remain permanently as they were laid down. I doubt very much whether they did. They probably expected that from time to time the frontiers would have to be adjusted. It is impossible to conceive that those people would be such supermen as to be able to see what would be the right frontiers for all time. The question is not whether those frontiers should be readjusted from time to time, but whether they should be readjusted by negotiation and discussion or be readjusted by war. Readjustment is going on, and in the case of the Hungarian frontier arbitration by Germany and Italy has been accepted by Czechoslovakia and Hungary for the final determination of the frontier between them. I think I have said enough about Czechoslovakia. . . ." There was, however, to be a later occasion.

★　　★　　★

I wrote on November 17, 1938:

Everyone must recognise that the Prime Minister is pursuing a policy of a most decided character and of capital importance. He has his own strong view about what to do, and about what is going to happen. He has his own standard of values; he has his own angle of vision. He believes that he can make a good settlement for Europe and for the British Empire by coming to terms with Herr Hitler and Signor Mussolini. No one impugns his motives. No one doubts his conviction or his courage. Besides all this, he has the power to do what he thinks best. Those who take a different view, both of the principles of our foreign policy and of the facts and probabilities with which our country has to deal, are bound to recognise that we have no power at all to prevent him, by the resources and methods which are at his disposal, from taking the course in which he sincerely believes. He is willing to take the responsibility; he has the right to take the responsibility; and we are going to learn, in a comparatively short time, what he proposes should happen to us.

The Prime Minister is persuaded that Herr Hitler seeks no further territorial expansion upon the Continent of Europe; that the mastering and absorption of the Republic of Czechoslovakia has satiated the appetite of the German Nazi *régime*. It may be that he wishes to induce the Conservative Party to return to Germany the mandated territories in British possession, or what is judged to be their full equivalent. He believes that this act of restoration will bring about prolonged good and secure relations between Great Britain and Germany. He believes further that these good relations can be achieved without weakening in any way the fundamental ties of self-preservation which bind us to the French Republic, which ties, it is common ground between us all, must be preserved. Mr. Chamberlain is convinced that all this will lead to general agreement, to the appeasement of the discontented Powers, and to a lasting peace.

But all lies in the regions of hope and speculation. A whole set of contrary possibilities must be held in mind. He may ask us to submit to things which we cannot endure; he may be forced to ask us to submit to things which we cannot endure. Or, again, the other side in this difficult negotiation may not act in the same spirit of goodwill and good faith as animates the Prime Minister. What we have to give, what we are made to give, may cost us dear, but it may not be enough. It may involve great injury and humbling to the British Empire, but it may not stay or even divert for more than a few months, if that, the march of events upon the Continent. *By this time next year we shall know whether the Prime Minister's view of Herr Hitler and the German Nazi Party is right or wrong. By this time next year we shall know whether the policy of appeasement has appeased, or whether it has only stimulated a more ferocious appetite.* All we can do in the meanwhile is to gather forces of resistance and defence, so that if the Prime Minister should unhappily be wrong, or misled, or deceived, we can at the worst keep body and soul together.

★   ★   ★

Whatever might be thought of "peace for our time", Mr. Chamberlain was more than ever alive to the need for dividing Italy from Germany. He hopefully believed that he had made friends with Hitler; to complete his work he must gain Mussolini's Italy as a counterpoise to the dear-bought reconciliation with Germany. In this renewed approach to the Italian Dictator he had to carry France with him. There must be love all round. We shall study the result of these overtures in the next chapter.

Late in November the Prime Minister and Lord Halifax visited Paris. The French Ministers agreed without enthusiasm to Mr. Chamberlain's suggestion of his visit to Rome; but he and Lord Halifax were glad to learn that the French were now planning to imitate the British declaration on the future of Anglo-German relations signed by Chamberlain and Hitler at Munich. On November 27, 1938, M. Bonnet sent a message to the French Ambassador in Washington describing this intention of the French Government: "Mr. Neville Chamberlain and Lord Halifax, in the course of discussions held in Paris yesterday, clearly expressed their satisfaction at a declaration which they regarded as being of a character, like that of the Anglo-German declaration, which would constitute an immediate contribution to the work of international appeasement."* For the purpose of these discussions Ribbentrop came to Paris, bringing with him Dr. Schacht. The Germans hoped not only for a general statement of good intentions, but for a concrete economic agreement. They obtained the former, which was signed in Paris on December 6, but even M. Bonnet was not prepared to accept the latter, in spite of considerable temptation to pose as the architect of Franco-German understanding.

The mission of Ribbentrop to Paris had also a deeper motive. Just as Mr. Chamberlain hoped to split Rome from Berlin, so Hitler believed that he could divide Paris from London. M. Bonnet's version of his talk with Ribbentrop on this subject is not without interest:

In regard to Great Britain, I indicated to M. Ribbentrop the *rôle* which the improvement of Anglo-German relations must play in any developments of the policy of European appeasement, which was considered as the essential object of any Franco-German undertaking. The German Foreign Minister made efforts to throw upon the British

* *Livre Jaune Français*, pp. 35, 37.

Government the responsibility for the present state of affairs. The
Government, and particularly the British Press, after having appeared
to show, on the morrow of Munich, a certain comprehension, had
adopted the most disappointing attitude towards the Government of
Berlin. . . . The manifestations multiplied in Parliament by Messrs.
Duff Cooper, Churchill, Eden, and Morrison, and certain newspaper
articles, have been strongly resented in Germany, where one had not
been able to restrain the reactions of the Press. I emphasised anew the
fundamental and unshakable character of Anglo-French solidarity,
indicating very clearly that a real Franco-German *détente* could not
be conceivable in the long run without a parallel Anglo-German
*détente.**

The question has been debated whether Hitler or the Allies
gained the more in strength in the year that followed Munich.
Many persons in Britain who knew our nakedness felt a sense of
relief as each month our Air Force developed and the Hurricane
and Spitfire types approached issue. The number of formed
squadrons grew and the ack-ack guns multiplied. Also the
general pressure of industrial preparation for war continued to
quicken. But these improvements, invaluable though they
seemed, were petty compared with the mighty advance in
German armaments. As has been explained, munitions production on a nation-wide plan is a four years' task. The first year
yields nothing, the second very little, the third a lot, and the
fourth a flood. Hitler's Germany in this period was already in
the third or fourth year of intense preparation under conditions
of grip and drive which were almost the same as those of war.
Britain, on the other hand, had only been moving on a non-
emergency basis, with a weaker impulse and on a far smaller
scale. In 1938–39 British military expenditure of all kinds reached
£304 millions,† and German was at least £1,500 millions. It is
probable that in this last year before the outbreak Germany manufactured at least double, and possibly treble, the munitions of
Britain and France put together, and also that her great plants
for tank production reached full capacity. They were therefore
getting weapons at a far higher rate than we.

The subjugation of Czechoslovakia robbed the Allies of the
Czech Army of twenty-one regular divisions, fifteen or sixteen
second-line divisions already mobilised, and also their mountain

* *Livre Jaune Français,* pp. 43–4.
† 1937–8, £234 millions. 1938–9, £304 millions. 1939–40, £367 millions.

fortress line, which in the days of Munich had required the
deployment of thirty German divisions, or the main strength of
the mobile and fully-trained German Army. According to
Generals Halder and Jodl, there were but thirteen German
divisions, of which only five were composed of first-line troops,
left in the West at the time of the Munich arrangement. We
certainly suffered a loss through the fall of Czechoslovakia
equivalent to some thirty-five divisions. Besides this the Skoda
works, the second most important arsenal in Central Europe, the
production of which between August 1938 and September 1939
was in itself nearly equal to the actual output of British arms
factories in that period, was made to change sides adversely.
While all Germany was working under intense and almost war
pressure, French labour had achieved as early as 1936 the long-
desired forty-hours week.

Even more disastrous was the alteration in the relative strength
of the French and German Armies. With every month that
passed, from 1938 onwards, the German Army not only increased
in numbers and formations and in the accumulation of reserves,
but in quality and maturity. The advance in training and general
proficiency kept pace with the ever-augmenting equipment. No
similar improvement or expansion was open to the French Army.
It was being overtaken along every path. In 1935 France, unaided by her previous allies, could have invaded and reoccupied
Germany almost without serious fighting. In 1936 there could
still be no doubt of her overwhelmingly superior strength. We
now know, from the German revelations, that this continued
in 1938, and it was the knowledge of their weakness which led
the German High Command to do their utmost to restrain Hitler
from every one of the successful strokes by which his fame was
enhanced. In the year after Munich, which we are now examin-
ing, the German Army, though still weaker in trained reserves
than the French, approached its full efficiency. As it was based
upon a population double as large as that of France, it was only
a question of time when it would become by every test the
stronger. In morale also the Germans had the advantage. The
desertion of an ally, especially from fear of war, saps the spirit
of any army. The sense of being forced to yield depresses both
officers and men. While on the German side confidence, success,
and the sense of growing power inflamed the martial instincts of

the race, the admission of weakness discouraged the French soldiers of every rank.

*   *   *

There is however one vital sphere in which we began to overtake Germany and improve our own position. In 1938 the process of replacing British biplane fighters, like the Gladiators, by modern types of Hurricanes and later Spitfires had only just begun. In September of 1938 we had but five squadrons remounted on Hurricanes. Moreover, reserves and spares for the older aircraft had been allowed to drop, since they were going out of use. The Germans were well ahead of us in remounting with modern fighter types. They already had good numbers of the Me.109, against which our old aircraft would have fared very ill. Throughout 1939 our position improved as more squadrons were remounted. In July of that year we had twenty-six squadrons of modern eight-gun fighters, though there had been little time to build up a full scale of reserves and spares. By July 1940, at the time of the Battle of Britain, we had on the average forty-seven squadrons of modern fighters available.

On the German side the figures of strength increased as follows:

1938	Bombers	1,466
	Fighters	920
1939	Bombers	1,553
	Fighters	1,090
1940	Bombers	1,558
	Fighters	1,290

The Germans had in fact done most of their air expansion both in quantity and quality before the war began. Our effort was later than theirs by nearly two years. Between 1939 and 1940 they made a 20 per cent. increase only, whereas our increase in modern fighter aircraft was 80 per cent. The year 1938 in fact found us sadly deficient in quality, and although by 1939 we had gone some way towards meeting the disparity we were still relatively worse off than in 1940, when the test came.

We might in 1938 have had air raids on London, for which we were lamentably unprepared. There was however no possibility of a decisive Air Battle of Britain until the Germans had occupied France and the Low Countries, and thus obtained the necessary bases in close striking distance of our shores. Without these bases they could not have escorted their bombers with the fighter air-craft of those days. The German armies were not capable of defeating the French in 1938 or 1939.

The vast tank production with which they broke the French front did not come into existence till 1940, and, in the face of the French superiority in the West and an unconquered Poland in the East, they could certainly not have concentrated the whole of their air-power against England as they were able to do when France had been forced to surrender. This takes no account either of the attitude of Russia or of whatever resistance Czechoslovakia might have made. I have thought it right to set out the figures of relative air-power in the period concerned, but they do not in any way alter the conclusions which I have recorded.

For all the above reasons, the year's breathing-space said to be "gained" by Munich left Britain and France in a much worse position compared with Hitler's Germany than they had been at the Munich crisis.

$$\star \quad \star \quad \star$$

Finally there is this staggering fact: that in the single year 1938 Hitler had annexed to the Reich and brought under his absolute rule 6,750,000 Austrians and 3,500,000 Sudetens, a total of over ten millions of subjects, toilers, and soldiers. Indeed the dread balance had turned in his favour.

CHAPTER XIX

PRAGUE, ALBANIA, AND THE POLISH
GUARANTEE
January–April 1939

Chamberlain's Visit to Rome – German Concentrations towards Czechoslovakia – Ministerial Optimism – Hitler Invades Czechoslovakia – Chamberlain's Speech at Birmingham – A Complete Change of Policy – My Letter to the Prime Minister of March 31 – The Soviet Government's Proposal for a Six-Power Conference – The British Guarantee to Poland – A Word with Colonel Beck – The Italian Landing in Albania, April 7, 1939 – Faulty Disposition of the British Mediterranean Fleet – My Speech in the House of Commons of April 13 – My Letter to Lord Halifax – Meeting of Goering, Mussolini, and Ciano on War Measures – German Strategic Advantages of the Annexation of Czechoslovakia – The Government Introduces Conscription – Weak Attitude of the Labour and Liberal Oppositions – Agitation for a National Government in Britain – Sir Stafford Cripps' Appeals – Mr. Stanley's Offer to Resign.

MR. CHAMBERLAIN continued to believe that he had only to form a personal contact with the Dictators to effect a marked improvement in the world situation. He little knew that their decisions were taken. In a hopeful spirit he proposed that he and Lord Halifax should visit Italy in January. After some delay an invitation was extended, and on January 11 the meeting took place. It makes one flush to read in Ciano's diary the comments which were made behind the Italian scene about our country and its representatives. "Essentially," writes Ciano, "the visit was kept in a minor key. . . . Effective contact has not been made. How far apart we are from these people! It is another world. We were talking about it after dinner to the

Duce. 'These men,' said Mussolini, 'are not made of the same stuff as Francis Drake and the other magnificent adventurers who created the Empire. They are after all the tired sons of a long line of rich men.' " "The British," noted Ciano, "do not want to fight. They try to draw back as slowly as possible, but they do not want to fight. . . . Our conversations with the British have ended. Nothing was accomplished. I have telephoned to Ribbentrop saying it was a fiasco, absolutely innocuous. . . . Chamberlain's eyes filled with tears as the train started moving and his countrymen started singing, 'For he's a jolly good fellow'. 'What is this little song?' asked Mussolini." And then a fortnight later: "Lord Perth has submitted for our approval the outlines of the speech that Chamberlain will make in the House of Commons in order that we may suggest changes if necessary." The Duce approved it, and commented: "I believe this is the first time that the head of the British Government has submitted to a foreign Government the outlines of one of his speeches. It's a bad sign for them."* However, in the end it was Ciano and Mussolini who went to their doom.

Meanwhile, on January 25 Ribbentrop was at Warsaw to continue the diplomatic offensive against Poland. The absorption of Czechoslovakia was to be followed by the encirclement of Poland. The first stage in this operation would be the cutting off of Poland from the sea by the assertion of German sovereignty in Danzig and by the prolongation of the German control of the Baltic to the vital Lithuanian port of Memel. The Polish Government displayed strong resistance to this pressure, and for a while Hitler watched and waited for the campaigning season.

During the second week of March rumours gathered of troop movements in Germany and Austria, particularly in the Vienna-Salzburg region. Forty German divisions were reported to be mobilised on a war footing. Confident of German support, the Slovaks were planning the separation of their territory from the Czechoslovak Republic. Colonel Beck, relieved to see the Teutonic wind blowing in another direction, declared publicly in Warsaw that his Government had full sympathy with the aspirations of the Slovaks. Father Tiso, the Slovak leader, was received by Hitler in Berlin with the honours due to a Prime Minister. On the 12th Mr. Chamberlain, questioned in Parlia-

* *Ciano's Diary*, 1939–43 (ed. Malcolm Muggeridge), pp. 9, 10.

ment about the guarantee of the Czechoslovak frontier, reminded the House that this proposal had been directed against unprovoked aggression. No such aggression had yet taken place. He did not have long to wait.

* * *

A wave of perverse optimism had swept across the British scene during these March days. In spite of the growing stresses in Czechoslovakia under intense German pressure from without and from within, the Ministers and newspapers identified with the Munich Agreement did not lose faith in the policy into which they had drawn the nation. For instance, on March 10 the Home Secretary addressed his constituents about his hopes of a Five Years' Peace Plan which would lead in time to the creation of "a Golden Age". A plan for a commercial treaty with Germany was still being hopefully discussed. The famous periodical *Punch* produced a cartoon showing John Bull waking with a gasp of relief from a nightmare, while all the evil rumours, fancies, and suspicions of the night were flying away out of the window. On the very day when this appeared Hitler launched his ultimatum to the tottering Czech Government, bereft of their fortified line by the Munich decisions. German troops, marching into Prague, assumed absolute control of the unresisting State. I remember sitting with Mr. Eden in the smoking-room of the House of Commons when the editions of the evening papers recording these events came in. Even those who like us had no illusions and had testified earnestly were surprised at the sudden violence of this outrage. One could hardly believe that with all their secret information His Majesty's Government could be so far adrift. March 14 witnessed the dissolution and subjugation of the Czechoslovak Republic. The Slovaks formally declared their independence. Hungarian troops, backed surreptitiously by Poland, crossed into the eastern province of Czechoslovakia, or the Carpatho-Ukraine, which they demanded. Hitler, having arrived in Prague, proclaimed a German protectorate over Czechoslovakia, which was thereby incorporated in the Reich.

On the 12th Mr. Chamberlain had to say to the House: "The occupation of Bohemia by German military forces began at six o'clock this morning. The Czech people have been ordered by their Government not to offer resistance." He then proceeded to state that the guarantee he had given Czechoslovakia no longer

307

in his opinion had validity. After Munich, five months before, the Dominions Secretary, Sir Thomas Inskip, had said of this guarantee: "His Majesty's Government feel under a moral obligation to Czechoslovakia to keep the guarantee [as though it were technically in force]. . . . In the event therefore of an act of unprovoked aggression against Czechoslovakia His Majesty's Government would certainly be bound to take all steps in their power to see that the integrity of Czechoslovakia is preserved." "That," said the Prime Minister, "remained the position until yesterday. But the position has altered since the Slovak Diet declared the independence of Slovakia. The effect of this declaration put an end by internal disruption to the State whose frontiers we had proposed to guarantee, and His Majesty's Government cannot accordingly hold themselves bound by this obligation."

This seemed decisive. "It is natural," he said in conclusion, "that I should bitterly regret what has now occurred, but do not let us on that account be deflected from our course. Let us remember that the desire of all the peoples of the world still remains concentrated on the hopes of peace."

Mr. Chamberlain was due to speak at Birmingham two days later. I fully expected that he would accept what had happened with the best grace possible. This would have been in harmony with his statement to the House. I even imagined that he might claim credit for the Government for having, by its foresight at Munich, decisively detached Great Britain from the fate of Czechoslovakia, and indeed of Central Europe. "How fortunate," he might have said, "that we made up our minds in September last not to be drawn into the Continental struggle! We are now free to allow these broils between countries which mean nothing to us to settle themselves without expense in blood or treasure." This would, after all, have been a logical decision following upon the disruption of Czechoslovakia agreed to at Munich and endorsed by a majority of the British people, so far as they understood what was going on. This also was the view taken by some of the strongest supporters of the Munich Pact. I therefore awaited the Birmingham declaration with anticipatory contempt.

The Prime Minister's reaction surprised me. He had conceived himself as having a special insight into Hitler's character, and the power to measure with shrewdness the limits of German action. He believed, with hope, that there had been a true meeting of minds at Munich, and that he, Hitler, and Mussolini had together saved the world from the infinite horrors of war. Suddenly as by an explosion his faith and all that had followed from his actions and his arguments was shattered. Responsible as he was for grave misjudgments of facts, having deluded himself and imposed his errors on his subservient colleagues and upon the unhappy British public opinion, he none the less between night and morning turned his back abruptly upon his past. If Chamberlain failed to understand Hitler, Hitler completely underrated the nature of the British Prime Minister. He mistook his civilian aspect and passionate desire for peace for a complete explanation of his personality, and thought that his umbrella was his symbol. He did not realise that Neville Chamberlain had a very hard core, and that he did not like being cheated.

The Birmingham speech struck a new note. "His tone," says his biographer, "was very different. . . . Informed by fuller knowledge and by strong representations as to opinion in the House, the public, and the Dominions, he threw aside the speech long drafted on domestic questions and social service and grasped the nettle." He reproached Hitler with a flagrant personal breach of faith about the Munich Agreement. He quoted all the assurances Hitler had given. "This is the last territorial claim which I have to make in Europe." "I shall not be interested in the Czech State any more, and I can guarantee it. We don't want any more Czechs." "I am convinced," said the Prime Minister, "that after Munich the great majority of the British people shared my honest desire that that policy should be carried further, but to-day I share their disappointment, their indignation, that those hopes have been so wantonly shattered. How can these events this week be reconciled with those assurances which I have read out to you?

"Who can fail to feel his heart go out in sympathy to the proud, brave people who have so suddenly been subjected to this invasion, whose liberties are curtailed, whose national independence is gone? . . . Now we are told that this seizure of territory has been necessitated by disturbances in Czechoslovakia. . . . If there were disorders, were they not fomented from without? . . . Is this the last attack upon a small State, or is it to be followed by another? Is this in fact a step in the direction of an attempt to dominate the world by force?"

It is not easy to imagine a greater contradiction to the mood and policy of the Prime Minister's statement two days earlier in the House of Commons. He must have been through a period of intense stress. On the 15th he had said: "Do not let us be deflected from our course." But this was "Right-about-turn."

Moreover, Chamberlain's change of heart did not stop at words. The next "small State" on Hitler's list was Poland. When the gravity of the decision and all those who had to be consulted are borne in mind, the period must have been busy. Within a fortnight (March 31) the Prime Minister said in Parliament:

I now have to inform the House that . . . in the event of any action which clearly threatened Polish independence and which the Polish Government accordingly considered it vital to resist with their national forces, His Majesty's Government would feel themselves bound at once to lend the Polish Government all support in their power. They have given the Polish Government an assurance to this effect.

I may add that the French Government have authorised me to make it plain that they stand in the same position in this matter as do His Majesty's Government. . . . [And later] The Dominions have been kept fully informed.

This was no time for recriminations about the past. The guarantee to Poland was supported by the leaders of all parties and groups in the House. "God helping, we can do no other," was what I said. At the point we had reached it was a necessary action. But no one who understood the situation could doubt that it meant in all human probability a major war, in which we should be involved.

* * *

In this sad tale of wrong judgments formed by well-meaning and capable people we now reach our climax. That we should all have come to this pass makes those responsible, however honourable their motives, blameworthy before history. Look back and see what we had successively accepted or thrown away: a Germany disarmed by solemn treaty; a Germany rearmed in violation of a solemn treaty; air superiority or even air parity cast away; the Rhineland forcibly occupied and the Siegfried Line built or building; the Berlin-Rome Axis established; Austria devoured and digested by the Reich; Czechoslovakia deserted and ruined by the Munich Pact, its fortress line in German hands, its mighty arsenal of Skoda henceforward making munitions for the German armies; President Roosevelt's effort to stabilise or bring to a head the European situation by the intervention of the United States waved aside with one hand, and Soviet Russia's undoubted willingness to join the Western Powers and go all lengths to save Czechoslovakia ignored on the other; the services of thirty-five Czech divisions against the still unripened Germany Army cast away, when Great Britain could herself supply only two to strengthen the front in France; all gone with the wind.

And now, when every one of these aids and advantages has been squandered and thrown away, Great Britain advances, leading France by the hand, to guarantee the integrity of Poland— of that very Poland which with hyena appetite had only six months before joined in the pillage and destruction of the Czecho-slovak State. There was sense in fighting for Czechoslovakia in 1938, when the German Army could scarcely put half a dozen trained divisions on the Western Front, when the French with nearly sixty or seventy divisions could most certainly have rolled forward across the Rhine or into the Ruhr. But this had been judged unreasonable, rash, below the level of modern intellectual thought and morality. Yet now at last the two Western demo-cracies declared themselves ready to stake their lives upon the territorial integrity of Poland. History, which, we are told, is mainly the record of the crimes, follies, and miseries of mankind, may be scoured and ransacked to find a parallel to this sudden and complete reversal of five or six years' policy of easy-going placatory appeasement, and its transformation almost overnight into a readiness to accept an obviously imminent war on far worse conditions and on the greatest scale.

Moreover, how could we protect Poland and make good our guarantee? Only by declaring war upon Germany and attacking a stronger Western Wall and a more powerful German Army than those from which we had recoiled in September 1938. Here is a line of milestones to disaster. Here is a catalogue of surrenders, at first when all was easy and later when things were harder, to the ever-growing German power. But now at last was the end of British and French submission. Here was decision at last, taken at the worst possible moment and on the least satisfactory ground, which must surely lead to the slaughter of tens of millions of people. Here was the righteous cause deliberately and with a refinement of inverted artistry committed to mortal battle after its assets and advantages had been so improvidently squandered. Still, if you will not fight for the right when you can easily win without bloodshed, if you will not fight when your victory will be sure and not too costly, you may come to the moment when you will have to fight with all the odds against you and only a precarious chance of survival. There may even be a worse case. You may have to fight when there is no hope of victory, because it is better to perish than live as slaves.

* * *

The Birmingham speech brought me much closer to Mr. Chamberlain. I wrote to him:

I venture to reiterate the suggestion which I made to you in the Lobby yesterday afternoon, that the anti-aircraft defences should forthwith be placed in full preparedness. Such a step could not be deemed aggressive, yet it would emphasise the seriousness of the action H.M. Government are taking on the Continent. The bringing together of these officers and men would improve their efficiency with every day of their embodiment. The effect at home would be one of confidence rather than alarm. But it is of Hitler I am thinking mostly. He must be under intense strain at this moment. He knows we are endeavouring to form a coalition to restrain his further aggression. With such a man anything is possible. The temptation to make a surprise attack on London, or on the aircraft factories, about which I am even more anxious, would be removed if it was known that all was ready. There could, in fact, be no surprise, and therefore the incentive to the extremes of violence would be removed and more prudent counsels might prevail.

In August 1914 I persuaded Mr. Asquith to let me send the Fleet to the North so that it could pass the Straits of Dover and the Narrow Seas *before* the diplomatic situation had become hopeless. It seems to me that manning the anti-aircraft defences now stands in a very similar position, and I hope you will not mind my putting this before you.

* * *

The Poles had gained Teschen by their shameful attitude towards the liquidation of the Czechoslovak State. They were soon to pay their own forfeits. On March 21, when Ribbentrop saw M. Lipski, the Polish Ambassador in Berlin, he adopted a sharper tone than in previous discussions. The occupation of Bohemia and the creation of satellite Slovakia brought the German Army to the southern frontiers of Poland. Lipski told Ribbentrop that the Polish man-in-the-street could not understand why the Reich had assumed the protection of Slovakia, that protection being directed against Poland. He also inquired about the recent conversations between Ribbentrop and the Lithuanian Foreign Minister. Did they affect Memel? He received his answer two days later (March 23). German troops occupied Memel.

The means of organising any resistance to German aggression in Eastern Europe were now almost exhausted. Hungary was in the German camp. Poland had stood aside from the Czechs, and was unwilling to work closely with Roumania. Neither Poland nor Roumania would accept Russian intervention against Germany across their territories. The key to a Grand Alliance was an understanding with Russia. On March 19 the Russian Government, which was profoundly affected by all that was taking place, and in spite of having been left outside the door in the Munich crisis, proposed a Six-Power Conference. On this subject also Mr. Chamberlain had decided views. In a private letter he wrote on March 26:

I must confess to the most profound distrust of Russia. I have no belief whatever in her ability to maintain an effective offensive, even if she wanted to. And I distrust her motives, which seem to me to have little connection with our ideas of liberty, and to be concerned only with setting everyone else by the ears. Moreover, she is both hated and suspected by many of the smaller States, notably by Poland, Roumania, and Finland.*

The Soviet proposal for a Six-Power Conference was therefore coldly received and allowed to drop.

The possibilities of weaning Italy from the Axis, which had loomed so large in British official calculations, were also vanishing. On March 26 Mussolini made a violent speech asserting Italian claims against France in the Mediterranean. Secretly he was planning for the extension of Italian influence in the Balkans and the Adriatic, to balance the German advance in Central Europe. His plans for invading Albania were now ready.

On March 29 Mr. Chamberlain announced in Parliament the

* Feiling, *op. cit.*, p. 403.

planned doubling of the Territorial Army, including an increase on paper of 210,000 men (unequipped). On April 3 Keitel, Hitler's Chief of Staff, issued the secret "Directive for the Armed Forces, 1939–40", in regard to Poland—"Case White" was the code name. The Fuehrer added the following direction: "Preparations must be made in such a way that the operations can be carried out at any time from September 1 onwards."

* * *

On April 4 the Government invited me to a luncheon at the Savoy in honour of Colonel Beck, the Polish Foreign Minister, who had come upon an official visit of significance. I had met him the year before on the Riviera, when we had lunched alone together. I now asked him: "Will you get back all right in your special train through Germany to Poland?" He replied: "I think we shall have time for that."

* * *

A new crisis now opened upon us.

At dawn on April 7, 1939, Italian forces landed in Albania, and after a brief scuffle took over the country. As Czechoslovakia was to be the base for aggression against Poland, so Albania would be the springboard for Italian action against Greece and for the neutralising of Yugoslavia. The British Government had already undertaken a commitment in the interests of peace in Northeastern Europe. What about the threat developing in the Southeast? The vessel of peace was springing a leak from every seam.

On April 9 I wrote to the Prime Minister:

I am hoping that Parliament will be recalled at the latest on Tuesday, and I write to say how much I hope the statements which you will be able to make will enable the same united front to be presented as in the case of the Polish Agreement.

It seems to me however that hours now count. It is imperative for us to recover the initiative in diplomacy. This can no longer be done by declarations or by the denouncing of the Anglo-Italian Agreement or by the withdrawal of our Ambassador.

It is freely stated in the Sunday papers that we are offering a guarantee to Greece and Turkey. At the same time I notice that several newspapers speak of a British naval occupation of Corfu. Had this step been already taken it would afford the best chance of maintaining peace. If it is not taken by us, of course with Greek consent, it seems to me that after the publicity given to the idea in the Press and the obvious needs of the situation Corfu will be speedily taken by Italy. Its recapture would then be impossible. On the other hand, if we are there first an attack even upon a few British ships would confront Mussolini with beginning a war of aggression upon England. This direct issue gives the best chance to all the forces in Italy which are opposed to a major war with England. So far from intensifying the grave risks now open, it diminishes them. But action ought to be taken to-night.

What is now at stake is nothing less than the whole of the Balkan Peninsula. If these States remain exposed to German and Italian pressure while we appear, as they may deem it, incapable of action, they will be forced to make the best terms possible with Berlin and Rome. How forlorn then will our position become! We shall be committed to Poland, and thus involved in the East of Europe, while at the same time cutting off from ourselves all hope of that large alliance which once effected might spell salvation.

I write the above without knowledge of the existing position of our Mediterranean Fleet, which should of course be concentrated and *at sea*, in a suitable but not too close supporting position.

The British Mediterranean Fleet was in fact scattered. Of our five great capital ships, one was at Gibraltar, another in the Eastern Mediterranean, and the remaining three were lolling about inside or outside widely-separated Italian ports, two of them not protected by their flotillas. The destroyer flotillas themselves were dispersed along the European and African shores, and a large number of cruisers were crowded in Malta harbour without the protection of the powerful anti-aircraft batteries of battleships. At the very time that the fleet was suffered to disperse in this manner it was known that the Italian Fleet was concentrated in the Straits of Otranto and that troops were being assembled and embarked for some serious enterprise.

I challenged these careless dispositions on April 13 in the House of Commons:

The British habit of the week-end, the great regard which the British pay to holidays which coincide with festivals of the Church, is studied abroad. Good Friday was also the first day after Parliament had dispersed. It was known too that on that day the British Fleet was carrying out in a routine manner a programme long announced. It would therefore be dispersed in all quarters. . . . I can well believe that if our Fleet had been concentrated and cruising in the southern parts of the

Ionian Sea the Albanian adventure would never have been undertaken. . . .

After twenty-five years' experience in peace and war, I believe the
British Intelligence Service to be the finest of its kind in the world.
Yet we have seen, both in the case of the subjugation of Bohemia and
on the occasion of the invasion of Albania, that Ministers of the Crown
had apparently no inkling, or at any rate no conviction, of what was
coming. I cannot believe that this is the fault of the British Secret
Service.

How was it that on the eve of the Bohemian outrage Ministers were
indulging in what was called "sunshine talk" and predicting "the dawn
of a Golden Age"? How was it that last week's holiday routine was
observed at a time when clearly something of a quite exceptional
character, the consequences of which could not be measured, was
imminent? . . . It seems to me that Ministers run the most tremendous
risks if they allow the information collected by the Intelligence Department, and sent to them, I am sure, in good time, to be sifted and
coloured and reduced in consequence and importance, and if they ever
get themselves into a mood of attaching weight only to those pieces
of information which accord with their earnest and honourable desire
that the peace of the world should remain unbroken.

All things are moving at the same moment. Year by year, month by
month, they have all been moving forward together. While we have
reached certain positions in thought, others have reached certain positions in fact. The danger is now very near, and a great part of Europe
is to a very large extent mobilised. Millions of men are being prepared
for war. Everywhere the frontier defences are being manned. Everywhere it is felt that some new stroke is impending. If it should fall,
can there be any doubt that we should be involved? We are no longer
where we were two or three months ago. We have committed ourselves in every direction, rightly in my opinion, having regard to all
that has happened. It is not necessary to enumerate the countries to
which directly or indirectly we have given or are giving guarantees.
What we should not have dreamt of doing a year ago, when all was
so much more powerful, what we should not have dreamt of doing
even a month ago, we are doing now. Surely then when we aspire
to lead all Europe back from the verge of the abyss on to the uplands
of law and peace we must ourselves set the highest example. We
must keep nothing back. How can we bear to continue to lead our
comfortable, easy lives here at home, unwilling to pronounce even the
word "compulsion", unwilling to take even the necessary measure by
which the armies which we have promised can alone be recruited and
equipped? The dark, bitter waters are rising fast on every side. How

can we continue—let me say with particular frankness and sincerity—with less than the full force of the nation incorporated in the governing instrument?

I reiterated my complaints about the Fleet a few days later in a private letter to Lord Halifax:

The dispositions of our Fleet are inexplicable. First, on Tuesday night, April 4, the First Lord showed that the Home Fleet was in such a condition of preparedness that the men could not even leave the anti-aircraft guns to come below. This was the result of a scare telegram, and was, in my opinion, going beyond what vigilance requires. On the other hand, at the same time the Mediterranean Fleet was, as I described to the House, scattered in the most vulnerable disorder throughout the Mediterranean; and, as photographs published in the newspapers show, the *Barham* was actually moored alongside the Naples jetty. Now the Mediterranean Fleet has been concentrated and is at sea, where it should be. Therefore no doubt all is well in the Mediterranean. But the unpreparedness is transferred to home waters. The Atlantic Fleet, except for a few anti-aircraft guns, has been practically out of action for some days owing to very large numbers of men having been sent on leave. One would have thought at least the leave could be "staggered" in times like these. All the minesweepers are out of action refitting. How is it possible to reconcile this with the statement of tension declared to be existing on Tuesday week? It seems to be a grave departure from the procedure of continuous and reasonable vigilance. After all, the conditions prevailing now are not in principle different from those of last week. The First Sea Lord is seriously ill, so I expect a great deal falls upon Stanhope.

I write this to you for your own personal information, and in order that you can check the facts for yourself. Pray therefore treat my letter as strictly private, as I do not want to bother the Prime Minister with the matter, but I think you ought to know.

* * *

On April 15, 1939, after the declaration of the German protectorate of Bohemia and Moravia, Goering met Mussolini and Ciano in order to explain to the Italians the progress of German preparations for war. The minutes of this meeting have been found. One passage reads—it is Goering who is speaking: "The heavy armament of Czechoslavakia shows, in any case, how dangerous it could have been, even after Munich, in the event of a serious conflict. By German action the situation of both Axis countries was ameliorated because, among other reasons, of the economic possibilities which resulted from the transfer to Germany of the great productive capacity of Czechoslovakia. That contributes towards a considerable strengthening of the Axis against the Western Powers. Furthermore, Germany now need not keep ready a single division for protection against that country in case of a bigger conflict. This too is an advantage by which both Axis countries will, in the last analysis, benefit. . . . The action taken by Germany in Czechoslovakia is to be viewed as an advantage for the Axis Powers. Germany could now attack this country [Poland] from two flanks, and would be within only twenty-five minutes' flying distance from the new Polish industrial centre, which has been moved farther into the interior of the country, nearer to the other Polish industrial districts, because of its proximity to the border."*

"The bloodless solution of the Czech conflict in the autumn of 1938 and spring of 1939 and the annexation of Slovakia," said General von Jodl in a lecture some years after, "rounded off the territory of Greater Germany in such a way that it now became possible to consider the Polish problem on the basis of more or less favourable strategic premises."†

On the day of Goering's visit to Rome President Roosevelt sent a personal message to Hitler and Mussolini urging them to give a guarantee not to undertake any further aggression for ten "or even twenty-five years, if we are to look that far ahead." The Duce at first refused to read the document, and then remarked: "A result of infantile paralysis!" He little thought he was himself to suffer worse afflictions.

*   *   *

On April 27 the Prime Minister took the serious decision to introduce conscription, although repeated pledges had been given by him against such a step. To Mr. Hore-Belisha, the Secretary of State for War, belongs the credit of forcing this belated awakening. He certainly took his political life in his hands, and several of his interviews with his chief were of a formidable character. I saw something of him in this ordeal, and he was never sure that each day in office would not be his last.

Of course the introduction of conscription at this stage did not give us an army. It only applied to the men of twenty years of

* *Nuremberg Documents*, Pt. II, p. 106.
† *Ibid.*, p. 107.

The German wars of Conquest

47 The invasion of the Rhineland, March 1936.
48 The entry of the Germans into Vienna, March 1938.

49 Hitler declaring in Vienna that Austria was no more than a part of the German Fatherland, 16th March, 1938.
50 The population of Salzburg enthusiastically welcomes the German Army, March 1938.

51 The invasion of Czechoslovakia: the Fuehrer personally crossing the border at Wildenau, 3rd October, 1938.
52 A German armoured-car entering the Sudetenland, 20th September, 1938.

53 German armed might in Hungary: a parade of light armoured-cars before
   Regent Horthy, 27th August, 1938.
54 Hitler's inspection of Czechoslovakia, 18th March, 1939.

age; they had still to be trained; and after they had been trained
they had still to be armed. It was however a symbolic gesture of
the utmost consequence to France and Poland, and to other
nations on whom we had lavished our guarantees. In the debate
the Opposition failed in their duty. Both Labour and Liberal
Parties shrank from facing the ancient and deep-rooted prejudice
which has always existed in England against compulsory military
service. The Leader of the Labour Party moved that:

Whilst prepared to take all necessary steps to provide for the safety
of the nation and the fulfilment of its international obligations, this
House regrets that His Majesty's Government, in breach of their
pledges, should abandon the voluntary principle, which has not failed
to provide the man-power needed for defence, and is of opinion that
the measure proposed is ill-conceived, and, so far from adding
materially to the effective defence of the country, will promote
division and discourage the national effort, and is further evidence
that the Government's conduct of affairs throughout these critical
times does not merit the confidence of the country or this House.

The Leader of the Liberal Party also found reasons for opposing
this step. Both these men were distressed at the course they felt
bound on party grounds to take. But they both took it, and
adduced a wealth of reasons. The division was on party lines,
and the Conservatives carried their policy by 380 to 143 votes.
In my speech I tried my best to persuade the Opposition to
support this indispensable measure; but my efforts were in vain.
I understood fully their difficulties, especially when confronted
with a Government to which they were opposed. I must record
the event, because it deprives Liberal and Labour partisans of any
right to censure the Government of the day. They showed their
own measure in relation to events only too plainly. Presently
they were to show a truer measure.

* * *

Though Mr. Chamberlain still hoped to avert war, it was plain
that he would not shrink from it if it came. Mr. Feiling says that
he noted in his diary, "Churchill's chances [of entering the
Government] improve as war becomes more probable, and *vice
versa*".* This was perhaps a somewhat disdainful epitome. There
were many other thoughts in my mind besides those of becoming

* Feiling, *op. cit.*, p. 406.

once again a Minister. All the same, I understood the Prime Minister's outlook. He knew, if there was war, he would have to come to me, and he believed rightly that I would answer the call. On the other hand, he feared that Hitler would regard my entry into the Government as a hostile manifestation, and that it would thus wipe out all remaining chances of peace. This was a natural but a wrong view. None the less, no one can blame Mr. Chamberlain for not wishing to bring so tremendous and delicate a situation to a head for the sake of including any particular member of the House of Commons in his Government.

In March I had joined Mr. Eden and some thirty Conservative Members in tabling a resolution for a National Government. During the summer there arose a very considerable stir in the country in favour of this, or at least for my and Mr. Eden's inclusion in the Cabinet. Sir Stafford Cripps, in his independent position, became deeply distressed about the national danger. He visited me and various Ministers to urge the formation of what he called an "All-in Government". I could do nothing; but Mr. Stanley, President of the Board of Trade, was deeply moved. He wrote to the Prime Minister offering his own office if it would facilitate a reconstruction.

Mr. Stanley to the Prime Minister   June 30, 1939
I hesitate to write to you at a time like this, when you are overwhelmed with care and worry, and only the urgency of affairs is my excuse. I suppose we all feel that the only chance of averting war this autumn is to bring home to Hitler the certainty that we shall fulfil our obligations to Poland and that aggression on his part must inevitably mean a general conflagration. All of us, as well, must have been thinking whether there is any action we can take, which without being so menacing as to invite reprisal will be sufficiently dramatic to command attention. I myself can think of nothing which would be more effective, if it were found to be possible, than the formation now of the sort of Government which inevitably we should form at the outbreak of war It would be a dramatic confirmation of the national unity and determination, and would, I imagine, not only have a great effect in Germany, but also in the United States. It is also possible that if at the eleventh hour some possibility of a satisfactory settlement emerged it would be much easier for such a Government to be at all conciliatory. You of course must yourself have considered the possibility, and must be much more conscious of possible difficulties than I could be, but I thought I would write both to let you know my views

and to assure you that if you did contemplate such a possibility, I—as I am sure all the rest of our colleagues—would gladly serve in any position, however small, either inside or outside the Government.

The Prime Minister contented himself with a formal acknowledgment.

As the weeks passed by almost all the newspapers, led by the *Daily Telegraph* (July 3), emphasised by the *Manchester Guardian*, reflected this surge of opinion. I was surprised to see its daily recurrent and repeated expression. Thousands of enormous posters were displayed for weeks on end on Metropolitan hoardings, "Churchill Must Come Back". Scores of young volunteer men and women carried sandwich-board placards with similar slogans up and down before the House of Commons. I had nothing to do with such methods of agitation, but I should certainly have joined the Government had I been invited. Here again my personal good fortune held, and all else flowed out in its logical, natural, and horrible sequence.

CHAPTER XX

THE SOVIET ENIGMA

Hitler Denounces the Anglo-German Naval Agreement – And the Polish Non-Aggression Pact – The Soviet Proposal of a Three-Power Alliance – Dilemma of the Border States – Soviet-German Contacts Grow – The Dismissal of Litvinov – Molotov – Anglo-Soviet Negotiations – Debate of May 19 – Mr. Lloyd George's Speech – My Statement on the European Situation – The Need of the Russian Alliance – Too Late – The "Pact of Steel" between Germany and Italy – Soviet Diplomatic Tactics.

WE have reached the period when all relations between Britain and Germany were at an end. We now know of course that there never had been any true relationship between our two countries since Hitler came into power. He had only hoped to persuade or frighten Britain into giving him a free hand in Eastern Europe, and Mr. Chamberlain had cherished the hope of appeasing and reforming him and leading him to grace. However, the time had come when the last illusions of the British Government had been dispelled. The Cabinet was at length convinced that Nazi Germany meant war, and the Prime Minister offered guarantees and contracted alliances in every direction still open, regardless of whether we could give any effective help to the countries concerned. To the Polish guarantee was added a Greek and Roumanian guarantee, and to these an alliance with Turkey.

We must now recall the sad piece of paper which Mr. Chamberlain had got Hitler to sign at Munich and which he waved triumphantly to the crowd when he quitted his aeroplane at Heston. In this he had invoked the two bonds which he assumed existed between him and Hitler and between Britain and Germany, namely, the Munich Agreement and the Anglo-German

Naval Treaty. The subjugation of Czechoslovakia had destroyed the first; Hitler now brushed away the second.

Addressing the Reichstag on April 28, he said:

Since England to-day, both through the Press and officially, upholds the view that Germany should be opposed in all circumstances, and confirms this by the policy of encirclement known to us, the basis of the Naval Treaty has been removed. I have therefore resolved to send to-day a communication to this effect to the British Government. This is to us not a matter of practical material importance—for I still hope that we shall be able to avoid an armaments race with England—but an action of self-respect. Should the British Government however wish to enter once more into negotiations with Germany on this problem, no one would be happier than I at the prospect of still being able to come to a clear and straightforward understanding.*

The Anglo-German Naval Agreement, which had been so marked a gain to Hitler at an important and critical moment in his policy, was now represented by him as a favour to Britain, the benefits of which would be withdrawn as a mark of German displeasure. The Fuehrer held out the hope to the British Government that he might be willing to discuss the naval problems further with His Majesty's Government, and he may even have expected that his former dupes would persist in their policy of appeasement. To him it now mattered nothing. He had Italy, and he had his air superiority; he had Austria and Czechoslovakia, with all that that implied. He had his Western Wall. In the purely naval sphere he had always been building U-boats as fast as possible irrespective of any agreement. He had already as a matter of form invoked his right to build 100 per cent. of the British numbers, but this had not limited in the slightest degree the German U-boat construction programme. As for the larger vessels, he could not nearly digest the generous allowance which had been accorded to him by the Naval Agreement. He therefore made fine impudent play with flinging it back in the face of the simpletons who made it.

In this same speech Hitler also denounced the German-Polish Non-Aggression Pact. He gave as his direct reason the Anglo-Polish Guarantee, "which would in certain circumstances compel Poland to take military action against Germany in the event of a conflict between Germany and any other Power, in which

* Hitler's Speeches, II, p. 1626.

England in her turn would be involved. This obligation is contrary to the Agreement which I made with Marshal Pilsudski
some time ago. . . . I therefore look upon the Agreement as having been unilaterally infringed by Poland and thereby no longer
in existence. I sent a communication to this effect to the Polish
Government. . . ."

After studying this speech at the time, I wrote in one of my
articles:

It seems only too probable that the glare of Nazi Germany is now
to be turned on to Poland. Herr Hitler's speeches may or may not be
a guide to his intentions, but the salient object of last Friday's performance was obviously to isolate Poland, to make the most plausible
case against her, and to bring intensive pressure upon her. The German
Dictator seemed to suppose that he could make the Anglo-Polish
Agreement inoperative by focusing his demands on Danzig and the
Corridor. He apparently expects that those elements in Great Britain
which used to exclaim, "Who would fight for Czechoslovakia?" may
now be induced to cry, "Who would fight for Danzig and the
Corridor?" He does not seem to be conscious of the immense change
which has been wrought in British public opinion by his treacherous
breach of the Munich Agreement, and of the complete reversal of
policy which this outrage brought about in the British Government,
and especially in the Prime Minister.

The denunciation of the German-Polish Non-Aggression Pact of
1934 is an extremely serious and menacing step. That pact had been
reaffirmed as recently as last January, when Ribbentrop visited
Warsaw. Like the Anglo-German Naval Treaty, it was negotiated at
the wish of Herr Hitler. Like the Naval Treaty, it gave marked advantages to Germany. Both Agreements eased Germany's position while
she was weak. The Naval Agreement amounted in fact to a condona-
tion by Great Britain of a breach of the military clauses of the Treaty
of Versailles, and thus stultified both the decisions of the Stresa front
and those which the Council of the League were induced to take. The
German-Polish Agreement enabled Nazi attention to be concentrated
first upon Austria and later upon Czechoslovakia, with ruinous results
to those unhappy countries. It temporarily weakened the relations
between France and Poland and prevented any solidarity of interests
growing up among the States of Eastern Europe. Now that it has
served its purpose for Germany, it is cast away by one-sided action.
Poland is implicitly informed that she is now in the zone of potential
aggression.

★   ★   ★

The British Government had to consider urgently the practical implications of the guarantees given to Poland and to Roumania. Neither set of assurances had any military value except within the framework of a general agreement with Russia. It was therefore with this object that talks at last began in Moscow on April 15 between the British Ambassador and M. Litvinov. Considering how the Soviet Government had hitherto been treated, there was not much to be expected from them now. However, on April 16 they made a formal offer, the text of which was not published, for the creation of a united front of mutual assistance between Great Britain, France, and the U.S.S.R. The three Powers, with Poland added if possible, were furthermore to guarantee those States in Central and Eastern Europe which lay under the menace of German aggression. The obstacle to such an agreement was the terror of these same border countries of receiving Soviet help in the shape of Soviet armies marching through their territories to defend them from the Germans, and incidentally incorporating them in the Soviet-Communist system, of which they were the most vehement opponents. Poland, Roumania, Finland, and the three Baltic States did not know whether it was German aggression or Russian rescue that they dreaded more. It was this hideous choice that paralysed British and French policy.

There can however be no doubt, even in the after-light, that Britain and France should have accepted the Russian offer, proclaimed the Triple Alliance, and left the method by which it could be made effective in case of war to be adjusted between allies engaged against a common foe. In such circumstances a different temper prevails. Allies in war are inclined to defer a great deal to each other's wishes; the flail of battle beats upon the front, and all kinds of expedients are welcomed which in peace would be abhorrent. It would not be easy in a Grand Alliance, such as might have been developed, for one ally to enter the territory of another unless invited.

But Mr. Chamberlain and the Foreign Office were baffled by this riddle of the Sphinx. When events are moving at such speed and in such tremendous mass as at this juncture it is wise to take one step at a time. The alliance of Britain, France, and Russia would have struck deep alarm into the heart of Germany in 1939, and no one can prove that war might not even then have been averted. The next step could have been taken with superior power on the side of the allies. The initiative would have been regained by their diplomacy. Hitler could afford neither to embark upon the war on two fronts, which he himself had so deeply condemned, nor to sustain a check. It was a pity not to have placed him in this awkward position, which might well have cost him his life. Statesmen are not called upon only to settle easy questions. These often settle themselves. It is where the balance quivers, and the proportions are veiled in mist, that the opportunity for world-saving decisions presents itself. Having got ourselves into this awful plight of 1939, it was vital to grasp the larger hope.

It is not even now possible to fix the moment when Stalin definitely abandoned all intention of working with the Western Democracies and considered coming to terms with Hitler. Indeed it seems probable that there never was such a moment. The publication in *Nazi-Soviet Relations, 1939-41*, by the American State Department of a mass of documents captured from the archives of the German Foreign Office gives us however a number of facts hitherto unknown. Apparently something happened as early as February 1939; but this was almost certainly concerned with trading and commercial questions affected by the status of Czechoslovakia after Munich which required discussion between the two countries. The incorporation of Czechoslovakia in the Reich in mid-March magnified these issues. Russia had some contracts with the Czechoslovak Government for munitions from the Skoda works. What was to happen to these contracts now that Skoda had become a German arsenal?

On April 17 the State Secretary in the German Foreign Office, Weizsaecker, records that the Russian Ambassador had visited him that day for the first time since he had presented his credentials nearly a year before. He asked about the Skoda contracts, and Weizsaecker pointed out that "a favourable atmosphere for the delivery of war materials to Soviet Russia was not exactly being created at present by reports of a Russian-British-French Air Pact and the like". On this the Soviet Ambassador turned at once from trade to politics and asked the State Secretary what he thought of German-Russian relations. Weizsaecker replied that it appeared to him that "the Russian Press lately was not fully participating in the anti-German tone of the American and some of the English papers". On this the Soviet Ambassador said,

"Ideological differences of opinion have hardly influenced the Russian-Italian relationship, and they need not prove a stumbling-block to Germany either. Soviet Russia has not exploited the present friction between Germany and the Western Democracies against her, nor does she desire to do so. There exists for Russia no reason why she should not live with Germany on a normal footing. And from normal relations might become better and better."

We must regard this conversation as significant, especially in view of the simultaneous discussions in Moscow between the British Ambassador and M. Litvinov and the formal offer of the Soviet on April 16 of a Three-Power Alliance with Great Britain and France. It is the first obvious move of Russia from one leg to the other. "Normalisation" of the relations between Russia and Germany was henceforward pursued, step by step, with the negotiations for a Triple Alliance against German aggression.

If, for instance, Mr. Chamberlain on receipt of the Russian offer had replied, "Yes. Let us three band together and break Hitler's neck," or words to that effect, Parliament would have approved, Stalin would have understood, and history might have taken a different course. At least it could not have taken a worse.

On May 4 I commented on the position in these terms:

Above all, time must not be lost. Ten or twelve days have already passed since the Russian offer was made. The British people, who have now, at the sacrifice of honoured, ingrained custom, accepted the principle of compulsory military service, have a right, in conjunction with the French Republic, to call upon Poland not to place obstacles in the way of a common cause. Not only must the full co-operation of Russia be accepted, but the three Baltic States, Lithuania, Latvia, and Esthonia, must also be brought into association. To these three countries of warlike peoples, possessing together armies totalling perhaps twenty divisions of virile troops, a friendly Russia supplying munitions and other aid is essential.

There is no means of maintaining an Eastern front against Nazi aggression without the active aid of Russia. Russian interests are deeply concerned in preventing Herr Hitler's designs on Eastern Europe. It should still be possible to range all the States and peoples from the Baltic to the Black Sea in one solid front against a new outrage or invasion. Such a front, if established in good heart, and with resolute and efficient military arrangements, combined with the strength of the Western Powers, may yet confront Hitler, Goering,

Himmler, Ribbentrop, Goebbels and Co. with forces the German people would be reluctant to challenge.

*　　*　　*

Instead, there was a long silence while half-measures and judicious compromises were being prepared. This delay was fatal to Litvinov. His last attempt to bring matters to a clear-cut decision with the Western Powers was deemed to have failed. Our credit stood very low. A wholly different foreign policy was required for the safety of Russia, and a new exponent must be found. On May 3 an official communiqué from Moscow announced that M. Litvinov had been released from the office of Foreign Commissar at his request and that his duties would be assumed by the Premier, M. Molotov. The German Chargé d'Affaires in Moscow reported on May 4 as follows: "Since Litvinov had received the English Ambassador as late as May 2 and had been named in the Press of yesterday as guest of honour at the parade, his dismissal appears to be the result of a spontaneous decision by Stalin. . . . At the last Party Congress Stalin urged caution lest the Soviet Union should be drawn into conflict. Molotov (no Jew) is held to be 'the most intimate friend and closest collaborator of Stalin'. His appointment is apparently the guarantee that the foreign policy will be continued strictly in accordance with Stalin's ideas."

Soviet diplomatic representatives abroad were instructed to inform the Government to which they were accredited that this change meant no alteration in Russian foreign policy. Moscow Radio announced on May 4 that Molotov would carry on the policy of Western security that for years had been Litvinov's aim. The eminent Jew, the target of German antagonism, was flung aside for the time being like a broken tool, and, without being allowed a word of explanation, was bundled off the world stage to obscurity, a pittance, and police supervision. Molotov, little known outside Russia, became Commissar for Foreign Affairs, in the closest confederacy with Stalin. He was free from all encumbrance of previous declarations, free from the League of Nations atmosphere, and able to move in any direction which the self-preservation of Russia might seem to require. There was in fact only one way in which he was now likely to move. He had always been favourable to an arrangement with Hitler. The Soviet Government were convinced by Munich and much else that neither Britain nor France would fight till they were attacked, and would not be much good then. The gathering storm was about to break. Russia must look after herself.

The dismissal of Litvinov marked the end of an epoch. It registered the abandonment by the Kremlin of all faith in a security pact with the Western Powers and in the possibility of organising an Eastern front against Germany. The German Press comments at the time, though not necessarily accurate, are interesting. A dispatch from Warsaw was published in the German newspapers on May 4 stating that Litvinov had resigned after a bitter quarrel with Marshal Voroshilov ("the Party boy", as cheeky and daring Russians called him in moments of relaxation). Voroshilov, no doubt on precise instructions, had declared that the Red Army was not prepared to fight for Poland, and, in the name of the Russian General Staff, condemned "excessively far-reaching military obligations". On May 7 the *Frankfurter Zeitung* was already sufficiently informed to state that Litvinov's resignation was extremely serious for the future of Anglo-French "encirclement", and its probable meaning was that those in Russia concerned with the military burden resulting from it had called a halt to Litvinov. All this was true; but for an interval it was necessary that a veil of deceit should cover the immense transaction, and that even up to the latest moment the Soviet attitude should remain in doubt. Russia must have a move both ways. How else could she drive her bargain with the hated and dreaded Hitler?

* * *

The Jew Litvinov was gone, and Hitler's dominant prejudice placated. From that moment the German Government ceased to define its foreign policy as anti-Bolshevism, and turned its abuse upon the "pluto-Democracies". Newspaper articles assured the Soviets that the German *Lebensraum* did not encroach on Russian territory; that indeed it stopped short of the Russian frontier at all points. Consequently there could be no cause of conflict between Russia and Germany unless the Soviets entered into "encirclement" engagements with England and France. The German Ambassador, Count Schulenburg, who had been summoned to Berlin for lengthy consultations, returned to Moscow with an offer of an advantageous goods-credit on a long-term basis. The movement on both sides was towards a compact.

This violent and unnatural reversal of Russian policy was a transmogrification of which only totalitarian States are capable. Barely two years since the leaders of the Russian Army, Tukhachevsky and several thousands of its most accomplished officers, had been slaughtered for the very inclinations which now became acceptable to the handful of anxious masters in the Kremlin. Then pro-Germanism had been heresy and treason. Now, overnight, it was the policy of the State, and woe was mechanically meted out to any who dared dispute it, and often to those not quick enough on the turn-about.

For the task in hand no one was better fitted or equipped than the new Foreign Commissar.

★ ★ ★

The figure whom Stalin had now moved to the pulpit of Soviet foreign policy deserves some description, not available to the British or French Governments at the time. Vyacheslav Molotov was a man of outstanding ability and cold-blooded ruthlessness. He had survived the fearful hazards and ordeals to which all the Bolshevik leaders had been subjected in the years of triumphant revolution. He had lived and thrived in a society where ever-varying intrigue was accompanied by the constant menace of personal liquidation. His cannon-ball head, black moustache, and comprehending eyes, his slab face, his verbal adroitness and imperturbable demeanour, were appropriate manifestations of his qualities and skill. He was above all men fitted to be the agent and instrument of the policy of an incalculable machine. I have only met him on equal terms, in parleys where sometimes a strain of humour appeared, or at banquets where he genially proposed a long succession of conventional and meaningless toasts. I have never seen a human being who more perfectly represented the modern conception of a robot. And yet with all this there was an apparently reasonable and keenly-polished diplomatist. What he was to his inferiors I cannot tell. What he was to the Japanese Ambassador during the years when after the Teheran Conference Stalin had promised to attack Japan once the German Army was beaten can be deduced from his recorded conversations. One delicate, searching, awkward interview after another was conducted with perfect poise, impenetrable purpose, and bland, official correctitude. Never a chink was opened. Never a needless jar was made. His smile of Siberian winter, his carefully-measured and often wise words, his affable demeanour, combined to make him the perfect agent of Soviet policy in a deadly world.

Correspondence with him upon disputed matters was always useless, and, if pushed far, ended in lies and insults, of which this work will presently contain some examples. Only once did I seem to get a natural, human reaction. This was in the spring of 1942, when he alighted in Britain on his way back from the United States. We had signed the Anglo-Soviet Treaty, and he was about to make his dangerous flight home. At the garden gate of Downing Street, which we used for secrecy, I gripped his arm and we looked each other in the face. Suddenly he appeared deeply moved. Inside the image there appeared the man. He responded with an equal pressure. Silently we wrung each other's hands. But then we were all together, and it was life or death for the lot. Havoc and ruin had been around him all his days, either impending on himself or dealt by him to others. Certainly in Molotov the Soviet machine had found a capable and in many ways a characteristic representative—always the faithful Party man and Communist disciple. How glad I am at the end of my life not to have had to endure the stresses which he has suffered; better never be born. In the conduct of foreign affairs Mazarin, Talleyrand, Metternich, would welcome him to their company, if there be another world to which Bolsheviks allow themselves to go.   *   *   *

From the moment when Molotov became Foreign Commissar he pursued the policy of an arrangement with Germany at the expense of Poland. It was not very long before the French became aware of this. There is a remarkable dispatch by the French Ambassador in Berlin, dated May 7, published in the *French Yellow Book*, which states that on his secret information he was sure that a Fourth Partition of Poland was to be the basis of the German-Russian *rapprochement*. "Since the month of May," writes M. Daladier in April 1946, "the U.S.S.R. had conducted two negotiations, one with France, the other with Germany. She appeared to prefer to partition rather than to defend Poland. Such was the immediate cause of the Second World War."* But there were other causes too.   *   *   *

* Quoted by Reynaud, *op. cit.*, I, 585.

On May 8 the British Government at last replied to the Soviet Note of April 16. While the text of the British document was not published, the Tass Agency on May 9 issued a statement giving the main points of the British proposals. On May 10 the official organ *Isvestia* printed a communiqué to the effect that Reuter's statement of the British counter-proposals, namely, that "the Soviet Union must separately guarantee every neighbouring State, and that Great Britain must pledge herself to assist the U.S.S.R. if the latter becomes involved in war as a result of its guarantees", did not correspond to fact. The Soviet Government, said the communiqué, had received the British counter-proposals on May 8, but these did not mention the Soviet Union's obligation to give a separate guarantee to each of its neighbouring States, whereas they did state that the U.S.S.R. was obliged to render immediate assistance to Great Britain and France in the event of their being involved in war under their guarantees to Poland and Roumania. No mention however was made of any assistance on their part to the Soviet Union in the event of its being involved in war in consequence of its obligations towards any Eastern European State.

Later on the same day Mr. Chamberlain said that the Government had undertaken their new obligations in Eastern Europe without inviting the direct participation of the Soviet Government on account of various difficulties. His Majesty's Government had suggested that the Soviet Government should make, on their own behalf, a similar declaration, and express their readiness to lend assistance, if desired, to countries which might be victims of aggression and were prepared to defend their independence.

Almost simultaneously the Soviet Government presented a scheme at once more comprehensive and more rigid, which, whatever other advantages it might present, must in the view of His Majesty's Government inevitably raise the very difficulties which their own proposals had been designed to avoid. They accordingly pointed out to the Soviet Government the existence of these difficulties. At the same time they made certain modifications in their original proposals. In particular, they [H.M.G.] made it plain that *if the Soviet Government wished to make their own intervention contingent on that of Great Britain and France, His Majesty's Government for their part would have no objection.*

It was a pity that this had not been explicitly stated a fortnight earlier.

It should be mentioned here that on May 12 the Anglo-Turkish Agreement was formally ratified by the Turkish Parliament. By means of this addition to our commitments we hoped to strengthen our position in the Mediterranean in the event of a crisis. Here was our answer to the Italian occupation of Albania. Just as the period of talking with Germany was over, so now we reached in effect the same deadlock with Italy.

The Russian negotiations proceeded languidly, and on May 19 the whole issue was raised in the House of Commons. The debate, which was short and serious, was practically confined to the leaders of parties and to prominent ex-Ministers. Mr. Lloyd George, Mr. Eden, and I all pressed upon the Government the vital need of an immediate arrangement with Russia of the most far-reaching character and on equal terms. Mr. Lloyd George began, and painted a picture of gloom and peril in the darkest hues:

The situation reminds me very much of the feeling that prevailed in the early spring of 1918. We knew there was a great attack coming from Germany, but no one quite knew where the blow would fall. I remember that the French thought it would fall on their front, while our generals thought it would fall on ours. The French generals were not even agreed as to the part of their front on which the attack would fall, and our generals were equally divided. All that we knew was that there was a tremendous onslaught coming somewhere, and the whole atmosphere was filled with, I will not say fear, but with uneasiness. We could see the tremendous activities behind the German lines, and we knew that they were preparing something. That is more or less what seems to me to be the position to-day. . . . We are all very anxious; the whole world is under the impression that there is something preparing in the nature of another attack from the aggressors. Nobody quite knows where it will come. We can see that they are speeding up their armaments at a rate hitherto unprecedented, especially in weapons of the offensive—tanks, bombing aeroplanes, submarines. We know that they are occupying and fortifying fresh positions that will give them strategic advantages in a war with France and ourselves. . . . They are inspecting and surveying, from Libya to the North Sea, all sorts of situations that would be of vital importance in the event of war. There is a secrecy in the movements behind the lines which is very ominous.

There is the same kind of secrecy as in 1918, in order to baffle us as to their objects. They are not preparing for defence. . . . They are not preparing themselves against attack from either France, Britain, or Russia. That has never been threatened. I have never heard, either privately or publicly, any hint or suggestion that we were contemplating an attack upon Italy or Germany in any quarter, and they know it quite well. Therefore all these preparations are not for defence. They are for some contemplated offensive scheme against someone or other in whom we are interested.

*　　*　　*

Mr. Lloyd George then added some words of wisdom:

The main military purpose and scheme of the Dictators is to produce quick results, to avoid a prolonged war. A prolonged war never suits dictators. A prolonged war like the Peninsular War wears them down, and the great Russian defence, which produced no great military victory for the Russians, broke Napoleon. Germany's ideal is now, and always has been, a war which is brought to a speedy end. The war against Austria in 1866 did not last more than a few weeks, and the war in 1870 was waged in such a way that it was practically over in a month or two. In 1914 plans were made with exactly the same aim in view, and it was very nearly achieved; and they would have achieved it but for Russia. But from the moment they failed to achieve a speedy victory the game was up. You may depend upon it that the great military thinkers of Germany have been working out the problem, what was the mistake of 1914, what did they lack, how can they fill up the gaps and repair the blunders or avoid them in the next war?

Mr. Lloyd George, pressing on from fact to fancy, then suggested that the Germans had already got "twenty thousand tanks" and "thousands of bomber aeroplanes". This was far beyond the truth. Moreover, it was an undue appeal to the fear motive. And why had he not been busy all these years with my small group ingeminating rearmament? But his speech cast a chill over the assembly. Two years before, or better still three, such statements and all the pessimism of his speech would have been scorned and derided. But then there was time. Now, whatever the figures, it was all too late.

The Prime Minister replied, and for the first time revealed to us his views on the Soviet offer. His reception of it was certainly cool, and indeed disdainful:

If we can evolve a method by which we can enlist the co-operation and assistance of the Soviet Union in building up that peace front, we welcome it; we want it; we attach value to it. The suggestion that we despise the assistance of the Soviet Union is without foundation. Without accepting any view of an unauthorised character as to the precise value of the Russian military forces, or the way in which they would best be employed, no one would be so foolish as to suppose that that huge country, with its vast population and enormous resources, would be *a negligible factor* in such a situation as that with which we are confronted.

This seemed to show the same lack of proportion as we have seen in the rebuff to the Roosevelt proposals a year before.

I then took up the tale:

I have been quite unable to understand what is the objection to making the agreement with Russia which the Prime Minister professes himself desirous of doing, and making it in the broad and simple form proposed by the Russian Soviet Government.

Undoubtedly, the proposals put forward by the Russian Government contemplate a Triple Alliance against aggression between England, France, and Russia, which alliance may extend its benefits to other countries if and when those benefits are desired. The alliance is solely for the purpose of resisting further acts of aggression and of protecting the victims of aggression. I cannot see what is wrong with that. What is wrong with this simple proposal? It is said: "Can you trust the Russian Soviet Government?" I suppose in Moscow they say: "Can we trust Chamberlain?" I hope we may say that the answer to both questions is in the affirmative. I earnestly hope so. . . .

This Turkish proposal, which is universally accepted, is a great consolidating and stabilising force throughout the whole of the Black Sea area and the Eastern Mediterranean. Turkey, with whom we have made this agreement, is in the closest harmony with Russia. She is also in the closest harmony with Roumania. These Powers together are mutually protecting vital interests. . . .

There is a great identity of interests between Great Britain and the associated Powers in the South. Is there not a similar identity of interests in the North? Take the countries of the Baltic, Lithuania, Latvia, and Esthonia, which were once the occasion of the wars of Peter the Great. It is a major interest of Russia that these Powers should not fall into the hands of Nazi Germany. That is a vital interest in the North. I need not elaborate the arguments about [a German attack upon] the Ukraine, which means an invasion of Russian territory. All along the whole of this Eastern front you can see that the major interests of

Russia are definitely engaged, and therefore it seems you could fairly judge that they would pool their interests with other countries similarly affected. . . .

If you are ready to be an ally of Russia in time of war, which is the supreme test, the great occasion of all, if you are ready to join hands with Russia in the defence of Poland, which you have guaranteed, and of Roumania, why should you shrink from becoming the ally of Russia now, when you may by that very fact prevent the breaking out of war? I cannot understand all these refinements of diplomacy and delay. If the worst comes to the worst, you are in the midst of it with them, and you have to make the best of it with them. If the difficulties do not arise, well, you will have had the security in the preliminary stages. . . .

His Majesty's Government have given a guarantee to Poland. I was astounded when I heard them give this guarantee. I support it, but I was astounded by it, because nothing that had happened before led one to suppose that such a step would be taken. I want to draw the attention of the Committee to the fact that the question posed by Mr. Lloyd George ten days ago and repeated to-day has not been answered. The question was whether the General Staff was consulted before this guarantee was given as to whether it was safe and practical to give it, and whether there were any means of implementing it. The whole country knows that the question has been asked, and it has not been answered. That is disconcerting and disquieting. . . .

Clearly Russia is not going to enter into agreements unless she is treated as an equal, and not only is treated as an equal, but has confidence that the methods employed by the Allies—by the peace front —are such as would be likely to lead to success. No one wants to associate themselves with indeterminate leadership and uncertain policies. The Government must realise that none of these States in Eastern Europe can maintain themselves for, say, a year's war unless they have behind them the massive, solid backing of a friendly Russia, joined to the combination of the Western Powers. In the main, I agree with Mr. Lloyd George that if there is to be an effective Eastern front—an Eastern peace front, or a war front as it might become—it can be set up only with the effective support of a friendly Soviet Russia lying behind all those countries.

Unless there is an Eastern front set up, what is going to happen to the West? What is going to happen to those countries on the Western front to whom, if we have not given guarantees, it is admitted we are bound—countries like Belgium, Holland, Denmark, and Switzerland? Let us look back to the experiences we had in 1917. In 1917 the Russian front was broken and demoralised. Revolution and mutiny had sapped the courage of that great disciplined army, and the conditions at the front were indescribable; and yet, until the treaty was made closing the front down, more than 1,500,000 Germans were held upon that front, even in its most ineffectual and unhappy condition. Once that front was closed down, 1,000,000 Germans and 5,000 cannon were brought to the West, and at the last moment almost turned the course of the war and forced upon us a disastrous peace.

It is a tremendous thing, this question of the Eastern front. I am astonished that there is not more anxiety about it. Certainly, I do not ask favours of Soviet Russia. This is no time to ask favours of countries. But here is an offer, a fair offer, and a better offer, in my opinion, than the terms which the Government seek to get for themselves; a more simple, a more direct and a more effective offer. Let it not be put aside and come to nothing. I beg His Majesty's Government to get some of these brutal truths into their heads. Without an effective Eastern front there can be no satisfactory defence of our interests in the West, and without Russia there can be no effective Eastern front. If His Majesty's Government, having neglected our defences for a long time, having thrown away Czechoslovakia with all that Czechoslovakia meant in military power, having committed us, without examination of the technical aspects, to the defence of Poland and Roumania, now reject and cast away the indispensable aid of Russia, and so lead us in the worst of all ways into the worst of all wars, they will have ill deserved the confidence and, I will add, the generosity with which they have been treated by their fellow-countrymen.

There can be little doubt that all this was now too late. Attlee, Sinclair, and Eden spoke on the general line of the imminence of the danger and the need of the Russian alliance. The position of the leaders of the Labour and Liberal Parties was weakened by the vote against compulsory national service to which they had led their followers only a few weeks before. The plea, so often advanced, that this was because they did not like the foreign policy was feeble; for no foreign policy can have validity if there is no adequate force behind it, and no national readiness to make the necessary sacrifices to produce that force.

*　*　*

The efforts of the Western Powers to produce a defensive alignment against Germany were well matched by the other side. Conversations between Ribbentrop and Ciano at Como at the beginning of May came to formal and public fruition in the so-called "Pact of Steel", signed by the two Foreign Ministers in

337

Berlin on May 22. This was the challenging answer to the flimsy British network of guarantees in Eastern Europe. Ciano in his diary records a conversation with Hitler at the time of the signature of this alliance.

Hitler states that he is well satisfied with the Pact, and confirms the fact that Mediterranean policy will be directed by Italy. He takes an interest in Albania, and is enthusiastic about our programme for making of Albania a stronghold which will inexorably dominate the Balkans.*

Hitler's satisfaction was more clearly revealed when on the day following the signing of the Pact of Steel, May 23, he held a meeting with his Chiefs of Staff. The secret minutes of the conversations are on record:

We are at present in a state of patriotic fervour, which is shared by two other nations—Italy and Japan. The period which lies behind us has indeed been put to good use. All measures have been taken in the correct sequence and in harmony with our aims. The Pole is no "supplementary enemy". Poland will always be on the side of our adversaries. In spite of treaties of friendship, Poland has always had the secret intention of exploiting every opportunity to do us harm. Danzig is not the subject of the dispute at all. It is a question of expanding our living space in the East and of securing our food supplies. There is therefore no question of sparing Poland, and we are left with the decision to attack Poland at the first suitable opportunity. We cannot expect a repetition of the Czech affair. There will be war. Our task is to isolate Poland. The success of the isolation will be decisive.

If it is not certain that a German-Polish conflict will not lead to war in the West, then the fight must be primarily against England and France. If there were an alliance of France, England, and Russia against Germany, Italy, and Japan, I should be constrained to attack England and France with a few annihilating blows. I doubt the possibility of a peaceful settlement with England. We must prepare ourselves for the conflict. England sees in our development the foundation of a hegemony which would weaken her. England is therefore our enemy, and the conflict with England will be a life-and-death struggle. The Dutch and Belgian air bases must be occupied by armed force. Declarations of neutrality must be ignored.

If England intends to intervene in the Polish war we must occupy Holland with lightning speed. We must aim at securing a new defence line on Dutch soil up to the Zuyder Zee. The idea that we can get off

* *Ciano's Diary,* p. 90.

cheaply is dangerous; there is no such possibility. We must burn our boats, and it is no longer a question of justice or injustice, but of life or death for eighty million human beings. Every country's armed forces or Government must aim at a short war. The Government however must also be prepared for a war of ten or fifteen years' duration.

England knows that to lose a war will mean the end of her world-power. England is the driving force against Germany.

The British themselves are proud, courageous, tenacious, firm in resistance, and gifted as organisers. They know how to exploit every new development. They have the love of adventure and the bravery of the Nordic race. The German average is higher. But if in the first World War we had had two battleships and two cruisers more, and if the Battle of Jutland had begun in the morning, the British Fleet would have been defeated* and England brought to her knees. In addition to the surprise attack, preparations for a long war must be made, while opportunities on the Continent for England are eliminated. The Army will have to hold positions essential to the Navy and Air Force. If Holland and Belgium are successfully occupied and held, and if France is also defeated, the fundamental conditions for a successful war against England will have been secured. †

On May 30 the German Foreign Office sent the following instructions to their Ambassador in Moscow: "Contrary to the policy previously planned, we have now decided to undertake definite negotiations with the Soviet Union." While the ranks of the Axis closed for military preparation, the vital link of the Western Powers with Russia had perished. The underlying discordance of view can be read into Foreign Commissar Molotov's speech of May 31 in reply to Mr. Chamberlain's speech in the Commons of May 19.

As far back [he said] as the middle of April the Soviet Government entered into negotiations with the British and French Governments about the necessary measures to be taken. The negotiations started then are not yet concluded. It became clear some time ago that if there was any real desire to create an efficient front of peaceable countries against the advance of aggression the following minimum conditions were imperative:

* *Nazi-Soviet Relations*, p. 15.
† *Nuremberg Documents*, I, pp. 167-8. Hitler was evidently quite ignorant of the facts of Jutland, which was from beginning to end an unsuccessful effort by the British Fleet to bring the Germans to a general action, in which the overwhelming gunfire of the British line of battle would soon have been decisive.

The conclusion between Great Britain, France, and the U.S.S.R. of an effective pact of mutual assistance against aggression, of an exclusively defensive character.

A guarantee on the part of Great Britain, France, and the U.S.S.R. of the States of Central and Eastern Europe, including, without exception, all the European countries bordering on the U.S.S.R., against an attack by aggressors.

The conclusion between Great Britain, France, and the U.S.S.R. of a definite agreement on the forms and extent of the immediate and effective assistance to be rendered to one another and to the guaranteed States in the event of an attack by aggressors.

The negotiations had come to a seemingly unbreakable deadlock. The Polish and Roumanian Governments, while accepting the British guarantee, were not prepared to accept a similar undertaking in the same form from the Russian Government. A similar attitude prevailed in another vital strategic quarter—the Baltic States. The Soviet Government made it clear that they would only adhere to a pact of mutual assistance if Finland and the Baltic States were included in a general guarantee. All four countries now refused, and perhaps in their terror would for a long time have refused such a condition. Finland and Esthonia even asserted that they would consider a guarantee extended to them without their assent as an act of aggression. On June 7 Esthonia and Latvia signed non-aggression pacts with Germany. Thus Hitler penetrated with ease into the final defences of the tardy, irresolute coalition against him.

CHAPTER XXI

ON THE VERGE

The Threat to Danzig – General Gamelin Invites Me to Visit the Rhine Front – A Tour with General Georges – Some Impressions – French Acceptance of the Defensive – The Position of Atomic Research – My Note on Air Defence – Renewed Efforts to Agree with Soviet Russia – Polish Obstruction – The Military Conversations in Moscow – Stalin's Account to Me in 1942 – A Record in Deceit – Ribbentrop Invited to Moscow – The Russo-German Non-Aggression Treaty – The News Breaks upon the World – Hitler's Army Orders – "Honesty is the Best Policy" – British Precautionary Measures – The Prime Minister's Letter to Hitler – An Insolent Reply – Hitler Postpones D-Day – Hitler's Letter to Mussolini – The Duce's Reply – The Last Few Days.

S UMMER advanced, preparations for war continued throughout Europe, and the attitudes of diplomatists, the speeches of politicians, and the wishes of mankind counted each day for less. German military movements seemed to portend the forcible settlement of the dispute with Poland over Danzig as a preliminary to the assault on Poland itself. Mr. Chamberlain expressed his anxieties to Parliament on June 10, and repeated his intention to stand by Poland if her independence were threatened. In a spirit of detachment from the facts the Belgian Government, largely under the influence of their King, announced on June 23 that they were opposed to Staff talks with England and France and that Belgium intended to maintain a strict neutrality. The tide of events brought with it a closing of the ranks between England and France, and also at home. There was much coming and going between Paris and London during the month of July. The celebrations of the Fourteenth of July were an occasion for a display of Anglo-French union. I was invited by the French Government to attend this brilliant spectacle.

As I was leaving Le Bourget after the parade General Gamelin suggested that I should visit the French front. "You have never seen the Rhine sector," he said. "Come then in August; we will show you everything." Accordingly a plan was made, and on August 15 General Spears and I were welcomed by his close friend, General Georges, Commander-in-Chief of the armies on the North-eastern front and *Successeur Eventuel* to the Supreme Command. I was delighted to meet this most agreeable and competent officer, and we passed the next ten days in his company, revolving military problems and making contacts with Gamelin, who was also inspecting certain points on this part of the front.

Beginning at the angle of the Rhine near Lauterbourg, we traversed the whole section to the Swiss frontier. In England, as in 1914, the carefree people were enjoying their holidays and playing with their children on the sands. But here along the Rhine a different light glared. All the temporary bridges across the river had been removed to one side or the other. The permanent bridges were heavily guarded and mined. Trusty officers were stationed night and day to press at a signal the buttons which would blow them up. The great river, swollen by the melting Alpine snows, streamed along in sullen, turgid flow. The French outposts crouched in their rifle-pits amid the brushwood. Two or three of us could stroll together to the water's edge, but nothing like a target, we were told, must be presented. Three hundred yards away on the farther side, here and there among the bushes, German figures could be seen working rather leisurely with pick and shovel at their defences. All the riverside quarter of Strasbourg had already been cleared of civilians. I stood on its bridge for some time and watched one or two motor-cars pass over it. Prolonged examination of passports and character took place at either end. Here the German post was little more than a hundred yards away from the French. There was no intercourse between them. Yet Europe was at peace. There was no dispute between Germany and France. The Rhine flowed on, swirling and eddying, at six or seven miles an hour. One or two canoes with boys in them sped past on the current. I did not see the Rhine again until more than five years later, in March 1945, when

I crossed it in a small boat with Field-Marshal Montgomery. But that was near Wesel, far to the north.

On my return I sent a few notes of what I had gathered to the Secretary of State for War, and perhaps to some other Ministers with whom I was in touch:

The French Front cannot be surprised. It cannot be broken at any point except by an effort which would be enormously costly in life, and would take so much time that the general situation would be transformed while it was in progress. The same is true, though to a lesser extent, of the German side.

The flanks of this front however rest upon two small neutral States. The attitude of Belgium is thought to be profoundly unsatisfactory. At present there are no military relations of any kind between the French and the Belgians.

At the other end of the line, about which I was able to learn a good deal, the French have done everything in their power to prepare against an invasion through Switzerland. This operation would take the form of a German advance up the Aar, protected on its right by a movement into or towards the Belfort Gap. I personally think it extremely unlikely that any heavy German attempt will be made either against the French Front or against the two small countries on its flanks in the opening phase.

It is not necessary for Germany to mobilise before attacking Poland. They have enough divisions already on a war footing to act upon their eastern front, and would have time to reinforce the Siegfried Line by mobilising simultaneously with the beginning of a heavy attack on Poland. Thus a German mobilisation is a warning signal which may not be forthcoming in advance of war. The French, on the other hand, may have to take extra measures in the period of extreme tension now upon us.

As to date, it is thought Hitler would be wise to wait until the snow falls in the Alps and gives the protection of winter to Mussolini. During the first fortnight of September, or even earlier, these conditions would be established. There would still be time for Hitler to strike heavily at Poland before the mud period of late October or early November would hamper a German offensive there. Thus this first fortnight in September seems to be particularly critical, and the present German arrangements for the Nuremberg demonstration—propaganda, etc.— seem to harmonise with such a conclusion.

*   *   *

What was remarkable about all I learned on my visit was the complete acceptance of the defensive which dominated my most responsible French hosts, and imposed itself irresistibly upon me. In talking to all these highly competent French officers one had the sense that the Germans were the stronger, and that France had no longer the life-thrust to mount a great offensive. She would fight for her existence—*Voilà tout!* There was the fortified Siegfried Line, with all the increased fire-power of modern weapons. In my own bones, too, was the horror of the Somme and Passchendaele offensives. The Germans were of course far stronger than in the days of Munich. We did not know the deep anxieties which rent their High Command. We had allowed ourselves to get into such a condition, physically and psychologically, that no responsible person—and up to this point I had no responsibilities—could act on the assumption—which was true—that only forty-two half-equipped and half-trained German divisions guarded their long front from the North Sea to Switzerland. This compared with thirteen at the time of Munich.

* * *

In these final weeks my fear was that His Majesty's Government, in spite of our guarantee, would recoil from waging war upon Germany if she attacked Poland. There is no doubt that at this time Mr. Chamberlain had resolved to take the plunge, bitter though it was to him. But I did not know him so well as I did a year later. I feared that Hitler might try a bluff about some novel agency or secret weapon which would baffle or puzzle the overburdened Cabinet. From time to time Professor Lindemann had talked to me about Atomic Energy. I therefore asked him to let me know how things stood in this sphere, and after a conversation I wrote the following letter to Kingsley Wood, with whom my fairly intimate relations have been mentioned:

Mr. Churchill to Secretary of State for Air　　　　　　*August 5,* 1939

Some weeks ago one of the Sunday papers splashed the story of the immense amount of energy which might be released from uranium by the recently discovered chain of processes which take place when this particular type of atom is split by neutrons. At first sight this might seem to portend the appearance of new explosives of devastating power. *In view of this it is essential to realise that there is no danger that this discovery, however great its scientific interest, and perhaps ultimately its practical importance, will lead to results capable of being put into operation on a large scale for several years.*

There are indications that tales will be deliberately circulated when international tension becomes acute about the adaptation of this process to produce some terrible new secret explosive, capable of wiping out London. Attempts will no doubt be made by the Fifth Column to induce us by means of this threat to accept another surrender. For this reason it is imperative to state the true position.

First, the best authorities hold that only a minor constituent of uranium is effective in these processes, and that it will be necessary to extract this before large-scale results are possible. This will be a matter of many years. Secondly, the chain process can take place only if the uranium is concentrated in a large mass. As soon as the energy develops it will explode with a mild detonation before any really violent effects can be produced.★ It might be as good as our present-day explosives, but it is unlikely to produce anything very much more dangerous. Thirdly, these experiments cannot be carried out on a small scale. If they had been successfully done on a big scale (*i.e.,* with the results with which we shall be threatened unless we submit to blackmail) it would be impossible to keep them secret. Fourthly, only a comparatively small amount of uranium in the territories of what used to be Czechoslovakia is under the control of Berlin.

For all these reasons the fear that this new discovery has provided the Nazis with some sinister, new, secret explosive with which to destroy their enemies is clearly without foundation. Dark hints will no doubt be dropped and terrifying whispers will be assiduously circulated, but it is hoped that nobody will be taken in by them.

It is remarkable how accurate this forecast was. Nor was it the Germans who found the path. Indeed they followed the wrong trail, and had actually abandoned the search for the Atomic Bomb in favour of rockets or pilotless aeroplanes at the moment when President Roosevelt and I were taking the decisions and reaching the memorable agreements, which will be described in their proper place, for the large-scale manufacture of atomic bombs.

I also wrote in my final paper for the Air Defence Research Committee:

August 10, 1939
The main defence of England against air raids is the toll which can be extracted from the raiders. One-fifth knocked out each go will soon bring the raids to an end. . . . We must imagine the opening attack as a large affair crossing the sea in relays for many hours. But it is not the first results of the air attack which will govern the future of the air war. It is not child's-play to come and attack England. A

★ This difficulty was of course overcome later by only very elaborate methods after several years of research.

heavy proportion of casualties will lead the enemy to make severe calculations of profit and loss. As daylight raiding will soon become too expensive, we have chiefly to deal with random night-bombing of the built-up areas.

* * *

"Tell Chamberlain," said Mussolini to the British Ambassador on July 7, "that if England is ready to fight in defence of Poland, Italy will take up arms with her ally, Germany." But behind the scenes his attitude was the opposite. He sought at this time no more than to consolidate his interests in the Mediterranean and North Africa, to cull the fruits of his intervention in Spain, and to digest his Albanian conquest. He did not like being dragged into a European war for Germany to conquer Poland. For all his public boastings, he knew the military and political fragility of Italy better than anyone. He was willing to talk about a war in 1942, if Germany would give him the munitions; but in 1939—no!

As the pressure upon Poland sharpened during the summer, Mussolini turned his thoughts upon repeating his Munich *rôle* of mediator, and he suggested a World Peace Conference. Hitler curtly dispelled such ideas. On August 11 Ciano met Ribbentrop at Salzburg. According to Ciano's diary:

> The Duce is anxious for me to prove by documentary evidence that an outbreak of war at this time would be folly. . . . It would be impossible to localise it in Poland, and a general war would be disastrous for everyone. Never has the Duce spoken of the need for peace so unreservedly and with so much warmth. . . . Ribbentrop is evasive. Whenever I ask him for particulars about German policy his conscience troubles him. He has lied too many times about German intentions towards Poland not to feel uneasy now about what he must tell me, and what they are really planning to do. . . . The German decision to fight is implacable. Even if they were given more than they ask they would attack just the same, because they are possessed by the demon of destruction. . . . At times our conversation becomes very tense. I do not hesitate to express my thoughts with brutal frankness. But this does not move him. I am becoming aware how little we are worth in the opinion of the Germans.*

Ciano went on to see Hitler the next day. We have the German minutes of this meeting. Hitler made it clear that he intended to

---

* *Ciano's Diary*, p. 123.

settle with Poland, that he would be forced to fight England and France as well, and that he wanted Italy to come in. He said, "If England keeps the necessary troops in her own country, she can send to France at the most two infantry divisions and one armoured division. For the rest she could supply a few bomber squadrons, but hardly any fighters, because the German Air Force would at once attack England, and the English fighters would be urgently needed for its defence." About France he said that after the destruction of Poland—which would not take long—Germany would be able to assemble hundreds of divisions along the West Wall, and France would thus be compelled to concentrate all her available forces from the colonies and from the Italian frontier and elsewhere on her Maginot Line for the life-and-death struggle. Ciano in reply expressed his surprise at the gravity of what he had been told. There had, he complained, never been any previous sign from the German side that the Polish quarrel was so serious and imminent. On the contrary, Ribbentrop had said that the Danzig question would be settled in the course of time. The Duce, convinced that a conflict with the Western Powers was unavoidable, had assumed that he should make plans for this event during a period of two or three years.

After these interchanges Ciano returned gloomily to report to his master, whom he found more deeply convinced that the Democracies would fight, and even more resolved to keep out of the struggle himself.

* * *

A renewed effort to come to an arrangement with Soviet Russia was made by the British and French Governments. It was decided to send a special envoy to Moscow. Mr. Eden, who had made useful contacts with Stalin some years before, volunteered to go. This generous offer was declined by the Prime Minister. Instead on June 12 Mr. Strang, an able official but without any special standing outside the Foreign Office, was entrusted with this momentous mission. This was another mistake. The sending of so subordinate a figure gave actual offence. It is doubtful whether he was able to pierce the outer crust of the Soviet organism. In any case all was now too late. Much had happened since M. Maisky had been sent to see me at Chartwell in August 1938. Munich had happened. Hitler's armies had had

a year more to mature. His munitions factories, reinforced by the
Skoda works, were all in full blast. The Soviet Government cared
much for Czechoslovakia; but Czechoslovakia was gone. Beneš
was in exile. A German Gauleiter ruled in Prague.

On the other hand, Poland presented to Russia an entirely
different set of age-long political and strategic problems. Their
last major contact had been the Battle of Warsaw in 1920,
when the Bolshevik armies under Kamieniev had been hurled
back from their invasion by Pilsudski, aided by the advice of
General Weygand and the British Mission under Lord
D'Abernon, and thereafter pursued with bloody vengeance. All
these years Poland had been a spear-point of anti-Bolshevism.
With her left hand she joined and sustained the anti-Soviet Baltic
States. But with her right hand, at Munich-time, she had helped
to despoil Czechoslovakia. The Soviet Government were sure
that Poland hated them, and also that Poland had no power to
withstand a German onslaught. They were however very conscious of their own perils and of their need for time to repair the
havoc in the High Commands of their armies. In these circumstances the prospects of Mr. Strang's mission were not exuberant.

The negotiations wandered around the question of the reluctance of Poland and the Baltic States to be rescued from Germany
by the Soviets; and here they made no progress. In its leading
article of June 13 *Pravda* had already declared that an effective
neutrality of Finland, Esthonia, and Latvia was vital to the safety
of the U.S.S.R. The security of such States, it said, was of
prime importance for Britain and France, as "even such a politician as Mr. Churchill" had recognised. The issue was discussed in
Moscow on June 15. On the following day the Russian Press
declared that "in the circles of the Soviet Foreign Ministry results
of the first talks are regarded as not entirely favourable". All
through July the discussions continued fitfully, and eventually
the Soviet Government proposed that conversations should be
continued on a military basis with both French and British representatives. The British Government therefore dispatched Admiral
Drax with a mission to Moscow on August 10. These officers
possessed no written authority to negotiate. The French Mission
was headed by General Doumenc. On the Russian side Marshal
Voroshilov officiated. We now know that at this same time the
Soviet Government agreed to the journey of a German negotiator

to Moscow. The military conference soon foundered upon the refusal of Poland and Roumania to allow the transit of Russian troops. The Polish atttitude was, "With the Germans we risk losing our liberty; with the Russians our soul".*

* * *

At the Kremlin in August 1942 Stalin, in the early hours of the morning, gave me one aspect of the Soviet position. "We formed the impression," said Stalin, "that the British and French Governments were not resolved to go to war if Poland were attacked, but that they hoped the diplomatic line-up of Britain, France, and Russia would deter Hitler. We were sure it would not." "How many divisions," Stalin had asked, "will France send against Germany on mobilisation?" The answer was, "About a hundred." He then asked, "How many will England send?" The answer was, "Two, and two more later." "Ah, two, and two more later," Stalin had repeated. "Do you know," he asked, "how many divisions we shall have to put on the Russian front if we go to war with Germany?" There was a pause. "More than three hundred." I was not told with whom this conversation took place or its date. It must be recognised that this was solid ground, but not favourable for Mr. Strang of the Foreign Office.

It was judged necessary by Stalin and Molotov for bargaining purposes to conceal their true intentions till the last possible moment. Remarkable skill in duplicity was shown by Molotov and his subordinates in all their contacts with both sides. As late as August 4 the German Ambassador Schulenburg could only telegraph from Moscow: "From Molotov's whole attitude it was evident that the Soviet Government was in fact more prepared for improvement in German-Soviet relations, but that the old mistrust of Germany persists. My overall impression is that the Soviet Government is at present determined to sign with England and France if they fulfil all Soviet wishes. Negotiations, to be sure, might still last a long time, especially since the mistrust of England is also great. . . . It will take a considerable effort on our part to cause the Soviet Government to swing about."† He need not have worried. The die was cast.

* * *

* Quoted in Reynaud, *op. cit.*, I, p. 587.
† *Nazi-Soviet Relations*, p. 41.

On the evening of August 19 Stalin announced to the Politburo his intention to sign a pact with Germany. On August 22 Marshal Voroshilov was not to be found by the Allied missions until evening. He then said to the head of the French Mission, "The question of military collaboration with France has been in the air for several years, but has never been settled. Last year, when Czechoslovakia was perishing, we waited for a signal from France, but none was given. Our troops were ready. . . . The French and English Governments have now dragged out the political and military discussions too long. For that reason the possibility is not to be excluded that certain political events may take place. . . ." The next day Ribbentrop arrived in Moscow.[*]

*　　*　　*

We now possess in the Nuremberg documents, and in those captured and recently published by the United States, the details of this never-to-be-forgotten transaction. According to Ribbentrop's chief assistant, Gauss, who flew with him to Moscow, "On the evening of August 23 the first conversation between Ribbentrop and Stalin took place. . . . The Reich Foreign Minister returned very satisfied from this long conference. . . ." Later in the day an agreement on the text of the Soviet-German Non-Aggression Pact was reached quickly and without difficulties. "Ribbentrop himself," says Gauss, "had inserted in the preamble a rather far-reaching phrase concerning the formation of friendly German-Soviet relations. To this Stalin objected, remarking that the Soviet Government could not suddenly present to their public a German-Soviet declaration of friendship after they had been covered with *pails of manure* by the Nazi Government for six years. Thereupon this phrase in the preamble was deleted." In a secret agreement Germany declared herself politically disinterested in Latvia, Esthonia, and Finland, but considered Lithuania to be in her sphere of influence. A demarcation line was drawn for the Polish partition. In the Baltic countries Germany claimed only economic interests. The Non-Aggression Pact and the secret agreement were signed rather late on the night of August 23.[†]

*　　*　　*

[*] Reynaud, *op. cit.*, I, p. 588.
[†] *Nuremberg Documents*, Pt. X, pp. 210 ff.

Despite all that has been dispassionately recorded in this and the foregoing chapter, only totalitarian despotism in both countries could have faced the odium of such an unnatural act. It is a question whether Hitler or Stalin loathed it most. Both were aware that it could only be a temporary expedient The antagonisms between the two empires and systems were mortal. Stalin no doubt felt that Hitler would be a less deadly foe to Russia after a year of war with the Western Powers. Hitler followed his method of "One at a time". The fact that such an agreement could be made marks the culminating failure of British and French foreign policy and diplomacy over several years.

On the Soviet side it must be said that their vital need was to hold the deployment positions of the German armies as far to the west as possible, so as to give the Russians more time for assembling their forces from all parts of their immense empire. They had burnt in their minds the disasters which had come upon their armies in 1914, when they had hurled themselves forward to attack the Germans while still themselves only partly mobilised. But now their frontiers lay far to the east of those of the previous war. They must be in occupation of the Baltic States and a large part of Poland by force or fraud before they were attacked. If their policy was cold-blooded, it was also at the moment realistic in a high degree.

The sinister news broke upon the world like an explosion. On August 21-22 the Soviet Tass Agency stated that Ribbentrop was flying to Moscow to sign a Non-Aggression Pact with the Soviet Union. Whatever emotions the British Government may have experienced, fear was not among them. They lost no time in declaring that "such an event would in no way affect their obligations, which they were determined to fulfil". Nothing could now avert or delay the conflict.

*   *   *

It is still worth while to record the terms of the Pact.

Both High Contracting Parties obligate themselves to desist from any act of violence, any aggressive action, and any attack on each other, either individually or jointly with other Powers.

This treaty was to last ten years, and if not denounced by either side one year before the expiration of that period would be automatically extended for another five years. There was much jubilation and many toasts around the conference table. Stalin spontaneously proposed the toast of the Fuehrer, as follows: "I know how much the German nation loves its Fuehrer; I should therefore like to drink his health." A moral may be drawn from all this, which is of homely simplicity. "Honesty is the best policy." Several examples of this will be shown in these pages. Crafty men and statesmen will be shown misled by all their elaborate calculations. But this is the signal instance. Only twenty-two months were to pass before Stalin and the Russian nation in its scores of millions were to pay a frightful forfeit. If a Government has no moral scruples it often seems to gain great advantages and liberties of action, but "All comes out even at the end of the day, and all will come out yet more even when all the days are ended."

* * *

Hitler was sure from secret interchanges that the Russian Pact would be signed on August 22. Even before Ribbentrop returned from Moscow or the public announcement was made he addressed his Commanders-in-Chief as follows:

We must be determined from the beginning to fight the Western Powers. . . . The conflict with Poland was bound to come sooner or later. I had already made this decision in the spring, but I thought I would first turn against the West and only afterwards against the East. . . . We need not be afraid of a blockade. The East will supply us with grain, cattle, coal. . . . I am only afraid that at the last minute some *Schweinhund* will make a proposal for mediation. . . . The political aim is set further. A beginning has been made for the destruction of England's hegemony. The same is open for the soldier, after I have made the political preparations.

* * *

On the news of the German-Soviet Pact the British Government at once took precautionary measures. Orders were issued for key parties of the coast and anti-aircraft defences to assemble, and for the protection of vulnerable points. Telegrams were sent to Dominion Governments and to the Colonies warning them that it might be necessary in the very near future to institute the precautionary stage. The Lord Privy Seal was authorised to bring the Regional Organisations to a war footing. On August 23 the Admiralty received Cabinet authority to requisition twenty-five merchantmen for conversion to armed merchant cruisers, and thirty-five trawlers to be fitted with Asdics. Six thousand reservists for the overseas garrisons were called up. The anti-aircraft defence of the Radar stations and the full deployment of the anti-aircraft forces were approved. Twenty-four thousand reservists of the Air Force and all the Air Auxiliary Force, including the balloon squadrons, were called up. All leave was stopped throughout the fighting services. The Admiralty issued warnings to merchant shipping. Many other steps were taken.

*　　*　　*

The Prime Minister decided to write to Hitler about these preparatory measures. This letter does not appear in Mr. Feiling's biography, but has been printed elsewhere. In justice to Mr. Chamberlain it should certainly be widely read.

Your Excellency will have already heard of certain measures taken by His Majesty's Government and announced in the Press and on the wireless this evening.

These steps have, in the opinion of His Majesty's Government, been rendered necessary by the military movements which have been reported from Germany, and by the fact that apparently the announcement of a German-Soviet Agreement is taken in some quarters in Berlin to indicate that intervention by Great Britain on behalf of Poland is no longer a contingency that need be reckoned with. No greater mistake could be made. Whatever may prove to be the nature of the German-Soviet Agreement, it cannot alter Great Britain's obligation to Poland, which His Majesty's Government have stated in public repeatedly and plainly, and which they are determined to fulfil.

It has been alleged that if His Majesty's Government had made their position more clear in 1914 the great catastrophe would have been avoided. Whether or not there is any force in that allegation, His Majesty's Government are resolved that on this occasion there shall be no such tragic misunderstanding. If the need should arise, they are resolved and prepared to employ without delay all the forces at their command, and it is impossible to foresee the end of hostilities once engaged. It would be a dangerous delusion to think that, if war once starts, it will come to an early end, even if a success on any one of the several fronts on which it will be engaged should have been secured.

At this time I confess I can see no other way to avoid a catastrophe that will involve Europe in war. In view of the grave consequences to humanity which may follow from the action of their rulers, I trust that Your Excellency will weigh with the utmost deliberation the considerations which I have put before you.*

Hitler's reply, after dwelling on the "unparalleled magnanimity" with which Germany was prepared to settle the question of Danzig and the Corridor, contained the following piece of lying effrontery:

The unconditional assurance given by England to Poland that she would render assistance to that country in all circumstances, regardless of the causes from which a conflict might spring, could only be interpreted in that country as an encouragement henceforward to unloose, under cover of such a charter, a wave of appalling terrorism against the million and a half German inhabitants living in Poland.†

On August 25 the British Government proclaimed a formal treaty with Poland, confirming the guarantees already given. It was hoped by this step to give the best chance of a settlement by direct negotiation between Germany and Poland in the face of the fact that if this failed Britain would stand by Poland. Said Goering at Nuremberg:

On the day when England gave her official guarantee to Poland the Fuehrer called me on the telephone and told me that he had stopped the planned invasion of Poland. I asked him then whether this was just temporary or for good. He said, "No, I shall have to see whether we can eliminate British intervention."‡

In fact Hitler postponed D-Day from August 25 to September 1, and entered into direct negotiation with Poland, as Chamberlain desired. His object was not however to reach an agreement with Poland, but to give His Majesty's Government every opportunity to escape from their guarantee. Their thoughts, like those of Parliament and the nation, were upon a different plane. It is a curious fact about the British Islanders, who hate drill and have not been invaded for nearly a thousand years, that as danger comes nearer and grows they become progressively less nervous; when it is imminent they are fierce; when it is mortal they are fearless. These habits have led them into some very narrow escapes.

* * *

* *Nuremberg Documents*, Pt. II, pp. 157-8.
† *Ibid.*, p. 158.
‡ *Ibid.*, p. 166.

A letter from Hitler to Mussolini at this time has recently been published in Italy:

Duce,

For some time Germany and Russia have been meditating upon the possibility of placing their mutual political relations upon a new basis. The need to arrive at concrete results in this sense has been strengthened by:

1. The condition of the world political situation in general.

2. The continued procrastination of the Japanese Cabinet in taking up a clear stand. Japan was ready for an alliance against Russia in which Germany—and in my view Italy—could only be interested in the present circumstances as a secondary consideration. She was not agreeable however to assuming any clear obligations regarding England—a decisive question from the German side, and I think also from Italy's. . . .

3. The relations between Germany and Poland have been unsatisfactory since the spring, and in recent weeks have become simply intolerable, not through the fault of the Reich, but principally because of British action. . . . These reasons have induced me to hasten on a conclusion of the Russian-German talks. I have not yet informed you, Duce, in detail on this question. But now in recent weeks the disposition of the Kremlin to engage in an exchange of relations with Germany—a disposition produced from the moment of the dismissal of Litvinov—has been increasingly marked, and has now made it possible for me, after having reached a preliminary clarification, to send my Foreign Minister to Moscow to draw up a treaty which is far and away the most extensive non-aggression pact in existence to-day, and the text of which will be made public. The pact is unconditional, and establishes in addition the commitment to consult on all questions which interest Germany and Russia. I can also inform you, Duce, that, given these undertakings, the benevolent attitude of Russia is assured, and *that above all there now exists no longer the possibility of any attack whatsoever on the part of Roumania in the event of a conflict.**

To this Mussolini sent an immediate answer:

I am replying to your letter, which has just been delivered to me by Ambassador Mackensen.

1. As far as the agreement with Russia is concerned, I completely approve.

2. I feel it would be useful to avoid a rupture or coolness with Japan and her consequent drawing together with the group of democratic States. . . .

* *Hitler e Mussolini, Lettere e Documenti,* p. 7.

3. The Moscow Pact blocks Roumania, and may change the position of Turkey, who has accepted an English loan but who has not yet signed the alliance. A new attitude on the part of Turkey would upset the strategic disposition of the French and English in the Eastern Mediterranean.

4. About Poland, I understand completely the German position and the fact that such a tense situation cannot continue indefinitely.

5. Regarding the practical attitude of Italy in the event of military action my point of view is the following:

If Germany attacks Poland and the conflict is localised Italy will give Germany every form of political and economic aid which may be required.

If Germany attacks Poland and the allies of the latter counter-attack Germany I must emphasise to you that I cannot assume the initiative of warlike operations, given the actual conditions of Italian military preparations, which have been repeatedly and in timely fashion pointed out to you, Fuehrer, and to von Ribbentrop.

Our intervention could however be immediate if Germany were to give us at once the munitions and raw materials to sustain the shock which the French and British would probably inflict upon us. In our previous meetings war was envisaged after 1942, and on this date I should have been ready on land, by sea, and in the air, according to our agreed plans.*

From this point Hitler knew, if he had not divined it already, that he could not count upon the armed intervention of Italy if war came. Any last-minute attempts by Mussolini to repeat his performance of Munich were brushed aside. It seems to have been from English rather than from German sources that the Duce learnt of the final moves. Ciano records in his diary on August 27, "The English communicate to us the text of the German proposals to London, about which we are kept entirely in the dark".† Mussolini's only need now was Hitler's acquiescence in Italy's neutrality. This was accorded to him.

* * *

On August 31 Hitler issued his "Directive Number 1 for the Conduct of the War".

1. Now that all the political possibilities of disposing by peaceful means of a situation on the Eastern frontier which is intolerable for Germany are exhausted, I have determined on a solution by force.

* *Hitler e Mussolini, Lettere e Documenti*, p. 10.
† *Ciano's Diary*, p. 136.

2. The attack on Poland is to be carried out in accordance with the preparation made for "Fall Weiss" [Case White], with the alterations which result, where the Army is concerned, from the fact that it has in the meantime almost completed its dispositions. Allotment of tasks and the operational targets remain unchanged.

The date of attack—September 1, 1939. Time of attack—04.45 [inserted in red pencil].

3. In the West it is important that the responsibility for the opening of hostilities should rest unequivocally with England and France. At first purely local action should be taken against insignificant frontier violations.*

* * *

On my return from the Rhine front I passed some sunshine days at Madame Balsan's place, with a pleasant but deeply anxious company, in the old château where King Henry of Navarre had slept the night before the Battle of Ivry. Mrs. Euan Wallace and her sons were with us. Her husband was a Cabinet Minister. She was expecting him to join her. Presently he telegraphed he could not come, and would explain later why. Other signs of danger drifted in upon us. One could feel the deep apprehension brooding over all, and even the light of this lovely valley of the Eure seemed robbed of its genial ray. I found painting hard work in this uncertainty. On August 26 I decided to go home, where at least I could find out what was going on. I told my wife I would send her word in good time. On my way through Paris I gave General Georges luncheon. He produced all the figures of the French and German Armies, and classified the divisions in quality. The result impressed me so much that for the first time I said, "But you are the masters." He replied, "The Germans have a very strong Army, and we shall never be allowed to strike first. If they attack, both our countries will rally to their duty."

That night I slept at Chartwell, where I had asked General Ironside to stay with me next day. He had just returned from Poland, and the reports he gave of the Polish Army were most favourable. He had seen a divisional attack exercise under a live barrage, not without casualties. Polish morale was high. He stayed three days with me, and we tried hard to measure the unknowable. Also at this time I completed bricklaying the kitchen

* *Nuremberg Documents*, Pt. II, p. 172.

of the cottage which during the year past I had prepared for our family home in the years which were to come. My wife, on my signal, came over *via* Dunkirk on August 30.

★   ★   ★

There were known to be twenty thousand organised German Nazis in England at this time, and it would only have been in accord with their procedure in other friendly countries that the outbreak of war should be preceded by a sharp prelude of sabotage and murder. I had at that time no official protection, and I did not wish to ask for any; but I thought myself sufficiently prominent to take precautions. I had enough information to convince me that Hitler recognised me as a foe. My former Scotland Yard detective, Inspector Thompson, was in retirement. I told him to come along and bring his pistol with him. I got out my own weapons, which were good. While one slept the other watched. Thus nobody would have had a walk-over. In these hours I knew that if war came—and who could doubt its coming?—a major burden would fall upon me.

APPENDICES

APPENDIX A

A CONVERSATION WITH COUNT GRANDI*

Mr. Churchill to Sir Robert Vansittart　　　　*September* 28, 1935

Though he pleaded the Italian cause with much address, he of course realises the whole position. . . .

I told him that since Parliament rose there had been a strong development of public opinion. England, and indeed the British Empire, could act unitedly on the basis of the League of Nations, and all parties thought that that instrument was the most powerful protection against future dangers wherever they might arise. He pointed out the injury to the League of Nations by the loss of Italy. The fall of the *régime* in Italy would inevitably produce a pro-German Italy. He seemed prepared for economic sanctions. They were quite ready to accept life upon a communal basis. However poor they were, they could endure. He spoke of the difficulty of following the movements of British public opinion. I said that no foreign ambassador could be blamed for that, but the fact of the change must be realised. Moreover, if fighting began in Abyssinia, cannons fired, blood was shed, villages were bombed, etc., an almost measureless rise in the temperature must be expected. He seemed to contemplate the imposition of economic sanctions which would at first be ineffective, but gradually increase until at some moment or other an event of war would occur.

I said the British Fleet was very strong, and, although it had to be rebuilt in the near future, it was good and efficient at the present moment, and it was now completely ready to defend itself; but I repeated that this was a purely defensive measure in view of our Mediterranean interests, and did not in any way differentiate our position from that of other members of the League of Nations. He accepted this with a sad smile.

I then talked of the importance of finding a way out: "He that ruleth his spirit is better than he that taketh a city." He replied that they would feel that everywhere except in Italy. They had to deal with two hundred thousand men with rifles in their hands. Mussolini's dictatorship was a popular dictatorship, and success was the essence of its strength. Finally, I said that I was in favour of a meeting between the political chiefs of the three countries. . . . The three men together could carry off something that one could never do by himself. After all, the claims of Italy to primacy in the Abyssinian sphere and the imperative need of internal reform [in Abyssinia] had been fully recognised by England and France. I told him I should support such an idea if it were agreeable. The British public would be willing to

* See p. 156.

try all roads to an honourable peace. I thought there should be a meeting of three. Any agreement they reached would of course be submitted to the League of Nations. It seemed to me the only chance of avoiding the destruction of Italy as a powerful and friendly factor in Europe. Even if it failed no harm would have been done, and at present we were heading for an absolute smash.

APPENDIX B

MY NOTE ON THE FLEET AIR ARM*

WRITTEN FOR SIR THOMAS INSKIP, MINISTER FOR THE CO-ORDINATION OF DEFENCE, IN 1936

1. It is impossible to resist an admiral's claim that he must have complete control of, and confidence in, the aircraft of the battle fleet, whether used for reconnaissance, gun-fire, or air attack on a hostile fleet. These are his very eyes. Therefore the Admiralty view must prevail in all that is required to secure this result.

2. The argument that similar conditions obtain in respect of Army co-operation aircraft cannot be countenanced. In one case the aircraft take flight from aerodromes and operate under precisely similar conditions to those of normal independent Air Force action. Flight from warships and action in connection with naval operations is a totally different matter. One is truly an affair of co-operation only, the other an integral part of modern naval operations.

3. A division must therefore be made between the Air Force controlled by the Admiralty and that controlled by the Air Ministry. This division does not depend upon the type of the undercarriage of the aircraft, nor necessarily the base from which it is flown. It depends upon the function. Is it predominantly a naval function or not?

4. Most of these defence functions can clearly be assigned. For instance, all functions which require aircraft of any description (whether with wheels, floats, or boats; whether reconnaissance, spotters or fighters, bombers or torpedo-seaplanes) to be carried regularly in warships or in aircraft-carriers naturally fall to the naval sphere.

5. The question thus reduces itself to the assignment of any type operating over the sea from shore bases. This again can only be decided in relation to the functions and responsibilities placed upon the Navy. Aircraft borne afloat could discharge a considerable function of trade protection. This would be especially true in the broad waters, where a

* See p. 143.

squadron of cruisers with their own scouting planes or a pair of small aircraft-carriers could search upon a front of a thousand miles. But the Navy could never be required—nor has it ever claimed—to maintain an air strength sufficient to cope with a concentrated attack upon merchant shipping in the Narrow Waters by a large hostile Air Force of great power. In fact, the maxim must be applied of Air Force *versus* Air Force and Navy *versus* Navy. When the main hostile Air Force or any definite detachment from it is to be encountered, it must be by the British Royal Air Force.

6. In this connection it should not be forgotten that a ship or ships may have to be selected and adapted for purely Air Force operations, like a raid on some deep-seated enemy base or vital centre. This is an Air Force operation, and necessitates the use of types of aircraft not normally associated with the Fleet. In this case the *rôles* of the Admiralty and the Air Ministry will be reversed, and the Navy would swim the ship in accordance with the tactical or strategic wishes of the Air Ministry. Far from becoming a baffle, this special case exemplifies the logic of the "division of command according to function".

7. What is conceded to the Navy should, within the limits assigned, be fully given. The Admiralty should have plenary control and provide the entire personnel of the Fleet Air Arm. Officers, cadets, petty officers, artificers, etc., for this force would be selected from the Royal Navy by the Admiralty. They would then acquire the art of flying and the management of aircraft in the R.A.F. training schools— to which perhaps naval officers should be attached—but after acquiring the necessary degree of proficiency as air chauffeurs and mechanics they would pass to shore establishments under the Admiralty for their training in Fleet Air Arm duties, just as the pilots of the Royal Air Force do to their squadrons at armament schools to learn air fighting. Thus, the personnel employed upon fleet air functions will be an integral part of the Navy, dependent for discipline and advancement as well as for their careers and pensions solely upon the Admiralty. This would apply to every rank and every trade involved, whether afloat or ashore.

8. Coincident with this arrangement whereby the Fleet Air Arm becomes wholly a naval Service, a further rearrangement of functions should be made, whereby the Air Ministry becomes responsible for active anti-aircraft defence. This implies, in so far as the Navy is concerned, that, at every naval port, shore anti-aircraft batteries, lights, aircraft, balloons, and other devices will be combined under one operational control, though the officer commanding would of course, with his command, be subordinate to the Fortress Commander.

9. In the same way, the control of the air defences of London and

of such other vulnerable areas as it may be necessary to equip with anti-air defences on a considerable scale should also be unified under one command and placed under the Air Ministry. The consequent control should cover not only the operations, but, as far as may conveniently be arranged, the training, the raising and administration of the entire personnel for active air defence.

10. The Air Ministry have as clear a title to control active antiair defence as have the Navy to their own "eyes". For this purpose a new department should be brought into being in the Air Ministry, to be called "Anti-Air", to control all guns, searchlights, balloons, and personnel of every kind connected with this function, as well as such portion of the Royal Air Force as may from time to time be assigned to it for this duty. Under this department there will be Air Force officers, assisted by appropriate staffs, in command of all active air defences in specified localities and areas.

11. It is not suggested that the Air Ministry or Air Staff are at present capable of assuming unaided this heavy new responsibility. In the formation of the Anti-Air Command recourse must be had to both the older Services. Well-trained staff officers, both from the Army and the Navy, must be mingled with officers of the existing Air Staff.

N.B.—The question of the recruitment and of the interior administration of the units handed over to the Anti-Air Command for operations and training need not be a stumbling-block. They could be provided from the present sources unless and until a more convenient solution was apparent.

12. This memorandum has not hitherto dealt with *matériel*, but that is extremely simple. The Admiralty will decide upon the types of aircraft which their approved functions demand. The extent of the inroad which they require to make upon the finances and resources of the country must be decided by the Cabinet, operating through a Priorities Committee under the Minister for the Co-ordination of Defence. At the present stage this Minister would no doubt give his directions to the existing personnel, but in the event of war or the intensification of the preparations for war he would give them to a Ministry of Supply. There could of course be no question of Admiralty priorities being allowed to override other claims in the general sphere of air production. All must be decided from the supreme standpoint.

13. It is not intended that the Admiralty should develop technical departments for aircraft design separate from those existing in the Air Ministry or under a Ministry of Supply. They would however be free to form a nucleus technical staff to advise them on the possibilities

of scientific development and to prescribe their special naval require-ments in suitable technical language to the supply department.

14. To sum up therefore we have:

First—The Admiralty should have plenary control of the Fleet Air Arm for all purposes which are defined as naval.

Secondly—A new department must be formed under the Air Ministry from the three Services for active anti-aircraft defence operations.

Thirdly—The question of *matériel* supply must be decided by a Priorities Committee under the Minister for the Co-ordination of Defence, and executed at present through existing channels, but eventually by a Ministry of Supply.

APPENDIX C

A NOTE ON SUPPLY ORGANISATION, JUNE 6, 1936*

1. The existing office of the Minister for the Co-ordination of Defence comprises unrelated and wrongly-grouped functions. The work of the Minister charged with strategic co-ordination is different, though not in the higher ranges disconnected, from the work of the Minister charged with (a) securing the execution of the existing programmes, and (b) planning British industry to spring quickly into war-time conditions and creating a high control effective for both this and the present purpose.

2. The first step therefore is to separate the functions of strategic thought from those of material supply in peace and war, and form the organisation to direct this latter process. An harmonious arrangement would be four separate departments—Navy, Army, Air Force, and Supply—with the Co-ordinating Minister at the summit of the four having the final voice upon priorities.

3. No multiplication of committees, however expert or elaborate, can achieve this purpose. Supply cannot be achieved without com-mand. A definite chain of responsible authority must descend through the whole of British industry affected. (This must not be thought to imply State interference in the actual functions of industry.) At the present time the three Service authorities exercise separate command over their particular supply, and the fourth, or planning, authority is purely consultative, and that only upon the war need divorced from present supply. What is needed is to unify the supply command of

* See p. 191.

the three Service departments into an organism which also exercises command over the war expansion. (The Admiralty would retain control over the construction of warships and certain special naval stores.)

4. This unification should comprise not only the function of supply but that of design. The Service departments prescribe in general technical terms their need in type, quality, and quantity, and the supply organisation executes these in a manner best calculated to serve its customers. In other words, the Supply Department engages itself to deliver the approved types of war stores of all kinds to the Services when and where the latter require them.

5. None of this, nor the punctual execution of any of the approved programmes, can be achieved in the present atmosphere of ordinary peace-time preparation. It is neither necessary nor possible at this moment to take war-time powers and apply war-time methods. An intermediate state should be declared called (say) the period of emergency preparation.

6. Legislation should be drafted in two parts—first, that appropriate to the emergency preparation stage, and, second, that appropriate to a state of war. Part I should be carried out now. Part II should be envisaged, elaborated, the principles defined, the clauses drafted and left to be brought into operation by a fresh appeal to Parliament should war occur. The emergency stage should be capable of sliding into the war stage with the minimum of disturbance, the whole design having been foreseen.

7. To bring this new system into operation there should first be created a Minister of Supply. This Minister would form a Supply Council. Each member would be charged with the study of the four or five branches of production falling into his sphere. Thereafter, as soon as may be, the existing Service sub-departments of supply, design, contracts, etc., would be transferred by instalments to the new authority, who alone would deal with the Treasury upon finance. (By "finance" is meant payments within the scope of the authorised programmes.)

MY STATEMENT ON THE OCCASION
OF THE DEPUTATION OF CONSERVATIVE MEMBERS
OF BOTH HOUSES TO THE PRIME MINISTER,
JULY 28, 1936 *

In time of peace the needs of our small Army, and to some extent of the Air Force and Admiralty, in particular weapons and ammunition are supplied by the War Office, which has for this purpose certain Government factories and habitual private contractors. This organisation is capable of meeting ordinary peace-time requirements, and providing the accumulating of reserves sufficient for a few weeks of war by our very limited regular forces. Outside this there was nothing until a few months ago. About three or four months ago authority was given to extend the scope of War Office orders in certain directions to ordinary civil industry.

On the other hand, in all the leading Continental countries the whole of industry has been for some time solidly and scientifically organised to turn over from peace to war. In Germany of course above all others this became the supreme study of the Government even before the Hitler *régime*. Indeed, under the impulse of revenge, Germany, forbidden by treaty to have fleets, armies, and an Air Force, concentrated with intense compression upon the perfecting of the transference of its whole industry to war purposes. We alone began seriously to examine the problem when everyone else had solved it. There was however still time in 1932 and 1933 to make a great advance. Three years ago, when Hitler came into power, we had perhaps a dozen officials studying the war organisation of industry, as compared with five or six hundred working continuously in Germany. The Hitler *régime* set all this vast machinery in motion. They did not venture to break the treaties about Army, Navy, and Air Force until they had a head of steam on in every industry which would, they hoped, speedily render them an armed nation unless they were immediately attacked by the Allies.

What is being done now? Nothing has been told to Parliament except some fragmentary items which by themselves are likely to mislead the ignorant. For instance, we were told last week that fifty-two firms had been inspected and offered contracts to make ammunition; that the old gun factory was to be reopened at Nottingham, and the Woolwich filling-station was to be moved to the West Coast. But no orders were given till three months ago, and none of this preparation

* See p. 204.

can reach a stage of mass deliveries for at least eighteen months from the date of the order. If by ammunition is meant projectiles (both bombs and shells) and cartridge-cases containing propellent, it will be necessary to equip all these factories with a certain amount of additional special-purpose machine-tools, and to modify their existing lay-out. In addition jigs and gauges for the actual manufacture must be made. . . . The manufacture of these special machine-tools, jigs, and gauges will have to be done in most cases by firms quite different from those to whom the output of projectiles is entrusted. After the delivery of the special machine-tools a further delay is required while they are being set up in the producing factories, and while the process of production is being started. Then, and only then, at first in a trickle, then in a stream, and finally in a flood, deliveries will take place. Not till then can the accumulation of war resources begin. This inevitably lengthy process is still being applied on a relatively minute scale. The fifty-two firms have been offered contracts. Fourteen had last week accepted contracts. At the present moment it would be no exaggeration to state that the German ammunition plants may well amount to four or five hundred, already for very nearly two years in full swing.

Turning now to cannon: by cannon I mean guns firing explosive shells. The processes by which a cannon factory is started are necessarily lengthy; the special plants and machine-tools are more numerous, and the lay-out more elaborate. Our normal peace-time output of cannon in the last ten years has, apart from the Fleet, been negligible. We are therefore certainly separated by two years from any large deliveries of field guns or anti-aircraft guns. Last year it is probable that at least five thousand guns were made in Germany, and this process could be largely amplified in war. Surely we ought to call into being plant which would enable us, if need be, to create and arm a national army of a considerable size.

I have taken projectiles and cannon because these are the core of defence; but the same arguments and conditions, with certain modifications, apply over the whole field of equipment. The flexibility of British industry should make it possible to produce many forms of equipment—for instance, motor lorries and other kindred weapons, such as tanks and armoured cars—and many slighter forms of material necessary for an army, in a much shorter time if that industry is at once set going. Has it been set going? Why should we be told that the Territorial Army cannot be equipped until after the Regular Army is equipped? I do not know what is the position about rifles and rifle ammunition. I hope at least we have enough for a million men. But the delivery of rifles from new sources is a very lengthy process.

Even more pertinent is the production of machine-guns. I do not

know at all what is the programme of Browning and Bren machine-
guns. But if the orders for setting up the necessary plant were only
given a few months ago one cannot expect any appreciable deliveries
except by direct purchase from abroad before the beginning of 1938.
The comparable German plants already in operation are capable of
producing supplies limited only by the national manhood available to
use them.

But this same argument can be followed out through all the processes
of producing explosives, propellent, fuzes, poison gas, gas-masks,
searchlights, trench-mortars, grenades, air-bombs, and all the special
adaptations required for depth-charges, mines, etc., for the Navy. It
must not be forgotten that the Navy is dependent upon the War
Office and upon an expansion of national industry for a hundred and
one minor articles, a shortage in any one of which will cause grave
injury. Behind all this again lies of course the supply of raw materials,
with its infinite complications.

What is the conclusion? It is that we are separated by about two
years from any appreciable improvement in the material process of
national defence, so far as concerns the whole volume of supplies for
which the War Office has hitherto been responsible, with all the
reactions that entails, both on the Navy and the War Office. But,
upon the scale on which we are now acting, even at the end of two
years the supply will be petty compared either with our needs in war
or with what others have already acquired in peace.

Surely if these facts are even approximately true—and I believe they
are mostly understatements—how can it be contended that there is no
emergency; that we must not do anything to interfere with the ordinary
trade of the country; that there is no need to approach the trade unions
about dilution of trainees; that we can safely trust to what the Minister
for Co-ordination of Defence described as "training the additional
labour as required on the job"; and that nothing must be done which
would cause alarm to the public, or lead them to feel that their
ordinary habit of life was being deranged?

Complaint is made that the nation is unresponsive to the national
need; that the trade unions are unhelpful; that recruiting for the Army
and the Territorial Force is very slack, and even is obstructed by
elements of public opinion. But as long as they are assured by the
Government that there is no emergency these obstacles will continue.

I was given confidentially by the French Government an estimate
of the German air strength in 1936. This tallies almost exactly with the
figures I forecast to the Committee of Imperial Defence in December
last. The Air Staff now think the French estimate too high. Personally
I think it is too low. The number of machines which Germany could

now put into action simultaneously may be nearer two thousand than fifteen hundred. Moreover, there is no reason to assume that they mean to stop at two thousand. The whole plant and lay-out of the German Air Force is on an enormous scale, and they may be already planning a development far greater than anything yet mentioned. Even if we accept the French figures of about fourteen hundred, the German strength at this moment is double that of our Metropolitan Air Force, judged by trained pilots and military machines that could go into action and be maintained in action. But the relative strength of two countries cannot be judged without reference to their power of replenishing their fighting force. The German industry is so organised that it can certainly produce at full blast a thousand a month and increase the number as the months pass. Can the British industry at the present time produce more than three hundred to three hundred and fifty a month? How long will it be before we can reach a war-potential output equal to the German? Certainly not within two years. When we allow for the extremely high rate of war wastage, a duel between the two countries would mean that before six months were out our force would be not a third of theirs. The preparation for war-time expansion at least three times the present size of the industry seems urgent in the highest degree. It is probable however that Germany is spending not less than one hundred and twenty millions on her Air Force this year. It is clear therefore that so far as this year is concerned we are not catching up. On the contrary, we are falling farther behind. How long will this continue into next year? No one can tell.

It has been announced that the programme of 120 squadrons and 1,500 first-line aircraft for Home Defence would be completed by April 1, 1937. Parliament has not been given any information how this programme is being carried out in machines, in personnel, in organisation, or in the ancillary supplies. We have been told nothing about it at all. I do not blame the Government for not giving full particulars. It would be too dangerous now. Naturally however, in the absence of any information at all, there must be great anxiety and much private discussion. . . . I doubt very much whether by July next year we shall have thirty squadrons equipped with the new types. I understand that the deliveries of the new machines will not really begin to flow in large numbers for a year or fifteen months. Meanwhile we have very old-fashioned and obsolete tackle.

There is a second question about these new machines. When they begin to flow out of the factories in large numbers fifteen months hence, will they be equipped with all necessary appliances? Take, for instance, the machine-guns. If we are aiming at having a couple of thousand of the latest machines, i e., 1,500 and 500 reserve, in eighteen months from now, what arrangements have been made for their machine-guns? Some of these modern fighting machines have no fewer than eight machine-guns in their wings. Taking only an average of four, with proper reserves, that would require 10,000 machine-guns. Is it not a fact that the large-scale manufacture of the Browning and Bren machine-guns was only decided upon a few months ago?

Let us now try the aeroplane fleet we have built and are building by the test of bombing-power as measured by weight and range. Here I must again make comparison with Germany. Germany has the power at any time henceforward to send a fleet of aeroplanes capable of discharging in a single voyage at least 500 tons of bombs upon London. We know from our war statistics that one ton of explosive bombs killed ten people and wounded thirty, and did £50,000 worth of damage. Of course, it would be absurd to assume that the whole bombing fleet of Germany would make an endless succession of voyages to and from this country. All kinds of other considerations intervene. Still, as a practical measure of the relative power of the bombing fleets of the two countries, the weight of discharge per voyage is a very reasonable measure. Now, if we take the German potential discharge upon London at a minimum of 500 tons per voyage of their entire bombing fleet, what is our potential reply? *They* can do this from now on. What can we do? First of all, how could we retaliate upon Berlin? We have not at the present time a single squadron of machines which could carry an appreciable load of bombs to Berlin. What shall we have this time next year? I submit for your consideration that this time next year, when it may well be that the potential discharge of the German fleet is in the neighbourhood of a thousand tons, we shall not be able to discharge in retaliation more than sixty tons upon Berlin.

But leave Berlin out of the question. Nothing is more striking about our new fleet of bombers than their short range. The great bulk of our new heavy and medium bombers cannot do much more than reach the coasts of Germany from this Island. Only the nearest German cities would be within their reach. In fact, the retaliation of which we should be capable this time next year from this Island would be puerile judged by the weight of explosive dropped, and would be limited only to the fringes of Germany.

Of course, a better tale can be told if it is assumed that we can operate from French and Belgian jumping-off grounds. Then very large and vital industrial districts of Germany would be within reach of our machines. Our Air Force will be incomparably more effective if used in conjunction with those of France and Belgium than it would be in a duel with Germany alone.

I now pass to the next stage: our defence, passive and active, ground and air, at home. Evidently we might have to endure an ordeal in our great cities and vital feeding-ports such as no community has ever been subjected to before. What arrangements have been made in this field? Take London and its seven or eight million inhabitants. Nearly two years ago I explained in the House of Commons the danger of an attack by thermite bombs. These small bombs, little bigger than an orange, had even then been manufactured by millions in Germany. A single medium aeroplane can scatter five hundred. One must expect in a small raid literally tens of thousands of these bombs, which burn through from storey to storey. Supposing only a hundred fires were started and there were only ninety fire brigades, what happens? Obviously the attack would be on a far more formidable scale than that. One must expect that a proportion of heavy bombs would be dropped at the same time, and that water, light, gas, telephone systems, etc., would be seriously deranged. What happens then? Nothing like it has ever been seen in world history. There might be a vast exodus of the population, which would present to the Government problems of public order, of sanitation and food-supply, which would dominate their attention, and probably involve the use of all their disciplined forces.

What happens if the attack is directed upon the feeding-ports, particularly the Thames, Southampton, Bristol, and the Mersey, none of which are out of range? What arrangements have been made to bring in the food through a far greater number of subsidiary channels? What arrangements have been made to protect our defence centres? By defence centres I mean the centres upon which our power to continue resistance depends. The problem of the civil population and their miseries is one thing; the means by which we could carry on the war is another. Have we organised and created an alternative centre of government if London is thrown into confusion? No doubt there has been discussion of this on paper, but has anything been done to provide one or two alternative centres of command, with adequate deep-laid telephone connections and wireless, from which the necessary orders can be given by some coherent thinking-mechanism? . . .

COMPARATIVE OUTPUT OF FIRST-LINE AIRCRAFT ★

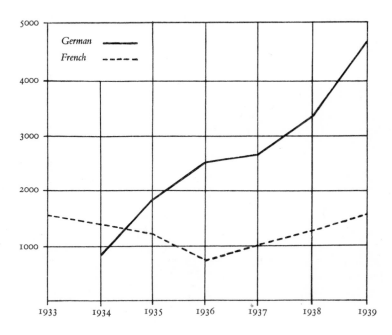

*Note: German figures derived from captured documents:
French figures from a French source.*

★ See p. 213.

INDEX

Aachen, 282, 295

Abdication crisis, 196-7

Abyssinia, Italian designs on, 97, 120, 148-53, 361; appeals to League of Nations, 117-18, 361; invasion of, 156, 361; plan to partition, 164-5; Italian conquest of, 166-8, 169; British recognition of conquest, 218, 226-8, 253-5

Admiralty, precautionary measures taken by, on announcement of German-Soviet Pact, 352-3; requires control of own Air Force, 362-65; and Ministry for Co-ordination of Defence, 365-6

Adowa, Battle of, 141

Aftermath, The, 35-7

Air attacks, to break morale, 137-8; in Spain, 193; main defence against, 345-6

Air Auxiliary Force, 353

Air Defence Research Committee, 135, 208; Churchill's memorandum for, 136-137; work of, 139-42; Churchill's final paper for, 345-6

Air defences, Churchill's adviser on, 72; inadequacy of, 84, 194, 208-10, 293, 372; research into, 133-42; strengthening of, 301; Churchill suggests manning of, 312; orders for assembling of, 352-353; Air Ministry control of, 363-4

Air Force—see under Fleet Air Arm and Royal Air Force; also French, German Air Force, etc.

Air Ministry, in error over strength of German Air Force, 107; and Air Defence Research Committee, 133-4, 141-142; constructs coastal chain Radar stations, 139; requires control of air defences, 363-4; and Ministry of Co-ordination of Defence, 365-6

Albania, Italian invasion of, 313-14; "a stronghold to dominate the Balkans," 338

Albert Hall meeting on rearmament, 195-6

Alexander, King of Yugoslavia, assassination of, 96

Amery, Rt. Hon. L. S., 106 n., 205

Anglo-German Naval Agreement, 124-8; effect of, on Allies, 125-6; Hitler denounces, 322-4

Anglo-Italian Agreement, 253-5

Anglo-Polish Guarantee, 246, 310-11,

323-324, 332, 336-7; practical implications of, 325, 336

Anglo-Roumanian Guarantee, 322, 325, 332, 337

Anglo-Turkish Agreement, 332, 335; ratification of, 333

Anti-aircraft guns, shortage of, 209-10, 293; German, 209-10; increase in number of, 301

Anti-Comintern Pact, 193

Anti-Submarine School, Portland, 147

Appeasement, an encouragement to dictators, 233; Churchill's speech on policy of, 298-9; reversal of policy of, 309-11; results of, 311

Argentina, protests against German violation of Peace Treaty, 120

Armaments, equality of, 58, 66-70; nationalising of, 113

"Arms and the Covenant" policy, 195-7

Army—see under British, French, German Army, etc.

Artillery, "offensive" weapon, 65; destruction of Allied heavy, 67-9

Asdics, 146-7; trawlers equipped with, 353

Asquith, Rt. Hon. H. H. (Earl of Oxford and Asquith), 21

Atomic bombs, 16; danger of propaganda war concerning, 344-5; Allies win race for, 345

Attlee, Rt. Hon. Clement R., denies need for increasing armaments, 103, 111, 160; on Collective Security, 111; leader of Labour Party, 157; supports Sanctions, 159-60; declines to appear on deputation to Prime Minister, 204-5; on Eden's resignation, 238; and need of Russian alliance, 337

Australia, protests against German violation of Peace Treaty, 120

Austria, German subversive activities in, 81-2, 85, 93-4, 185, 234-5; Nazism in, 82-3, 185; Italian interest in, 81-2, 85, 185; Allied Declaration on independence of, 85; signs Rome Protocols, 85; abortive Nazi revolt in, 93; affected by fortified Rhineland, 184-5; Hitler signs pact with, 185; German plans for occupation of, 185, 232; man-power in, 212; active

German intervention in affairs of, 229–230, 234–7; reasons for German absorption of, 234; ultimatums presented to, 236, 240–1; German occupation of, 241–245, 273; troop movements in, 306
Austria-Hungary, break-up of, 9

Bacteriological warfare, 38
Baldwin, Rt. Hon. Stanley (Earl Baldwin of Bewdley), 18, 19; Administrations of, 20, 21, 23–4, 29, 122, 161–2; political eminence of, 19–20; precipitates second election, 21; offers Chancellorship to Churchill, 21; and payment of war debts, 22–3; Churchill's relations with, 23; signs Treaty of Locarno, 28; great party manager, 30, 162–3, 181; Indian policy of, 30–1, 71; his breach with Churchill, 30–1; in National Coalition, 33, 60; disarmament policy of, 76, 83–4, 103; his aversion to foreign problems, 80; and East Fulham by-election, 100; pledges increase in Air Force, 102, 108; denies approaching air parity of Germany, 107, 114; his confession of error, 111, 113; appoints Minister for League of Nations Affairs, 123–4; and Air Defence Committee, 133–5; Sanctions principles of, 157–8; determined against being drawn into war, 157–60, 162–4, 177; election policy of, 159–61; speaks for rearmament and denies its need, 161; excludes Churchill from office, 162, 179–180; and Hoare-Laval Pact, 165–6; against conscription, 167; general policy of, 170; Flandin's discussion with, 171–2, 177; confesses putting party before country, 194–5; and Abdication crisis, 196–7; retirement of, 198; appreciation of, 199–200; receives Conservative deputation, 204–7, 367–72; failing health of, 206
Baldwin-Coolidge debt settlement, 22–3
Balearic Islands, 222
Balfour, Rt. Hon. Arthur J. (Earl), 19
Balfour Note on war debts, 22–3
Balkan States, Italian threat to, 314–5, 338
Balloon squadrons, 353
Balsan, Madame, 357
Baltic Sea, German mastery of, 125–6, 136, 306
Baltic States, in proposed Eastern Pact, 95; aligned to France, 173; affected by

fortified Rhineland, 184; fear of Russia in, 324–5, 348–9; British need for co-operation of, 327; refuse guarantees from Russia, 340. See also Esthonia, Latvia, Lithuania
Barcelona, 166
Barham, H.M.S., 317
Barthou, Louis, 95–7
Baruch, Bernard M., 222
Battleships, Treaty limitations to size of, 84, 125, 145; German advantage in construction of, 125; question of design of, 142–6; Queen Elizabeth class, 143
Bavaria, Hitler attempts to seize power in, 49–50; Austrian Nazis trained in, 82, 93
Beatty, Admiral of the Fleet Earl, 247
Beaverbrook, Lord, 19
Beck, Colonel, Polish Foreign Minister, 306, 314
Beck, General von, 279, 280
Belgium, and Western Pact, 25, 27; Germany suggests pact with, 172; German menace to, 183–4; Hitler plans attack on, 338; opposes Staff talks with Britain and France, 341, 343; as base for Royal Air Force, 371
Beneš, Dr. Eduard, Hitler's offer to, 258; faithful ally of France, 258, 272; informs Stalin of conspiracy, 258–9; negotiates with Henlein, 264; appeals for calm, 275; resignation of, 289
Berchtesgaden, Halifax at, 224; Schuschnigg summoned to, 235–6; Chamberlain's visit to, 269, 292
Berehaven, 247–9
Berlin, Hitler's triumph in, 64; suppression of Roehm plot in, 89–90
Bevin, Rt. Hon. Ernest, 156–7, 159
Birkenhead, Earl of, 19
Bismarck, 146; strongest vessel afloat, 125
Blackshirts (S.S.), 53, 63, 94; faithful to Hitler, 88
Blockade, Hitler not afraid of, 352
Blomberg, General von, 87, 233
Blum, Léon, 118, 193, 211; declares France will honour Czechoslovakian guarantee, 252, 270–1; conversation of, with Churchill, 252; fall of Government of, 253
Bodenschatz, Colonel, 281
Bohemia and Moravia, German protectorate of, 317
Bonnet, Georges, 253, 266–7; De Washington au Quai d'Orsay of, 266 n.; favours cession of Sudetenland, 271; on British communiqué promising support, 278;

signs Franco-German declaration, 300;
his talk with Ribbentrop, 300–1
Boothby, Robert, 106 *n.*, 278
Bracken, Rt. Hon. Brendan, 74, 278
Brauchitsch, General, 280
Bremen, the, 318
Brenner Pass, Italian troops on, 93, 151
Briand, Aristide, 26
British Army, need to strengthen, 84;
German views on, 167; compulsory
service in, 318–19
Brockdorff, General, 280
Brownshirts (Storm Troops, S.A.), first
units of, 49; development of, 53, 86;
Hitler prepared to liquidate, 54; Roehm
and, 55, 86–90; Roehm leader of, 62;
Hitler mistrusts growth of, 86–8;
merged with Reichswehr, 87; reduced
to obedience, 94; compulsory service
in, 129
Bruening, Heinrich, and rearming of Ger-
many, 45; becomes Chancellor, 56;
policy of, 56–8; downfall of, 58
Bukharin, M., 259
Bullitt, William C., 185
Burckel, Gauleiter, 241

Cadogan, Rt. Hon. Sir Alexander, head of
Foreign Office, 217, 227; hears of inva-
sion of Austria, 243
Canada, and Western Pact, 26
Canaris, Admiral, 241
Cannes, 219–20
Cecil, Lord (Viscount Cecil of Chel-
wood), 152, 278
Chamberlain, Rt. Hon. Sir Austen, and the
1922 election, 19; announces German
suggestion of pact, 25–6; and Western
Pact, 26, 28; and German menace, 74;
and air defences, 133; and Italy's attack
on Abyssinia, 156; not offered Foreign
Office, 166; disbelieves in Hitler's sin-
cerity, 176; supports offer of office to
Churchill, 179; member of Conservative deputation to Prime Minister,
204–5, 206–7
Chamberlain, Rt. Hon. Neville, Chancellor of Exchequer, 60–1, 198; and
British aid to France after reoccupation
of Rhineland, 176; refuses Ministry of
Co-ordination of Defence, 179; becomes
Prime Minister, 198; appreciation of,
199–200; confirms Churchill's estimate

of German expenditure on armaments,
203–4; not member of Conservative
deputation, 206; reasons for foreign
policy of, 207; dismisses Lord Swinton,
Air Minister, 208–9; his strong views on
foreign affairs, 216–18, 229, 298–9; his
differences with Eden, 216–18, 225, 227,
230–1; dismisses Vansittart from the
Foreign Office, 217; seeks better relations with Dictators, 217–18, 253, 298–
300; his approaches to Italy, 217–18,
226–7, 229–30, 253, 300; supports Eden
at Nyon Conference, 222; approves
Halifax's visit to Germany, 224; rebuffs
Roosevelt's overture, 226–9, 237; gives
luncheon to Ribbentrop, 243–4; aban-
dons idea of guarantee to Czechoslovakia, 245–6; decides his policy as
regards Europe, 246–7; makes pact with
Italy, 253–5; suggests sending mediator
to Prague, 260; foreign policy in hands
of, 268–9, 270, 299–300; visits Hitler,
269, 271, 275–7, 281, 283–6; his opinion
of Hitler, 270, 299; presses cession of
Sudetenland, 270–2; Churchill confers
with, on Czech crisis, 277–8; unknow-
ingly defeats plot against Hitler, 281;
broadcasts to nation, 283; at Munich,
284–6; his agreement with Hitler, 285–6,
300–1, 322; Duff Cooper expresses
disagreement with, 291–2; perseverance and moral courage of, 292; on
dismemberment of Czechoslovakia, 298,
306–7; visits Paris, 300; visits Italy,
305–6; submits speech to Mussolini,
306; on occupation of Czechoslovakia,
307–10; reversal of policy of, 308–10,
322, 324; his guarantee to Poland, 310,
341, 344; his distrust of Russia, 313;
Churchill's letters to, 314–15; introduces conscription, 318–19; on Churchill's
"chances" of office, 319–20; Stanley
urges National Government on, 320–1;
answer of, to Russian proposal for
Triple Alliance, 332; on Russian alliance,
334–5; Molotov's reply to speech of,
339–40; sends Strang to Russia, 347;
writes to Hitler on British preparations
for war, 353–4; War Cabinet of, 313–14
Chartwell Manor, 72; visitors to, 72–3
Chatfield, Admiral of the Fleet Lord, First
Sea Lord, 142; shows Churchill the
Asdics, 146–7; at Nyon Conference,
220; on relinquishment of Irish bases,
248; mentioned, 222
Chemical warfare, 38

INDEX

Chile, protests against German violation of Peace Treaty, 120

China, Japanese aggression in, 78–80; repercussions of Anglo-German Naval Agreement on, 127

C.H.L. stations, 140

Churchill, Randolph, 178, 263

Churchill, Rt. Hon. Winston S., his relations with Baldwin, 18, 30; loses office as Dominions Secretary, 19; Chancellor of Exchequer, 21, 27, 45; rejoins Conservative Party, 21–33; opposes disarmament, 27–8, 65–6, 68–70, 91–2, 104–6; opposes Indian independence, 30–1, 61, 71; out of office, 33–4, 71–2; writes on possibilities in future wars, 35–39; lecture tour in United States, 71; accident to, 71; literary work of, 71–2, 180–1; building works of, 72, 357–8; friends of, 72–4; sources of information of, 73–4; speeches of, on German menace, 74, 77, 83–5, 92, 101, 104–9, 126–7, 183–4, 188–9, 203, 244–5, 273; Hitler fails to meet, 75–6; protests against plan of having two Foreign Ministers, 123; condemns Anglo-German Naval Agreement, 126–7; on Committee on Air Defence Research, 133–8, 142, 210; writes to Air Minister on Radar, 141–2; keeps in touch with naval affairs, 142–3; corresponds with First Lord on battleship design, 143–5; shown use of Asdics, 146–7; consulted on Italian aggression in Abyssinia, 151; writes to Foreign Secretary on Mediterranean crisis, 153–4; speaks to City Carlton Club on Abyssinian crisis, 155–156; Conservative Party Conference resolution of, 160; desires office, 160–2; election campaign of (1935), 161; absence of, during Hoare-Laval Pact crisis, 166; paintings of, 166, 357; excluded from Ministry of Co-ordination of Defence, 179–81; writes on potential power of League, 181–2; speaks on consequences of fortified Rhineland, 183–4; his principles of foreign policy, 186–90; Edward VIII consults, 196; loses influence in House, 197; George VI's letters to, 197–8; his meeting with Ribbentrop, 200–1; continues to urge rearmament, 202–3, 204–10; speaks on German war expenditure, 203–4; leads Conservative deputation to Prime Minister, 204–5, 367–72; speaks on inadequacy of air defences, 208–10;

his correspondence with Daladier on German rearmament, 211–12; writes on Spanish war, 219; his correspondence with Eden on Nyon Conference, 220–3; refuses invitations to meet Hitler, 224–5; capacity for sleep, 231; on Eden's resignation, 231, 238–9; at farewell lunch to Ribbentrop, 243–4; speaks on occupation of Austria, 244–5; urges Franco-British-Russian alliance, 245; speaks on relinquishment of Irish bases, 249; conversations of, with French leaders, 252–3; his correspondence with Eden on Anglo-Italian pact, 254–5; speeches of, on Czech crisis, 261–262, 273; letters of, to Halifax, on Czech crisis, 262–6, 277; confers with Chamberlain on Czech crisis, 277–8; speech of, on Munich Agreement, 293–4; German resentment to attitude of, 294–5; Epping's vote of confidence in, 296; exchanges letters with Duff Cooper, 296–7; speech of, on Chamberlain's foreign policy, 298–299; suggests manning of air defences, 312; his letters to Prime Minister, 314–315; complains of disposition of Mediterranean Fleet, 315–17; his "chances" of office, 319–20; tables resolution for National Government, 320; popular desire for return of, to office, 321; writes on German threat to Poland, 324; on need for Russian alliance, 327–8, 335–7; visits Rhine front, 342–4; his conversation with Grandi, 361–2

Churchill, Mrs. Winston S., 357–8

Ciano, Count, at Hitler and Mussolini's first meeting, 86; on Chamberlain's visit to Mussolini, 305–6; Goering explains German preparations for war to, 317–18; signs Pact of Steel, 337–8; argues with Ribbentrop against war, 346; hears from Hitler of imminence of war, 347; on the secrecy of Germany's intentions, 356

Citrine, Rt. Hon. Sir Walter (Baron), 196

Clemenceau, Georges, 11

Collective Security, through the League, 110–12; Hoare on, 154–5; breakdown of, 169; still time for assertion of, 171

Collins, Michael, 247

Colvin, Ian, 74

Communism, victorious in Russia, 13; in Hungary, 13; in Germany, 13, 48–9; in Spain, 191–2

Communist Party, French, and extended military service, 118, 121

Communist Party, German, 62–3

Conscription, forbidden in Germany by the Treaty, 39–40; Baldwin pronounces against, 167; introduction of, in Britain, 318–19

Conservative Party, returned to power (1922), 19–20; returned to power (1924), 21; supports Churchill, 21; Churchill rejoins, 21; after 1929 election, 29; and disarmament, 76, 104; blameworthy conduct of, 80; election manifesto of (1935), 159; Conference of (1935), 160; Baldwin sacrifices country for, 194–5; against National Defence contribution, 198; deputation from, to Prime Minister, 204–5, 367–72; supports relinquishment of Irish bases, 248–9; split in, on Munich 290–3, 296

Coolidge, Calvin, President, 22

Cooper, Rt. Hon. Sir Alfred Duff, 150; First Lord of the Admiralty, 198; demands mobilisation of Fleet, 278; resignation of, 291–2; German resentment at attitude of, 295, 301; exchanges letters with Churchill, 296–7

Co-ordination of Defence, Ministry of, 179–80, 369; and Air Force *matériel*, 365; note criticising functions of, 365–6

Corbin, André, letter from Churchill to, 193

Corfu, occupation of, 314–15

Cot, Pierre, 193, 252

Cranborne, Viscount, 237

Cripps, Rt. Hon. Sir Stafford, urges formation of "All-in Government", 320

Croft, Rt. Hon. Sir Henry (Baron Croft), and German menace, 74; urges rearmament, 76; member of Conservative deputation to Prime Minister, 205

Cruisers, armed merchant, 352–3

Cunliffe-lister, Rt. Hon. Sir Philip—*see* Swinton, Viscount

Curzon of Kedleston, Lord, 19–20

Cyprus, 254

Czechoslovakia, independence of, 14; German Arbitration Treaty with, 27; French guarantee to, 27, 176, 246, 252, 259–60, 263–4, 266, 270–2; in proposed Eastern Pact, 95; protests against German violation of Peace Treaty, 120; aligned to France, 173, 175, 258; affected by fortified Rhineland, 184; Austria the door to, 234, 251–2, 273; isolation of, 245–6, 263–4; no British guarantee to,

246; Germany's political offensive against, 250–1; German minority in, 251, 255–6; plans for destruction of, 251; Goering's assurance to, 252; Mussolini's acceptance of German action in, 255; mobilises Army, 256, 276, 278–9; German preparations to attack, 257; Hitler seeks to separate from France, 258; relations with Russia, 257–9, 263–4, 266, 274, 348; Runciman mission to, 260–2; seeks to conciliate Sudetens, 261–2, 269; cession of Sudetenland by, 266, 269–73; establishes martial law, 267; effect of Chamberlain's German visits on, 269; Franco-British pressure on, 271–3; railway connections between Russia and, 274; German estimate of strength of, 282; Hitler's guarantee to, 283; Munich decision on, 284–5, 286, 289; dismemberment of, 289–90, 293–4, 298, 306–7; Polish demands on, 289–90, 298, 348; Hungarian demands on, 290, 298; Army and arsenal of, lost to Allies, 301–2, 311, 317–18, 337; German occupation of, 307–9, 318; Russian contracts with, 325–7; uranium in, 345. *See also* Little Entente

D'Abernon, Viscount, 348

Daily Herald, 176

Daily Telegraph, 321

Daladier, Edouard, Churchill's correspondence with, on German rearmament, 211–12; Government of, 253; renews assurances to Czechoslovakia, 259, 272; desires Anglo-French approach to Hitler, 269; favours cession of Sudetenland, 270–1; at Munich, 284; on Russian negotiations with Germany, 331; mentioned, 95

Danzig, German declaration of sovereignty over, 306, 324; threat to, 341; mentioned, 98, 338, 347

Davis, Norman, 58

Delbos, Yvon, 223

Denmark, protests against German violation of Peace Treaty, 120. *See also* Scandinavia

Destroyers, Irish bases of, 249

De Valera, Eamon, agreement with, on naval bases, 247–9

Disarmament, of Germany, II; naval, British and American 12; urged on

France, 12, 55–6, 76, 83–5, 92, 118; general, and Western Pact, 26–8; British, 30, 64–70, 76, 100–1; "equality of armaments" and, 58, 66–70; "qualitative", Churchill on, 65; Labour and Liberal Parties uphold, 111–13

Disarmament Conference, in Washington, 12; in Geneva, 58; German demands before (1932), 66; German withdrawals from 67, 70; adjournment of, 91–2

Dollfuss, Dr., reaches understanding with Mussolini, and disarms Socialists, 82; German pressure on, 85; murder, of 93, 234

Dominions, and Locarno Conference, 22–23; warned of approaching war, 352

Doumenc, General, 348

Doumergue, Gaston, 95

Dowding, Air Chief Marshal Lord, 139

Drax, Admiral the Hon. Sir R.A.R., 348

East Fulham by-election (1933), 100, 194–5

Eastern Pact, 28; France proposes, 95; sabotaged by Germany, 171

Ebert, Friedrich, 24

Eden, Rt. Hon. Anthony, in Berlin, 87, 108, 118; early career, 118; in Moscow, 119; Minister for League of Nations Affairs, 122–3; and Italy's aggression against Abyssinia, 151; and Sanctions against Italy, 154, 216; becomes Foreign Secretary, 166; Flandin's discussions with, 171–2; and German proposal for pact, 173; and reoccupation of Rhineland, 175; demands Staff talks with France, 183, 216; his differences with Chamberlain, 215–18, 225, 228, 230; foreign policy of, 216, 218, 237–8; and Vansittart, 217; his relations with Churchill, 218–20, 262; at Nyon Conference, 220–3; corresponds with Churchill, 220–3; and Halifax's visit to Germany, 224; and rebuff of American offer, 226–9; and talks with Italy, 229–230; resignation of, 230–1, 237–8; his correspondence with Churchill on Anglo-Italian pact, 254–5; German resentment at attitude of, 295, 301; supports resolution for National Government, 320; on need for Russian alliance, 333, 337; suggests going to Russia, 347

Edward VIII, King, 196–7

Egypt, Socialist policy in, 30

Eire, Britain renounces rights to naval bases in, 248–9; question of neutrality of, 248–9

"Equality of armaments", 58, 66–70

Ernst, Karl, 89–90

Esthonia, need for co-operation of, 327; should not fall into the hands of Germany, 335; signs non-aggression pact with Germany, 340; Russian need for neutrality of, 345; Germany politically disinterested in, 350. See also Baltic States

Eyres-Monsell, Sir Bolton (Viscount Monsell), 126

Falmouth, 248

Far East, growth of Japanese power in, 78–9; repercussions of Anglo-German Naval Agreement in, 127; dangers of war in, 267

Fascism, rise of, 13–14

Faucher, General, 272

Feiling, Professor Keith, Life of Neville Chamberlain of (extracts), 176, 179–80, 228, 230–1, 245–6, 253, 270, 283, 313, 319

Fey, Major, 82

Finland, fear of Russia in, 325; refuses guarantee by Russia, 340; Russian need for neutrality of, 348; Germany politically disinterested in, 350

Fisher, Admiral of the Fleet Lord, 143–4

Fitzalan, Viscount, 205

Flandin, Pierre, at Stresa Conference ,119; in London, 171–2, 175–6; and reoccupation of Rhineland, 174–7; trial of, 178; out of office, 253; mentioned, 211

Fleet Air Arm, question of naval control of, 143, 362–65

Foch, Marshal, 6, 10–11, 13

Forbes, Admiral of the Fleet Sir Charles, Commander-in-Chief, 147

France, and threat of German aggression, 5–6, 10, 76, 96, 176; and Treaty of Versailles, 6, 10–11; repudiation of Anglo-American guarantee to, 10–11; disarmament urged on, 12, 64–70, 76, 83–4, 92, 118; and Western Pact, 25–8; guarantees assistance to Poland, 27, 310; guarantees assistance to Czechoslovakia, 27, 176, 246, 252, 259–60, 263–4, 271; fails to prevent second war, 38, 46, 70, 106, 131, 171, 174; "equality of armaments" between Germany and, 58, 66–70; strongest military Power, 69, 187; German approach to, before First World War, 83; Italian relations with, 94–7, 163–4; seeks security in East, 95–6; declares extension of military service, 117–118, 121; Communists in, 118, 121; and Stresa Conference, 118–20; protests against German violation of Peace Treaty, 120; approaches Russia, 121–2, 171; and Anglo-German Naval Agreement, 125, 163; and Abyssinian war, 151, 156, 163; anxiety of, about Rome-Berlin Axis, 163; promises armed support to League, 172; Germany suggests pact with, 172; seeks British aid on reoccupation of Rhineland, 172–3, 175–7; fails to mobilise, 175, 235–6, 239; Staff conversations between Britain and, 183; menace of fortified Rhineland to, 183–4; a peaceful and fearful nation, 187–8; Britain's need for defensive association with, 189–90, 205; and Spanish Civil War, 192–3, 218–19; co-operates with Britain in anti-submarine patrols of Mediterranean, 220–3; Hitler plans to precipitate war with, 233; British obligations to, 247; Hitler certain of inaction of, 251–2, 257; urges Czechs to be reasonable, 255; Czechoslovakia's commitments to, 258; validity of her treaty wih Czechoslovakia, 259–260; approaches Russia on Czech crisis, 263–4, 274; asks British position in event of German attack, 266–7; suggests Anglo-French approach to Hitler, 269; favours cession of Sudetenland, 270–1; "ultimatum" of, to Czechs, 271–3; partial mobilisation of, 277, 279–80; Britain declares she will support, 278; further concessions of, to Hitler, 284; and Munich conference, 284–8; fails to honour her agreement, 288, 294; signs declaration of amity with Germany, 300; Ribbentrop's mission to, 300–1; forty-hours week in, 302; Italian claims against, 313; Russia suggests Triple Alliance to, 325–7, 339–40; draws nearer Britain, 341–2; Rhine frontier of, 342–3; purely defensive attitude of, 343–4; Hitler on course of war against, 347; military conversations of, with Russia, 348–50; number of divisions of, 349; failure of foreign policy of, 351; Hitler leaves opening of hostilities to, 357; as base for Air Force 371

Franco, General, rises in revolt, 192; successes of, 245

François-Poncet, André, 284

Franco-Soviet Pact, 121–2, 172; German case against, 182; Russia seeks discussion on, 245

French Air Force, post-1918, 14; reduction of, 112; culpable neglect of, 212–13

French Army, strength of, 14, 39, 69, 187; centre of life of France, 65; planned reduction of, 67–70, 83; extension of compulsory service in, to two years, 118, 121; compared with German, 130, 302–303, 357; artillery of, 252; partial mobilisation of, 277, 279–80; purely defensive tactics of, 344

French Navy, Treaty limitations on, 125; need for reconstruction, 126; superiority of, over German Navy, 128; battleship design in, 146; co-operates with British, 220–3

Fritsch, General von M., 233, 242

Gamelin, General, 252–3; suggests that Churchill should visit the Rhine front, 342

Gandhi, Mahatma, at London Conference, 30

Gaulle, General de, 253

Gauss, Herr, 350

G.C.I. stations, 140

General Election of 1922, 19–20; of 1923, 20–1; of 1929, 29; of 1931, 34; of 1935, 156

Geneva Disarmament Conference, 58

George VI, King, coronation of, 197; letters to Churchill, 197–8

George, Rt. Hon. David Lloyd (Earl of Dwyfor), and Treaty of Versailles, 10, 11; rift between Poincaré and, 12; end of Coalition of, 18–19; on Hindenburg, 25; plan of, to limit German Army, 39; failure of, in the "locust years", 80; on reoccupation of Rhineland, 174; conversation of, with Churchill, 219–21; misled by Hitler, 225; on need of arrangement with Russia, 333–4; asks question on Anglo-Polish guarantee, 336; mentioned, 19, 20, 29, 33, 166

Georges, General, 96; shows Churchill Rhine front, 342; shows figures of French and German Armies, 357

German Air Force, re-creation of, 43–4, 99 et seq., 170; prohibition of, 68; approaches parity with British, 105–7; reaches parity, 108–9, 114–16; officially constituted, 117; possible policy of, in event of war, 136–7; enlargement of, 190; strongest in Europe, 207; estimates of strength of, 211, 369–70; compared with British, 303, 369–71

German Army, Treaty limits to, 39–40; plans to re-create, 40–2, 99; exceeds Treaty limits, 42; equality of, with French Army, 58, 66–70, 83; compulsory service for, 117, 128–9, 190; function of, in Nazi Germany, 128–9; organisation of, 129; expansion of, 113–114, 190; compared with French, 130, 302–3, 357; strongest in Europe, 207; Churchill's estimates of strength of, 211–12; defects shown in, during invasion of Austria, 242; generals on deficiencies of, 281–2

German colonies, question of return of, 200, 218, 225, 276–7, 299

German Navy, Treaty limits to, 14, 44, 68, 123; illicit building up of, 44, 99, 108–9; exceeds Treaty limits, 123–4; as permitted by Anglo-German Naval Agreement, 124–6; battleship design in, 146

German Workers' Party, 48–9

Germany, after First World War, 4, 10–12; France threatened by, 4–6; reparations from, 6, 8–9, 23; loans to, 8–9, 10, 29, 52; total disarmament of, 11, 4–16, 29, 43; economic chaos in, 11–12, 55–6, 58; British sympathy for, 12; Communism in, 13, 48–9; hideous crimes of, 15–16; Hindenburg's Presidency, 24–5; suggests Rhineland Pact, 25; enters League, 25–7; Arbitration Treaties of, 27; dissatisfied with Eastern frontiers, 28; withdrawal of Inter-Allied Control Commission from, 43; rearming of, 41–46, 64, 70, 76, 101–2, 117, 128–31, 136–7, 170, 210–13, 367; anti-Semitism in, 45, 48, 52, 69, 91; Hitler's conception of, 47–8, 50–1; rise of Nazi Party in, 49–50, 51–4; question of revival of monarchy in, 56–7; "equality of armaments" between France and, 58, 66–70, 83, opposition to Hitler in, 63, 74, 86–7; Hitler achieves power over, 63–4; demands right to rearm, 66, 68–9; quits Disarmament Conference, 67, 70; quits League, 70; Churchill visits, 75; deliveries of metals to, 77; absorbs Austria, 81, 93–4, 240–5, 273; approach to France before First World War, 83; Nazi unity preserved in, 90–1; concentration

camp system in, 91; Churchill on power of dictatorship in, 92; opposes Eastern Pact, 95; Saar returns to, 97–8; relations of, with Russia, 102, 171; approaches air parity with Great Britain, 105–7; reaches air parity, 108, 114; British naval agreement with, 124–8, 170; function of Army in Nazi, 128–9; Italy on side of, 148, 163, 171; contempt for Britain felt by, 167–8; prepares for war, 170, 190–1, 317–18, 344; suggests twenty-five-year pact, 172; reoccupies Rhineland, 173–9; Hitler's prestige enhanced in, 179, 184; defies League, 182–3; fortifies Rhineland, 183–4, 196; draws up plans for reoccupation of Austria, 185, 232; British duty to oppose, 188; subscribes to Non-Intervention, 192; intervenes in Spanish war, 193, 219; asks for free hand in Eastern Europe, 200–1; "living space" for, 200, 232, 251, 338; expenditure of, on armaments, 203–4, 301; strongest military Power, 207; anti-aircraft guns in, 209–10; absorption by, of all German minorities, 251; prepares to attack Czechoslovakia, 257; cession of Sudetenland to, 269–73, 275–7; Godesberg ultimatum of, 276–7, 283; poor morale in, 281–2; mobilisation of, denied, 282; resents Britain's attitude of mistrust, 295, 301, 323; arbitrates on Czecho-Hungarian frontier, 298; signs declaration with France, 300; increase in population of, 304; troop movements in, 306; annexes Czechoslovakia, 307; gains of, through appeasement, 310–11; gains of, through occupation of Czechoslovakia, 317–18; Russian relations with, 326–7, 329; needed speedy victory, 334; signs Pact of Steel with Italy, 337–8; negotiates with Russia, 339, 348–9; Baltic non-aggression pacts with, 340; fails to make atomic bomb, 345; determined on war, 346–7; signs pact with Russia, 350–352; her secret agreement with Russia, 350; invades Poland, 356–7; war potential of, 367–73

Gestapo, 94

Gibraltar, British fleet at, in Abyssinian crisis, 155

Gilmour, Colonel Rt. Hon. Sir John, 205

Glaise-Horstenau, General, 241

Gneisenau, built in defiance of Treaty limitations, 123–4; escorts troopships to Narvik, 352

Godesberg ultimatum, 276–7, 283–5

Goebbels, Dr., organises election campaign for Hitler, 63; at arrest of Roehm, 89; plot to arrest, 281

Goering, Hermann, in the *Putsch*, 49; Minister of Interior, 63; in suppression of Roehm plot, 89–90; Laval meets, 122; invites Halifax to Germany, 224; demands calling off of plebiscite, 240; gives assurances to Czechoslovakia, 252; suggested London visit of, 260; plot to arrest, 281; explains German preparations for war to Mussolini, 317–18; on effect of British treaty with Poland, 354

Gold Standard, abandonment of, 34

Grandi, Count, conversations of, with Chamberlain, 217–18, 229–30; conversation of, with Churchill, 361–2

Great Britain, loans by, to Germany, 8, 29, 45; and Treaty of Versailles, 10–11; German sympathies of, 12; disarmament policy of, 12, 30, 64–5, 76, 100–101; American debts of, 22–3, 34; and Western Pact, 25–8; two-way guarantee of, 228; financial crisis in, 32–4; fails to prevent second war, 37, 46, 70, 83, 106, 131, 170–1; economy ruling on Service estimates of (1919–32), 45–6; and Japanese aggression in China, 78–9; Italian relations of, 95; desire for peace in, 100–1; German air parity with, 105–109, 114, 119, 131; protests against German violation of Peace Treaty, 120; makes Naval Agreement with Germany, 124–8; reaction of, to Abyssinian war, 150–1; undertakes to uphold League action against Italy, 152–60, 163–4; evades effective action, 157–9, 163–4; lost prestige of, 167–8; new atmosphere in, 169; asked to support France in possible violation of Locarno Treaty by Germany, 171–2; Germany suggests pact with, 172; evades action on re-occupation of Rhineland, 174–7, 239; Staff conversations between France and, 183; Churchill's principles of foreign policy for, 186–90; needs defensive association with France, 189–90, 205; keeps agreement for Non-Intervention in Spanish war, 192–3; plan for rearmament of, 195; Germany's declared wish for friendship with, 200; French cooperation with, in anti-submarine patrols, 220–3; Hitler plans to precipitate war with, 233; gives guarantee to

Poland, 246, 310–11, 323–4, 336, 341, 344, 353–4; obligations of, in Central Europe, 247; Hitler certain of inaction of, 251–2, 257; makes pact with Italy, 253–5; urges Czechs to be reasonable, 255; asked by France to clarify position in event of German attack, 266–7; "ultimatum" of, to Czechs, 271–2; rejects Godesberg terms, 277; declares she will support France, 278; and Munich conference, 284–7; encourages France in her treatment of Czechoslovakia, 288; ill-prepared for war, 293, 295–6, 367–372; Hitler's speech on, 294–5; Ribbentrop seeks to detach France from, 300–1; military expenditure of, compared with German, 301; not bound by guarantee to Czechoslovakia, 307–8; losses to, through appeasement, 310–11; conscription introduced in, 318–19; gives guarantee to Roumania, 322; in alliance with Turkey, 322, 333, 335; Russia suggests Triple Alliance to, 325–7; answers Russian proposals, 323; German minutes on war against, 338–40; draws nearer to France, 341–2; Hitler on war against, 347, 352; sends mission to Russia, 347–50; military conversations of, with Russia, 348–50; number of divisions of, 349; failure of foreign policy of, 351; precautionary measure taken by, on announcement of German-Soviet Pact, 352–3; proclaims treaty with Poland, 354; Hitler leaves opening of hostilities to, 357; German Nazis in, 358; war organisation of industries of, compared with German, 367–70

Greece, Italian threat to, 314–15

Grigg, Rt. Hon. Sir Edward (Baron Altrincham), 74, 205, 278

Guarantee, Treaty of, 11

Guernica, bombing of, 193

Guest, Captain Rt. Hon. F. E., 106 *n.*, 205

Hacha, Dr., President of Czechoslovakia, 298

Halder, General von, and the attack on Czechoslovakia, 252, 302; Chief of Army General Staff, 279; plots against Hitler, 280–1; mentioned, 302

Halifax, Earl of, as Viceroy, 30–1; on private armament firms, 112–13; his kinship of outlook with Chamberlain, 216; visits Hitler, 224; appointed

Foreign Secretary, 231; and Czech crisis, 260–1, 268, 277–8, 284, 286; Churchill's letters to, on Czech crisis, 262–6, 277; answer of, to French request for clarification of position, 266–7; visits Paris with Chamberlain, 300; visits Italy with Chamberlain, 305–6; Churchill's letter to, on disposition of Mediterranean Fleet, 317; mentioned, 175, 294, 238
Hanfstaengl, Herr, 75–6
Hanneken, General von, 281
Hawkey, Sir James, 296
Heimwehr, suppresses Austrian Socialist army, 82
Heligoland, evasion of Treaty obligations in, 44
Helldorf, Graf von, 280, 281
Henderson, Admiral Sir Reginald, 142–3
Henderson, Sir Nevile, and Czech crisis, 256, 276
Henlein, Herr, demands autonomy in Sudetenland, 255; interview of, with Churchill, 256; negotiates with Beneš, 260, 264; flees to Germany, 267, 269; demands union of Sudetenland with Reich 269
Herriot, Edouard, German memorandum to, 25; Premier, 58; "Plan" of, 67; mentioned, 252
Hess, Rudolph, in the *Putsch*, 49
Himmler, Heinrich, leader of Blackshirts, 88, 94; plot to arrest, 281
Hindenburg, Marshal, 10; President of Germany, 24–5, 52; successor to, 53–4; re-election of, 56–7; staunch monarchist, 57; dismisses Bruening, 58; meets Hitler, 62; appoints Hitler Chancellor, 63; death of, 94
Hindenburg Line, 184
Hindu-Moslem antagonism in India, 61
History of the English-Speaking Peoples, 180
Hitler, Adolf, 13; temporary blindness of, 47–8; early life of, 47; anti-Semitism of, 48, 50, 75–6, 295; becomes "the Fuehrer", 49; *Putsch* of, 49–50, 53; main pillars of policy of, 49–51; gains allegiance of Reichswehr, 54–5; as successor to Hindenburg, 54; campaigns against Young Plan, 55–6; stands for Presidency, 57; and Chancellorship, 62–3; opens first Reichstag of Third Reich, 64; granted emergency powers, 64; withdraws Germany from League, 70; loses opportunity to meet Churchill, 75–6; Austrian aims of, 81, 85; his first meeting with Mussolini, 85–6; Roehm's

plot against, 86–90; executes Roehm and his following, 90–1; succeeds Hindenburg, 94; announces air parity with Great Britain, 109, 114, 119; openly repudiates Treaty of Versailles, 117–18; on date of war with England, 125, 233; Army under personal leadership of, 128; opens Staff College, 129; his estimate of British decadence, 159; free to strike, 190; opposed to co-operation of West with Russia, 171–9; offers non-aggression pact, 172–3, 176; reoccupies Rhineland, 173–9; differences between generals and, 175, 178–9; 233, 242, 257, 279–83; enhanced prestige of, 179, 286–287; signs pact with Austria, 185; Four Years' Plan of, 190; comes to terms with Mussolini, 190; gambles of, 190–1; Chamberlain seeks better relations with, 217–18; Halifax visits, 224; Lloyd George misled by, 225; his plans for the future of Germany, 232–3, 250–1; assumes direct control over Army, 233–234, 279; puts pressure on Schuschnigg, 235–6; speech of, on Austrian submission to his demands, 236–7; acknowledges his obligation to Mussolini, 241–242; his entry into Vienna, 242; opens Czechoslovakian campaign, 251, 255–6, 260, 266, 269; requires Italy's acceptance of Czechoslovakian campaign, 255; his offer to Beneš, 258; Churchill urges Joint Note to, 262; Chamberlain's visits to, 269, 270, 274–6, 281, 283–5; demands cession of Sudetenland, 269–70, 276; further demands of, 275–7; plot by generals against, 279–81; denies intent to mobilise, 282; offers guarantee to Czechoslovakia, 283; and Munich conference, 284–7; signs agreement with Chamberlain, 285–6, 300; and Horthy, 290; instances of bad faith of, 292, 309–310; speech of, on warmongers of Britain, 294–5; "appeasement" of, 299; hopes to divide Britain and France, 300–301; annexes Czechoslovakia, 307; fixes date for invasion of Poland, 314; Roosevelt's message to, 318; denounces Naval Agreement, 322–3; denounces Polish Non-Agression Pact, 323–4; and war on two fronts, 326; on Pact of Steel, 338; determined on war, 346; 352; demands Italian aid, 347; Chamberlain's letter to, on British preparations for war, 353–4; postpones invasion of

Poland, 354; informs Mussolini of pact with Soviet, 355; issues Directive No. 1 for conduct of war, 356–7

Hitler and Mussolini's Letters and Documents, 354 n., 355 n.

Hitler Youth, 129

Hoare, Rt. Hon. Sir Samuel (Viscount Templewood), and India Bill, 71; Foreign Minister, 122; on Anglo-German Naval Agreement, 127–8; First Lord of Admiralty, 142; Churchill corresponds with, on battleship design, 144; consultations with, on Italian aggression in Abyssinia, 151; Churchill writes to, on Mediterranean crisis, 153–4; on League action against Italy, 154–5; meets Laval, 162; resignation of, 165–6; question of new office for, 179; takes Home Office, 199

Hoare-Laval Pact, 162, 165, 169

Hoeppner, General, 280

Holland, German menace to, 183–4; Hitler plans attack on, 338–9

Hood, H.M.S., 155

Hore-Belisha, Rt. Hon. Leslie, urges conscription, 318

Horne, Rt. Hon. Sir Robert (Lord Horne), and German menace, 74; member of Conservative deputation to Prime Minister, 205; mentioned, 19, 106 n., 278

Horthy, Admiral, 290

Hugenberg, Herr, 56, 63

Hull, Cordell, 227

Hungary, Communism in, 13; signs Rome Protocols, 85; transport of Russian troops across, 274; claims of, on Czechoslovakia, 290, 298, 307; in German camp, 313

Hurricane fighters, 115, 301–3

I.F.F. apparatus, 139

Imperial Defence, Committee of, 45–6, 133

Incendiary bombs, 372

India, Socialist policy in, 30–1; Churchill opposes Government policy in, 30–1, 61, 71, 74

India Bill, MacDonald's, 71, 160

India Defence League, 71, 74

Innitzer, Cardinal, 94

Innsbruck, German leaflets dropped on, 82

Inskip, Rt. Hon. Sir Thomas (Viscount Caldecote), on the question of the Fleet Air Arm, 143, 362–3; Minister for Co-ordination of Defence, 180, 191; on measures for rearmament, 206; on guarantee to Czechoslovakia, 308; mentioned, 60 n., 204

Inter-Allied Military Commission of Control, 41–5

International Settlements, Bank for, 55

Ireland, Southern—*see* Eire

Ironside, Field-Marshal Lord, on Polish Army, 357

Italian Navy, reconstruction of, 126; and British Mediterranean Fleet, 153, 158–9, 163; concentration of, 315

Italy, Communism in, 13–14; and Western Pact, 25–8, 46; conflict between interests of, and German plans, 81; supports Austrian independence, 82, 85, 93, 97; imperialist programme of, in Africa, 95, 97, 148–50; French agreements with, 96–7, 151, 163; makes trade agreement with Russia, 102; designs of, towards Abyssinia, 117–18, 120, 149–51, 152–3, 361–2; and Stresa Conference, 118–20; protests against German violation of Peace Treaty, 120; sides with Germany, 148, 163, 169, 190, 361; and Abyssinian membership of League, 149; Churchill consulted on British policy concerning, 151; "Sanctions" against, 154–8, 361; invades Abyssinia, 156; impotent in war against Britain, 158–9, 163; annexes Abyssinia, 166–8; Germany suggests pact with, 172; and reoccupation of Rhineland, 183; subscribes to Non-Intervention, 192; intervenes in Spanish war, 193, 218–20, 230, 254–5; Chamberlain seeks to improve relations with, 217–18, 226–7, 229–30, 253, 300; submarine piracy of, 220–3; fortification of Mediterranean by, 222; Eden's resignation claimed as victory for Mussolini, 238; pact of, with Britain, 253–5; attempts to change alignment of, 253–5, 298, 313; arbitrates on Czecho-Hungarian frontier, 298; claims against France, of, 313; invades Albania, 313–14; signs Pact of Steel with Germany, 337–8; not prepared for war, 346–7, 356; neutrality of, 356; under popular dictatorship, 361

Japan, annulment of British alliance with, 13; naval power of, 13; economic crisis in, 78; occupies Manchuria, 78–80;

withdraws from League, 80; and London Treaty, 84 *n.*; and Anglo-German Naval Agreement, 127; joins Anti-Comintern Pact, 193–4; repercussions in, of recognition of Italian position in Abyssinia, 227; in state of patriotic fervour, 338; Hitler on procrastination of, 355; Mussolini desires to avoid rupture with, 355

Jehol, annexed to Manchukuo, 78

Jews, Hitler's hatred of, 48, 50, 75–6, 295; Nazi persecution of, 69

Jibuti-Addis-Ababa Railway, 97

Joad, C. E. M., and Oxford Union resolution, 77, 150

Jodl, General, diary of, 236, 240–1; on annexation of Czechoslovakia, 318; mentioned, 302

Jutland, Battle of, Hitler on, 339

Kahr, Otto, von 90

Kamieniev, M., 348

Keitel, Field-Marshal, Hitler's directive to, on Czechoslovakia, 260; on Munich, 286; issues "Directive for Armed Forces", 314; mentioned, 241

Keyes, Admiral of the Fleet Sir Roger (Lord Keyes), 205

King George V, H.M.S., 146

King George V, class of battleship, 145

Kun, Bela, 13

Labour Party, first Government of, 21; second Government of, 29–33; Indian policy of, 30–1, 71; MacDonald's separation from, 60, 122; and disarmament, 76; pacifism of, 80, 100; opposes strengthening of Air Force, 102–6; and Baldwin's confession, 111; changed outlook of, 156–7; divided as to policy, 159; supports action by League, 182; against Munich agreement, 292; opposed to conscription, 319, 337

La Chambre, Guy, 213

Lamlash, 248

Lansbury, Rt. Hon. George, leader of Labour Party, 61, 92; on disarmament, 100; resigns leadership, 157

Latvia, need for co-operation of, 327; should not fall into the hands of Germany; 335; Russian need for neutrality of, 348; Germany politically disinterested in, 350. *See also* Baltic States

Laval, Pierre, foreign policy of, 96; signs agreement with Italy, 97, 163; makes bargain with Hitler, 98; at Stresa Conference, 119; his interview with Stalin, 121; and Hoare-Laval Pact, 162, 165; opposed to Franco-Soviet Pact, 171; mentioned, 223

Law, Rt. Hon. Andrew Bonar, 19, 22

League of Nations, origin of, 3; repudiated by United States, 12; potential strength of, 14–16, 70, 83, 106, 110, 131, 171, 181–182, 188–90; German entry into, 25–8; and withdrawal of Inter-Allied Control Commission, 43; German withdrawal from, 70, 100; and Japanese aggression in China, 79–80; Russia joins, 95; hands over Saar to Germany, 97–8; collective security through, 110–2; Abyssinia appeal to, 117–18; and German violations of Peace Treaty, 117–21; impotence of, without force, 120–1, 181–2; Anglo-German Naval Agreement a blow to, 125; Abyssinian membership of, 149; possible action of, in Abyssinian war, 149–50, 151, 361–2; Covenant of, and Peace Ballot, 152–3; imposes Sanctions against Italy, 154, 156, 361; British Navy as arm of, 158, 361; Hoare-Laval plan laid before, 165; damaged by Baldwin's policy, 168, 169–70; France appeals to, 175, 181–2; failure of, 182–183; a British conception, 188–9; Russia advises invoking Council of, on Czech crisis, 264; Litvinov's speech to, on Czech crisis, 273–4

League of Nations Affairs, Ministry for, 122–3

Leeb, General Ritter von, 281

Leeper, Sir Reginald, 278

Liberal Party, in 1923, 20–1; in 1929, 29–30; break-up of, 33; pacifism of, 80, 100; opposes strengthening of Air Force, 103–106; and Baldwin's confession, 111; supports action by League, 182; against Munich agreement, 291–2; opposed to conscription, 319, 337

Libya, France gives Italy territory in, 97; withdrawal of Italian troops from, 254

Lindemann, Professor Frederick (Baron Cherwell), friendship with, 72; on Air Defence Research Committee, 133–5, 138, 210; mentioned, 166, 256, 344

Lindsay, Rt. Hon. Sir Ronald, 226

Linz, 242

Lipski, M., 312–13

Lithuania, need for co-operation of, 327; should not fall into the hands of Germany, 335; in German sphere of influence, 350; mentioned, 306, 313. *See also* Baltic States

Little Entente, anxiety in, concerning Germany, 76; anxiety in, concerning Russia, 95; ranged with France, 173, 175; lesson to be learned by, through reoccupied Rhineland, 179, 184; effect of German control of Vienna upon, 244; collectively a Great Power, 244–5. *See also* Czechoslovakia, Roumania, Yugoslavia

Litvinov, M., and League of Nations, 95; on joint action in Czech crisis, 263–4, 266, 273–4; suggests Triple Alliance, 325, 327; removed from office, 328–9, 355

Lloyd, Lord, urges rearmament, 76; member of Conservative deputation to Prime Minister, 205; mentioned, 150, 154, 278

Locarno Treaty, 27–8; and withdrawal of Control Commission, 43; German breach of, 173 *et seq.*

London, threat to, from the air, 115, 371–2; alternative centre of government to, 118

London Conference on India, 30

Londonderry, Marquess of, Minister for Air, 113–15

Lothian, Marquess of, 176–7

Ludendorff, General von, in the *Putsch*, 49

Lytton Report, 79

MacDonald, Rt. Hon. J. Ramsay, his political brotherhood with Baldwin, 20; first Administration of, 21; second Administration of, 29–30, 32–3; National Government of, 33–4, 46, 60, 66–71; at Geneva Disarmament Conference, 58; disarmament policy of, 64–70, 76, 83, 104, 122; India Bill of, 71; on German rearmament, 108–9; lays down office, 115, 122; at Stresa Conference, 119; Churchill interviews, on air defence research, 133; mentioned, 73

MacDonald Plan, 68–70

Machine-guns, classed as defensive weapons, 65; British production of, compared with German, 368–9; for aircraft, 370–1

Machine tools, war-time production of, 368

Mackensen, Field-Marshal von, 42

Maginot Line, Churchill visits, 342–3; Hitler on concentration of French troops on, 347

Maisky, I. M., communicates Russian views on Czech crisis to Churchill, 263, 274

Malta, lacks A.A. defences, 153

Manchester Guardian, 321

Manchukuo, 78–9

Manchuria, Japanese occupation of, 78–9

Mandel, Georges, 272

Marin, Louis.252

Marlborough: His Life and Times, 33, 72, 75

Marrakesh, 166, 258

Marseilles, assassination of King Alexander in, 96

Martini, General, 140

Marx, Herr, 24

Masaryk, Jan, 256

Me.109, 303

Mediterranean, repercussions of Anglo-German Naval Agreement in, 126–7; Fleet in, during Abyssinian crisis, 153–7, 164, 361; question of evacuating, 153–4; submarine piracy in, 220–3; Anglo-French co-operation in, 221–3; Italian fortification of, 222, 254; disposition of Fleet in, at occupation of Albania, 315–17; Italy promised free hand in, 338

Mein Kampf, main thesis of, 50–1; on German Army, 128–9

Memel, German occupation of, 306, 313

Merchant ships, conversion of, into A.M.C., 352–3

Mexico, protests against German violation of Peace Treaty, 120

Miklas, Dr., Austrian President, 93; refuses to nominate Nazi Chancellor, 240–1

Milne, Field-Marshal Lord, 205

Molotov, Vyacheslav, Commissar for Foreign Affairs, 328; German leanings of, 328, 331; his qualities, 330–1; replies to Chamberlain's speech on the proposed Russian alliance, 339–40; skill of, in duplicity, 349

Moore-Brabazon, Lieut.-Col. Rt. Hon. John (Baron Brabazon of Tara), 205

Morocco, 166

INDEX

Morrison, Rt. Hon. H. S., German resentment at attitude of, 301

Morton, Major Sir Desmond, 72–3

Moslem-Hindu antagonism in India, 61

Mueller-Hillebrandt, General, 281

Mukden, Japanese occupation of, 78

Munich, Communism in, 49; Churchill visits, 75; suppression of Roehm plot in, 89–90

Munich crisis, wisdom or folly of Britain and France in, 250–1, 287–8; the story of, 268–87; British reactions to, 290–1; debate on, 292–5

Munitions, insufficient supply of, 367–9

Mussolini, Benito, rise of, 13–14; and rise of Hitler, 81; supports Austrian independence, 82, 85, 93, 148, 235; first meeting with Hitler, 85–6; imperialist African programme of, 95; at Stresa Conference, 119–20; Abyssinian programme of, 120, 125, 148–9; and Anglo-German Naval Agreement, 125; sides with Hitler, 148, 170–1, 234–5; his estimate of Britain, 150; and Sanctions, 156; seeks compromise on Abyssinia, 164; estranged from Britain, 171; Chamberlain's approaches to, 218, 298–9; calling bluff of, 221–3; Eden's resignation claimed as victory for, 238; approves Schuschnigg's submission, 239; warns against plebiscite, 239; Hitler's gratitude to, over Austria, 241–2; makes pact with Britain, 253; supports Hitler in Czech crisis, 261, 275; Chamberlain appeals to, 283; and Munich conference, 284–5; Chamberlain visits 305–6; asserts Italian claims against France, 313; Goering explains German preparations for war to, 317–18; on message from Roosevelt, 318; anxious to avoid war, 346–7; informed of pact with Soviet, 355; tells Hitler that Italy will not fight, 355–6; correspondence of, with Hitler, 355–6; learns of final moves from England, 356; popular dictatorship of, 361

Mutual Guarantee, Treaty of, 27

National Coalition Government, end of war-time (1916–22), 18–19; Mac-Donald-Baldwin, 33–4, 60; Indian policy of, 61, 71, 74; blameworthy conduct of, 80

National Socialist Party—see Nazi Party

Nationalist Party, German, 63

Navy—see under Royal Navy; also French, German Navy, etc.

Nazi Party, rise of, 49–50, 52–3; Reichswehr joins forces with, 54–5; campaigns against "Young Plan", 55–6; loses seats, 62; majority vote for, 63–4; in Saar valley, 97; plot to arrest leaders of, 280–81

Nazi Party, Austrian, German aid to, 82, 94, 234; abortive revolt of, 93, 234; represented in Austrian Cabinet, 236

Nazi-Soviet Relations, 1939-41, 326

Nelson, H.M.S., 143

Neurath, Freiherr von, suggests non-aggression pact, 172; on importance to Germany of Rhineland fortifications, 185; announces Anti-Comintern Pact, 193–4; alarmed at Hitler's plans, 233; takes over Foreign Office, 241

New Statesman, 66

New York, Churchill's accident in, 71

New Zealand, and Western Pact, 26

"Night of the Long Knives", 90

Non-aggression pact, Germany proposes, 172–3

Non-Intervention policy in Spain, 192–3

North Sea, British Fleet tied to, 127

Norway, protests against German Treaty violation, 120

Nuremberg trials, 250, 286; extracts from documents, 236, 240–1, 251, 317–318, 338–9, 350, 353–4, 356–7

Nyon Conference, 220–3

O'Neill, Rt. Hon. Sir Hugh, 205

Oxford Union, pacifist resolution of 77, 150

"Pact of Steel", 337–9

Papen, Franz von, as Chancellor, 62; sides with Hitler, 63; in the Roehm purge, 90; organises overthrow of Austrian republic, 93–4, 234, 236; on the Fuehrer, 236

Peace Ballot, 152, 157, 180 n., 182

Peace Society, Baldwin's speech to, 161

Pembroke Dock, 248

Philip of Hesse, Prince, 241–2

Phipps, Rt. Hon. Sir Eric, 266

Pilsudski, Marshal, 324, 348

388

Poincaré, Raymond, 12

Poison gas, development of, 36, 38

Poland, Russian repulse in, 13; independence of, 14; France's guarantee to, 27; German Arbitration Treaty with, 27; opposes Eastern Pact, 95; protests against German violation of Peace Treaty, 120; aligned to France, 173; affected by fortified Rhineland, 184; German need to absorb, 200, 232; British guarantee to, 246, 310–11, 323–5, 336, 341, 344, 353–4; demands cession of Teschen, 289–90, 298, 311–12; heroism and sufferings of, 289–90; German encirclement of, 306, 313, 318; refuses transit to Russian troops, 313, 349; date for German invasion of, 314, 343, 357; Hitler denounces agreement with, 323–4; fear of Russia in, 325; Russian arrangement with Germany concerning, 331, 350; German policy with regard to, 338, 346–7, 354–7; refuses guarantee from Russia, 340; anti-Bolshevism of, 348; British treaty with, effect of, 354; invasion of, 356–7

Polish Army, favourable reports of, 357

Polish Corridor, 200, 324

Portland, Anti-Submarine School at, 147

Portugal, protests against German violation of Peace Treaty, 120

Prince of Wales, H.M.S., 146

Prussia, Socialist Government of, driven from office, 62

Putsch of 1923, 49–50

Queen Elizabeth class, 143

Queenstown, 247–9

Rabenau, General von, 41–2

Radar (R.D.F.), the technique of, 138; coastal chain stations for, 139–40; German system of, 140; calling up of defence for stations, 353

Radio-beams, bombers guided by, 135. See also Radar

Radio-location, 139–40, See also Radar

Raeder, Admiral, 125; warns Hitler, 282

Rathenau, Herr von 44–5, 56

R.D.F.—see Radar

Rearmament, British, 195, 202–3; Churchill continues to urge, 204–10, 367–72; Chamberlain's attitude towards, 218,

225; demand for, after Munich, 295–6; in year following Munich, 302

Reichenau, General von, 242

Reichstag, Nazi Party in, 52; agrees to "Young Plan", 56; burning of building of, 63; Hitler addresses, after suppression of Roehm plot, 91; election of 1933, 100

Reichswehr, secret building up of, 42; Ministry, 42, 43; amassing of arms by, 45; real power in Germany, 52–3; Hitler's bargain with, 54–5, 94; at opening of Hitler's first Reichstag, 64; Storm Troops merged with, 87; liaison of, with Red Army, 102; becomes Wehrmacht, 128; alleged bad condition of, 281–2

Renown, H.M.S., 155

Reparations, payment of, under the Peace Treaty, 6, 8; "Young Plan" for, 55–6; cancellation of, 58

Reparations Commission, abolition of, 55

Reynaud, Paul, La France a Sauvé l'Europe of, 286, 331, 350; mentioned 252, 272

Rhine, river, as French frontier, 6, 10; Churchill visits fortifications along, 342–344

Rhineland, French seek independent, 11; Germany seeks pact on, 25; evacuation of, by Allies, 29, 56; Germany suggests demilitarisation of frontiers of, 172; German reoccupation of, 172–9, 181–4, 235, 239; Germany declines to limit troops in, 182–3; fortification of, 184–5, 190

Ribbentrop, Frau von, 243

Ribbentrop, Joachim von, his meeting with Churchill, 200–1; hands ultimatum to Schuschnigg, 236; farewell luncheon to, in London, 243; mission of, to Paris, 300–1; opens diplomatic offensive against Poland, 306, 312–13; reaffirms German-Polish Non-Aggression Pact, 324; signs Pact of Steel, 337; Ciano argues with, against war, 346; signs pact with Stalin, 350–2, 355; mentioned, 241, 261

Rieth, Dr., 93

Rodney, H.M.S., 143

Roehm Ernst, in the 1923 Putsch, 49; Chief of Staff of S. A., 53; Schleicher plots with, 54–5, 62; plots against Hitler, 86–9; arrest and execution of, 90

Rome Protocols, 85

Rome-Berlin Axis, inception of, 171, 190

Roosevelt, Franklin D., speech of, against

dictatorships, 222; proposes using American influence to improve situation in Europe, 225–9, 311; possible intervention of, in Czech crisis, 262; seek non-aggression assurance from Dictators, 318; and atomic bombs, 345; mentioned, 170, 178

Rosenberg, Herr, in the 1923 *Putsch*, 49

Rothermere, Viscount, 166

Roumania, aligned to France, 173, 175; affected by fortified Rhineland, 184–5; oil of, 244; question of transport of Russian troops across, 264, 274, 313, 349; British guarantee to, 322; fear of Russia in, 325; Turkish relations with, 335; refuses guarantee from Russia, 340; effect of Soviet-German Pact on, 356. *See also* Little Entente

Royal Air Force, neglect of, 66, 101, 213; reduction of, 68; need to strengthen, 84, 101, 106–9, 206; Opposition vote of censure on proposals to strengthen, 102–103; German Force approaches parity with, 105–7; parity achieved, 108, 114–116, 213; expansion of, 116, 301–4, 370–1; German views of, 167; compared with German, 303, 370–1; call-up of reservists of, 353; and Fleet Air Arm, 362–3; deficiency of bombers in, 371

Royal Navy, reduction in strength of, 12–13; Treaty limitations to, 84, 125; rebuilding of, 126, 143–6; value of Radar to, 141–2; as arm of League, 158, 361; not capable of meeting Italian Navy, 158, 164; French co-operation with, 220–3; loses bases in Ireland, 247–9; fleet movements of, as deterrent in Czech crisis, 263; mobilisation of, 279–280, 282, 291; disposition of Mediterranean Fleet of, during Italian invasion of Albania, 315–17; requires own Air Force, 362–5; dependent on War Office for supplies, 369

Royal Observer Corps, 140

Ruhr, French invasion of, 11, 49; accessible to air attack, 136

Runciman, Viscount, Czech mission of, 260–2

Russia, Soviet, rise of, 13; extermination of populations by, 16; desirability of German pact with, 28; Hitler's enmity for, 51, 171; and proposed Eastern Pact, 95; enters League, 95; relations between Dictatorships and, 102; protests against German violation of Peace Treaty, 120;

French approach to, 121–2, 171–2, 263–4; subscribes to Non-Intervention, 192; intervention of, in Spanish war, 193, 219; Eden's wish for better relations with, 216; offers of collaboration from, 229; proposes conference after occupation of Austria, 245–6; relations of, with Czechoslovakia, 258–259; Army and political purge in, 258–9, 330; advises action on Czech crisis, 263–4, 273–4; declares resolve to fulfil obligations to Czechoslovakia, 264, 273–4; and guarantee of new Czech frontiers, 271; offer of, ignored, 274–5, 311; Conservatives desire co-operation with, 278; German fear of attack by, 280; not represented at Munich, 285; Hitler on Jewish influence in, 295; suggests Six-Power Conference, 313; Chamberlain's distrust of, 313; British talks with, 325; suggests Triple Alliance, 325–7, 339–40; relations of, with Nazi Government, 326; turns towards Germany, 328–30; arranges new partition of Poland, 331, 351; Britain's answer to proposals of, 332; Turkey's relations with, 335; need for alliance with, 333–7; renewed Franco-British approach to, 347–9; her attitude to Poland, 348; Franco-British military talks with, 348–50; negotiates with Germany, 350–1; number of divisions of, 349; signs pact with Germany, 350–3; her secret agreement with Germany, 350; realistic policy of, 351; retribution suffered by, 352; Japan ready for alliance against, 355

Russian Air Force, Czechoslovakian base taken from, 251

Russian Army, liaison of, with Reichswehr, 102; purged of pro-German elements, 330; not prepared to fight for Poland, 329

Russian Revolution, 4, 5, 13

S.A.—*see* Brownshirts

Saarbrucken fortifications, 282, 295

Saar Valley, plebiscite in, 97–8

St. Germain, Treaty of, 9

Salisbury, Marquess of, 205

Salzburg, German leaflets dropped on, 82

Samuel, Rt. Hon. Sir Herbert (Viscount Samuel), 33, 103

Sanctions, Britain opposed to, against

Germany, 119; imposed against Italy, 154–6, 361–2; Baldwin's conception of, 157

Sanjurjo, General, 192

Sarraut, Albert, 174

Scandinavia, apprehensive of Germany rearmed, 76, 120; and Anglo-German Naval Agreement, 125–6. *See also* Denmark, Norway, Sweden

Schacht, Dr., 130, 300

Scharnhorst, built in defiance of Treaty limitations, 123–4

Schleicher, General Kurt von, plots with Roehm against Hitler, 54–5, 62–3, 88; secures downfall of Bruening, 58; makes a bid for power, 62–3; becomes Chancellor, 62; death of, 90

Schmidt, Dr. Guido, 235

Schubert, General von, 240

Schulenburg, Count von, 329, 349

Schuschnigg, Dr. Kurt von, takes control of the Administration, 93; submits to German demands, 230, 236–7; his interviews with Hitler, 235–6; announces holding of plebiscite, 239–40; resignation of, 240; Mussolini refuses aid to, 241

Seeckt, General von, plans re-creation of German Army, 41–2, 129–30; plans re-creation of Air Force, 43–4, 99–100

Seyss-Inquart, Dr., 230, 236, 240–1

Shanghai, Japanese landing near, 78

Shipping, radio-location of, 141–2; range-finding on, 141. *See also* Merchant ships

Siegfried Line—*see* West Wall

Simon, Rt. Hon. Sir John (Viscount), disarmament policy of, 64–5, 69–70; hears of German air parity, 108, 114, 119; visits Berlin, 108, 118; foreign policy of, 119; a Stresa Conference, 119; moves to Home Office, 122; mentioned, 269

Simon Commission, report of, 71

Sinclair, Rt. Hon. Sir Archibald, on disarmament and the German menace, 112–113; supports rearmament, 196; declines to appear on deputation to Prime Minister, 205; at talk with Henlein, 255–256; and need of Russian alliance, 337

Skoda works, 302, 311; Russian contracts for munitions from, 326

Slovakia, autonomy of, 298; secession of, 306–7; German protection of, 313

Smuts, Field-Marshal Rt. Hon. J. C., and Western Pact, 26

Snowden, Lord, 60–1, 174

Socialist Party, Prussian, driven from office, 62; German, 64; Austrian, 82. *See also* Labour Party

Somaliland, 97

Sotelo, Señor, 192

Soviet-Czech Pact, 274

Soviet-German Non-Aggression Pact, 350–2; Mussolini informed of, 355–6

Spain, protests against German violation of Peace Treaty, 120; Churchill in, 166; growing strength of Communism in, 191; outbreak of Civil War in, 192; policy of Non-Intervention in, 192–3; foreign intervention in, 193, 219–20, 230, 254–5; Franco's successes in, 245

Spears, Major-General Sir Edward, 342

Spitfire fighters, 115, 301, 303

S.S.—*see* Blackshirts

Stalin, Generalissimo, Eden's interview with, 119; Laval's interview with, 121; conspiracy to overthrow, 258–9; gives up attempt to work with Western democracies, 326–7, 329; changes his Foreign Commissar, 328–9; on position of Russia (1939) with Britain and France, 349; signs pact with Germany, 350–2; proposes toast of Fuehrer, 352

Stanley, Rt. Hon. Oliver, urges National Government on Mr. Chamberlain, 320–321

Starhemberg, Prince, 93

Stimson, H. L., at Geneva Disarmament Conference, 58; on Lytton Report, 79–80

Storm Troops—*see* Brownshirts

Stoyadinovitch, M., 224

Strakosch, Sir Henry, 203

Strang, Sir William, mission of, to Russia 347–9

Strasbourg, 342

Strasser, Gregor, 86, 88, 90

Stresa Conference, 118–20

Stresemann, Gustav, 25, 28, 52, 56

Stuelpnagel, General, 280

Submarines, Anglo-German agreement on, 125–6; abolition or restriction of use of, 126, 128; value of R.D.F. to, 141; location of, by Asdics, 146–7; piracy of Italian, 220–3. *See also* U-boats

Sudeten Germans, Hitler on, 251; demand autonomy, 255–6; Czech attempts to conciliate, 261, 269; claim union with Reich, 270; mentioned, 258, 266

Sudetenland, autonomy demanded for, 255–6, 269; failure of German-provoked revolt in, 269; cession of, to Germany, 270–3; evacuation of, 277, 285

Suez Canal, movement of Italian troopships through, 152–3, 158

Supply, Ministry of, need for, 191, 365–6; and Air Force *matériel*, 364–5

Suvich, Signor, on Austrian independence, 82; Dollfuss appeals to, 85; at Stresa Conference, 119

Sweden, protests against German Treaty violation, 120. *See also* Scandinavia

Swilly, Loch, 247–9

Swinton, Viscount (Rt. Hon. Sir Philip Cunliffe-Lister), Air Minister, 115, 134, 142; dismissal of, 208; Churchill's tribute to, 209

Switzerland, possibility of invasion through, 343

Syrovy, General, 275

Tangier, 166

Tanks, classed as offensive weapons, 65

Tardieu, M., 58

Territorial Army, German opinion of, 167; doubling of, 313–14; supply of equipment to, 368

Teschen, Polish acquisition of, 289, 298, 312

Thaelmann, Herr, 24, 57

Thomas, General, 280

Thompson, Inspector, 358

Thorez, M., 118

Times, the, supports German right to rearm, 66; believes in Hitler's sincerity, 176; on relinquishment of Irish bases, 249; on partition of Czechoslovakia, 266

Tirpitz, strongest vessel afloat, 125

Tirpitz, Grand-Admiral von, 24

Tiso, Father, 306

Tizard, Sir Henry, 138, 141

Toledo, defence of, 192

Torpedoes, direction of, by Radar, 141

Trade unions, reaction of, to Abyssinian crisis, 157; not making full effort, 369

Trawlers, Asdic-equipped, 352–3

Trenchard, Viscount, 205

Trianon, Treaty of, 9

Tukhachevsky, Marshal, 259, 330

Tunisia, status of Italians in, 97

Turkey, protests against German violation of Peace Treaty, 120; at Nyon Conference, 222; British alliance with, 322, 333, 335, 356; effect of Soviet-German Pact on, 356

U-boats, building of, 44, 323; Britain concedes German right to build, 124–5; use of Asdics in locating, 146–7

Ukraine, German need to absorb, 200, 232; mentioned, 335

Unemployment, in United States, 32; in Germany, 56

United States, loans of, to Germany, 8–9, 10, 14, 29, 45; and Treaty of Guarantee, 11; repudiates League of Nations, 12; Isolationist policy of, 12, 70, 76, 79, 118, 170, 229; disarmament policy of, 12, 65; British war debts to, 22–3, 34; economic crisis in, 31–2, 55; fails to prevent second war, 37–8, 70; Churchill's lecture tour in, 70–1; and Japanese aggression in China, 79; "non-realistic" policy of, 94; repercussions of Anglo-German Naval Agreement on, 127; offers assistance in improving international relations, 225–228; possible effects of European intervention, 229; and joint action in Czech crisis, 264

United States Navy, Treaty limitations of, 84, 125; battleship design in, 146

Uranium, potential powers of, 344–5

Vansittart, Rt. Hon. Sir Robert (Baron Vansittart), and German menace, 163, 217; and Hoare-Laval Pact, 164, 217; leaves Foreign Office, 217; at Nyon Conference, 220; Churchill's letter to, on Grandi's conversation, 361–2; mentioned, 150

Versailles Peace Conference, 3–4

Versailles, Treaty of, territorial provisions of, 6, 97, 172; economic clauses of, 6, 8; disarmament clauses of, 14–15, 29, 39–41, 44–5, 66; German breaches of, 42–5, 76, 97, 101, 105, 108, 117–20, 123–4, 128, 170. 172–3; readjustment of frontiers laid down by, 298

Vienna, after First World War, 9; Nazi revolt in, 93; Hitler's entry into, 242; advantages to Germany of mastery of, 244

Voelkischer Beobachter, 49

Voroshilov, Marshal, 329, 348, 350

Vyshinsky, A. J., 258

Wallace, Mrs. Euan, 357

War debts, 22–3, 34

War Office, and Ministry for Co-ordination of Defence 365–6; supplies Services, 367, 369

Warsaw, Battle of (1919), 348

Washington Disarmament Conference (1920), 12

Washington Naval Agreement, 13, 125, 145

Watson-Watt, Sir Robert, 138

Wehrmacht, 128–9

Weimar Republic, foundation of, 10; Hitler's antagonism to, 49; biennial elections in, 52; power behind, 52–3

Weizsaecker, Herr, 326

Welles, Summer, 225, 228

West Wall, fortification of, 190; incomplete, 252, 257, 259; defects of, 282; additional fortifications of, 295; "hundreds of divisions" along, 347

Western Pact, 25–8

Weygand, General, 348

White Russia, German need to absorb, 200, 232

Wiedemann, Captain, 260

Wiessee, arrest of Roehm at, 88–9

Wigram, Ralph, friendship with, 73; and reoccupation of Rhineland, 175–6, 178; death of, 178

Wilhelm II, Kaiser, 57

Wilmot, Rt. Hon. John, 100

Wilson, Sir Horace, adviser to Chamberlain, 217, 268; and Czech crisis, 276–7, 283–4, 292

Wilson, President Woodrow, 3, 11, 12

Winterton, Earl, 74, 106 n., 205

Witzleben, General, 280–1

Wolmer, Viscount, 205

Wood, Rt. Hon. Sir Kingsley, memorandum from Churchill to, on Radar, 141–142; Secretary of State for Air, 210; letter from Churchill to, on atomic energy, 344–5

Work Battalions, of German Army, 129–130

World War, First, Europe at close of, 3–6, 15; plans for 1919 campaign, 36–7; German study of lessons of, 41; German approach to France before outbreak of, 83–4

Wu-Sung, 78

"Young Plan", 55–6

Yugoslavia, assassination of King of, 96; aligned to France, 173; affected by fortified Rhineland, 184; raw materials of, 244; Italian threat to, 314. See also Little Entente

Zeppelin, Radar-detecting flight of, 140

Zinoviev, M., 259

SOURCES OF THE ILLUSTRATIONS

1 Clemenceau signs the Treat of Versailles 28th June, 1919. (B.N. Prints)
2 The occupation of the Rhineland, 1920. (Keystone)
3 A session of the League of Nations, under the chairmanship of Mr. Viviani, February 1923. (Meurisse photo, Sirot collection)
4 Gandhi in London, surrounded by crowds. (Radio-Times, London)
5 The anti-tank defences of the Maginot Line. (Army Cinematographic Service)
6 An armoured gun emplacement in action on the Maginot Line. (Army Cinematographic Service)
7 The underground caverns of the Maginot Line. (B.N. Prints)
8 Before the scuttling of the captured German Fleet at Scapa Flow, 21st June, 1919. (Keystone)
9 Mussolini's entry into Rome (centre foreground), 29th October, 1922. (B.N. Prints)
10 The assassination of the President of the French Republic, Paul Doumer, by Gorguloff, 12th May, 1932. (B.N. Prints)
11 The assassination of King Alexander of Yugoslavia, 10th October, 1934. The photo shows the body of the assassin at the feet of police agents. (B.N. Prints)
12 The ceremonial laying of the first stone of the Maginot Line at Bar-le-Duc. (N.B. Prints)
13 The financial crash of 1929 at the New York Stock Exchange. (Keystone)
14 Stanley Baldwin. (Sirot collection)
15 One of the first clandestine meetings of the Hitler Party in the cellars of Kalkberge. (Keystone)
16 A Nazi demonstration in front of the house of a Jew, Karl Liebknecht, in Berlin, January 1933. (Keystone)
17 An attitude typical of Hitler, during a speech, 1935. (Safara photo)
18 Hitler marching in the streets of Weimar on the occasion of the first meeting of the National Socialist (Nazi) Party, 5th July, 1926. (Keystone)
19 On board the battleship "Cavour", 7th May, 1938. From left to right: von Ribbentrop, Mussolini, Count Ciano, Hitler. (Trampus photo)
20 Munich, 1937: SS men swearing an oath of allegiance to Hitler. (Safara photo)
21 Training the German Army with tanks of tin and cardboard. The Treaty of Versailles did not permit the German Army to use tanks. (Keystone)
22 Hindenburg and General von Seeckt reviewing the German Army in front of the Reichstag. (Illustrated Press photo, Sirot collection)
23 General von Seeckt, 1923, the man who reshaped and reorganized the German Army. (Meurisse photo, Sirot collection)

24 A parade by the German Army, about 1930. (Keystone)

25 German soldiers in front of the Munich Memorial, 1935. (Keystone)

26 A march-past by the German Army at the Congress of Nuremberg, 16th September, 1935. (B.N. Prints)

27 British artillery. (War Office)

28 British "Tommies". (War Office)

29 French infantrymen. (Mondial photo)

30 Russian riflemen. (B.N. Prints)

31 Italian artillery at Santa Marinella. (B.N. Prints)

32 Nuremberg: demonstration of an attack by the German Army. (Keystone)

33 A parade by the Chinese Army. (Safara photo)

34 A march-past by Japanese troops, led by Prince Chichibu, brother of the Emperor. (Mondial photo)

35 Churchill reviewing the Home Fleet at Spithead. (Radio-Times, London)

36 Emperor Haile Selassie of Ethiopia. (Rol photo)

37 Stalin and von Ribbentrop. (B.N. Prints)

38 Konrad Henlein, leader of the Sudetenland. (Trampus photo)

39 The Spanish Civil War: a machine-gun nest on the Madrid Front. (B.N. Prints)

40 The Spanish Civil War: inhabitants of the village of Villanova held under close guard by soldiers of Franco. (B.N. Prints)

41 The Spanish Civil War: the evils of war; the bullet-ridden body of a young girl. (B.N. Prints)

42 The Spanish Civil War: Barcelona in ruins, March 1938. (B.N. Prints)

43 The Sino-Japanese War: Chinese Communist soldiers with American sten guns. (Keystone)

44 The Sino-Japanese War: Japanese tanks entering Nankin, January 1938. (Keystone)

45 The Ethiopian War: the arrival of an Italian expeditionary force. (B.N. Prints)

46 The Ethiopian War: the capture of Lake Tana by the Italian Army, 24th April, 1936. (Mondial photo)

47 The invasion of the Rhineland, March 1936. (Keystone)

48 The entry of the Germans into Vienna, March 1938. (B.N. Prints)

49 Hitler declaring in Vienna that Austria was no more than a part of the German Fatherland, 16th March, 1938. (Trampus photo)

50 The population of Salzburg enthusiastically welcomes the German Army, March 1938. (World and Camera photo)

51 The invasion of Czechoslovakia: the Fuehrer personally crossing the border at Wildenau, 3rd October, 1938. (Trampus photo)

52 A German armoured-car entering the Sudetenland, 20th September, 1938. (Safara photo)

53 German armed might in Hungary: a parade of light armoured-cars before Regent Horthy, 27th August, 1938. (Trampus photo)

54 Hitler's inspection of Czechoslovakia, 18th March, 1939. (B.N. Prints)

This book, designed by
Werner Schelling
is a production of
Edito-Service S.A., Geneva

Printed in Switzerland